CONTENTS

FOREWORD

Although *new media technology* conjures up images of individuals—technophiles and technophobes alike—connecting with or combating various hardware and software applications, it is something more than its most practical manifestations.

At the same time that some commentators are overly technical about technology (an approach usually accompanied by gushing enthusiasms), others are deeply immersed in futurist theorizing, much of it darkly discouraging in context and tone. Thus, technology cheerleaders bump up against modern Luddites, whose essential message is that technological change isn't important after all.

Awash with contradictions, the literature of new media technology ranges from industry puff pieces about the new world aborning to dire warnings from those who essentially fear change. Along with this comes the work of forecasters—those who use charts, graphs, and quantitative measures, however fanciful—and other humanistic critics, often equally fanciful in their predilections. Over the last fifty years or so, voices from these two quarters and others have had at least one thing in common: they have mostly been wrong in their speculations about the future. Predictions of new technologies such as facsimile newspapers, the electronic home and office, the wired city with hundreds of channels of television and other video services have either not materialized at all or come decades later than anyone expected and in a form far different from what even the best students of new media suggested.

In the midst of such confusion, it is not inappropriate to ask where one can turn for sound, commonsense information that draws both on industry realities and scholarly assessments. Happily, this book is a good place to start. Although written by a scholar deeply immersed in communication theory, it is a practical account of new media technologies as they actually exist in the 1990s, with some speculative material (presented cautiously) about possible future scenarios and directions.

John V. Pavlik, with whom I've had the pleasure of working at the Freedom Forum Media Studies Center at Columbia University for six years, has produced a useful book that outlines the world of new media technology in the present tense but also reflects back on historical antecedents and the climate in which new ventures, technologies, and enterprises actually arose. Recognizing that technology and technological change must be more than vague musings, Pavlik then focuses on the actual technologies as they have existed, drawing on some of the best industry sources about the next generation of hardware and software now being developed. The definition of technology is followed by a consideration of what it does, and this takes the reader into the world of cyberspace. Up to this point, the book has been long on ideas and inventory and short on people and institutions. However, what follows is a useful account of the new "masters of the universe," to borrow a phrase from Tom Wolfe. The players—corporate, governmental, and institutional forces that own, operate, and direct this world—come into sharp relief. That leads to the most human of all communications operations: the editorial process. This largely content-oriented approach is augmented with a discussion of the realities of marketing electronic "publications."

Because no consideration of the world of new media is complete without a discussion of the realities of the world around us that can block or facilitate change, the book takes up the legal–regulatory environment as well as the social and cultural consequences of what is happening in the world of new media and new media technology. Finally, there is a lively speculative chapter that deals intelligently with the future, raising questions that students and teachers alike will want to debate. The book also blessedly offers its readers a much-needed glossary for anyone not familiar with technical terms that are de rigueur these days in any conversation about new media.

During the time that we worked together at Columbia University, John Pavlik lived in two worlds—those of the media industries and of media studies and scholarship. He connected the two with ingenuity and creative force in a series of technology studies seminars that engaged high-level media executives and scholars alike. At the same time, he worked with young media professionals and students, always learning from them all and contributing as well. It is this unique venue and set of experiences that especially qualify John Pavlik to map and navigate the material he presents so well in this book. Happily for higher education,

Dr. Pavlik is now Director of the School of Communication at San Diego State University, an institution with long experience connecting the various elements of the media industries with scholarly enterprise.

This is a distinctive book, broad in scope, deep in insight, and written in a fashion that is user friendly for students, media professionals, scholars, and others in the general public who have a hunger for intelligent sense-making in this field, which is so often fragmented and confusing. Here, the reader gets a coherent picture of the field, one that is often tentative and exploratory because dogmatism would be both foolish and misleading. In a field in which so much is new, this well-structured and effectively written text ought to find an eager audience. There is no book quite like it to date, and it will no doubt break new ground. It offers satisfying information while giving readers latitude to make their own conclusions.

This is a book worth reading, studying, and saving. Much of what is written here will change, but the structural framework offered probably won't. That is the value of the work and the questions it raises. Designed for courses in media technology in schools of communication, journalism, media studies, and related areas, it also has value for anyone interested in media industries and their connection to technological change and societal forces.

Everette E. Dennis, Executive Director
The Freedom Forum Media Studies Center
Columbia University
New York, New York

PREFACE

*All modes of communication we humans have devised
since the beginnings of humanity are coming together
into a single electronic system, driven by computers.*
                                                    —*JOHN WICKLEIN*

As the science fiction–like technologies of virtual reality, cyberspace, and the information superhighway become today's realities, visions of the new media landscape range from the utopian to the Orwellian. While many industry and government voices proclaim that building a national information infrastructure is the key to the economic and cultural fortunes of the United States, many scholarly voices caution against creating an electronic nightmare in which individual privacy is lost and only a few global conglomerates control access to information technology. Bowman Cutter, deputy assistant to the President for economic policy, claims the information highway is "the basic building block in the economy of the future." The Clinton Administration's commitment to this view is reflected in the President's appointment of Secretary of Commerce Ron Brown to head a twenty-seven-member information-policy advisory council. "The NII (National Information Infrastructure)," Brown observes, "can transform the lives of American people—ameliorating the constraints of geography, disability, and economic status—giving all Americans a fair opportunity to go as far as their talents and ambitions will take them."

Ohio University's John Wicklein, in contrast, cautions that the convergence of all communications in a digital world may create nothing less than an electronic nightmare for those living in it. Charles Martin, professor at Mills College, similarly concludes that the social cost of new media technologies will be high. He expects social inequities to increase as high-priced new media technologies limit access to information, thus broadening the gap between the information haves and have-nots.

Important questions about the future of new media technologies include:

- How much will it cost to build a new information infrastructure?
- What will happen to those who can't afford the price?
- Who will control access to information in an increasingly electronic, pay-as-you-go media system?
- What content will fill the digital airwaves and wires?

THE SHAPE OF THINGS TO COME: ROUND

Regardless of the view one subscribes to, one thing is certain: the onrush of new media technologies is inevitable. They are, in fact, already here. Publishers are distributing best-selling books on CD-ROM. Author Michael Crichton's novel *Jurassic Park* was published in 1991 as a Macintosh HyperCard™ stack, complete with squawking velociraptors, long before moviegoers saw a single frame of Steven Spielberg's film adaptation. Writers are even venturing into a new form of nonlinear text known as hyperfiction, in which notions of beginning, middle, and end have little meaning and the reader enters the realm of story creator.

Interactive television is being offered in a number of markets throughout North America, bringing an abrupt end to the legacy of the couch potato. Families in test communities in California are playing "Jeopardy!" via computer in simultaneous competition with the competitors seen on television each evening. Viewers in Montreal, Canada, are selecting stories of their own choice each evening on nightly newscasts and playing armchair director during telecasts of Montreal Canadian hockey games, choosing camera angles and instant replays as they desire. Despite all the tests and research, one question no one has adequately answered about this new technology is, How much interactivity do people really want? After nearly a half century of passive entertainment, will TV viewers suddenly want to become active participants in the communication process? "The consumer doesn't want to work to be entertained," observes Francine Sommer, a securities analyst and expert on new technologies.

Many people around the globe have already demonstrated an interest in accessing an electronic superhighway, however. For example, more than fifteen million people in more than forty countries already send and receive electronic messages around the world on the global Internet, a worldwide web of computer networks. Use of the Internet is growing by as much as 15 percent a month, with almost no end in sight. Everything from an electronic evangelical network to direct electronic access to the White House exists on the Internet. The Internet even offers a 24-hour radio station, RTFM, offering gavel-to-gavel audio broadcasts from the House and Senate floors.

THE PURPOSE OF THIS BOOK

New Media Technology and the Information Superhighway is devoted to a systematic exploration of the commercial and cultural implications of the rapidly evolving new media landscape. In the ten chapters that follow, the discussion systematically and critically reviews not only the technologies themselves, but the ways they are affecting how people live, work, and communicate. Chapter 1 outlines the broad contours and parameters of the new media landscape and communication industry. Chapter 2 places new media technology into an historical context. Chapter 3 examines the emerging technologies themselves, the infrastructure of the information age. Chapter 4 reviews the fundamental concepts and applications driving the development of new media technology. Chapter 5 identifies the principal players on the new media landscape, the emerging new media barons. Chapter 6 outlines key considerations in publishing in the new media environment, and Chapter 7 reviews marketing considerations. Chapter 8 discusses legal and regulatory concerns, and Chapter 9 examines the social and cultural consequences of new media technology. Chapter 10 provides a summary and gazes into the hazy future of new media technology. An appendix offers additional tabular information on the state of new media technologies and industries. A glossary provides a road map to key terms in the field of new media technology. A complete bibliography of references cited in this book is also included.

SCOPE OF THIS BOOK

The boundaries of the new media landscape are in a constant state of flux and are extremely difficult to pin down. As the traditional distinctions between print and broadcast media technologies rapidly vanish, we are witnessing the emergence of "a united state of media," concludes Everette E. Dennis, executive director of the Freedom Forum Media Studies Center. In agreement is Walter Wriston, former chairman and chief executive officer of Citicorp and author of *Twilight of Sovereignty: How the Information Revolution Is Transforming Our World,* who states, "The law of technology is the law of convergence." Journalist and technology seer George Gilder refers to this convergence as the *telecosm,* a process in which telecommunications and computing blend into one seamless state.

Thus, included within the scope of this book are electronic media technologies that, driven by computers, are rapidly merging into a single digital communication environment. Moreover, included in this book are communication technologies whose nature and impact are largely unsettled, primarily because they are still developing both in their form and function. Certain technologies, although decades old, have undergone significant changes in recent years and are included here because of their unsettled nature. For the most part, however, the media technologies discussed in this book are relatively recent inventions and are only beginning to exert their cultural and commercial influence in global society.

For updates, see the author's home page on the World Wide Web at: http://rohan.sdsu.edu/dept/schlcomm/index.html

Acknowledgements

Many people have contributed greatly to this book. I am especially thankful to Everette E. Dennis, the executive director of the Freedom Forum Media Studies Center and senior vice president of the Freedom Forum, who was my mentor, colleague, and boss during my six years as associate director for Research and Technology Studies at the Freedom Forum Media Studies Center. Several other current and former Center staff also deserve thanks, including Shirley Gazsi, Mark A. Thalhimer, Debbie Rogers, Wendy Boyd, Judy Annozine, and Marcella Steingart, as well as my former research assistants, Sujoya Roy and Bruce Cronin.

Several anonymous reviewers provided invaluable commentary on earlier drafts of this book; I am deeply grateful for their time and effort. I am also grateful to veteran news executive Adam Clayton Powell, III, now director of Technology Studies and Programs for the Freedom Forum Media Studies Center, and telecommunications consultant John Carey, director of Greystone Communications, for their frank and useful comments on the book. Thanks also to all the scholars, journalists, and colleagues whose groundbreaking work on new media technology precedes this writing and is cited extensively within these chapters. Special thanks go to series editor Albert N. Greco, professor and director, Publishing Studies, Gallatin Division at New York University, for inviting me to write this book; Steven P. Hull, senior editor at Allyn & Bacon, with whom I originally worked on this book; and to Joe Opiela, vice president and editor in chief, Humanities, at Allyn & Bacon, Simon and Schuster Education Group, who saw this book through to its completion.

Finally, my sincerest thanks go to my friendliest critic, best friend, and wife, Jackie Dina Oregel Pavlik, who gave me the time to work on this book, while caring for our two lovely daughters, Tristan Mariana, born May 13, 1993, and Orianna Magdalena, born June 6, 1994.

1

NEW MEDIA TECHNOLOGY: AN INDUSTRY OVERVIEW

'Tis true, There's magic in the web of it.
—WILLIAM SHAKESPEARE[1]

CONTOURS OF THE NEW MEDIA LANDSCAPE

From virtual reality to the information highway, the new media technology landscape is as diverse as it is fast changing. These new technologies are radically transforming almost every aspect of how we communicate and with whom, as well as just about any other dimension of our lives, from dating to making money to health care. Each year the pace of technological change seems to accelerate, as bold new technological advances are announced nearly every day. Likewise, regulatory changes have opened new technology vistas and the world has moved startlingly closer to realizing Marshall McLuhan's global village.[2] Although nearly 200 years elapsed between Gutenberg's invention of movable type in 1450 and the arrival of the printing press in America in 1639, the past century alone has seen the invention of the telephone, radio and television, satellite communications, the computer, and countless other technologies, each one revolutionizing some aspect of human communication.

A CONCEPTUAL ROAD MAP TO NEW MEDIA TECHNOLOGIES

A conceptual framework is useful to help organize and make sense of the dimensions, qualities, and consequences of these new media

1

technologies. One way to map these new technologies is by their primary technical function:

- production
- distribution
- display
- storage

Although this approach is limited by the convergence of media technologies and the blurring of lines among different media functions, it still has usefulness in charting the most distinctive or distinguishing contours of the landscape of new media technologies. Its value is articulated by Anthony Smith, who writes, "The impact of electronics upon our ways of creating, storing and disseminating text goes through our whole culture, since the composition and use of text permeates everything we are as a civilization. The electronic transformation of text does not, however, displace our values or identity so much as superimpose itself on what has gone before; it is useful to remind ourselves what the traditional method of printing itself offered our culture when it arrived some centuries ago."[3] Today, however, the world of multimedia communication extends well beyond text-based communication, and the impact of digital technology is truly transforming all forms of human communication.

Production

Production technologies refer to those used in gathering and processing information. These technologies include computers, electronic photography, optical scanners, and remote sensing technologies. Electronic production technologies have not only created new ways to collect and interpret information, they have also enabled us to gather new kinds of information, solve new problems, and solve old problems more rapidly and efficiently. Conversely, these same technologies have sometimes replaced human workers, posed a serious threat to individual privacy, oftentimes greatly increased the cost of information, and raised thorny questions about the ownership of information. Moreover, they have invariably outpaced human ability to cope with the new possibilities created by these technologies. Use of computer technologies in the workplace has also been linked to an increase in the occurrence of repetitive stress injury (RSI), such as carpal tunnel syndrome, among persons spending long, uninterrupted periods typing on a computer keyboard.

Distribution

Distribution technologies refer to those involved in the transmission or movement of electronic information. Included are six primary technology systems:

- over-the-air broadcasting
- land-based telecommunications (including twisted pair, optical fiber, the switched telephone network, the advanced intelligent network (AIN), integrated services digital network (ISDN), asymmetrical digital subscriber line (ADSL))
- coaxial cable (for example, cable TV)
- satellite communications, including direct broadcast satellite (DBS)
- wireless transmission, including personal communication networks or services (PCN or PCS)
- electrical power lines

These technologies have both positive and negative cultural and commercial consequences. They have made information globally available at the speed of light. They have made video on demand a practical reality. They have brought target marketing and audience specialization to unprecedented levels. Moreover, they have made telecommuting more practical than ever before. Research shows that more than 10 percent of Americans conduct at least some of their work from home offices made possible by these technologies; 1 percent now telecommute full time.[4]

Meanwhile, these distribution technologies have contributed to a number of social ills, making, for instance, the piracy of electronic information a multibillion dollar industry worldwide. Some argue that these technologies have contributed to growing social fragmentation, the division between society's information rich and information poor, and the formation of an information underclass.

Display

Display devices refer to a variety of technologies for presenting information to the end user, audience member, or consumer of information. They include devices for presenting electronic information in a variety of formats, such as video, audio, text, data, or any combination of these. Some even present information in tactile, or touch-sensitive, format. Many of these technologies are dependent on or interconnected to the technologies of distribution, production, or storage and are separated here only conceptually. Examples include various multimedia computer displays, such as personal digital appliances (PDAs) or flat-panel screens, a new generation of display telephones, emerging forms of interactive television, high-definition television (HDTV), and virtual reality technologies of the dataglove and the bodysuit. The cultural and commercial consequences of these technologies are not yet clear and often interact with other factors, such as the nature of the content as well as the characteristics of the user. Collectively, however, these technologies make it increasingly easy to access vast amounts of information while on the move. Flat-panel display technologies, already commonly used by overnight delivery carriers, hold the promise of bringing about a "mediamorphosis," or the electronic transformation of the newspaper. Many of these multimedia display devices act as enabling technologies, facilitating communication between and among persons with or without disabilities.

Conversely, these same technologies may also pose an array of potential negative consequences. Video display terminals (VDTs), for instance, present potential public health risks by exposing users to large doses of electromagnetic radiation, sometimes linked to cancer, miscarriage, and stress. Many are alarmed by the potential mental health risks posed by heavy exposure to violent or sexist computer games. Some are concerned that an increasingly heavy reliance on electronic media has contributed to a steady erosion in America's literacy rate.

Storage

Storage technologies refer to those media used in housing information in electronic format. These media are evolving from largely magnetic to optical in format. While the standard computer storage device has been the floppy magnetic diskette and the magnetic hard drive, the compact disk is emerging as the storage medium of choice for large amounts of information, such as data, text, audio, video, and combined multimedia information. The compact disc–read only memory (CD-ROM) is the most common CD format, although the interactive format (CD-I) is growing in use. Laserdiscs have also been used primarily for storing video information and for distributing movies. The lasercard is a likely candidate for storing information for use in PCNs, such as the Apple Newton or the Casio/Tandy Zoomer. Video servers are an increasingly important storage technology for the development of interactive television and video on demand. Video servers, a class of powerful minicomputers, are the engines that will drive not only the availability of large libraries of video but also the emergence of tapeless television stations and TV networks, which today rely largely on analog videotape file servers. By 2000, most stations and networks will use digital video servers to play back previously recorded programming and advertising content.

MAPPING THE CONSEQUENCES OF NEW MEDIA TECHNOLOGIES

The rapid pace of technological change and convergence has made it increasingly difficult to develop a coherent framework for understanding the nature and shape of new media technologies. We organize our analysis by asking four fundamental questions:

- How does technological change affect the way communication professionals do their work?
- How does new technology influence the nature of the communication product or content?
- How does changing technology affect the structure of communication industries?
- How do new media technologies affect the nature of the media audience and society at large?

Table 1-1 presents a conceptual framework for mapping these four types of consequences of new media technologies. The dimensions are the nature of the consequences, intended or unintended, and the level of impact on the communication worker, the communication product, the media structure, and on society, the ultimate media audience. Intended consequences of new media technologies for the communication worker include greater efficiency and flexibility. Unintended social consequences of new technologies include, by contrast, an increasing loss of privacy and an inability for social institutions to keep pace with technological change. Table 1-1 includes selected examples of these consequences, and is not a comprehensive listing of all of the effects of technological change. It is offered as an analytical framework for mapping the consequences of new media technologies.

TABLE 1-1 Mapping the Consequences of Technological Change

	Communication worker	Product	Structure	Society
Intended consequence	Increased efficiency, lower cost, greater speed, Flexibility	Interactivity User control Multimedia Content	Decentralization Virtual newsroom Telecommuting	Economic benefit, freedom
Unintended/ unexpected consequence	Health effects Fewer jobs	Information more costly, intellectual property rights hard to define	Redefined roles Organization	Privacy lost, pace of technological change faster than society's ability to cope

Changing How Communication Professionals Do Their Work

Journalists, public relations practitioners, and advertisers all use new technology to do their work more effectively. They use new technologies to increase their work efficiency and speed, as well as to reduce cost. Moreover, new technologies can enable communication professionals to do things in new and creative ways or even do entirely new things.

There are seemingly endless examples of how the work of journalists has been irretrievably transformed by a variety of technologies, from desktop publishing technologies that have spawned a new era in information graphics to speech recognition and synthesis technologies for persons with disabilities. One noteworthy example comes from the annals of television coverage of the 1988 presidential campaign. ABC News developed a new anchor information system for its 1988 election coverage by creating a hypertext computer database on all the candidates including their voting records, speeches, and positions on the issues. MAGNA (ABC News's Macintosh General News Almanac, created by then executive producer David Bohrman and Apple Computer's Larry Wood) also included a complete database on the Republican and Democratic Party Conventions.[5] MAGNA was created using HyperCard®, a hypertext software authoring system for the Macintosh computer. MAGNA replaced an old card file system that ABC News had previously used on the candidates, as had the other television networks. Unlike previous campaigns, MAGNA enabled *ABC World News Tonight* anchor Peter Jennings to come equipped to the debates and other news events with an exhaustive database at his fingertips in fully electronic, instantly searchable form on a laptop computer. Although in years past it was impossible to verify statements by the candidates the moment they made them while in the field, MAGNA changed all that. What's more, MAGNA eventually led to the creation of an entirely new unit at ABC. Called ABC Interactive, the new unit spun off the hypertext framework developed for MAGNA and linked it to the full-motion video archives of ABC News. The unit's first product was *The '88 Vote*, which included both the MAGNA software and nearly an hour of audio and video on the 1988 presidential campaign. Since then, the unit has produced interactive laser disks on the Middle East (called *The Holy Land*), Martin Luther King, and several other subjects. ABC Interactive functions as an educational service arm of ABC News, primarily targeting high schools and universities as the consumers of its product line. A major user has been the state of Florida public school system, which has widely tested and adopted the innovative multimedia products. As a result of the educational focus, ABC Interactive has generated only modest revenues to date.

Surveying the Newsroom Consequences

To systematically assess the impact of new technology in the newsroom, the Freedom Forum Media Studies Center surveyed a panel of executives from dozens of news organizations represented at technology studies seminars hosted by the center between 1991 and 1993.[6] The survey suggests that technological convergence is driving today's newsroom. Table 1-2 summarizes the technologies that those responding to the survey report have transformed their newsrooms.

Those surveyed also mention a number of telecommunications advances, from cellular telephones to fax communications to advanced radio communications, as well as computer-based technologies for investigative reporting, electronic image scanning and processing, video capture, and electronic mail. Survey respondents point to the benefits of technology convergence in the newsroom, such as improved efficiency and speed, greater access to information, and new abilities.

Technology convergence also presents a variety of challenges to newsroom management, from new staffing requirements to maintaining compatibility between alternative platforms. Some newspaper editors foresee the need for new editorial and design skills and probably for increased editorial staffing. Pagination, for example, shifts the page-makeup function from back shop to newsroom and may require more editors who are "technically coordinated."

Pagination refers to computerized page design and layout technologies. It is the newspaper analog to desktop publishing. The 1980s saw

TABLE 1-2   Technologies Affecting the Newsroom

Technologies	News editors mentioning a technology (percent)
Personal computers for reporters, including portable PCs, pagination systems	80%
Digital photo processing and digital darkrooms	70%
Online databases, online libraries	70%
Telecommunications, such as celphones, fax	60%
Macintosh computers for graphics editors	50%
Satellite news and data transmissions	40%

pagination systems widely adopted in the newspaper industry, though not without problems. Typically, electronic pagination was introduced to streamline production and reduce costs. In the process, however, many newspapers did not anticipate the consequence of moving back-room production and layout processes into the newsroom, where editors suddenly found themselves learning a new technical system, as well as having responsibility for the design of the daily newspaper. This meant spending less time editing text for content and style. In the 1980s, one newspaper company in Westchester County, NY, experimented with applying artificial intelligence to its pagination technology in an effort to fully automate the page design process. Although admirable in its philosophy, the experiment was ahead of its time and failed after a few years' trial.

News executives are also concerned about the ethical questions raised by technological convergence and digitization. Although computerization may provide greater access to information, it must be weighed against each citizen's right to privacy. Electronic image processing also poses important ethical questions in today's newsroom. Synthetic images or manipulated pictures are easier to create and are virtually undetectable in the electronic darkrooms now prevalent in the newsroom. It is inevitable that distorted news photos will appear in newspapers and television news reports. One recent case involved a manipulated Pulitzer Prize–winning photo. As more and more readers and viewers become aware of the use of digital image processing, what will be the effect on the credibility of visual news?

News executives foresee a number of profound technologically driven changes looming on the newsroom horizon. These changes include:

- a possible redefinition of news based on the development of real-time news information
- a new definition of what it means to be a journalist, where editors may soon have to function as compositor, production quality control supervisor, and, to an extent, production manager
- a reconceptualization of the audience in terms of specialized interests
- the advent of news on demand, delivered through the information highway

The results of this survey demonstrate how the communication product has been indelibly altered by the face of new technology. We have seen the emergence of new communication products that are more and more computer based, nonlinear (for example, hypertext), multimedia (incorporating text, data, video, and audio), and user controlled (both in terms of form, function, and time). Moreover, more communication products are reaching the end user in real time via online and satellite technology. It is perhaps this final quality that will prove the most important in transforming human communication. As more information is received the moment it is transmitted, whether by electronic mail, satellite communications, or cellular transmission, decisions will be instantly made based on that real-time information. We will return to this theme later in the book. An interesting historical precedent suggests that large news organizations may be poised once again to redefine news, driven in part by the availability of relatively costly news services to a small, but important, minority of the organization's customers. The major commercial networks, ABC, NBC, and CBS, cut back on coverage of some events in 1980 and 1981 because of coverage available on then fledgling CNN. At the time, CNN reached only a small minority of U.S. television households; however it was an elite minority made up of higher-income, well-educated audience members. Even today, CNN is seen on a regular basis by only a small portion of TV households, but around the world the CNN audience includes many opinion leaders, decision makers, and relatively affluent audience members.

Technological Transformations of the Media Product

Media Industry Case Studies

Oftentimes the effects of technologies have been hidden and long-term, while on other occasions the effects have been more direct, intended, and dramatic. Two commercially successful examples of direct, intended, and dramatic technology applications in the news industry include *USA Today* and *Bloomberg Business News*. Founded a decade ago, *USA Today* capitalized on satellite technologies to make possible the first truly national newspaper in the United States. *Bloomberg Business News,* founded a decade ago as well, has capitalized on the convergence of computing and telecommunications technology to make possible a successful real-time multimedia information service. A more recent example comes from the world of magazine publishing and reflects the role of new technology in developing new communication products as well as transforming the way the communication professionals do their work. During the last week of April in 1992, 99 publishing pioneers gathered in the lower levels of the Time-Life building in midtown New York to create *Open,* the product of the Electronic Magazine project.[7] These editors, designers, and production specialists came together to create an electronic, interactive magazine of the future and published it on CD-ROM.

Although many of these consequences have been intentional, others have been unexpected. Network news executive Adam Clayton Powell III has studied the unexpected consequences of technological change in the television newsroom.

Powell has found that as new technology gains ground in television newsrooms, it often becomes largely invisible to its users. It is analogous to learning to ride a bicycle, he says, "You do not need to think about the process while you are pedaling." As a result, the extent of the changes brought about by new technology has often come as a surprise to many network producers and executives. Powell states:

> *As recently as 1976, television news teams covered the world on film. During the Vietnam War, for example, film was usually shipped by air to the United States, where it was developed, edited and fed into the final broadcast. This process consumed at least a day, often two. Viewers saw yesterday's news today, and then only if the networks moved quickly.*
>
> *Things have changed: Film has been replaced by videotape and live satellite feeds, and yesterday's pictures are now overset. Interestingly, many network news producers and executives questioned about the demise of film maintained that nothing else had changed: Good pictures are good pictures, they said, and good journalism is still good journalism.*[8]

Powell's study of network news coverage suggests that the demise of film in broadcast news actually exerted a profound, although subtle, effect. Looking at a 1976 network newscast, Powell found that the graphics were flat and the editing almost leisurely—"some pictures are allowed to run for several seconds, a rarity today," since the introduction of videotape and satellite technologies.

An important question, Powell asks, is whether flashy graphics and fast-paced editing are synonymous with better journalism. The answer, he says, can be found in a summer 1986 article in *Niemen Report*.[9] In the article, Burton Benjamin, executive producer of the *CBS Evening News* during the 1970s asked, "Are we in danger of emulating MTV with NTV—News TV? What does it profit you when no shot is longer than three seconds and the total is zero?"

Looking to the future, Powell contends that one of the major changes looming on the television news horizon is the digitization of moving images. Although there have been celebrated cases of the digital manipulation of still images, such as the *National Geographic* case in which editors manipulated a digitized image of the great pyramids to get an improved aspect ratio on the magazine's cover, few viewers or even news executives realize the same thing can be done seamlessly with moving pictures in today's digital darkrooms.

"Totally synthetic news events are now within reach," Powell writes.[10] Using composite video, editors can make synthetic news events look absolutely real. Digital darkrooms, he concludes, symbolize nothing less than the end of truth in video photography. The implications for the credibility of television news are alarming. Don E. Tomlinson, an associate professor of journalism at Texas A&M University, agrees.[11] He contends that the digital revolution will directly lead to the manipulation of images and sounds and with dire consequences. "Soon, then, the capability will be such that the recorded, digitized, sampled voice of, say, the President of the United States could be made to sound perfectly as if he had said something he in fact had not said. All it would require, once a representative sample of his voice's binary codes have been fed into the computer, is their rearrangement."

Digital image processing, of course, has transformed far more than just the news. Anyone who has seen a Hollywood movie, a television commercial, or a music video in the 1990s has almost certainly seen hundreds, perhaps thousands, of images that have been digitally altered or rearranged in some way. Almost routinely now, movie and television special effects are created digitally by computer. Everything from Arnold Schwartzenegger's *Terminator II* to Michael Jackson's latest video owe much of their video magic to the digital darkroom. In a 1994 political campaign spot run on TV by Sam Cravotta, a Republican House candidate in West Virginia, an image of his opponent, Representative Bob Wise, is transformed digitally into one of President Clinton. Technological advances now make the digital imaging process virtually seamless, with no significant degradation of the original image, and invisible even to a well-trained eye. If you're not convinced, just watch *Jurassic Park* and see if you can find a dinosaur or any other digital effect that looks anything less than real.

Although many would say these technological advances have led to ever better communication products, some have pointed out the possible downside. Technology critics argue that the growth of electronic communication signals the death of literacy, or at least verbal literacy. Interactive multimedia hold the potential for a reduced role of linear narrative, one in which storytelling may become a nostalgic relic of the past. When immersed in a sea of data, a reader may see no beginning, middle, or end. Important questions include:

- What will be the grammar of interactive media?
- What will become the storytelling conventions of virtual reality?
- Will literacy as we know it be as irrelevant to the post-Gutenberg era as the art of illumination?

Communications analyst Benjamin Compaine suggests that we need to think in terms of media literacy, a literacy based on fluency with all media, especially those based on images and sound.[12] Posing both a potential commercial bonanza as well as a cultural threat is the development of a new digital editor that can superimpose ads in real time over action video. The planned use for the technology is to put commercial banners in the scenes at sporting events. For example, imagine you're watching a basketball game and a billboard for Coke appears behind the basket. In the next play, the billboard might be advertising Canon cameras. None of these messages would actually appear at the sporting event. They would all be superimposed electronically, either by a central network location, or by any local station. The digital editor could provide the ultimate in custom tailoring commercial messages in real time. It also means a further erosion of the reality of the television image.

Even the advent of the electronic newspaper has alarmed some, who are concerned that one of the greatest social benefits of the newspaper, at least since the days of the penny press, its low cost and widespread availability, will be forever lost in an electronic world where expensive electronic devices will be needed to read the morning newspaper. Arthur Ochs Sulzberger, publisher of The New York Times Company, says his company has had mixed results with high-tech information delivery and is a "long way from saying good-bye to our newsprint suppliers".[13] Although electronic news delivery will serve an important place in the future, Sulzberger said computerized news-on-demand services will never entirely replace newspapers.

In agreement is Charles Brumback, chair and CEO of The Tribune Company. "People won't abandon newspapers in our lifetime," Brumback said.[14] "But advertising will flow to other distribution channels."

Restructuring Media Organizations

Technology has also affected the structure of communication industries. The convergence of computers and telecommunications has created an era of wired and nonwired network computing. This distributed computing environment has enabled media organizations from newsrooms to advertising agencies to rethink the structure of their offices. Decentralization is the primary shift in the structure of these media organizations. No longer need all employees work at the same location, in the same city, or even in the same country. With satellite communications, fiber optics, and powerful desktop computers, communication workers can work together, sharing files, sending messages, and creating new communication products simultaneously from all parts of the world.

Virtual Spaces

During Operation Desert Storm each of the network news divisions created "virtual newsrooms" linking offices in New York City with correspondents on assignment in the Persian Gulf. "Through the use of advanced communication technologies—laptop computers, modems, cellular phones and beepers—journalists now can hook into an electronic 'virtual newsroom' wherever they go, keeping in touch with editors and sources, searching databases and researching, writing and filing stories on the road from their newsrooms without walls."[15]

Similarly, such virtual structures are being adopted in other media organizations. One major advertising agency has already gone virtual. Chiat/Day's Venice, California, headquarters converted to a virtual workplace on January 3, 1994.[16] Envisioned only eight months earlier by company chairman Jay Chiat, the virtual agency houses its electronic nerve center in its Frank Gehry–designed signature building, featuring a variety of high-tech applications ranging from an "intelligent switchboard" to an advanced computing system. Through these technologies, agency executives and other personnel are able to conduct virtually all of their business without ever coming physically to the agency's Venice headquarters. Bob Grossman, senior vice president–group account director at Chiat/Day, who lives in Los Angeles and has been confronted by earthquake-snarled commuter traffic, links easily into his office electronically from a home-based computer just a few steps from his kitchen. Grossman, like other Chiat executives, can do a lot more than simply have his phone calls forwarded to his home. Using a computer and a modem, he can connect to Chiat's central computer and select from any of the system's menu-driven applications, such as word processing, electronic calendar (including automatically scheduling meetings), file management, and electronic mail. But it is neither the hardware nor its applications that make this virtual agency so remarkable, *Advertising Age* points out. The Chiat office building actually houses no private offices and hard-wired phones any longer for its executives. Rather, it provides "work spaces" and portable phones. "What makes Chiat/Day virtual is the extent to which it pushes technology. The modern office shifts employees' bottom line to the work, rather than attendance."[17]

The New Media Audience: Technology's Child

Ultimately, these technological changes have important implications for media audiences and society in general. Technology critic Neil Postman writes, "a technology . . . is merely a machine"; it "becomes a medium as it employs a symbolic code, as it finds its place in a particular social setting."[18] "A medium," he notes, "is the social and intellectual environment a machine creates." Thus, as new technologies create new social and intellectual environments, one would expect society to be irrevocably changed.

Many of the new technologies are opening up new means of human interaction. Whether you are exploring a virtual world or simply accessing an electronic bulletin board, people around the world are talking to each other, sharing experiences, and generally going where no man or woman has gone before—electronically.

Daniel Kennedy, reporter and editor at the *Boston Phoenix,* a leading alternative weekly newspaper, recently assessed the potential harmful cultural consequences of a technological Frankenstein created and driven by commercial interests. When corporate titans such as Time-Warner build information superhighways delivering five hundred television channels to the home, what is the social cost? Kennedy contends that "as information becomes increasingly decentralized, there's a danger that consumers of that information—all of us, in other words—will become more and more isolated from society and from each other."[19]

:) (smile)

Of course, some of the unintended, or at least unexpected, consequences are relatively harmless. One cultural example is the creation of "emoticons" on computer networks. As computer users have entered the online world of cyberspace, they have invented a graphical iconic language of their own to represent a whole range of emotions using a standard QWERTY keyboard. Commonly used emoticons, or smileys, are shown in Table 1-3.

Such keyboard keystrokes have also developed into a form of humor, as well. Making the rounds at MIT, says Adam Clayton Powell III, is this computer joke:

DOS prompt in Canada: EH:\

("EH" is a Canadian verbal expression commonly added to the end of a sentence in conversation, and :\ the accompanying facial expression.)

Some see the use of emoticons as nothing more than online clichés. Neal Stephenson, author of the science fiction novel *Snow Crash,* suggests that emoticons are the "electronic equivalent of spin doctors: commonly inserted at the end of a sentence that is meant to be interpreted as sarcasm."[20]

THE CHANGING PLAYERS

With the technological convergence of the computer, television, and telecommunications in a digital communication environment, the major players in the communication industry come from a wide variety of fields. At the time of this writing, the key players vying for control of the information highway include telephone, cable television,

TABLE 1-3   Emoticons on the Information Highway

Emotion	Meaning
:)	Smile
:(	Frown
:'	Cry
;)	Wink
:D	Laughter
:-O	Yell
:-	Anger
:X	My lips are sealed
:P	Stick out tongue
:Q	Smoking
:*	A kiss

Can you decipher this one %-) ? (It means confusion, with the % indicating a crinkled brow.)

entertainment, broadcasting, and newspaper companies, as well as satellite and computer companies. Thus, depending on how one defines the field, the list of top companies varies, although many lists include most of the same key players since those companies tend to have multimedia holdings.

Although it is impossible to develop a single short list of the most important communication companies, it is still useful to identify a few of the companies leading the development of new media technologies. These companies come from a variety of industries and divide generally along the lines of being either content producers or technology creators, although these lines are rapidly blurring. A selected list of the most important communication companies with a major stake in new technology includes:

- international multimedia titans Time-Warner Inc., USA; News Corporation, Australia; Verlagsgruppe Bertelsmann GmbH, Munich, Germany; Capital Cities/ABC, USA and Sony, Japan
- U.S. cable TV behemoth TCI
- Japan's public broadcaster NHK and Japanese audiovisual company Matshushita Electrical Industrial
- U.S. telephone companies Bellsouth and Bell Atlantic
- U.S. computer hardware manufacturers IBM and Hewlett-Packard
- U.S. software giant Microsoft

Importantly, a growing number of mergers, acquisitions, and corporate alignments are redefining the nature and number of industry players. Some $75 billion has changed hands in 160 recent multimedia deals.[21] Bell Atlantic's planned acquisition of TCI, the struggle for Paramount, and other as yet undetermined alignments may completely reshape the corporate landscape in information technology. The formerly separate worlds of publishing, broadcasting, cable, entertainment, computing, and telecommunications are rapidly converging, both in terms of ownership and in cross-industry collaboration. As companies have recognized the necessity to join forces and capitalize on the synergistic potential between companies with differing expertise in the information industry, they have come together to form strategic alliances for the multimedia world of the next millennium.

No longer do even the greatest of corporate giants prefer to go it alone on the information highway. Behemoths such as Bell Atlantic, Tele-Communications Inc., IBM, AT&T, and Time-Warner all announced collaborative efforts with companies in 1993 that only a few months earlier they would have treated as competitive threats.[22] Telephone companies have aligned with newspaper publishers. Cable companies are cooperating with entertainment companies. Computer manufacturers are combining with software developers. In each instance, one company is complementing its knowledge, skills, and resources with those of its former adversary.

Nevertheless, there are dangerous ramifications of this game of increasing industry collaboration and mergers. Media critics such as Ben Bagdikian contend that the increasing concentration of media ownership and the growth of global media companies based on the capabilities of the electronic superhighway are leading to fewer and fewer hands controlling greater and greater amounts of information. Soon, many fear, virtually the entire flow of information will be controlled by a few communication behemoths. Bagdikian points to the shrinking ownership of major media corporations in the United States, from about fifty companies in 1983 to twenty in 1992. Technology visionary Anthony Smith has argued convincingly that the 1990s have already seen the growth of just seven media giants: Time-Warner, Bertelsmann, Sony, Disney, Hachette, News Corp, and . . . telecom giants AT&T, and cable.[23]

In addition, most of the major players fighting for control of the information are companies from the fields of entertainment, cable TV, telecommunications, and computers. Few are from the newspaper industry or broadcast television, with the exception of companies like Cox Enterprises, which in addition to its newspaper holdings, also owns cable TV systems. "Phone companies, cable systems and entertainment producers are rushing headlong into the new interactive electronic world while the print media try to figure out how they fit in," observes Philip Moeller, former business editor and electronic news editor at the *Sun* in Baltimore and a communication consultant in West Hartford, Connecticut.[24] The question is: Who will control the information infrastructure? For more than three hundred years, newspapers in America have controlled their own printing presses. Broadcasters have controlled the airways for much of the twentieth century under the watchful eye of the Federal Communications Commission. Both newspapers and broadcasters have held news in high regard, almost as a public trust necessary to a democracy. If the information highway infrastructure is controlled by media without that tradition of news (with some exceptions such as Turner's CNN and local cable news, such as Cablevision's pioneering Rainbow 12 on Long Island), how will news fare? NBC was originally 50 percent owned by the General Electric Company. In fact, the musical notes G-E-C are well-known to anyone in America who has ever watched NBC. GE, however, sold off NBC early on to RCA, and it was only a decade ago that GE reacquired the television network. As author, journalist, and media critic Ken Auletta makes clear in his classic work, *Three Blind Mice*, the impact of the reacquisition of the network by a nonmedia, nonjournalistic company was profound.[25] It changed completely the corporate culture that existed at NBC, replacing a value system that placed high priority on news at any cost, with a bottom-line orientation that treated news like any other area of network programming or, for that matter, like any product produced by GE. What are the implications of such ownership prospects for the future of the information superhighway? Will corporate interests and the government treat the information highway as a national public resource and require its owners to serve as a common carrier, as the phone companies are required to do today?

U.S. government agencies, such as the Federal Communications Commission (FCC), the Federal Trade Commission (FTC), and the Justice Department have so far paid little attention to any potential antitrust considerations in this era of collaboration. In 1993, the FTC found itself deadlocked regarding the propriety of the competitive practices of one software giant, Microsoft, accused of collaborating with computer manufacturers to assure itself of an industry-standard platform compatible to only Microsoft operating systems, such as MS-DOS (Microsoft Disk Operating System) and Windows, a graphical user interface for IBM-compatible personal computers (PCs).

In the fall of 1993, Viacom Inc. filed the first antitrust lawsuit in the media wars. Viacom owner Sumner Redstone found himself in an escalating bidding war with QVC Home Shopping Network's CEO John Malone for Paramount Communications, a man Vice President Al Gore once called Darth Vader.[26] In response to TCI's $9.9 billion bid for Paramount, which exceeded Viacom's opening bid by some $2 billion, Redstone filed his antitrust suit against not only rival bidder QVC, but also Tele-Communications Inc. (TCI), Liberty Media Inc., and Encore Media Corp., all of which are owned or controlled by Malone. The implications of the suit, however, go far beyond the battle for Paramount. "While QVC's attempt to wrestle the studio away triggered the filing, Viacom broadly charges that TCI president and Liberty chairman John Malone and the companies with which he is affiliated have tried to secure a chokehold on programming delivery," reports John M. Higgins.[27] This antitrust suit may be just the first salvo in a new era of mergers, acquisitions, and the resulting antitrust litigation in the age of the information superhighway.

Just when media and financial analysts began to make sense out of this complicated and potentially hostile corporate takeover, Bell Atlantic and TCI stunned those same analysts by announcing the $33 billion acquisition of TCI by Bell Atlantic. The largest media merger ever—the largest merger or acquisition of any type in the United States since 1981, and one of the largest in history—demonstrated American industry's seriousness about building the highly touted "information superhighway" of the future. Others add that the megamerger may have other consequences. "There could be a new period of peace and quiet," said Eli M. Noam, director of Columbia University's Institute for Tele-Information (CITI), admitting the potential oligopoly model. "But the other possibility—the possibility I consider more likely—is that it will lead to more aggressive competition within each market segment."[28]

Unfortunately for Bell Atlantic and TCI, the deal fell through on February 23, 1994, just four months after it was announced. The exact reasons for the failed deal are unclear, but many industry analysts have offered several possibilities, including: Malone got cold feet about selling the cable TV behemoth he spent years building; the plummeting stock prices of TCI and Bell Atlantic since the announced merger decreased the value of the deal to the point where it made little economic sense. Malone, Smith, and some media analysts put the blame on the FCC's decision to reregulate the price of cable TV, reducing the potential cash flow of an acquired TCI. Others, including telecommunications scholar Michael Noll said the failed deal is the first death knell in the impending collapse of the information superhighway.[29] In Noll's view, there is no need or demand for an information superhighway.

An analysis in the *New York Times* echoes this view, arguing that the notion of an information superhighway is fundamentally flawed, since unlike the national highway system, government has no intention of building the information superhighway. A more appropriate model is that of the railroad, which was built by corporations in the nineteenth century, and was subject to the vagaries of profit drives and marketplace fancies.

Had the Bell Atlantic–TCI merger gone through, the new company would have had electronic access to 42 percent of United States homes.[30] Although current regulations prohibit a telephone company from owning any cable interests in its local telephone service area, less than 15 percent of TCI's customers would have been affected. Perhaps more important, the deal would have given the would-be corporate giant both the multichannel cargo-carrying capacity and content of the nation's largest cable television system and programmer and the "magical" switching capability of the telephone company, which lets "anyone on the network communicate with anyone else.[31] Bell Atlantic's Chairman Smith believed that the merger would have created an environment in which even a five hundred–channel cable system would be a misnomer. "It's the infinite channel," Smith said. "We won't be talking about channels in the year 2000. That will be sort of quaint." Smith added that the model will be that of the telephone company, but in a new form. "All of this will be telco. Only it will be broadband, interactive telco. Not narrowband telco. It will be switched, we will be delivering it exactly to your home," he explained, adding, "It will be common carrier when it starts from the telephone plant."[32] As a government regulated monopoly, telephone companies are currently required to serve as a common carrier, providing open access to all content providers seeking to use the telephone infrastructure.

Critics of the merger, such as Viacom, voiced concern about the awesome power the new corporate titan would have wielded over the nation's information infrastructure. The day after the merger announcement, Viacom issued a statement that "the deal raises many new and troubling questions about the Malone group's market dominance and monopolistic intentions." Some scholarly voices agreed. "If the Supreme Court accepts TCI's claim that a media company cannot be compelled to allow access to competitors, it would give a Bell Atlantic–TCI conglomerate an open path to monopolization," wrote C. Edwin Baker, a professor of law at the University of Pennsylvania, on the Op-Ed page of the *New York Times*.[33] Some have pointed out the dangers of applying principles of common carrier practices to the information superhighway. If the telephone companies are required to treat all video suppliers as equal— which is implied under common carrier rules—then the Walt Disney Channel and The Orgasm Channel might be right next to each other on a video dial-tone menu.

Despite the failed Bell Atlantic–TCI merger, the information superhighway is likely to be built. The potential for industry collaboration is still real, even if not in the form of mergers or acquisitions. As investment banker Richard MacDonald of C.S. First Boston suggests, if the deals made sense before, they still make sense now.[34] They may simply take another shape, perhaps being executed on a contractual basis. Like the railroad of a century ago, the new data network is likely to find entrepreneurs to finance its construction, public relations practitioners who will promote it, and passengers who will ride on it. There are still six other Regional Bell Operating Companies, not to mention AT&T, that have considerable interest in developing a nationwide advanced, broadband, switched telecommunications network.

William Gates, Microsoft CEO and America's wealthiest entrepreneur (and second richest person—*Forbes,* 1993), has involved his company in a number of alliances. The rationale is clear. "Anyone who invests in this area is making a bet on interactivity," says Gates.[35] Gates stunned many observers by announcing in early 1994 a joint effort with McCaw Cellular to build a global satellite network to provide a wireless superhighway.

One area where new deals are taking shape is in wireless communications. Some of the major deals announced in 1994 include AT&T's $11.5 billion acquisition of McCaw Cellular; the alliance of Sprint and three cable TV companies: Telecommunications Inc., Comcast, and Cox Cable; and the joint effort of Bell Atlantic, Nynex, US West, and Air Touch.

The giant players in the new media game are joined by a growing number of small entrepreneurs. As the new technologies have made possible global multimedia communications, they have also reduced many of the barriers to market entry. Much of the new technology is considerably less expensive and simpler to use than earlier generations of technology. As a result, new companies have found ways to compete with much larger companies for specialized market niches. *Newsweek* declares, "Forget the big mergers. In the race to control the interactive highway, the real winners may be the (lesser-known) firms that will build it bit by byte."[36]

Since the divestiture of AT&T in 1984, thousands of small and hungry companies have emerged to provide competitive alternative long-distance telephone services. Although most of these companies have captured little market share from AT&T, MCI and Sprint have made sizable inroads. There are many other interesting examples of small, pioneering companies in the new technology marketplace. One innovative upstart is RoundBook Publishing Group of Scotts Valley, California, a company specializing in CD-ROM publishing. Although publishing giants such as Ziff Communications maintain control over much of the the CD-ROM publishing field in the United States, RoundBook has captured a very important market niche. With the end of the Cold War and the opening up of the former Soviet Union to foreign business investment, RoundBook has taken its entrepreneurial spirit to the museums and art world of Russia. Although many companies sought the rights to publish images of Russia's vast art collections on CD-ROM, RoundBook convinced Russia's museum and art directors to grant them exclusive rights to the material. Founded on March 1, 1993 by CD-ROM gurus Greg Smith and Francis Juliano, RoundBook secured the confidence of Russia's art world by agreeing to keep all Russian art in Russia and to work with Russian artists to photograph all the art. Smith and Juliano have more than twelve years' experience developing CD-ROM products at Sony and Meridian Data, creating many of the products available for the Sony Data Diskman and the MMCD player, including "the highly respected *Mayo Clinic Family Health Book.*"[37] Compton's NewMedia will distribute the forthcoming RoundBook products to more than 5,000 outlets. Round-Book and Compton's NewMedia recently signed an agreement worth $18 million that will deliver at least twenty CD-ROM titles to stores in 1994. The deal will catapult RoundBook from obscurity into one of the largest publishers of CD-ROMs in the world.[38]

In 1991, the Minority Television Project launched an innovative new public television station in the San Francisco Bay Area. Under the direction of founding station manager Adam Clayton Powell III, the station was able to operate on a shoestring budget of just $100,000 for the first three months of transmission. Although KMTP captured a small share of the Bay Area viewers, it has been able to survive and grow largely because of the new technology of new wave television, including the multichannel nature of the marketplace and the low cost of 8mm videotape technology.

Another startup taking advantage of both breakthroughs in wireless technology and loosening of the regulatory environment is Cellularvision.[39] The small New York–based company uses wireless cellular transmitters to send cable television programming to consumers in Brighton Beach, Brooklyn, and will soon expand into the larger markets of Queens and midtown Manhattan.

Media giants have also succeeded at employing the new technology to successfully launch new media efforts. Time Warner used the technology of high-8 video equipment to launch its 24-hour cable news channel, New York One in New York City. *Time* magazine first experimented with high-8 equipment during the Persian Gulf war.[40] *Time* sent one of its boldest reporters into the Gulf equipped with a light-weight, inexpensive high-8 video camera, small enough to fit into the palm of the hand of the operator. He was able to shoot the first video of the Kuwaiti oil well fires seen on American television on ABC's *Nightline.*

THE STAKES

At stake is a potentially huge and lucrative global marketplace. Industry projections are that by the year 2000, revenues on the information highway in the United States alone will be 10 to 20 times the $25 billion cable market or the $12 billion video rental market. The global marketplace is even bigger, exceeding a trillion dollars worldwide. "The gold rush to a $3.5 trillion multimedia market is on," proclaims technology visionary and author George Gilder.[41] These financial stakes are driving many large and small corporations to invest millions, in some cases billions, of dollars in infrastructure, software development, and experimental projects.

There are interesting historical parallels to the massive investment in new media technology today. As recently as a decade ago, many news and information companies invested heavily in the development of videotex, or text delivery over the air or by cable for presentation on television screens. Knight-Ridder invested heavily in its Viewtron experiment, for example, only to see its ultimate failure at a cost of many millions of dollars. Walter Baer, deputy vice president of domestic research for RAND, physicist, and director of the Times Mirror's videotex experiments, has commented on the lessons learned from the videotex failures. He observed that the videotex experiments of the early 1980s taught us how to become a millionaire—all you needed was to start with $40 million.[42] One might say the current efforts to build the information highway will teach us how to become a billionaire. . . .

Although many of the traditional media and information companies have seen their revenues plateau and experienced little growth throughout the 1980s, many electronic information services have seen their revenues grow dramatically. Real-time information service providers, such as Dow Jones's Telerate, Reuters, *Bloomberg Business News,* and Knight-Ridder, for example, have seen dramatic annual growth rates of more than 10 percent since 1982.[43] In 1992 alone, the net profit of Dow Jones's Telerate reached $90 million, an amount in excess of the net profit of the entire daily newspaper industry in the United States, which totaled just $88 million in 1992. Bloomberg has grown at an annual rate of more than 13 percent since its inception in just 1983 and is now a company with annual revenues of more than $37 billion.[44, 45]

On Wall Street, media analysts have found that a fundamental sea change is occurring in the revenue base of the media. Traditionally, media industries have been largely supported by advertising revenues. Newspapers, magazines, television, and radio have received the majority of their revenues, between 60 and 75 percent, from advertising support. In today's new media environment, advertiser-supported media are experiencing flat or declining revenues. Meanwhile, user-supported media are experiencing revenue growth. Cable television, online services, and pay-per-view are growing rapidly. Some projections show a rate of growth in excess of 20 percent.

Although the commercial stakes loom large on the financial horizon, the cultural stakes may be even greater. For at least three centuries, since the first newspaper, *Publick Occurrences,* was founded in the Western Hemisphere in Boston, Massachusetts, media markets have been defined largely by geography and limited by political and cultural boundaries. In recent decades, new technology has begun to change all that, as computers, modern telecommunications, and satellite communications have spawned an era of target marketing based on demographics and other audience characteristics. The convergence of telecommunications, computing, and media is completing the transformation of the communications marketplace. We are witnessing the creation of online telecommunities existing only in cyberspace. These are the communities of mind, linking individuals with common interests, able to communicate across geographic, political, and cultural boundaries.

Inventing the Future

With the stakes looming so large, important questions arise regarding the different roles of government, industry, education, and the public in shaping the future of new media technology and the information superhighway. Should the role of government be that of a neutral referee, simply making sure that all participants play fairly and by the same rules? Or, should government be an active participant in the development of information technology? For example, is it appropriate for the government to introduce and support a "free" (to users) Internet system? Does such a role advance or hinder the development of the technology?

In comparison, what should be the role of industry-led research, development, and implementation? In the United States, industry has often lead the way in developing new technology, with social consequences being considered more as an afterthought than as a part of the plan. What are the consequences of such an approach? In contrast, the approach taken in developing new information technologies in the European Union has been much more cautious, with government and official bodies taking the lead and industry following suit. More often in Europe, social consequences are analyzed before technologies are tested or implemented. What are the implications of such an approach for the development of new media technologies? Are there important implications for future economic growth? How are these considerations affected by the growth of the global economy and the global information society?

Economic Forces

A wide variety of indicators point to the growth and strength of the information technology sector of the U.S. economy. Information technology leads capital investment, with steady growth from 17 percent of private equipment investment in 1974 devoted to computers and other information technology to 45 percent in 1994 devoted to the information technology sector.[46] Meanwhile, industrial machinery as a percent of private equipment investment has dropped from about 32 percent in 1974 to 19 percent in 1994. Computer and telecommunication equipment has grown dramatically as a U.S. export in recent years, rising from about 7.0 percent of U.S. exports in 1980 to twice that level (14 percent) in 1993. Information sector jobs have grown steadily over the past two decades as well, rising from about 150,000 jobs in computer software, data processing, and information retrieval to about 900,000 such jobs in 1994, now surpassing the total employed in motor vehicles and parts manufacture. Consumer spending on multimedia products as a share of disposable income has also risen recently, from about 2.8 percent in 1980, to about 3.4 percent in 1993.[47]

INDUSTRY OVERVIEW

The information and communication industry is a broad and rapidly growing sector of the U.S. and global economies. The U.S. Department of Commerce identifies seven primary subindustries within this broad industry.[48] They are ranked by total revenues in Table 1-4.

TABLE 1-4   Subindustries in the Information and Communication Industry: Revenue Ranking

Subindustry	Revenues (in billions)
Telecommunications services	$175.0
Printing and publishing	$172.0
Computer equipment and software	$160.3
Information services	$102.1
Telephone and telegraph equipment	$66.0
Radio communications and detection equipment	$55.3
Entertainment (not including over the air TV advertising revenues)	$43.29

Telecommunications services ($175 billion) and printing and publishing ($172 billion) are the largest of these seven subindustries, with the information services subindustry running a strong fourth, at $102.1 billion. Although fourth in total revenues, the information services sector is the fastest growing, with growth of nearly 20 percent in 1992. Printing and publishing is growing at a rate of just 2 percent, in contrast. Recent data confirm that business is booming in the online market. Revenue and subscriber totals are both on the rise and show no signs of stopping for at least the rest of the 1990s (see Figures 1-1 and 1-2).[49] Of course, revenue and subscriber levels eventually will plateau, and their growth curves will likely follow the general pattern of cable growth. The growth curve will probably follow an S-shaped curve, with a period of rapid growth continuing for the next decade or so, followed by a gradual decrease in growth. The potential for online subscriptions worldwide could reach the hundreds of millions some day, perhaps equaling that of telephone subscription. Much, however, depends on the diffusion of a variety of technologies, including optical fiber and home computers and information appliances. Moreover, advances in wireless and satellite-based mobile communications may further enlarge the potential subscriber base for online communication services. If these technologies do not progress as rapidly as one might expect in the next decade, then the potential for online subscriptions might plateau at roughly 50 million by 2000.

The U.S. Department of Commerce divides the information services industry into three main sectors: electronic information services ($10.2 billion), data processing and network services ($35.6 billion), and

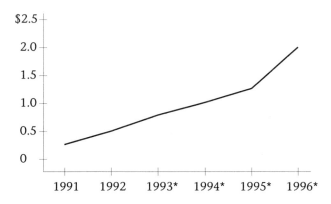

FIGURE 1-1   Online Revenue in Billions

Source: The Yankee Group
*Projection

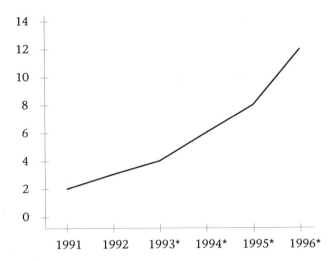

FIGURE 1-2   Online Subscribers in Millions

Source: The Yankee Group
*Projection

computer professional services ($56.3 billion). In 1991, the U.S. Depart-
ment of Commerce projected that the revenues of the electronic information services sector of the U.S. economy would grow by 20 percent in
1992. The projected growth for data processing and network services for
this same period was 13.5 percent and for computer professional services,
almost 14 percent.

Electronic information services include five major media: online
computer communications, compact disk–read only memory (CD-ROM),
magnetic tape, floppy disk, and audiotex, reports the Commerce Department. Online computer services provide the lion's share of electronic
information services revenue (78 percent), with audiotex and CD-ROM
growing rapidly. Use of magnetic tape and floppy disk for delivery of
information services is on the decline.

Although important in the control and creation of the information
highway, the other six subindustries within the communication and
information industry are less central to the discussion of new media technologies. Therefore, we will provide only a thumbnail sketch of the revenue and structure of these subindustries. Telecommunications services,
the largest subindustry with annual revenues of $175 billion, is also expe-
riencing rapid growth. Although revenues for domestic telecommunications services ($169.9 billion) are growing at just 5.5 percent, revenues
from international services ($11.6 billion) are growing at 17.7 percent.
Revenues from cellular mobile telephone services ($5.5 billion) are

growing at a rate of about 13 percent. Satellite services revenue ($1.5 billion) is growing more slowly at 4.5 percent. This subindustry serves 88 million households and 30 million businesses nationwide.

Printing and publishing, the second largest subindustry with $172 billion in annual revenues, comprises four main sectors: newspapers, periodicals, book publishing, and commercial printing (U.S. Commerce Department). Newspapers ($34.7 billion) face the gloomiest future of these sectors, with an expected growth of 1–2 percent. Periodicals ($21.3 billion) experienced unprecedented growth in the past decade, but saw a slight drop in receipts in constant dollars in the early 1990s. Still, international prospects are good, and growth is expected to be about 2 percent. Book publishing ($16 billion) is growing at about 3 percent, with the marketplace shifting from heavy purchases by state and local schools, as government funding has decreased, to increased personal consumption. Commercial printing is both the largest ($55.7 billion) and fastest-growing sector of the printing and publishing subindustry, with an annual growth rate of about 3.5 percent.

Computer equipment and software have total revenues of approximately $160 billion and are made up of seven specific industries (U.S. Commerce Department). In computer equipment, the four industries are electronic computers, computer storage devices, computer terminals, and computer peripheral equipment. The three software industries are computer programming services, prepackaged software, and computer integrated systems design. Electronic computers include supercomputers, mainframes, midrange, personal, and portable computers. Computer storage devices include magnetic, optical, and tape storage devices. Computer terminals also include teleprinters. Computer peripheral equipment includes printer, plotter, and graphics display technology.

In the software sector, computer programming services include computer assisted design, manufacturing, and engineering (U.S. Commerce Department). Prepackaged software includes a variety of consumer and professional off-the-shelf programs, ranging from word processing software such as Microsoft Word to desktop publishing software such as QuarkXPress. Computer integrated systems design includes a variety of developing software applications, such as artificial intelligence (AI), including expert systems, fuzzy logic, and neural networks. AI applications have ranged from military diagnostic systems in Desert Storm to insurance underwriting programs. Although AI revenues were only about $300 million in 1991, rapid growth is projected in the rest of the 1990s. In Europe, revenues are expected to top $2.4 billion for expert systems in 1994; the global market for neural networks is expected to reach $1 billion by 1995.

Telephone and telegraph equipment can be grouped into two categories: network equipment, such as transmission systems and switches, and customer premises equipment (CPE), such as telephone sets, key systems, and private branch exchanges (PBXs) (U.S. Commerce Department). Total market revenues were $66 billion in 1992, although consumer demand has been decreasing and industry shipments are expected to decline about 1 percent.

Radio communications and detection equipment is a $55.3 billion industry, with annual growth expected at about 5 percent (U.S. Commerce Department). Four sectors in this industry are particularly notable: satellite communications, mobile cellular radiotelephone systems, wireless personal communications, and fiber optics. The United States controls 65 percent of the world communications satellite market, with France (14 percent), Italy (6 percent), the United Kingdom (5 percent) and Japan (2 percent) trailing far behind. In 1991, U.S. companies held contracts to build fifty-seven of the world's eighty-seven satellite orders. The nine commercial communications satellites built by U.S. firms in 1990 were valued at $1.3 billion. The mobile cellular radiotelephone systems sector is poised for explosive growth in the decade ahead. Cellular phone prices have fallen dramatically (low-end celphones are priced at less than $100) and the number of users has risen rapidly (7.4 million users at the end of 1991 with 30 percent annual growth), with total revenues of some $5.5 billion in 1991.

Wireless personal communications services (PCNs), although currently still on the drawing board, are likely to experience rapid growth in the decade ahead as the FCC auctions off 160 megahertz of bandwidth for personal communications services, more than three times the spectrum allotted to cellular telephone systems (U.S. Commerce Department). The pocket-sized phones will be available after 1996.[50] Demand for PCNs is estimated at 60 to 100 million users by 2000, with PCN devices costing as little as $90 to $200. "The growth potential for wireless data service is enormous," says Benjamin L. Scott, chief operating officer for Bell Atlantic Mobile. "In our markets alone, $1.3 billion is up for grabs."[51] Market analysts at Arthur D. Little predict that the United States wireless market could quintuple during the next decade. Gregory Pottie, a wireless technology researcher at the University of California at Los Angeles, estimates the total capacity for the technology at 150 million wireless customers in the United States. Convergence is also an important factor in the wireless market as digital PCN technology is developed, facilitating direct access to the Internet. See Chapter 3 for further discussion of the possible services available through PCNs.

The fiber optics industry has grown at roughly 20 percent in recent years, despite the economic recession (U.S. Commerce Department). Companies in the United States have installed more than 8.2 million fiber-kilometers for telecommunications applications. The majority of these fiber-kilometers have been installed by the telephone companies, although cable companies have installed several hundred thousand fiber-kilometers. The total U.S. market was $1.7 billion in 1991, about 40 percent of the world market. There has been much debate about whether fiber is needed to the home to provide a full range of communication services, with the general consensus that fiber backbone and trunk lines and fiber to the curb is all that is needed, given compression technologies and the availability of coaxial cable to the home. This combination of technologies would allow for true video-on-demand, or the video dial tone. Estimates for the cost of fiber to every home in the United States range from $200 billion to $1 trillion, with fiber costing roughly $100 million for every 3,200 kilometers. Fiber is being rapidly deployed around the world, including European countries such as France, Germany, the United Kingdom, and the Netherlands, and in East Asia, especially in Japan.

Entertainment, not including over-the-air TV advertising, is a $43.14 billion industry (U.S. Commerce Department). Included are the motion picture ($5.01 billion with 1 percent annual growth), music ($7.54 billion, with 7 percent annual growth), and home entertainment subindustries, including home video ($10.8 billion, 4 percent growth), which is really a part of the same industry that produces and distributes motion pictures, and cable television ($19.79 billion, with about 15 percent annual growth). As of 1992, approximately three-fifths of all TV households subscribed to cable TV in the United States. Sixty-one percent of U.S. TV households subscribe to basic cable, up from 46 percent in 1985. Subscription revenues were up 14.5 percent in 1990, with advertising revenues up 25.8 percent. Overall revenue was up 10.5 percent in 1992. New media technologies have important implications for the entertainment industry. The motion picture industry is competing successfully with the home video market, although any gains are due not to increased admissions but to increased admission prices and increased revenues in the international market, where motion pictures remain one of the United States' strongest exports, with more than $6.35 in revenues in 1990. The music subindustry has been transformed by the compact disk (CD); 1991 was a milestone year for the music industry, with CD sales ($3.9 billion) surpassing sales of cassettes. CD unit sales surpassed cassette sales, as well, with 370 million cassettes sold that year, while the number of CD unit sales reached 382 million. Protecting intellectual property rights continues to be one of the greatest challenges facing the music industry. Copyright infringement, including piracy and counterfeiting, have plagued the music industry on the international front, and the problem is likely to worsen as digital technologies take hold, making high-quality copying and illegal distribution easier.

Employment

The communication and information industry officially employs some 4.165 million persons in the United States, according to the 1987 United States Department of Commerce census. Growth trends suggest that by 1994, the number employed in this field is likely to easily top five million. Table 1-5 breaks down the 1987 employment figures by subindustry.

Number of Firms

Some 24,223 establishments provide electronic information services, although the number is rapidly growing. There are three times as many printing and publishing firms, 60,000, although there is less growth in this sector. Approximately 2,000 firms provide telecommunications services in the United States. By mid-1991 there were 1,029 cellular radiotelephone systems; however, there ultimately will be 1,468 firms, with 2 in every market. In the entertainment sector, there were 23,700 theater screens and 387 new releases, and theater attendance was 1.06 billion (U.S. Department of Commerce, 1989). As of 1992, some 100,000 establishments sold and rented videocassettes in 1990, although most did not specialize in videocassette sales and rentals. The number of videocassette specialty stores decreased from 29,400 in 1989 to 29,000 in 1990. Blockbuster is the leading provider in this market, with nearly 3,500 stores and $2.9 billion in revenue in 1992—seven times the volume of its closest retail competitor—and 11 percent of the retail sector.[52] There are 1,505 cable television systems in the United States. Most are part of larger companies called multiple system operators (MSOs), the largest being John Malone's Denver-based Tele-Communications Inc. (TCI).

TABLE 1-5   Employment in the Communication and Information Industry

Subindustry	Number employed
Printing and publishing	1.5 million
Information services	1 million
Telecommunications services	890,000
Entertainment	413,000
Computer equipment and software	362,900
Radio communications and detection equipment	63,057

Source: Employment and Wages Annual Averages, 1993. U.S. Department of Labor, bulletin 2449, U.S. Government Printing Office, Washington, DC.

International Distribution

Unlike many U.S. industries, the information services industry has always had a positive trade balance, and the U.S. Department of Commerce expects this trend to continue. Electronic information services derive 30 percent of their revenue from international markets. Databases are an important part of this global picture. Cuadra Associates, publishers of an annual directory of databases, reports that there are 6,200 databases available worldwide, with 4,700 online and 1,500 in portable format, compared to only 3,369 available in 1987.[53] The United States is easily the largest producer and consumer of databases, producing more than 50 percent of the databases available in the world.

Projected Publishing on a Global Information Highway

Projections for the market size of the global information superhighway range from more than $1 trillion to more than $3.5 trillion in the United States alone by 2000, with the international market even greater. The United States is not alone, however, in building information superhighways. Projects in Europe, Asia, Latin America, and Australia are also underway to construct broadband information systems. Two Europewide systems are already under development. Europe has planned a two-year trial to link seventeen now incompatible telephone networks into a pan-European digital network. A similar European Community project began in the fall of 1993 to test broadband services including financial transactions and medical and computer-aided design applications.

Britain, France, and Germany have also planned information highway projects, many involving U.S. companies. In Britain, cable and telephone companies are laying fiber optics throughout most neighborhoods. Some of the companies are Regional Bell Operating Companies (RBOCs), such as Nynex, SBC Communications (formerly Southwestern Bell), and US West, along with two international telephone companies, Singapore Telecom and Bell Canada, as well as U.S. cable operators Tele-Communications Inc. (TCI), Jones Intercable, Cox Cable, and Comcast.

In France, France Telecom has launched four pilot projects to evaluate high-capacity fiber-optic systems to offices and homes. Plaisance Television has planned two interactive cable-TV home shopping channels that will also carry video games. Of course, France's government-sponsored Minitel nationwide videotex service continues to provide home shopping, banking, and other services such as an electronic telephone directory. Interestingly, one of the most popular services on Minitel, like many other new technologies, is the blue services, or adult-oriented bulletin boards.

Germany's Berlin and Deutsche Bundespost Telekom are testing a variety of services, such as one that will let physicians conduct video-conferences involving patient X-rays and medical histories.

U.S. telephone giant Bell Atlantic has also announced a preliminary deal with Italy's Stet SpA to form an interactive television venture.[54] The agreement calls for the two companies to study the application of video on demand in the Italian market. Down under, Australia is launching an innovative over-the-air cable television system that will bring the information highway to the entire continent, reports Richard MacDonald, leading media analyst and investment banker.[55]

As these global conglomerates, media magnates, and upstart entrepreneurs race headlong into the future of new media technology, one can't help wondering how these new media barons will explore and develop the unknown boundaries of the electronic frontier. Will their commercial interests completely overwhelm public interests? What balance will they strike between the needs of the few and the needs of the many? Recalling the words of former FCC Chairman Newton Minow, will the new media landscape become anything more than a cultural wasteland exploited for pure commercial profit?[56]

NOTES

1. William Shakespeare, *Othello,* George L. Kitredge, ed. Ginn, 1941 (1621), act 3, sc. 4, line 69.

2. Marshall McLuhan, *Understanding Media: The Extensions of Man.* New York: McGraw-Hill, 1964.

3. Anthony Smith, "From Books To Bytes: The Computer and the Library," in John V. Pavlik and Everette E. Dennis, eds., *Demystifying Media Technology.* Mountain View, CA: Mayfield Publishing, 1993.

4. Sandra D. Atchison "The Care and Feeding of 'Lone Eagles,'" *Business Week,* 5 November 1993, 58.

5. David Bohrman and Larry Wood, "Hypermedia at ABC News: Magna: An Electronic Anchor Information System," in John V. Pavlik and Everette E. Dennis, eds., *Demystifying Media Technology.* Mountain View, CA: Mayfield Publishing, 1993.

6. John Pavlik, "Newsroom Convergence," in John V. Pavlik and Everette E. Dennis, eds., *Demystifying Media Technology.* Mountain View, CA: Mayfield Publishing, 1993.

7. Lorne Manly, "The 6 Days of Creation," *Folio,* 15 June 1993, 49, 92.

8. Adam Clayton Powell III, "Getting the Picture," in John V. Pavlik and Everette E. Dennis, eds., *Demystifying Media Technology.* Mountain View, CA: Mayfield Publishing, 1993.

9. Burton Benjamin, *Niemen Report,* Summer 1986.

10. Adam Clayton Powell III, Speech, Technology Studies seminar hosted by the Freedom Forum Media Studies Center, 27 October 1993.

11. Don E. Tomlinson, "Computer Manipulation and Creation of Images and Sounds: Assessing the Impact," Monograph, The Annenberg Washington Program, Communications Policy Studies, Northwestern University, 1993.

12. Benjamin Compaine, *Understanding New Media: Trends and Issues in Electronic Distribution of Information.* Cambridge, MA: Ballinger, 1984.

13. Mark Thalhimer and Marcella Steingart, eds., *Media Industry News Roundup,* compiled from the Associated Press, the Freedom Forum Media Studies Center, 31 May 1994.

14. Tom Fenton, Freedom Forum report on a speech by Charles Brumback at the 47th World Newspaper Congress and FIEJ Annual General Meeting May 29–June 1 1994, Vienna, Austria.

15. Mark Thalhimer, "The Virtual Newsroom," *Media and Campaign '92: The Homestretch,* the Freedom Forum Media Studies Center: 70.

16. *Advertising Age,* "A Day in the 'Virtual' Life of a Chiat/Day Executive," 14 March 1994.

17. *Advertising Age,* "A Day in the 'Virtual' Life of a Chiat/Day Executive," 14 March 1994, 19.

18. Neil Postman, *Amusing Ourselves to Death.* New York: Penguin Books, 1986, p. 86.

19. Daniel Kennedy, "Lost in Space," *Boston Phoenix,* 7 May 1993, 40.

20. Neal Stephenson, "Smiley's People," *The New Republic,* 13 September 1993, 26.

21. Janice Hughes, "The Changing Multimedia Landscape," The Media Studies Journal, the Freedom Forum Media Studies Center, Winter 1994.

22. Edmund L. Andrews, "Sudden Synergy Among Communications Rivals," *New York Times,* 21 October 1993, D1, D10.

23. Anthony Smith, *Age of Behemoths.* New York: The 20th Century Fund, 1992.

24. Philip Moeller, "The age of convergence," *American Journalism Review,* January/February 1994, 22.

25. Ken Auletta, *Three Blind Mice: How the Networks Lost Their Way.* New York: Random House, 1991.

26. Ken Auletta, "John Malone: Flying Solo," *New Yorker,* 7 February 1994.

27. John M. Higgins, *Multichannel News,* September 1993, 1.

28. Edmund L. Andrews, "Sudden Synergy Among Communications Rivals," *New York Times,* 21 October 1993, D1, D10.

29. Michael Noll, "Is All That Fiber Necessary?" *New York Times,* 19 October 1993.

30. Geraldine Fabrikant, "$23 Billion Media Acquisition Reporter to Be Near Completion," *New York Times,* 13 October, 1993, A1.

31. John Markoff, "A Phone-Cable Vehicle for the Data Superhighway," *New York Times,* 14 October 1993, A1.

32. *Information & Interactive Services Report,* "Bell Atlantic Chairman Sketches Map of Information Superhighway," 5 November 1993, 9.

33. C. Edwin Baker, "Tollbooths on the Information Superhighway," *New York Times,* 26 October 1993.

34. Richard MacDonald, Technology Studies Seminar, the Freedom Forum Media Studies Center, 6 April 1994.

35. Jeff Greenfield, "American Agenda," *ABC World News Tonight* with Peter Jennings, September 1993.

36. *Newsweek,* "Forget the Big Mergers," 24 January 1994, 44.

37. Paul Hilts, "RoundBook Rounds Up Russian Art Treasures," *Publishers Weekly,* 19 July 1993, 24.

38. *Publish,* "Soviet Art via CD-ROM," January 1994, 13.

39. Kirk Johnson, "Acorns Sprout Among the Oaks Of the Telecommunications Field," *New York Times,* 5 July 1994, A1, B2.

40. Joe Quinlan, interview with John Pavlik, 1992.

41. George Gilder, "Telecosm: Digital Darkhorse—Newspapers," *Forbes ASAP,* 25 October 1993, 138–149.

42. Walter Baer, Technology Studies Seminar hosted by the Freedom Forum Media Studies Center, 1991.

43. Russell G. Todd, Communication and Society Seminar, the Freedom Forum Media Studies Center, 1992.

44. Michael Bloomberg, "The Next Generation," Technology Studies Seminar for Newsroom Managers hosted by the Freedom Forum Media Studies Center, 15 September 1993.

45. Matthew Winkler, Speaker, "Real-Time Information Services," Technology Studies Seminar, the Freedom Forum Media Studies Center, 15 September 1993.

46. Michael J. Mandel, "The Information Economy: The Digital Juggernaut," *Business Week,* Special 1994 Bonus Issue, 22, 23.

47. U.S. Commerce Department, Bureau of Labor Statistics, Morgan Stanley & Co., January 1982.

48. "U.S. Industrial Outlook '92: Business Forecasts for 350 Industries," U.S. Department of Commerce, January 1992.

49. "Wired," *The Wall Street Journal Reports,* 15 November 1993.

50. Thomas McArroll, "Betting on the Sky," *Time,* 22 November 1993:57.

51. Wayt W. Gibbs, "When Cells Divide: Making Space for the Next Wave of Wireless Communications," *Scientific American,* December 1993: 44–45.

52. Larry Rohter, "Florida Entrepreneur Plans to Challenge Disney World," *New York Times,* 4 April 1994.

53. Cuadra Associates, Directory of On Line Databases, Boston, 1994.

54. Mary Hardie, *ENS,* 18 November 1993:3; *WSJ,* 18 November 1993:A16.

55. Richard MacDonald, "Patterns of Media Entrepreneurship," Fellows presentation, the Freedom Forum Media Studies Center, 15 December 1993.

56. Newton Minow, "Vast Wasteland Revisited," the Freedom Forum Media Studies Center, 1991.

2

HISTORICAL PERSPECTIVES: MEDIA AT THE MILLENNIUM

Once a new technology rolls over you, if you're not part
of the steamroller, you're part of the road.
—*STEWART BRAND*[1]

Historians may one day recall the late twentieth century as the era of "Mortal Kombat," LambdaMOO and the Pentium PC. But without actually traveling back to the future, one way to make sense of today's bewildering array of media technologies is to examine the history of many still-evolving media technologies to see what lessons emerge. This chapter looks at that history, drawing on both the technological successes and failures of the past.

FROM CAVE PAINTINGS TO THE INFORMATION HIGHWAY

Since the days of the earliest known aboriginal petroglyphs in Australia in 80,000 B.C. and the cave paintings in Altamira, Spain, sixty thousand years later, people have used technology as a medium to communicate across space and time.[2, 3] In the modern world, some trace the origins of new media technology to the birth of the information society in 1956, when for the first time more than 50 percent of the U.S. workforce was employed in the service sector; the Burroughs Corporation manufactured the E101, the first desktop computer; videotape was introduced to the world of television; and the Soviet Union launched Sputnik, the first artificial satellite.[4, 5] In the four decades since then, the world's communication system has changed dramatically, bringing us ever closer to Marshall McLuhan's notion of a global village.[6] "By the end of the 1980s, 'globalization' had become the term for accelerating interdependence. . . . The primary agent of globalization is the transnational corporation. The primary driving force is the revolution in information and communication technologies," writes Sylvia Ostry.[7]

Arguably, the technical foundation of this global village rests largely in science fiction writer Arthur C. Clarke's 1945 prediction of the communications satellite, which was published in *Wireless World* in an article titled "Extraterrestrial Relays."[8] In making his prediction of a global broadcasting system based on satellites, Clarke, who earlier helped the British develop radar technology during World War II, defined the exact height of the orbit necessary to match the movement of the satellite with the earth's rotation, called a *geosynchronous orbit*. Four years after the Soviet Union's Sputnik, the United States put Echo I, the first communications satellite, into orbit on October 4, 1960. It was a passive satellite, designed only to reflect, and not transmit signals. Since then, satellite technology has advanced significantly, providing two-way transmission capabilities around the world. Communication satellites have redefined the nature of global communications, making possible everything from worldwide financial trading to global television, such as the Cable News Network (CNN).[9] The importance of this system of transmission is eloquently explained by Walter Wriston, former chief executive officer of Citicorp, the United States' largest banking institution. "The single most powerful development in global communications has been the satellite, born a mere thirty-one years ago. . . . Satellites now bind the world for better or worse, in an electronic infrastructure that carries news, money, and data anywhere on the planet at the speed of light".[10]

As a result, the technology of the global village has produced far-reaching effects in today's post–Cold War world, where everything from foreign policy to debates on free trade are played out simultaneously around the world. Some even talk of a resultant new form of telediplomacy, illustrated during the Persian Gulf War when Presidents George Bush and Saddam Hussein used television to deliver their messages to worldwide audiences, or more recently in the United Nations' ill-fated humanitarian efforts in Somalia. "A clearer demonstration of the global village that modern communications have created, and the land mines that American Presidents face as a result, would be difficult to imagine," wrote veteran political reporter R. W. Apple, Jr.[11] "After more than a dozen American soldiers were killed in street fighting in Somalia ten days ago,

President Clinton argued that it would be dangerous for the United States to pull out its troops at once, because doing so would only encourage 'aggressors, thugs, and terrorists' all over the world," presumably as a consequence of watching the withdrawal live on television throughout the world.

Of course, not everyone agrees that new technology has brought us closer to anything resembling a global village. Among those who question this conclusion is noted communication scholar Herbert I. Schiller, professor emeritus of communication at the University of California, San Diego. Schiller argues that the new technology is essentially a tool for transforming the societies of the world into commercial markets. "Contrary to the conventional wisdom that recent advances in communications have led to the emergence of the 'global village,' I do not believe that globalization of the media industries sector has resulted in the formation of an international civil society as such," Schiller writes.[12] "Rather, this process has resulted in an international order organized by transnational economic interests that are largely unaccountable to the nation-states in which they operate." Gary Selnow, who has studied the effects of high technology on political campaigns, argues that computer technology has produced something more akin to a global cacophony than a global village, with politicians using databases to target individualized messages to potential voters everywhere.[13]

The Computer Revolution

Another technical foundation of the information society is the computer. By changing the way we live, work, and play, the computer has irrevocably altered the fabric of society. From the living room to the board room, computers have changed both how we spend our time and how we make our money. The computer has become both a metaphor and a direct representation of the automation of thinking and processing of information.

Although it is in many ways the ultimate symbol of the postmodern information society of the twentieth century, the computer has a history that stretches back to at least the early 1600s (see Table 2-1). German mathematician Wilhelm Schickard created in 1623 arguably the original automatic computing device, the first mechanical calculator employing a set of metal wheels to tabulate numbers. Two centuries later, in 1823, English inventor Charles Babbage conceived a steam-powered digital calculating machine, although the device was not built until 1880 by Herman Hollerith who named it the "electromechanical tabulator." Also in 1880, Scottish physicist Lord Kelvin introduced the idea for an analog computer whose "modus operandi" entailed the use of mechanical

TABLE 2-1   Milestones in the Computer Revolution

1623	German mathematician Wilhelm Schickard creates the first mechanical calculator, employing a set of metal wheels to tabulate numbers.
1823	English inventor Charles Babbage conceives a steam-powered digital calculating machine
1880	Herman Hollerith builds the first working model of Babbage's invention, naming it the "electromechanical tabulator."
	Scottish physicist Lord Kelvin introduces the idea for an analog computer using mechanical devices to process and manipulate numbers and information entered in numerical format.
1930	American engineer Vannevar Bush builds a prototype analog computer called the "differential analyzer."
1939	Iowa State University professor John Atanasoff creates the first electronic digital computer based on use of a binary code of 0s and 1s.
1945	Rear Admiral Grace Murray Hopper removes a 2-inch moth from a navy computer, giving rise to the use of the term *bug* to describe all types of mysterious computer failures.
1948	Bell Labs unveils the transistor, invented by research team Walter Brattain, John Bardeen, and William Shockley, who shared a Nobel Prize in 1956 for their invention.
1951	The Univac (Universal Automatic Computer), the first commercially manufactured computer, is installed at the U.S. Census Bureau in Philadelphia.
1964	American Gilbert Hyatt builds the first silicon microchip.
1981	IBM introduces its first personal computer.
1983	Apple Computer introduces the Lisa, the first desktop computer system to use icons and a mouse.

devices to process and manipulate numbers and information that could be entered in numerical format. His idea was not translated into a working device, however, until 1930 when American engineer Vannevar Bush built a prototype analog computer called the differential analyzer. Also important in the story of the computer is Thomas Watson, the founder of IBM, whose vision launched a company with a machine for tabulating numbers in the late 1800s that eventually evolved into the global standard for business and personal computing. In 1939, John Atanasoff, an Iowa State University professor, created the first electronic digital computer. Rather than use the standard base of 10 that had been attempted in the past, his computer was based on use of a binary code of 0s and 1s to process information. Although originally capable only of addition and subtraction of about eight numbers, by 1946, Professor Atanasoff had developed the basis for modern computer technologies. The first commercially manufactured computer, the Univac (Universal Automatic Computer), was installed in 1951 at the U.S. Census Bureau in Philadelphia. Simultaneously, the Ferranti Mark I was installed at Manchester University, England.

A Bug in the Machine

On a warm August night at Harvard in 1945, Rear Admiral Grace Murray Hopper made an important contribution to the common lexicon of computing. Hopper was having trouble getting her computer to function properly. "Things were going badly," Hopper said. "There was something wrong in one of the circuits of the long, glass-enclosed computer. Finally, someone located the trouble spot and, using ordinary tweezers, removed the problem, a two-inch moth. From then on, when anything went wrong with a computer, we said it had bugs in it." Today, the term *bug* is widely used to describe all types of mysterious computer failures. Hopper also helped invent COBOL, a programming language widely used in business, and the first practical compiler for modern computers. A compiler translates code written by humans into more specific code read directly by computers. A computing pioneer, Hopper died on January 2, 1992.[14]

The Falling Price of Computing Power

> It is generally simpler . . . for people to consider the impact of a ten percent rise in gasoline prices than it is for them to consider the impact of a tenfold increase in the capacity of computer memory chips. Material changes are concrete and imaginable; information changes seem very abstract and mystical.
>
> —JOSHUA MEYROWITZ[15]
> No Sense of Place: The Impact of
> Electronic Media on Social Behavior

Since its inception, the computer has undergone a revolution, from mere computational device to a sophisticated multimedia global communications tool. Driving the revolution in computing has been the dramatically falling price of computing power. By most estimates, the price of computing power has been falling by a factor of 1,000 every twenty years. In more mundane terms, this means that to buy $1,000 of early 1970s computing power today would cost just $1. The pocket calculator provides a simple example. When introduced in the early 1960s, the pocket calculator was something of a luxury item with only limited computing power. Today's pocket calculators are so common and affordable that even the Educational Testing Service, administrators of the SAT

TABLE 2-2   The Falling Price of Computing Speed

		Approximate number of instructions per second	Price
1975	IBM Mainframe	10,000,000	$10,000,000
1976	Cray 1	160,000,000	20,000,000
1979	Digital VAX	1,000,000	200,000
1981	IBM PC	250,000	3,000
1984	Sun Microsystems 2	1,000,000	10,000
1994	Pentium-chip PC	66,000,000	2,000

Sources: Company reports; the *New York Times*[16]

(Scholastic Aptitude Test), recently ruled in favor of allowing students to use a calculator when taking their college entrance exams. Moreover, the average pocket calculator of today can make instant calculations of complex problems that would exceed the ability of many mainframe computers of the early 1960s.

As is seen in Table 2-2, the most powerful IBM mainframe computer in 1975 cost about $10 million, and could perform about 10 million instructions per second, a cost of about $1 per instruction per second. By 1994, the Pentium-chip PC, the fastest processor, cost about $2,000 and could process 66 million instructions per second. This translates into a cost of about $1 per 33,000 instructions per second, meaning that consumers now have on their desktops 33,000 times more computing power than an IBM mainframe of twenty years ago.

Long-time news media executive Adam Clayton Powell III, now a producer for Quincy Jones Entertainment, offers another way to view the falling price of computing power. "In 1976, a Cray Supercomputer cost some $8 million," Powell observes.[17] "Today, a Silicon Graphics workstation with roughly the same computing power of the 1976 Cray costs just $4,995.00." The implications, Powell says, are profound for the development of new media and the information highway. If the trend in the falling price of computing power continues, twenty years from now most homes will have a device in their living room with the power of today's supercomputers—but at a cost of just $500. For the creators of multimedia software, interactive television and other new media content, the implications are that all software—programming—can be vastly different than today. Rather than endless reruns of *Gilligan's Island,* the interactive TV future might offer viewers the opportunity to trek across the North Pole or converse with William Shakespeare. The limits will be only those of our own imaginations.

The Transistor and a Revolution in Computing

Central to the revolution in computing is the transistor, invented in 1948 by the AT&T Bell Labs research team of Walter Brattain, John Bardeen, and William Shockley. The invention marked the beginning of the era of miniaturization of electronics. Transistors fundamentally changed the nature of computing because the small components could control the transmission of electrical currents without producing much heat. The first transistors were known as "point-contact devices." Brattain, Bardeen, and Shockley shared a Nobel Prize in 1956 for their invention.

Enabled by the development of the transistor, IBM introduced its first personal computer in 1981, ushering in the era of desktop computing and establishing the PC as the preferred platform for most business applications. In 1983, Apple Computer introduced the Lisa, the first desktop computer system to use icons and a mouse, propelling a revolution in graphical user interfaces (GUIs) and "user-friendliness" in computing, most recently illustrated by the introduction of the Windows operating system for the PC and the graphic interface of Mosaic for network applications on the Internet. The PC's success in the marketplace is largely attributable to IBM's decision to provide an open licensing arrangement for the PC's disk operating system (DOS), which enabled other manufacturers to produce "clone" PCs at a very competitive price, also encouraging the development of much software for the DOS platform. Microsoft's disk operating system (MS-DOS) has became the standard for the PC industry. Not until September of 1994 did Apple announce it would begin licensing its operating system and permit Macintosh clone production.

Law of the Microcosm

Perhaps just as important to the transformation of the computer has been the miniaturization of the computer chip. Thirty years ago Intel chairman Gordon E. Moore noted that by reducing by 10 percent a year the size of the tiny silicon lines that form transistor circuits, chipmakers create a new generation of chips every three years with four times as many transistors.[18] This means the capacity of dynamic random-access memories (DRAMs) quadruples every three years as does the speed and overall performance of computer chips. If theses trends continue, the thinnest circuit line or transistor element will shrink from 0.5 microns in 1993 to 0.35 in 1996 and 0.10 in 2008. At that final size, a string of 2,500 transistors would be needed to encircle a single human hair.

Writing in the 1994 *Forbes ASAP,* George Gilder observes that we are rapidly moving toward an era in which the fastest computer will soon be based on a *single* silicon chip.[19] Gilder calls this "the law of the microcosm." In a sense, it is the process of computing miniaturization taken to its ultimate extreme, at least within the existing computing paradigm.

Advances in microcomputing technology will soon make it possible to pack billions of microcircuits on a single computer chip. Thus, rather than creating supercomputers based on millions of microchips, the fastest computers will contain only a single chip with millions, even billions, of circuits. These chips will cost only a few dollars. The implications are that devices as powerful as today's most advanced supercomputers or parallel processors will fill less space than a penny. Wristwatch videophones once the stuff of Dick Tracy comic books may be just around the twenty-first-century corner.

Creating a Sexy Robot

In the history of the computer one also finds the history of computer graphics and animation. In its earliest days in the 1960s, computer graphics took the form of vector graphics, or simple line drawings. Vector graphics formed the basis of computer-aided design, or CAD, and dominated the field for more than a decade. Pioneering work in this period was conducted at Xerox Parc in Silicon Valley, where visionaries such as Alan Kay developed the graphical user interface (GUI), now the standard in the world of computing. Among the earliest uses of vector graphics in creating media content was by film pioneer Robert Abel in the Walt Disney classic, *The Black Hole*, produced in 1977.[20] At about the same time, computer programmers developed the next generation of computer graphics, known as raster optics. Raster optics enabled the addition of color, shading, and texture to computer graphics, offering a revolution in the application of computer graphics to film production and media content in general. Unfortunately, early raster optics required many millions of bytes of computer storage, and even the most powerful mainframe computers had difficulty processing raster images. In the 1980s, the merging of vector graphics and raster optics along with improvements in computing power made digital movie effects increasingly standard fare. Among the most notable early examples of digital image rendering was Robert Abel's "The Sexy Robot" television commercial produced in 1982. Abel began his production by using vector graphics to digitize images of a live model. He then added color and movement through the application of raster optics. The result was an Emmy award-winning television commercial. Abel's firm, CGI, has won 33 Clios (the advertising industry's highest award) and two Emmys for its special effects productions.

THE NATURE OF "NEW" TECHNOLOGIES

To understand the nature of new technologies, one must look beyond the realm of the computer, as well. One of the most interesting "new" technologies is the fax, or facsimile machine. Used to scan and transmit images (that is, fax or telecopier), the fax is an example of a technology that simply wouldn't die. Although many think of the fax as a new technology of the 1980s, it was actually invented in 1842 by Scotsman Alexander Bain.[21] Bain based his original invention on electrochemical telegraph processes developed earlier in the nineteenth century. When Bain applied for a U.S. patent on his invention in 1848, he found that Samuel Morse had already applied for a patent for a very similar device. Bain sued Morse and the court ruled in favor of Bain because he had held a patent in England prior to Morse's application.

What's more, fax newspapers were being transmitted as early as the 1930s. The *Milwaukee Journal,* the *New York Times,* and many others transmitted to department stores and other locations fax newspapers in the 1930s and 1940s by use of radio frequencies. None of these fax efforts succeeded, however. Novel though they were, each failed for a variety of reasons, some of which were technologically based. The fax technology of a half century ago was slow, unreliable, expensive, and printed on a paper stock that was difficult to read. Fax printers were available in few locations, as well, such as department stores and on board ships. Perhaps more importantly, the content of early fax newspapers offered readers little that they couldn't just as easily get in the regular newspaper.

Almost miraculously, the fax had a renaissance in the late 1980s. The success of the new fax machine can be attributed to a confluence of circumstances, including the emergence of a viable fax technology transmitted over telephone wires, a cheaper, more reliable fax receiver and printer, and an application in the business market, where greater resources were available to acquire and use the technology effectively. Recent efforts to create fax newspapers have as a result fared somewhat better, especially since publishers have made a greater effort to offer something special in the content of the current generation of fax newspapers. As a result, fax newspapers were reintroduced. The *New York Times* began publishing a fax newspaper in 1992, primarily aimed at cruise ships, and in 1993 expanded via Nynex to a broader consumer market. The *Hartford* (Connecticut) *Courant* launched the successful *FaxPaper* in 1990 to a predominantly business audience interested in getting a twelve-hour advance copy of tomorrow's news.[22] Fax newspapers are not likely to ever become major vehicles for the distribution of news, however, because electronic, online technologies have already eclipsed them in terms of speed and accessibility. Rather, the fax has found an important niche in easy, low-cost, instant business-to-business or personal communications and has emerged as an effective alternative to postal delivery or express mail services when an original document is not needed. One of the advantages of fax communications over online file transfer is that there is a universal technical standard that allows any fax machine any-where in the world to communicate with any other fax machine. Thus, images and documents look the same on the sender and receiver end of a fax transmission. Conversely, a fax image is simply that—an image. It cannot be read as a text file, unlike a document sent via e-mail. The con-clusion to draw from the history of the fax: *olde* technologies never die, they just *morph*.

Time-Shift: Introducing the VCR

The introduction of the videocassette recorder (VCR) is another useful case study in the evolution of new technologies of communication.[23] Launched more than two decades ago, the VCR transformed how people watch television, allowing people to control what they watch and when (sometimes called time-shifting). A variety of factors contributed to the successful introduction of the VCR in the marketplace. The price dropped dramatically from the early 1980s, when VCRs often cost $1,000, the technology became easier to use, and videocassette rentals became even more popular than videocassette sales. The introduction of the VCR also took many unexpected twists and turns. The first of these twists was the evolving format of the VCR. The forerunner to the modern VCR was Elec-tronic Video Recording (EVR), introduced by CBS in 1967. EVR allowed material recorded on video to be replayed on a TV set. The black-and-white cartridge that contained the film was electronically coded, and pic-tures and sounds were stored right on it, allowing the cassette to be played on a specially made TV set.

In 1972, the Sony Corporation introduced the Betamax, a one-half inch-VCR. For most of the next decade, a battle ensued in the consumer marketplace between the technically superior Beta and commercially successful VHS format VCRs. Though technically inferior, VHS gained a slight edge in the marketplace, often capturing better shelf display space in the department and video stores. Moreover, more movies were often available in VHS format. This slight economic advantage trans-lated into what one economist calls positive feedback, allowing VHS to ultimately win the marketplace.[24] A second important factor was the completely unexpected evolution of the so-called "Mom & Pop" video rental store, initially resisted by the major film studios, and later allowed by court order.[25] These ubiquitous video stores drove much of the success of the videocassette by making videocassette rentals easily accessible and affordable in virtually every neighborhood in America. Finally, the introduction of the VCR was driven by the strong early con-sumer demand for pornography. Many of the earliest adopters of the technology were willing to pay the high early price of the VCR in order to gain private access to erotic video material. This stage of adoption helped drive down the price of the technology to make it more affordable to a general consumer market.

Origins of the High-Speed Data Network

A different story unfolds when looking at the history of the data network. Although many would point to the development of modern telecommunications in the twentieth century, the first nationwide optical data networks were built more than two hundred years ago.[26] Much older long-distance, high-speed communication networks existed as well. In 450 B.C. carrier pigeons were used for fast communication between Greek city-states, and Chinese emperors used geese flying as much as 50 mph to carry messages.[27]

Many eighteenth century European countries had fully operational nationwide communications systems capable of transmitting messages over hundred of kilometers in a matter of minutes. These systems consisted of hundreds of semaphore towers linked via line of sight over vast distances, such as one in France from Paris to Lyons separated by some 400 kilometers. The history of this optical telegraphy has been almost forgotten in the era of modern digital communications. French clergyman Claude Chappe and Swedish nobleman Abraham Niclas Edelcrantz built the first optical telegraph system in 1791 linking the castle in Brulon and a private residence in the neighboring town of Parcé some 16 kilometers distant. They completed the first nationwide system in 1795. The first message transmitted was a sentence selected by the local Doctor M. Chenou, "Si vous réussissez vous serez bientot couvert de gloire" ("If you succeed, you will soon be back in glory"). Napoleon Bonaparte, who seized power in 1799, immediately recognized the profound importance of this technology, and ordered construction of a new and vast optical telegraph line completed in 1804 linking Paris and Milan, covering some 720 kilometers. The systems worked in a relatively simple but effective manner. Holzmann and Pehrson explain:

> *Each station consisted simply of a modified pendulum clock and a large panel painted black on one side and white on the other. The clockfaces were divided into 10 parts, each used to designate a number. A single hand, or pointer, made one complete rotation of the clockface at least twice a minute.*
>
> *At the start of a transmission, the sender turned the panel to indicate when the hand of his clock reached the zenith; that allowed the receiver, watching through a telescope, to set the clock on the other end. Subsequent numbers were sent by flipping the panel from white*

to black each time the pointer of the sender's clock passed over the appropriate position. By looking at the position of the local clock, the receiver could determine what number the sender intended. Messages were encoded with the help of a numbered dictionary of letters, words, and phrases. The speed of the telegraph was regulated by the rate at which the clock pointer turned.[28]

Although it was labor intensive and required operation solely during daylight hours, the optical telegraph represented the first functional data transmission system for rapid nationwide communications.

The Information Superrailroad

Even the notion of a national electronic communication infrastructure has its roots stretching back nearly a century and a half, to when two entrepreneurial visionaries issued a public call to build an information superrailroad. In 1853 Hiram O. Alden and James Eddy lobbied the U.S. Congress for "a right of way through the public lands of the United States, for the construction of a subterranean line of telegraph." On behalf of the House of Representatives Committee on Territories, Ephraim Farley, a Whig from Maine, subsequently issued a report on their proposal.[29] Farley's report, which outlines many of the benefits of the proposed enterprise, foreshadows today's arguments in support of the information superhighway. Even the notion of universal service is present in its suggestion that every home "would be in immediate communication with each other." Farley suggests, "Connect the Atlantic to the Pacific coasts by telegraph communication, and the impulse which it will give to business, and that great tide of emigration setting towards California, will add up to the necessity for railroad communication . . . But it is in its social bearing that the advantages of a telegraph to the Pacific will be most strikingly seen. Every hamlet, it might almost be said every home, in the thirty States of the Union, has its representative on the Pacific shore. By the aid of the telegraph, they would be in immediate communication with each other."

Farley also outlines the cost of such a proposed information railroad. "A subterranean line of two wires, such as the bill provides for, is estimated to cost eleven hundred and fifty dollars per mile. Calling the distance twenty-four hundred miles, the entire cost of the line, including the buildings necessary at the working stations, together with incidental expenses to be incurred in its construction, such as explorations and engineering, land transportation of materials, cost of supplies, and erection of forts to protect way stations, would be not less than two million seven hundred and sixty thousand dollars."

Had the government decided to provide the right of way for the proposal, perhaps today's debate about building a national information infrastructure would have a decidedly different tone.

Important lessons also emerge from the evolution of the so-called information highway. Beginning with American Samuel Morse's invention of the telegraph in 1835, to Time Warner's Full Service Network in 1993, technology has increasingly enabled people to communicate across vast distances in real time, forever changing the economic, political and social structures of the world's societies.[30] Table 2-3 traces some of the major milestones on the road to the information highway.

Although this timeline represents the milestones in a linear, sequential fashion, the development of the information highway should not be thought of as a series of systematic advances, culminating in today's high-powered optical networks. Rather, many of the developments are unrelated to earlier developments, often running on parallel tracks. Others are the result of serendipity, and some are the result of completely unexpected and unintended uses of the technology. One such unanticipated use of the technology of the telegraph occurred during the Mexican revolution nearly a century ago.

Information Railroads and the Mexican Revolution. Latin-American folk hero Francisco "Pancho" Villa employed then state-of-the-art technology to help fight for the cause of social justice during the Mexican Revolution of the early 1900s. Villa tapped into telegraph lines running through the Sierra Madre mountains, intercepting messages from his enemies, including U.S. generals. In an effort to confuse and mislead his enemies, Villa also sent false messages over the telegraph lines.[31]

Lost in Cyberspace. Today, many suggest the information highway is already demonstrated in the world of online computer network communications, what some call cyberspace. The earliest such system was developed by the U.S. Department of Defense, which created the first nationwide computer network called ARPAnet in 1969. ARPAnet was based on the principle of packet switching, which could provide continuous communications even during a time of nuclear attack. ARPAnet eventually led to today's global computer network known as Internet. As of September, 1993, more than four million U.S. households had signed on with the major online computer services, according to a survey by *Information and Interactive Services Report,* with more than 50,000 signing up each month.[32] Conservative estimates project that some fifteen to twenty million people now use the Internet worldwide, and that as many as fifty million will do so by 2000.[33]

TABLE 2-3 Information Highway Timeline

1795	French clergyman Claude Chappe and Swedish nobleman Abraham Niclas Edelcrantz build the first data network—the optical telegraph.
1835	American Samuel Morse invents the electromagnetic telegraph.
1842	Scotsman Alexander Bain invents the facsimile transmission.
1866	Englishman William Thomson—who becomes Lord Kelvin for this feat—directs the laying of the first transatlantic cable.
1876	American Alexander Graham Bell invents the telephone.
1886	German Heinrich Hertz experiments with electromagnetic waves.
1895	Hertz discovers radio waves.
1899	Italian Guglielmo Marconi invents radio telegraphy.
1934	The *Milwaukee Journal* publishes the first facsimile newspaper.
1936	The BBC creates the first television network.
1945	Arthur C. Clarke invents the communication satellite.
1948	The first cable television systems are created in the United States.
1957	The Soviet Union launches the first communication satellite, Sputnik ("traveling companion"), which contains a radio receiver.
1961	Western Electric introduces push-button and touch-tone telephone service.
1964	AT&T unveils the videophone; it fails, but is reintroduced in 1993.
1969	ARPAnet, the first national computer network, is founded by the U.S. Defense Department.
1970	Optical fiber is invented by Corning Glass Works.
1975	NASA experiments with direct broadcast satellites.
1979	The British government introduces Prestel, the first videotext service.
1980	CNN begins the first 24-hour TV news network
1983	The U.S. government creates the Internet, NSFnet.
1989	World Wide Web created at CERN, Geneva, Switzerland.
1993	The Clinton/Gore administration publishes a position paper calling for the creation of the information highway.
1993	BellCore transmits full-motion video over standard twisted-pair telephone wire.
1993	Time Warner announces plans to build a full service network in Orlando, Florida, the first information highway capable of providing a video dialtone and other communication services.
1994	Albert Gore, Jr., is the first vice president to participate in a live news conference by computer network.

It is important to recognize that the information highway is coming about because of a broad array or confluence of forces, including not only technological, but also political, social, and economic forces. Among the technological forces are the convergence of computing and telecommunications, the digital revolution that is enabling multimedia communications to blossom, and compression technologies that squeeze vast amounts of video and other information into small electronic spaces. Political forces include the opening of national borders and political leadership that is unleashing telephone and cable companies to enter the information business and opening up radio frequencies for new uses such as wireless personal communication networks. Social forces include the relentless push toward democracy in many societies hungry for communications, and individuals drawn by the enabling and empowering nature of new media technologies.[34] "Laptop computers, cellular modems, satellite dishes, and electronic mail allow the global proliferation of information at ever cheaper and faster rates," writes Kristi K. Kahrenburg."[35] "Fiber-optic networks, transporting data at thousands of times the speed of their digital predecessors, already link personal computers to everything from libraries to news wires to video stores. As a result, anyone with a television, fax machine, or PC has access to a staggering array of new information sources." But perhaps even more important is the economic force of giant financial behemoths—transnational corporations—pushing to ensure their place as a player in the global marketplace. Transnational media-information corporations such as Time Warner, Disney, Reuters, Sony, News Corp, and Bertelsmann have moved rapidly since the 1960s to achieve a worldwide market share.[36] Although many of the forces outlined above are complementary, others are countervailing. Similarly, although some are positive, others pose significant threats to individual freedom and choice.[37]

Origins and Pitfalls of the Highway Metaphor.   The highway metaphor for the high-capacity information infrastructure has evolved slowly and naturally from a confluence of events and circumstances. In the 1950s, Senator Al Gore, Sr., whose son later became Vice President of the United States, introduced legislation to build a national highway system that today stands nearly complete. In fact, with the 1993 construction of the Century Highway in Los Angeles, only 114 miles of the national highway system are left to be built.

Several decades later, Senator Al Gore, Jr., introduced legislation to build the national research and educational network (NREN). Almost as a natural result, journalists, scholars, and policy makers dubbed this the information highway, inspired by the national highway system spearheaded by now Vice President Gore's father. The Vice President has used the term himself to describe the information infrastructure described in his NREN legislation.[38] The Clinton administration has used the term, as well.[39, 40, 41] Dordick and Lehman write that "The comparison appears in most all telecommunications infrastructure studies, including the report by the National Telecommunications and Information Administration (NTIA, 1991)."[42] The NTIA report states, "Several parties repeated the oft-stated analogy that telecommunication facilities and services will be as important to the future performance of the U.S. economy as transportation systems have been in the past." Kahin asks, "Is the Interstate Highway System precedent for the NREN? . . . the transportation infrastructure as a whole compares to the emerging information infrastructure in terms of scope and heterogeneity."[43]

The metaphor of a highway fits the information infrastructure well in a number of respects. It connotes a larger conduit to provide room for more information. It also suggests that there will be faster travel. And, much as the national highway system had important social consequences, so too will the information highway. Some of these consequences may be intentional and positive, while others may be unexpected or negative.

Conversely, the highway metaphor is problematic, as well. Professors Herbert Dordick and Dale Lehman argue that the highway metaphor is not only wrong, but it encourages policy makers, scholars, journalists, and anyone else interested in the information infrastructure to think in the wrong terms.[44] Even the term *infrastructure* implies certain assumptions that Dordick and Lehman find troubling.

Indeed, the relatively recent use of the term "infrastructure" rather than "network" tends to support the need for a single, centrally managed and controlled electronic communications "highway" favored by the major carriers. It can be argued that by meeting the needs of the more informationally and technologically advanced segments ("the information literate") the benefits will trickle down to all through enhanced economic growth.

The cornucopia of human services that will benefit mankind is overwhelming, but first must come the electronic highway, the infrastructure, from which the manna will trickle down. Before we unquestionably succumb to this theory, let us realize that there is an alternative view of infrastructure. The weak link theory would lead us to address the needs of the least well off members of our society, those who are the least information literate, often poorer, less well educated, and least efficient. On what basis can this be sound public policy?

Coverage of the Information Superhighway. Few topics were of greater interest in the media of the early 1990s than the information highway. A bibliometric study, or the science of word counting, shows that major daily newspapers in the United States began placing the information highway high on their news agenda in early 1993.[45] As Figure 2-1 shows, although few major newspapers reported regularly on the information highway in the fall of 1992, attention began picking up in January 1993. Then in February, when newly inaugurated President Bill Clinton and Vice President Al Gore, Jr., released their paper on rebuilding America's infrastructure, with an emphasis on the need to build a new information infrastructure—the information highway—coverage exploded. The phrase *information highway* or *information superhighway* appeared in twenty-five stories during that month in fifteen major American daily newspapers. These phrases appeared in the lead paragraphs of six stories in the *New York Times* alone that month (see Figure 2-2). While coverage of the information highway slacked off slightly in March, it has grown steadily since then to a record number of forty-nine stories in September 1993 in fifteen major dailies, and in eighteen lead paragraphs in

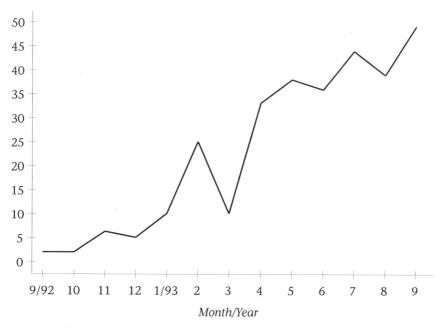

Number of articles in fifteen major daily newspapers mentioning information highway or information superhighway

FIGURE 2-1   Press Coverage of the Information Highway

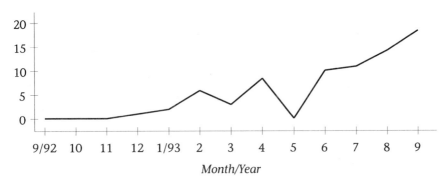

Number of articles in the *New York Times* mentioning information highway or information superhighway in lead paragraph.

FIGURE 2-2 *New York Times* **Coverage of the Information Highway**

the *New York Times*. This great attention coincides with the latest report by Clinton/Gore outlining their proposed goals for the information highway released also in September.

The newspapers included in this bibliometric search conducted on Dialog are:

- *Boston Globe*
- *Chicago Tribune*
- *Christian Science Monitor*
- *Cleveland Plain Dealer*
- *Dallas Morning News*
- *Detroit Free Press*
- *Los Angeles Times*
- *Miami Herald*
- *Minneapolis Star Tribune*
- *Newsday/New York Newsday*
- *Philadelphia Inquirer*
- *San Francisco Chronicle*
- *USA Today*
- *Wall Street Journal*
- *Washington Post*

GOOD-BYE GUTENBERG: FROM MOVABLE TYPE TO DIGITAL BIT STREAMS

Although many Westerners attribute the invention of movable type to Johannes Gutenberg of Mainz, Germany, in 1450, the first documented use of movable type was actually in 1234 in Korea under the Koryo rule. The Koreans' invention allowed the printing and dissemination of Buddhist texts and Confucian writings by Korean scholars. Gutenberg was the first European to print using movable type. His invention used replica-casting in molten metal with a converted winepress to reproduce composed pages of type.[46]

Regardless of whether it was the Koreans in the early thirteenth century or Gutenberg in the fifteenth century, the concept of publication has been defined almost universally in terms of pressing ink onto paper and distributing the printed result to some broader audience.

In an electronic, digital information environment, publication takes on an entirely new meaning.[47] There is no ink, no paper. Words and images—even sounds—exist in an ethereal electronic space, a digital bit-stream where each datum is infinitely changeable, reproducible, fluid.

The New Nature of Publication

In this context, the critical question becomes: at what point is an electronic "document" published? Some might say the answer to that question is simple and largely unaltered from the printed document. They might say an electronic document goes through all the same stages of publication that a printed document must. Message creation, editing, and presentation to the public are the necessary steps. But the wrinkle in this reasoning is that today, nearly all documents are created and edited at least in part electronically. While some are "published" electronically, others are transferred to paper at the final stage. This suggests that publication consists exclusively in terms of whether the publisher says it is published or not. Thus, as I write these words, they are published, if I say they are. Clearly, this is not an acceptable standard for a court of law where matters of libel are settled.

Another way to look at the situation is with a case study. On Sunday, September 17, 1993, horror novelist Stephen King had his latest story published on the Internet, and only on the Internet. King wrote the story, "Umney's Last Case." Editors edited it. And Viking Press distributed the story to anyone interested in downloading the story off the Internet. Since the Internet is really nothing more than a loosely connected network of networks and is not owned or controlled by any single person or institution, who is liable should King's story be found libelous? King himself? His publisher? The story was simply made available electronically to anyone interested in obtaining it. It really wasn't published until another user of the Internet downloaded it. In essence, each user of the Internet publishes it when the user downloads the story. In this sense, anyone who downloads the story could be held liable as the publisher. Even more interestingly, if King's story was published on the Internet, how is it any different than any of the millions of messages that float around in the cyberspace of the Internet each day? Why is King's story published, while the rest of the messages downloaded, accessed, saved, printed, read, viewed, or listened to are not? Is a newspaper published on the Internet any less subject to laws pertaining to libel than that same document published on paper? Is the real issue a matter of the nature of the audience? Is the issue the size and scope of the intended audience? What happens if the message is intended for a wide audience, but no one downloads and reads it? What happens if the source of an electronic publication is hidden? Some electronic bulletin boards now feature anonymous publishing in which the identity of the original creator of a message is obscured electronically. In such a case, it would be impossible to identify the source of any potentially libelous messages. Current federal copyright and intellectual property right law states, "'Publication' is the distribution of copies or phonorecords of a work to the public by sale or other transfer of ownership, or by rental or lease, or lending. The offering to distribute copies or phonorecords to a group of persons for purposes of further distribution, public performance, or public display, constitutes publication. A public performance or display of a work does not of itself constitute publication."[48] Thus, according to current law, simply putting a message on the Internet does not necessarily constitute publication—the key is the transfer of ownership. Further complicating the issue is the notion of a "final edition." Traditionally recognized as the last, complete version of a newspaper or magazine, what constitutes a final edition in electronic form, to which changes can continually be made? This subject is examined more fully in Chapter 8 on the legal and regulatory context of new media.

Consequences for "Old" Media

The emergence of a new electronic publishing environment has important consequences for the "old" media of newspapers, television, radio, magazines, and books. Many contend that the old media will go the way of the dinosaurs. Writer Michael Crichton, author of *Jurassic Park, The Andromeda Strain,* and *Rising Sun,* told the National Press Club in Washington D.C., on April 6, 1993, "In my own mind, it's likely that what we now think of as the mass media will be gone in ten years—vanished without a trace."[49] Subsequently, Crichton completed views on the subject in an article titled "Mediasaurus" for the high-tech magazine *Wired.* He likened mass media to the dinosaurs of the Jurassic period. Newspapers and other mass media, he suggested, have become large, bulky creatures generally surpassed by the new environment of the electronic world. Crichton asks, "Who will be the GM or IBM of the '90s? The next great American institution to find itself obsolete and outdated? I suspect one answer would be the *New York Times* and the commercial networks." He concludes that today's mass media are "tomorrow's fossil fuel." Crichton is not alone in proclaiming traditional media dead. Ted Turner, founder of Turner Broadcasting and the Cable News Network, in 1981 told those assembled at the annual meeting of the American Newspaper Publishers Association (ANPA) that newspapers simply wouldn't exist in ten years. A decade later, although newspapers continued to exist, Turner returned to address the ANPA, only this time no one was laughing.[50]

Although this view of the lumbering mediasaurus is seductive and in certain respects accurate, it ignores the fact that newspapers and other traditional media are still very profitable, among the most profitable of all industries.

Adaptive Strategies and New Technology

Still, lessons from the past suggest that the old media will likely adapt to changes brought about by the development of new media technologies. Just as radio adapted to the introduction of television, one of the most likely changes is increased specialization. As new technologies have been introduced, old media have tended to adapt by identifying special interest, core audiences and targeting them. This adaptive strategy has served as both a coping mechanism as well as a consequence of the principle of relative constancy, first articulated by newspaper baron Charles E. Scripps and later tested by professor Maxwell McCombs.[51, 52, 53] Scripps observed that from 1929 to 1957 advertisers and consumers in the United States tended to spend a relatively constant amount of money on the mass media. McCombs's research demonstrated that since 1929, Americans have spent a relatively constant portion of the Gross National Product (GNP) on media and communication products and services, approximately 4–5 percent. Moreover, as the amount of leisure time has also remained relatively constant during that period, and media choices have increased dramatically, there has been a greatly increased level of competition for the media audience. These factors explain much of the precipitous decline in the television networks share of the television audience, as well as the decline in newspaper household penetration. People have relatively fixed amounts of time and money for media and communication, and are presented with an increasingly complex multichannel communications environment. As a result, each medium is capturing less of the communication pie. The only major exception has been the telephone company.

Consequently, existing, as well as new, media have often opted for a strategy of audience specialization. Still, Robert Iger, president of the ABC Television Network, admonishes TV critics not to blow taps just yet for the networks. Iger observes, "In a world in which there is massive choice, there's still going to be a need for someone to create order." This will be the role of the networks, Iger says.[54] History suggests he is probably right, since the past introduction of new media has not caused existing media to disappear, although their audience and revenue base have often been eroded.

Recent data compiled by telecommunications authority John Carey suggest that the average household spends about $205 a month for communication products and services.[55, 56] By comparison, average gasoline expenditures (among those households with an automobile) are about $107 a month; household food averages $362 a month. The largest communication expenditures are for telephone service ($62 a month), followed by expenditures on radio sets, television sets, and recorded music ($57), cable television service ($33), and newspapers and magazines ($23). Videocassette rentals and purchases are about $13 a month, followed by books and maps ($18) and admission to movie theaters ($5). If McCombs's relative constancy hypothesis holds, then new media technologies will be vying for an increasingly competitive communications dollar. To increase overall expenditures on communication products will require either growth in the nation's economy, or a reallocation of expenditures from some other category, such as food or gasoline. This latter alternative is unlikely. Recent data do show a modest increase in spending on information products, although it is unclear whether this is a shift in long-term patterns or a momentary reallocation of consumer dollars.

A second likely development in the new media is the extension of existing information services, especially in the creation of new electronic services, which will often consist of repackaging existing information in new formats. Newspapers, for example, have greatly increased their use of voice information services (that is, audiotext services), especially voice personals and classifieds. Between 1988 and 1993, the number of newspapers offering audiotext services rose from about a dozen to more than 450, or from less than 1 percent to 25 percent of the 1,600 daily newspapers in the United States in just five years. Much of the reason for the increased newspaper interest in audiotext services is that audiotext makes it easy for newspapers to experiment with new technology.[57] Tens of millions of American homes have all the equipment necessary to receive sophisticated audiotext services (a Touch-Tone phone), and all the equipment newspapers need to set up an audiotext service is relatively inexpensive computer systems to deliver recorded information on demand. "Audiotext may be the Rodney Dangerfield of the interactive age," says Chris Jennewein, general manager of the Mercury Center at the San Jose (California) *Mercury News*.[58] Much current media attention is focused on online services, multimedia publications, and interactive television, and they have ignored the "lowly" telephone. Although newspapers have sponsored dial-up weather and sports lines for years, true audiotext services combining Touch-Tone phones and computer servers first appeared in the 1980s. Newspaper audiotext services fall into three main categories: free-to-caller services, where the caller dials a local number, punches in a four-digit code, and gets stock quotes, weather reports, sports scores, soap opera updates, and more, with information generally preceded by a brief sponsorship message; 900-number services, which grew out of people's need to respond to personal ads, require the caller to pay a fee for the call, and provide a revenue stream to the newspaper; and, N11 services, which are similar to local 411 directory assistance numbers and offer audio and fax for a fee, ranging from 35 cents a call at the Palm Beach (Florida) *Post* to $2.95 for unlimited calls and up to five fax documents a month at the Mercury Center's News Call service.[59] The jury is still out on whether newspapers are better served by free or for-a-fee audiotext services, but it is clear that audiotext helps newspapers connect better with readers.

Go Ahead, Make My Disk
Similar forms of new media content will emerge in other areas of media industry. For example, much as musical artists have often released retrospectives on CD-ROM and earlier on LPs, many Hollywood stars are taking an interest in releasing their collected works on CD-ROM. Among them are superstar Clint Eastwood, whose life and films will be available on CD-ROM in 1995. Says Eastwood, to the pleasure of his fans in cyberspace, "The idea of experimenting with this medium is very attractive to me."[60]

Direct-Response Content
As the technologies of new media evolve, so too will their content. One likely aspect of this evolution has already been foreshadowed in the field of fashion and other fields of marketing. In that field, information technology has allowed for the development of what is called quick-response marketing. Jeffrey Buchman, chairman of the Advertising and Marketing Communications Department at the Fashion Institute of Technology (FIT), explains how technology has enabled companies like Wal Mart in the United States and Italy's Bennetton to introduce a new form of marketing to their consumers.[61] Using information technologies, Wal Mart monitors product sales each day at each store so that individual stores need not maintain large amounts of stock on premises. Rather, depending on each day's purchases, in-store merchandise is replaced overnight on an as-needed basis. Not only are brands and types of products monitored in this fashion, but particular consumer preferences for colors

and styles are monitored, and each store can provide just what customers want. Bennetton likewise transmits data from its U.S. stores back to a central office in Italy, where sales patterns are similarly monitored, and stock is provided to match consumer purchase patterns. Moreover, specific types and styles of clothing, patterns, and colors are manufactured in quick response to variations in consumption patterns.

Just as Bennetton, Wal Mart, and other companies have applied technology to provide quick response to the vagaries of the marketplace, so too will media companies of the future be able to use technology to provide quick-response media content to the tastes of the audience. Imagine sitting in front of your wall-screen television in 2001 and seeing a news story about a fire swept out of control by the Santa Ana winds in southern California. Using your voice recognition TV response system, you ask for more video about the fires, which instantly comes up. But, acting as an assignment editor, you ask for information about the estimated cost of battling the fire, the communities affected, and the number of similar fires in the area in the past twenty years. You even ask how many involved possible arson. Your response is processed in a central news bureau, which receives similar questions from more than two thousand viewers. The bureau assigns a reporter to the story you have requested, and the next day that story is transmitted to your digital video recorder for later viewing. Quick-response media can be applied even more effectively to other forms of media content, such as entertainment, sports, and information programming, where specific viewer preferences can easily be targeted. These applications need not even involve human intervention, especially in areas such as sports or financial reporting, which are often heavily statistical. Much of the quick-response content can be identified and targeted automatically by computer.

Economic Forces and Media Adaptation

What really drives the system, however, is not the news, entertainment, and information applications of quick-response media. Driving the system are the economic incentives for advertising, public relations, publicity and other marketing advantages to quick-response media. Advertisers, for example, will be able to achieve the ultimate in niche marketing, by targeting their messages not just to those people with the appropriate demographics, psychographics, and buying habits, but to those who are actively interested in buying the product.

Computer-Assisted Investigative Reporting

To a limited degree, media organizations are also adapting to the new media environment by developing their own new media applications that change how their own staff do their work. One important example comes from the newsroom, where investigative reporters have increasingly employed the computer as an investigative tool. With the advent of the computer era, the government began storing public records electronically, often on nine-track magnetic computer tapes on mainframe computers. Investigative journalists were often hindered in their efforts to explore and examine these records by a number of factors, including limited access to electronic records of government, the complexity of the data and the mainframe computers required to read them, and a lack of financial and other resources needed to analyze computer records. Mainframe computers, although immensely powerful, are especially complex to use and program. Few investigative reporters, who were generally trained in journalism, not computer science, had the programming skills to set up mainframe applications to analyze massive databases of public records. New technology helped changed all this.

In reporting that helped the *Detroit Free Press* win a Pulitzer Prize, professor Philip E. Meyer pioneered the use of the computer in journalism in 1967. Meyer's computerized study of survey data from riot-area blacks following the 1967 civil rights riots in Detroit produced a front-page series titled "The People Beyond 12th Street." It spawned a form of reporting later described as precision journalism by distinguished journalism educator Everette E. Dennis.

Meyer's pioneering effort was followed by former *New York Times* investigative reporter David Burnham's 1972 computer analysis of crime data in New York City. Burnham, the author of award-winning books and articles, attained legendary status in New York City for his investigative work with police officer Frank Serpico, a narcotics officer whose testimony before the Knapp Commission revealed widespread corruption and graft in the New York City police department. Burnham was the first journalist to use the computer to analyze public records, marking the beginning of what we today call computer-assisted reporting (CAR). Burnham used the *New York Times*'s mainframe computer to sort crime data by police precinct, revealing the first public mapping of the variation in crime rates throughout New York City.

Computer-assisted investigative reporting (CAIR, or CAR, for computer-assisted reporting) developed slowly during the next two decades, and few newspapers or other news organizations warmly embraced the field. CAR did not begin to become a part of mainstream journalism until Pulitzer Prize–winning investigative reporter Elliot Jaspin developed NineTrack Express®, software for computer-assisted investigative reporting that allows reporters to analyze public records using their personal computers. Prior to Jaspin's creation of NineTrack Express® at the Freedom Forum Media Studies Center in 1989, reporters had to rely on mainframe computers for their investigative analyses. Because of the complexity of mainframe computing, this was a cumbersome and slow process, especially since most newspaper mainframes were not traditionally used by the editorial department; they were part of the business department for payroll processing and circulation data. NineTrack Express® allowed journalists to transfer data from the magnetic tapes commonly used by government agencies when storing data processed on mainframe to desktop computers. This new technology enabled investigative journalists to use spreadsheet and other database packages to analyze vast electronic files of public records that in the past were available either in paper form or required an expensive and complex mainframe computer to analyze.

Since 1989, every Pulitzer Prize for investigative reporting has been awarded to a journalist whose research was based upon a computer analysis of public records. One story in New York dramatized the impact of this new technology. *New York Newsday* investigative reporter Peggy Baer used NineTrack Express to uncover a major loophole in New York City property tax law. Baer had learned during a conversation over dinner in Greenwich Village that property tax law in New York did not require the city to inform property owners when they were owed a refund. Baer obtained the data records on magnetic tape that stored the city's property tax records. Using the computer to analyze the data, Baer determined that the city owed property owners a whopping $273 million in tax refunds, refunds the city had no intention of repaying unless requested. *Newsday* ran a front-page story proclaiming the city's $273 IOU, and then ran a complete listing of every property owner owed a refund as well as the amount they were owed. Since this story ran in 1991, the city has refunded more than $100 million in over-paid property taxes.

Today, dozens of newspapers and television newsrooms operate computer-assisted reporting programs. Some of those news organizations are listed in Table 2-4. Despite this trend, many news organizations still relegate CAR to "special project" status, and have not integrated it into the mainstream of their reporting. Full integration of CAR into American journalism will likely depend not only on a commitment of resources, but also on a new mindset about the role of the computer in reporting and perhaps even a reorganization of the newsroom to make use of computers in investigative reporting as routine as picking up the phone.

Informational Graphics

A second example of how media organizations have applied computer technology as an adaptive strategy in the use of transformation of content comes from the field of graphic arts. Here, the Macintosh computer has been used to develop what are now widely called informational graphics, a class of graphics used by newspapers, news magazines, and television news programs to present news visually rather than through

TABLE 2-4   News Media Operating CAR Programs[62]

Daily Newspapers

Akron Beacon Journal	*Orange County Register*
Asbury Park Press	*Orlando Sentinel*
Atlanta Journal & Constitution	*Palm Beach Post*
Boston Globe	*Philadelphia Inquirer*
Boston Herald	*Pittsburgh Press*
Cleveland Plain Dealer	*Providence Journal*
Dallas Morning News	*Raleigh News & Observer*
Dayton Daily News	*Record of Hackensack*
Detroit Free Press	*Roanoke Times and News Report*
Greensboro News & Record	*San Francisco Chronicle*
Hartford Courant	*Seattle Post-Intelligencer*
Kansas City Star	*St. Louis Post Dispatch*
Los Angeles Times	*St. Petersburg Times*
The Morning News Tribune	*Syracuse Herald Journal*
(Tacoma, Washington)	*The* (Toledo) *Blade*
Minneapolis Star/Tribune	*USA Today*
New York Times	*Wall Street Journal*
New York Newsday	

Television Stations

WNBC-TV News	WRC-TV (Washington, D.C.)

words alone. Informational graphics emerged in their current form in the mid-1980s out of the tradition of graphic arts as applied to newspapers and news magazines, but were enabled by the development of the Macintosh computer.[63] The development of information graphics is, of course, really much older than the past decade. They are a product of the graphics revolution, which historian Daniel Boorstin traces to the invention of a much older technology, that of photography in the nineteenth century.

News industry visionary Roger Fidler, a veteran newspaper designer, pioneered the modern development of information graphics while working for Knight-Ridder Newspapers in Miami, Florida. Fidler saw the development of information graphics in newspapers as an opportunity to tell many complex stories more effectively and efficiently through a blend of visual illustrations and textual information. The introduction of information graphics into newspapering and other news media was rapid and paralleled the diffusion of the Macintosh computer, with its graphical user interface and simple applications for desktop publishing.

Illustrative of the impact of informational graphics is the national newspaper *USA TODAY*, which was launched in 1980 and based its whole approach on this revolution in newspaper design enabled by Macintosh technology. Even "the old gray lady" of American journalism, the *New York Times,* has changed dramatically in its design from the 1970s. Not only does it feature a completely different look, but it incorporates a far greater use of information graphics. It's worth noting, as well, that the entire graphic arts department at the *Times* is equipped with Macintosh computers, while the rest of the editorial side of the newspaper uses an Atex system.

Turning Something Old into Something New

Finally, new media content is likely to be based on the content of old media. For example, early television shows were often based directly on old radio programs, including soap operas, variety shows, comedy, and western series. While this pattern may ease the transition in the short run, it is likely to fail in the long run, suggests new media expert David Shefrin, former IBM executive who led the company's early multimedia efforts, head of the Shefrin Group, and pioneer in the experimental fax newspapers of the 1940s. Shefrin explains that as new media are being envisioned, "The models are still being thought out in terms of past experiences. You can see that with Diller and Paramount and investments in online services."[64] Shefrin contends that these megamergers are designed to create greater vertical integration in the hopes of preserving old mass media values in the new media of distribution. Unfortunately, the content created for the new media may fail to exploit the full range of qualities of the new media.

Magazines: A Case Study in Technology Adaptation
One medium already undergoing extensive adaptation to the new delivery media is magazines. The first magazine, the *American Magazine,* was published in 1741. Benjamin Franklin's *General Magazine* was the second, and began publication shortly after the *American Magazine.* Franklin was proud of the *General Magazine* readership of his magazine and printed on the magazine's pages a complete list of its subscribers, which included many of the founding fathers of the United States, including George Washington, Thomas Jefferson, and Alexander Hamilton.[65] In the two and a half centuries since then, magazines have undergone a series of sweeping changes in their nature. Printing technologies of the late-1800s and early-1900s allowed magazines to become mass media. The introduction of radio, television, and film drew audience and advertising revenue away from magazines, and magazines adapted by specializing.

Today's information highway offers magazine publishers an opportunity for a "new lease on life," says Clay Felker, founder of *New York*

Magazine, former editor-in-chief and CEO of the *Village Voice,* former editor, publisher, and CEO of *Esquire,* and pioneer in the development of the new journalism. Felker has explained that magazine publishing is being assaulted by escalating costs for printing and postage. Not only has the number of magazines published and distributed in the United States grown to more than 10,000, but many other publications printed on the same coated paper stock and distributed via the U.S. mail have emerged, including direct mail and preprinted newspaper inserts. The electronic highway has presented a new opportunity for magazine publishing. Already, several established magazines, including the number one magazine in America, *Time,* are offering electronic versions. Depending on the development of the technology, several scenarios are possible. In the short term, text versions of magazines are likely to be increasingly delivered over the information highway. "Readers" will use their computers to "open" the electronic magazines of their choice, perhaps printing the stories, or even entire magazines. Time Warner announced in September 1993 that it is working with Hewlett-Packard to develop a $400 printer that it will place free of charge, with a free stock of paper, in all of the homes in the Orlando, Florida, test market where it is implementing its initial full-service network. Using the printer, readers could print their own magazines, saving the cost and time of printing and distribution for the magazine publishers. Revenue will be generated from advertising support for the service, as well as subscription fees.

An alternative scenario, perhaps more long-term, depends on the refinement of the flat panel computer display.[66] The flat panel will eventually have the display quality of ink on paper, will be highly portable, being about the size and weight of a notepad, and may cost less than $200. With flat panels, electronic magazines need not be printed at all. Instead, readers would simply download and read at their leisure electronic magazines that would look exactly like their printed counterparts of today. Moreover, advertisers could introduce a variety of new features, such as fully interactive ads, in which readers could not only request more information about a product, or book a hotel reservation, but could even make an electronic purchase. Moreover, advertisers could achieve the ultimate in target marketing, and could collect data about exactly who reads their ads, who responds to them, and who purchases the product as a direct response to the ad. The pricing structure of magazine advertising could be redefined based upon impact assessment. At the same time, however, magazines and other publishers are facing competition from other forms of new commercial media, such as computer-generated point-of-sale coupons, or supermarket-issued shopper IDs, which allow stores to generate their own specialized data bases of individual consumer purchase patterns and highly targeted direct mail advertising, potentially circumventing traditional media outlets, even in electronic form.

These electronic publishing scenarios would allow magazine publishers to publish their products on new time schedules. Weeklies could become dailies, with even more frequent updates on breaking news events or depending on reader interest. Moreover, magazines could become fully multimedia, incorporating text, data, sound, and full-motion video. One of the challenges of these multimedia magazines will be to develop simple navigational tools to let readers glide as easily through electronic magazine choices as they do with printed magazines. Many companies are working on navigational tools, such as Stargazer for interactive TV from Bell Atlantic, which organizes content by categories like entertainment, news and education, but none have been tested with real media products.

Each scenario, but especially the electronic, flat panel model, could allow magazines to provide stories of much greater depth, since story length becomes almost irrelevant in the digital world. Depth becomes a matter of user demand, not limited by space or pages. With the exception of magazines like the *New Yorker* under editor Tina Brown, few publications can devote extensive space to most stories, observes publishing pioneer Clay Felker. The problem is that the rising costs of printing and distribution via the postal service have forced magazines to reduce their size, both in terms of numbers of pages and trim size (that is, the size of the actual page). Large circulation magazines such as *Time* or *Newsweek*, for example, save millions of dollars each year by reducing their trim size by a quarter inch. Advertisers will pay the same amount for a full-page ad, regardless of the exact size of the page, and the reduced page size reduces the printing cost and the postage cost because of the reduced weight. Electronic distribution can change all that. By radically reducing the cost of distributing the product and by eliminating the cost of printing it, magazine publishers could completely reinvent their magazines. They could reintroduce long-form journalism, they could expand on "news you can use," which has become the hallmark of *U.S. News and World Report,* which as Felker explains, now devotes 50 percent of its pages to such user-friendly news.

However, there are dangers. Electronic magazines, Felker cautions, have the danger of becoming media for the elite. In the new model, many magazines may become increasingly specialized and expensive, especially when costly electronic devices are needed to receive and print them. Ironically, the information highway of 1994 may help recreate the elitist magazines of two centuries ago, when the core subscribers to Ben Franklin's *General American* were the signers of the Declaration of Independence.

LEARNING FROM HISTORY: A SUMMARY

From the evolution of the fax to the introduction of the flat panel display, history offers considerable insight into the future of new media technologies. Some lessons to be learned include:

- Few media technologies are truly new, and even fewer are immediately successful on their initial introduction to the marketplace.
- The success of all new technologies is dependent on a confluence of circumstances, including price, reliability, simplicity—sometimes called "user friendliness"—and a clear use or application.
- Many attempts to introduce new media technologies are destined to fail and to cost their creators great sums of money—so watch carefully those who go before you and learn from their successes and failures.
- A variety of unanticipated circumstances, or what telecommunications expert John Carey calls the serendipity factor, often make marketplace predictions completely unreliable—so be prepared to follow your instincts at times and to adapt to unforeseen circumstances.[67]
- There are valuable lessons to be learned from past failures in the realm of new media technologies. "For every new technology success in the 1980s, there were ten failures," notes Bruce Maggin, executive vice president, Capital Cities/ABC, Inc. Video Enterprises.[68] Today's ventures in new media technology follow on the heels of many attempts and failures from the 1970s and 1980s, such as videotex, teletext, Qube, and so on. We might learn something valuable, he adds, when venturing into the uncharted waters of new media technology from a most unlikely source: penguins in the Antarctic. Antarctic penguins, he explains, form two lines when entering the water. The second line pushes the first line into the water, and if they come up with fish in their mouths, then the second line dives into the water. If they come up in the mouths of sharks, then the second line stays out of the water. "It pays to be in the second line when introducing new technology," Maggin concludes.

NOTES

1. Stewart Brand, *The Media Lab: Inventing the Future at MIT*. New York: Viking, 1987.

2. Wilbur Schramm, *The Story of Human Communication: Cave Painting to Microchip*. New York: Harper and Row, 1988.

3. Jan V. White, *Graphic Design for the Electronic Age*. New York: Guptill Publications, 1988.

4. Herbert S. Dordick and Georgette Wang, *The Information Society: A Retrospective View.* Newbury Park, CA: Sage Publications,1993.

5. John Pavlik, *Media Technology Chronology.* Software published by Wayne Danielson Software, 1992.

6. Mike Featherstone, ed., *Global Culture.* Newbury Park, CA: Sage Publications, 1990.

7. Sylvia Ostry, "The Domestic Domain: The New International Policy Area," *Transnational Corporations 1,* no. 1 (February 1992):7.

8. Arthur C. Clarke, "Extraterrestrial Relays," *Wireless World,* 1945.

9. Hamid Mowlana, George Gerbner, and Herbert I. Schiller, *Triumph of the Image: The Media's War in the Persian Gulf: A Global Perspective.* Boulder, CO: Westview Press, 1992.

10. Walter Wriston, *Twilight of Sovereignty: How the Information Revolution Is Transforming Our World.* New York: Scribners, 1992, p. 12.

11. R. W. Apple Jr., "Policing a Global Village," *New York Times,* 13 October 1993:A1.

12. Herbert I. Schiller, "Transnational Media: Creating Consumers Worldwide." *Journal of International Affairs,* Summer 1993, no. 1:47.

13. Gary W. Selnow, *High-Tech Campaigns: Computer Technology in Political Communication.* Westport, CT: Praeger, 1993.

14. John Markoff, "Rear Adm. Grace Hopper Dies; Innovator in Computers Was 85," *New York Times,* 3 January 1992:A17.

15. Joshua Meyrowitz, *No Sense of Place: The Impact of Electronic Media on Social Behavior.* New York: Oxford University Press, 1985. See also Ethan Katsch, "Law in a Digital World: Computer Networks and Cyberspace," *Villanova Law Review,* Vol. 38, No. 2, 1993:417.

16. John Markoff, "Toys Now, Computers Tomorrow," *New York Times,* 20 April 1994:D1, D6.

17. Adam Clayton Powell, III, speech at Technology Studies seminar hosted by the Freedom Forum Media Studies Center, 27 October 1993.

18. Ibid.

19. Gilder, George. "Law of the Microcosm," *Forbes ASAP,* 1994.

20. "Movie Magic," the Discovery Channel, 16 June 1994.

21. David Shefrin, "History of the Fax Newspaper," in John Pavlik and Everette E. Dennis, eds., *Demystifying Media Technology: Disk Edition.* Mountain View, CA: Mayfield Publishing, 1993.

22. Bill Williams, "FaxPaper," in John Pavlik and Everette E. Dennis, eds., *Demystifying Media Technology: Disk Edition.* Mountain View, CA: Mayfield Publishing, 1993.

23. Mark Levy, ed., *The VCR Age: Home Video and Mass Communication.* Newbury Park, CA: Sage Publications, 1989.

24. Brian Arthur, "Positive Feedback in Economic Modeling," *Scientific American,* December 1991.

25. John Carey, "Back to the Future: How New Communication Technologies Enter American Homes," Technology Studies seminar, the Freedom Forum Media Studies Center, 26 October 1993.

26. Gerard J. Holzmann and Bjorn Pehrson, "The First Data Networks," *Scientific American,* January 1994.

27. Jan V. White, *Graphic Design for the Electronic Age,* New York: Guptill Publications, 1988.

28. Holzmann and Pehrson, op. cit.

29. "Historical Premonitions of the Information Superhighway," *Wired,* August 1994:64.

30. James Carey, *Communication as Culture.* London: Unwin Hyman, 1989.

31. "Treasure Hunters," the Discovery Channel, 1 February 1994.

32. *Information & Interactive Services Report,* Washington, DC: BRP Publications, Inc., 27 September 1993.

33. Jack Donegan, San Diego Supercomputer Center, Cities of the Future conference, 13 December 1994.

34. Steven Levy, "We Have Seen the Content, and It Is Us," *The Media Studies Journal,* Winter, 1994.

35. K. K. Kahrenburg, "Power of the Media in the Global System," *Journal of International Affairs,* Summer 1993:i.

36. *Business Week,* "The 1993 Business Week 1000: U.S. Companies Ranked by Industry."

37. Neil Postman, *Technopoly: The Surrender of Culture to Technology.* New York: Random House, 1992.

38. Albert Gore, Jr., "Information for the Global Village," *Scientific American,* 1991.

39. W. J. Clinton and A. Gore, *Technology for America's Economic Growth, a New Direction to Build Economic Strength.* Washington, DC: Office of the President of the United States, February 1993.

40. W. J. Clinton and A. Gore, *National Information Infrastructure. . . .* Washington, DC: Office of the President of the United States, September 1993.

41. John Markoff, "Traffic Jams Already on the Information Highway," *New York Times,* 3 November 1993.

42. Herbert S. Dordick and Dale E. Lehman, "Information Highways: 'Trickle Down' Infrastructure?" in Fred Williams and John V. Pavlik, eds., *The People's Right to Know: Media, Democracy, and the Information Highway.* Hillsdale, NJ: Lawrence Erlbaum Associates, 1994.

43. B. Kahin, *Information Infrastructures.* New York: McGraw-Hill, Inc., 1992.

44. Dordick and Lehman, op. cit.

45. John Pavlik and Everette E. Dennis, "Traveling the Information Superhighway," the Freedom Forum Media Studies Center, 1994.

46. Pavlik, op. cit. 1992.

47. Anthony Smith, *Goodbye Gutenberg.* New York: Oxford University Press, 1980.

48. Copyright Law of the United States of America, contained in Title 17 of the United States Code, Revised to March 1, 1991.

49. Michael Crichton, speech to the National Press Club, Washington, D.C. on 6 April 1993; "Mediasaurus," *Wired,* 1993.

50. Rupert Murdoch, Keynote Address, Center for Communication, Communicator of the Year Award Luncheon, 11 April 1994.

51. Donald L. Shaw, "The Rise and Fall of American Mass Media," *Journal of Communication,* 1993.

52. M. E. McCombs and C. H. Eyal, "Spending on Mass Media," *Journal of Communication* 30(1), 1980:153–158.

53. M. E. McCombs and J. Nolan, "The Relative Constancy Approach to Consumer Spending for Media," *Journal of Media Economics* 5(2), 1992:43–52.

54. Jeff Greenfield, "American Agenda," *ABC World News Tonight* with Peter Jennings, September 1993.

55. John Carey, "Back to the Future: How New Communication Technologies Enter American Homes," Technology Studies seminar, the Freedom Forum Media Studies Center, 26 October 1993.

56. U.S. Department of Commerce, Bureau of Labor Statistics, Morgan Stanley & Co., 1992.

57. Chris Jennewein, "Audiotext gives a growing number of dailies the chance to experiment with new technologies," *ASNE Bulletin,* January/February 1994.

58. Ibid.: 16.

59. Ibid.

60. "Hear This," *International Herald Tribune,* 8 July 1994:8.

61. Jeffrey Buchman, speech, Technology Studies seminar, the Freedom Forum Media Studies Center, 23 October 1993.

62. John V. Pavlik and Mark A. Thalhimer, "A Brief History of Computer-Assisted Investigative Reporting," the Freedom Forum Media Studies Center, 1992.

63. Roger Fidler, "Information Graphics," in John Pavlik and Everette E. Dennis, eds., *Demystifying Media Technology: Disk Edition,* Mountain View, CA: Mayfield Publishing, 1993.

64. *Mediaweek,* 27 September 1993.

65. Clay Felker, fellows seminar at the Freedom Forum Media Studies Center,13 October, 1993.

66. Roger Fidler, "Mediamorphosis," in Frederick Williams and John V. Pavlik, eds., *The People's Right To Know: Media, Democracy, and the Information Highway,* Hillsdale, NJ: Lawrence Erlbaum Associates, 1994..

67. Carey, op. cit., 1993.

68. Bruce Maggin, "Riding the Information Highway," speech at the Center for Communications, 30 September 1993.

3

THE TECHNOLOGY

*All this may seem more like science fiction than reality.
Indeed, in the history of the world, it has been only a
few hundred years since gunpowder transformed
human warfare and less than a century since television
connected the world. But just as those inventions
brought us to the twentieth century, so will digital
information transmit us into the next, transforming
everything from how we learn to how we work.*
                                    —*VICE PRESIDENT AL GORE*[1]

New media technologies beckon more enticingly than ever. More than
merely offering an improvement on existing forms of communication,
new media technologies are creating what telecommunications scholar
Frederick Williams calls a "virtually new medium of public communication."[2] Enabled by the convergence of telecommunications, computing,
and media, the new media landscape offers true interactivity, full user
control, and multimedia communications. Virtual reality, already being
applied in medicine, employee training, and video arcades, may transform mediated communication into a total sensory experience. The so-
called information superhighway promises access to a universal video
dial tone, untold treasures of data and knowledge, and a broad array of
information and entertainment unparalleled in history.

But how much of this is hype and how much is reality? Which technologies will succeed and help remake society, and which will become little more than objects of curiosity, artifacts in a technology museum of the
future? Identifying which technologies will transform the media and
communications world is a slippery slope, in which many ultimately

important technologies will be excluded and other technologies receiving much attention will eventually fade into obscurity. Moreover, although many of these technologies may offer social, cultural, educational, and commercial benefits, they bring with them a variety of costs, and there is little guarantee that their availability will reach every strata of society on an equitable basis. This chapter systematically examines the hardware now available, as well as that on the media technology horizon. Chapter 4 will then review the key concepts and applications central to understanding the new media landscape. Chapter 5 will subsequently examine the key players developing these technologies.

NEW MEDIA TECHNOLOGY MAP

As Columbus's 1492 encounter with the Americas required European cartographers to redraw their maps of the world, so too has the development of new, digital, computer-based technologies required us to redraw the conceptual map of the media world. No longer do old organizational frameworks apply when analyzing media industries. What were once separate and distinct media, such as newspapers, broadcasting, cable, and telephony, are now becoming increasingly indistinct and overlapping as the old lines blur. Similarly, the scholarly domain of media studies is undergoing a similar transformation as a new communication paradigm emerges, one based on a unified, global mediamorphosis.

A new conceptual map is needed to understand the contours and topography of the new media landscape. In this chapter we will use the media technology map developed in the opening chapter of the book to guide our discussion of each emerging media technology. This framework emphasizes digital, computer-based technologies and how they are changing the way information is

- gathered, processed and produced
- transmitted
- stored
- received and displayed

The Creation Machines

This section reviews technologies used in the gathering, production, and processing of media and communications content. The discussion is grouped into two parts: part one includes electronic information processing technologies, particularly computers and related computer technologies, and part two reviews electronic information gathering devices, such as image capturing and related technologies, as well as speech recognition and synthesis technologies.

Part I: Electronic Information Processing Technologies

The Computer
As the basis of all electronic information processing technologies, the computer comes in all shapes, sizes, and prices, from low-priced, lap-top personal computers (PCs) to powerful room-size supercomputers and parallel processors that cost more than half a million dollars (see Table 3-1). This discussion concentrates on the personal computer and other consumer-related computer products, although the section also looks at video servers, the computer engines driving interactive television and video on demand.

Warp Speed.   The twentieth century's fastest PCs arguably are based on the new Intel Pentium microprocessor.[5] They are 75 percent faster than the 66-megahertz (MHz) 486DX2 PCs, previously the fastest desktop computers. "These machines are like dragsters," says John C. Dvorak, a widely read computer columnist. "There are no bells and whistles, they just go fast," writes technology reporter John Markoff.[6] Models include

TABLE 3-1   Qualities of Computer Market Segments, Ranked by Price

Market segment	Price range	Processing speed	Primary function
Personal computers	$700–$10,000	20–50 MIPS	Desktop applications, word processing, spreadsheets
Workstations	$5,000–$60,000	20–350 MIPS	Desktop applications, high-resolution graphics, simulations
Mainframes and mini-computers	$25,000–$500,000	50–375 MIPS	Central processors for data from linked terminals
Supercomputers	$500,000 or more	Up to 26,000 MIPS	Numerical processing massive data

MIPS refers to millions of instructions per second.

Sources: Transnational Data and Communications Report, 1994;[3] The U.S. International Trade Commission.[4]

the IBM ValuePoint P60/D, Compaq Deskpro 5/60M, and the Gateway 2000 P5-60. They're fast, but they're also usually expensive, though there are exceptions. The Deskpro begins at $8,758, while the Gateway 2000 starts at just $2,995. Gateway is a small company started in a garage in South Dakota, and its products are available via mail order. Among its offerings is the Gateway 2000 Handbook 486 computer, loaded with 130 megabytes of memory, up to 8 megabytes of RAM, a 14.4 Kbps fax modem on a credit-card-sized insert device, at a weight of 2.5 pounds, and at a cost of just $1,995.

Increasing Processing Power.   The current generation of 100-megahertz Pentium microprocessors offers the latest support for what is called Moore's Law.[7] In terms of processing power, today's Pentium micro-processor has in a single microchip DRAM capacity of 16 megabits, the equivalent of 500 pages of text. By 1996, the DRAM capacity of a single chip will increase to 64 megabits, the equivalent of 1,500 pages of text. By 2008 the DRAM capacity would reach 64 gigabits, or the equivalent of roughly 45,000 pages of text.

Caveat Emptor: Let the Buyer Beware!   Any discussion of the Intel Pentium chip would be remiss without acknowledging the flaw identified in Intel's highly touted chip. On October 30, 1994, Dr. Thomas R. Nicely, a mathematics professor at Lynchburg College, Virginia, reported on the Internet that the Pentium chip occasionally made errors in mathemati-cal division operations involving long strings of numbers.[8] The problem was due to an error in the chip's so-called "look-up table," where all cal-culations are checked for accuracy by the computer. Every number in the look-up table is normally accurate to sixteen decimal places, but in the case of the Pentium chip, some numbers were accurate to only five places, thus occasionally producing the equivalence of rounding error. Intel sub-sequently admitted that they knew of the error since July of 1994 but had not considered the problem serious enough to disclose. Public confusion, IBM's discontinuation of selling Pentium-based PCs, and the falling price of Intel stock all led Intel to announce a chip replacement program. Intel has since corrected the problem, but not before the error had spurred a series of Pentium jokes that quickly made the rounds on the Internet, including:

Q: *How many Pentium designers does it take to screw in a light bulb?*
A: *1.99904274017, but that's close enough for nontechnical people.*
Q: *What's another name for the "Intel Inside" sticker they put on Pentiums?*
A: *The warning label.*

Q: Why didn't Intel call the Pentium the 586?
A: Because they added 486 and 100 on the first Pentium and got 585.999983605.

Top of the Heap. Challenging the Pentium as master of the desktop is the PowerPC, based on a fast, inexpensive PowerPC chip that is also largely compatible with many existing applications, whether of MS-DOS or Macintosh design. At least that is the promise. Early tests suggest full compatibility has not quite arrived. IBM, Apple Computer, and Motorola are hoping that their jointly designed PowerPC family of RISC (reduced instruction set computer) computers will draw consumers away from the Pentium line, which is based on CISC (complex instruction set computer) chip technology, produced by Intel.[9]

RISCy Business. Because of their enhanced efficiency and speed, RISC computers are considered technically superior to CISC computers, or complex instruction set computers. Until recently, RISC computers have had limited utility in the PC marketplace, largely because Microsoft Windows, the dominant PC platform in business settings, has not been compatible with the RISC technology. The recent development of the UNIX-based Windows NT by Microsoft, however, changes that situation. Windows NT operates with RISC computers using the MIPS chip developed by Silicon Graphics, Inc. Intel says its CISC chip has been able to keep pace with the RISC technology through a redesign that lets each software instruction run in a single tick of the computer's clock.[10]

In 1963, computer pioneer Seymour Cray of Control Data Corporation (CDC) invented the CDC 6600, the world's first commercially available computer capable of executing three million program instructions per second. It represents the first use of reduced instruction set computing (RISC). In 1968, Cray developed the next generation in RISC computers, the CDC 7600, capable of fifteen million instructions per second.

True Believers: Enter the PowerPC. One of the first computers to use the PowerPC chip, the new Power Macintosh, has already drawn many true believers. "The PowerPC is the light side of the force," observes John Battelle, managing editor for *Wired* magazine.[11] "It's the chip with a heart," he adds. Crusaders for the Power Macintosh are convinced it will lead the way into the future of computing, driving the merger of computers and technologies such as handheld devices and digital set-top devices.

To many, the Power Macintosh represents the beginning of the end of an almost holy quest for a unified computing platform capable of running software for both the IBM PC and the Macintosh desktop computer.

A single machine to run various versions of software would make it "the ideal lab computer," says Pamela S. Vogel of Brown University.[12] Still, differences remain between the two platforms, such as the RISC vs. CISC technology, and the quest continues. Table 3-2 compares the relative attributes of the two desktop computing platforms.

Video Servers.   Silicon Graphics is the principle provider of video servers, although a number of other companies have developed competing platforms. Video servers are the digital library driving the video-on-demand service promised in the current round of interactive TV trials.

Notebook, Laptop, Sublaptop, and Palmtop Computers.   Reflecting the trend toward miniaturization in the computing world is the development of ever-smaller, lighter, and more portable PCs. Notebook, laptop, sublaptop and palmtop computers represent the decreasing size and weight of the family of portable computers. Each is progressively lighter and more portable, but typically has greater limitations, such as less power or speed, less storage capacity, and less battery life. They also vary in price, as reflected in Table 3-1. Over time, the power, speed, and overall performance of even the smallest and lightest of these computers is increasing, and within the next decade, the tiniest of these computers is likely to have the power of 1995's most powerful parallel processing computer. One complicating factor is the size of the keyboard. Still the dominant medium for inputting text, the keyboard can be reduced in size only to a certain degree before becoming unusable as a typing interface. With the development of speech recognition technology, however, it may be possible to input text and other information by voice command to even the smallest super-small computers that may not even need to include a keyboard as a standard item. Palmtop computers, in fact, do

TABLE 3-2   CISC versus RISC

	Pentium P54C	PowerPC 601
Speed	100 MHz	80 MHz
Size	163 sq. mm	121 sq. mm
Transistors	3.3 million	1.6 million
List price	$995	$520
Available	April 1994	March 1994
Manufacturer	Intel	Motorola, IBM, Apple Consortium

Adapted from the *New York Times*.[13]

not include a full-size keyboard, although none in 1995 recognize voice command.

Desktop Publishing.   Coinciding with the rise of the desktop computer is the technology today known collectively as *desktop publishing*. The term refers to a collection of hardware and software applications that developed in the 1980s to allow computerized publishing on personal computers. The advent of the MacIntosh computer drove the desktop publishing field, making integrated text and graphics processing simple and inexpensive. Author Steven Levy describes the impact of the Macintosh computer as profound. In *Insanely Great: The Life and Times of Macintosh, the Computer that Changed Everything,* Levy argues that not only did the Macintosh spur the graphics revolution, but it brought the computer out of its exclusive domain and into the mainstream of society by popularizing desktop computing.[14]

The Digital Darkroom.   Paralleling the meteoric rise of desktop publishing is the emergence of the digital darkroom, the video analog of desktop publishing. The digital darkroom refers to a computerized version of a chemical darkroom used to develop and process emulsion film. A digital darkroom, however, is not used to develop images. Rather, images are either scanned in from film or ported directly in from a digital camera or another digital medium and are then manipulated in the digital darkroom. A digital darkroom can perform all the processing functions of a chemical darkroom, such as cropping or shading. In addition, a digital darkroom can be used to seamlessly manipulate images in a variety of other ways, such as adding or deleting portions of the existing image, combining two images, or creating totally synthetic images based on real photographs. All of these functions are possible in a chemical darkroom but are not as easy, simple, or seamless as in the digital darkroom. Moreover, because of digital image capturing technology, there is no longer necessarily a film negative to document the existence of an original image.

Desktop Video.   Advances in desktop computing have also made it possible to seamlessly process full-motion video using a Macintosh or a PC. Especially important in this desktop video is the notion that the manipulation of the video is not only simple and fast, but because it is in digital format, it is nonlinear. In contrast to editing analog videotape, desktop video allows the editor to move instantly from one image or sequence to another, to remove, add, resequence, or modify any images in a database or image file in the same manner a writer can edit text in a word processor.

Part II: Electronic Information Gathering

Digital technologies are rapidly transforming the process of gathering information of all types. From electronic photography to speech recognition, new media technologies are providing a direct electronic link between external stimuli such as images and sounds and computer processing devices.

Electronic Photography

Digital technology has begun to transform the manner in which visual information is captured and stored. Although the quality has much improved, the fundamental principle of using chemical processes to capture images on film has changed little since the invention of still photography in the early part of the nineteenth century. Credited with the invention of still photography, Frenchmen Louis-Jacques-Mande Daguerre and Joseph Niepce developed in 1839 the first practical photographic technology known as the daguerreotype. The daguerreotype allowed for the production of a permanent image on a silver-coated copper plate treated with iodine vapor. Digital photography represents an entirely new approach to capturing images without chemicals. Instead, digital cameras use an electronic charge-coupled device (CCD) to capture and store images electronically.

Introduced as an analog technology in the early 1970s by RCA, the charge-coupled device (CCD) eventually lead to the replacement of tubes in video cameras. CCD-based cameras employ a photo sensor to capture an image in an analog format and then digitally transfer the image to an output amplifier. Such CCD-based cameras offer several advantages over conventional emulsion-film based cameras, including no film processing delay, maintained image resolution when either the camera or image is moving, no aging of the CCD, no warm-up time, smaller and lighter cameras, and less temperature and light sensitivity (although many tube cameras have been rendered useless by pointing them directly at the sun or another bright light, CCD cameras are much less susceptible to this malady).

The first broadcast-quality CCD-based cameras were developed in 1986, when *USA Today*, the *Chicago Tribune,* and *Newsday* inaugurated the use of still video (or CCD) cameras in news reporting by using the electronic cameras for their photographic coverage of the Republican National Convention. Using Canon's RC701, the papers captured images via a CCD-based camera for recording onto a magnetic disc. Images were then sent by modem directly into the newsroom, bypassing processing in a chemical darkroom.

Digital/Electronic Photography

The latest generation of CCD cameras and photographic technologies now capture and store images in a digital format. It makes possible the complete processing of any images—still or full motion—in a computerized, nonlinear environment. With wide commercial applications in advertising, public relations, and journalism, it also raises a variety of thorny ethical questions about establishing the authenticity, veracity, and credibility of the photographic image, since digital cameras do not provide a film negative and electronic images can be easily manipulated. One of the major drawbacks of the digital video camera has been the quality of the image. When introduced, these cameras could produce images with no more than about 600,000 pixels (the smallest picture element in a computer image) of resolution, versus the equivalent of some 35 million pixels in an emulsion-film photograph. The latest generation of digital cameras, however, has substantially improved image resolution, with Kodak's 1994 digital camera storing images with about 3.5 million pixels. The human eye cannot easily distinguish between images at this level of resolution. Moreover, few media reproduce images at this level of resolution, whether the highest quality magazine or high definition television.

Electronic News Gathering (ENG)

Introduced by pioneering CBS engineer Joseph Flaherty in the early 1970s, electronic news gathering (ENG) refers to the use of portable electronic video systems and audio apparatus in news collection.[15] 1973 marked the turning point for ENG because of the creation of the timebase corrector, which could convert the product of a videotape recorder into an image that was clear enough to broadcast directly without the need for further processing. Reports indicate that by 1973 just 3 percent of local TV news stations had begun using modern ENG equipment in collecting information. By the late 1970s, virtually every local station and national network was using ENG equipment, and ENG had become the de facto standard in television news.

ENG coverage offered a number of advantages over film, the traditional medium for television news, including speed (due to the elimination of the film processing time), labor savings, reduced personnel necessary for an on-site taping, cost savings through the reusability of video, and easy transportation. ENG also brought with it some unexpected consequences, including new styles of editing with more rapid pacing.[16]

Satellite News Gathering (SNG)

A cousin of electronic news gathering, SNG technology links the technology of electronic cameras with advances in satellite communications.

Today's SNG technology enables reporters anywhere in the world to transmit video to any other part of the world instantly and at low cost. Thus, for better or worse, SNG has made "going live" the standard in local and network TV news coverage.

High-8 Millimeter Video/Camcorders

A similarly important technological development in the area of electronic photography is the high-8 millimeter videocamera. Also based on the use of a CCD sensor, high-8 cameras record images in analog format, but on 8 millimeter (mm) tape, rather than the much larger 16 mm or 35 mm VHS tape or Beta formats previously used for most broadcast-quality video content. The high-8 cameras are also much smaller, lighter, and less expensive than conventional video cameras, making them considerably more portable and versatile. As a result, high-8 cameras, which vary in size from a shoulder pack camera to a palm-size camcorder and range in price from about $1,000 to $20,000, have been used to cover stories in remote and dangerous locations—the first video of the oil-well fires in Kuwait at the end of the Persian Gulf War was shot using a high-8 camera. Increasingly, print news organizations are even equipping their reporters with high-8 cameras, because of their low cost and portability, to provide video coverage of breaking news events.

Importantly, the competing S-VHS (super-VHS) format produces nearly identical resolution as the half-inch high-8 format, with both providing 400+ lines of resolution instead of the 260+ for standard VHS. Many stations use S-VHS instead of or in addition to high-8 cameras, including Fox Network News.

Optical Scanners

Optical scanners are computer input devices that use optical technology to digitize visual information such as pages of text, images, and other documents and bring that visual information into a computer processing or transmission environment. Using optical character reader (OCR) software, some scanners can decipher text, as well, although few low-end (that is, inexpensive) products are capable of reading characters with high reliability. Typically, most OCR scanners are most accurate with typewritten text using a uniform font or typeface. Handwritten text is especially problematic and requires considerable subsequent error correction using spelling checking software or human editing.

Remote Sensing Technology

Reading the newspaper and watching television are things most of us do every day, and they don't seem like much of a technological achievement.

But if you've seen the movie *Patriot Games,* then you know that satellite technology has changed all that. With the latest image-enhancement software, reading the license plate of a car driving on the Washington Beltway is now something the CIA—or anyone with access to the right remote-sensing satellite—can do from more than five hundred miles away.

Most of us, of course, don't have access to the CIA's spy satellites with super-high-resolution sensors and advanced image-enhancement technology. Journalists in particular have been frustrated by the lack of access to these technologies. Nevertheless, reporters have found creative ways to use the available satellite images to tell important stories. The *New York Times* has reported that the CIA may soon give its consent to commercial sales of spy satellite equipment and images.[17] R. James Woolsey, the Director of Central Intelligence, is seriously considering "advancing CIA's position from 'no, never' to considering support for international sales of hardware and perhaps imagery," said David French, an agency spokesman.[18]

From Amazonia to the Persian Gulf.   Since the early days of Tiros 1, the U.S. weather satellite launched in 1960, scientists have used remote-sensing satellite imaging to observe planet Earth. These satellites have provided space-based images of phenomena as diverse as diamond deposits on the coast of Namibia, or pineapples and coconut palms on the South Pacific island of Marinduque.[19-27]

The technology of remote-sensing imagery is essentially a more sophisticated version of today's handheld video cameras. Meteorologists, geologists, ecologists, and others have used remote sensing for many applications. Earliest uses were for weather forecasting. Other uses include mapmaking and resource mapping and measuring, agricultural land-use planning, geological and mineral prospecting, and archaeological analysis.

The first commercially available remotely sensed images were provided by the first U.S. civilian Earth Resources Technology Satellite (ERTS), launched in 1972. These images, however, were too slow, with a two-month delay, and crude, with 80-meter resolution (that is, only objects at least 80 meters in size—nearly the size of a football field—could be discerned), to be useful to the news media. By the 1990s, the news media had begun to make increasing use of remote sensing images in news coverage, as timeliness and image resolution improved. Images now are available within a 48-hour turnaround, and with 5-meter resolution (that is, about the size of a car). A recent online database search reveals that hundreds of news stories that were either about or had used remote-sensing imaging have appeared in the past year in leading newspapers, magazines, and other publications as well as on news broadcasts and wire services.

The type of sensing technology is one of the critical factors in determining the usefulness of remote sensing to the news. Remote-sensing technology involves two primary sensor systems. One is a television camera that takes pictures of earth using visible light. The other is a multispectral scanner that uses both visible and infrared light. Both technologies are useful for news gathering, although the first is the simplest and most straightforward in its application. Infrared images, however, can be striking visually. Their dramatic impact can be seen in the blockbuster movie, *Patriot Games*, based on spy-master novelist Tom Clancy's book. In this film, director Philip Noyce tantalizes the audience with stunning special effects captured by remote-sensing satellite technology. Noyce recently said, "The scene I like best is a live infrared satellite broadcast of an attack on a terrorist training camp in the North African desert; it is seen above the subject in infrared from a camera 80,000 miles away."[28]

Although civilians traditionally have not had access to these spy data, the end of the Cold War may change the situation. Then Tennessee Senator Al Gore, Jr., spearheaded a drive to make public secret CIA data from spy satellites. These data include remote-sensing imagery of missile silos in the former Soviet Union, imagery that also recorded snowfall data, containing possible clues to global temperature changes.[29] The release of these government data could prove invaluable to journalists covering the earth's environment.

When Bernard Kalb, distinguished network correspondent and former State Department spokesman, returned from taping a documentary on the Earth Summit in Rio, he made an impassioned plea in a speech to the Freedom Forum trustees to take the steps necessary to save the Earth's environment. After all, he said, "We cannot trade this planet in for another one."[30] The environmental story is finally emerging as the greatest news story on Earth.

Remote-sensing technology provides the perfect medium to investigate human impact on the environment, and through which to tell the environmental story. Remote sensing has been used to cover a wide variety of environmental stories, often by juxtaposing images taken at different points in time or multiple locations. Such stories include fires in Amazonia spewing smoke for more than a million square miles, from Bolivia to Antarctica; the spread of crop disease and pests such as the gypsy moth; and deforestation in Gifford Pinchot National Forest in the state of Washington, in Mount Hood National Forest in Oregon, and in the state of Amazonas in Brazil.

Environmental coverage is not the only news application for remote sensing. Another is coverage of archaeological stories, such as the ancient Frankincense routes in southern Oman, the land T. E. Lawrence (known to many as Lawrence of Arabia) called, "the Atlantis of Arabia"; or, stories on thousand-year-old footpaths in Costa Rica, long-lost Mayan causeways running through the jungle of Guatemala, and prehistoric Indian religious sites in western Colorado.

Interestingly, one of the earliest precursors to remote-sensing imagery involved an aerial archaeological survey conducted in 1929 by renowned aviator, Charles Lindbergh. Lindbergh had flown over the Chaco canyon and snapped some black-and-white photos. Forty years later archeologists analyzing these photos discovered faint straight lines crossing the desert, providing the first evidence of the roads of the mysterious Anasazi Indians of the southwestern United States.

Remote sensing was also used in news coverage of the war in the Persian Gulf. ABC News used several Soviet satellite photos in their dramatic special, "A Line in the Sand," in which they combined remote-sensing imagery with computer mapping software to depict the geography of the region. A dramatic remote-sensing story on the war ran in the *St. Petersburg Times* on January 6, 1991.[31, 32] *Times* correspondent Joan Heller wrote, "Soviet satellite photos of Kuwait taken five weeks after the Iraqi invasion suggest the Bush administration might have exaggerated the scope of Iraq's military threat to Saudi Arabia." The photos showed no evidence of a large Iraqi military buildup in Kuwait. ABC News also acquired Soyuzkarta photos of Kuwait and found little evidence of a massive Iraqi buildup along the Kuwaiti border. Unfortunately, other news organizations did not confirm this story, partly because other satellite images were not available to corroborate the evidence from the Soviet satellite. Nevertheless, this story provides a compelling example of how remote-sensing images can be used in the most critical of news events: war.

This example also underscores the dramatic importance of extending full First Amendment rights of freedom of speech and of the press to the outer limits of Earth's environment, even to outer space.[33, 34] To date, American and other journalists have been denied access to many of the most timely and highest-resolution satellite images. By law, the U.S. Congress has restricted access to the highest-resolution satellite technology to military applications. Moreover, because of the expense of launching a satellite capable of taking remote-sensing imagery, no single media organization can afford its own private remote-sensing satellite, what some have called the MediaSat. In 1987, the United States Congress' Office of Technology Assessment estimated that it would cost as much as $470 million to launch and operate a MediaSat. Only through a consortium of media companies could a MediaSat be launched and operated.

France's remote-sensing satellite company, SPOT Image, was concerned about these images falling into the hands of the Iraqi military, who might have purchased the images through a third party.[35] In early August 1990, SPOT denied several news media requests for images from the Gulf region. As a result, news organizations could get images of the Gulf region from only Soyuzkarta and on a delayed basis. This meant the American people were denied the full story on why we went to war. Without the full First Amendment guarantees of disclosure and access to information, journalists cannot effectively cover the increasingly global story of planet Earth. Without this coverage, Earth's citizens may be denied access to the Earth's greatest news story.

Table 3-3 provides a comparative overview of the three principal remote-sensing image providers for news media. These firms are France's SPOT Image, the worldwide market leader, Russia's Soyuzkarta, and NASA's Landsat. The chart compares each provider in terms of a number of factors, including ground resolution of the images, image cost, and lead time required to obtain images. Each of these factors affects when, how, and how often news organizations can use remote-sensing imagery.

Voice Recognition and Speech Synthesis

Computer voice recognition and speech synthesis have been a hallmark of science fiction for generations and are slowly becoming a central part of the real-world computing environment. Isaac Asimov's 1950s science-fiction novel *I, Robot,* featured not just the immortal three laws of robotics, but also robots that fully understood human speech and could talk fluently. The 1950s Hollywood classic motion picture, *Forbidden Planet,* featured a robot that could both speak and understand voice commands. The *Enterprise*'s computer on television's 1960s sci-fi classic *Star Trek* spoke in a female voice and understood Captain Kirk's every voice command.

The reality of computer speech and voice recognition has lagged behind the realm of science fiction, with early efforts of the 1970s and 1980s fairly primitive, clunky, and slow. Even those speech-recognition systems that had a fairly effective range of understanding took many hours of training and required the speaker to pronounce his or her commands in a staccato style, with a momentary pause between each word spoken. Most had highly restricted vocabularies and were limited to specialized applications, such as medicine. Most of the current generation of commercial speech-recognition systems, such as one designed by Dragon Systems, Inc., of Newton, Massachusetts, are really nothing more than voice typewriters, translating spoken words into printed ones. Some can respond to simple, preset commands, such as "open file," but have no

TABLE 3-3   News Applications of Remote Sensing:
A Comparative Framework

	SPOT Image[36]	Soyuzkarta	Landsat[37]/EOSAT[38]
Resolution	10 meters (photo, black and white), 20 meters (high-resolution visible color), fully digital	5 meters (photo, not digital)	15 meters (photo) 30 meters (thematic mapper), 80 meters (multispectral scanner),[39] 120 meters , fully digital
Types	High-resolution visible, infrared, 3 bands of data[40]	Infrared	Multispectral scanner has 4 bands, thematic mapper and enhanced thematic mapper, panchromatic infrared, 7 bands of data
Access	Very easy	Difficult	Very Easy
Skills needed	Depends on need[41]	Depends on need	Depends on need
Cost	$600–$3,000	$2,000–$3,000	$2,500–$4,400[42]
Flexibility[43]	Very easy	Difficult[44]	Very easy[45]
Lead time	3 days, archive 3 weeks, custom	Variable	3 weeks
Orbital path	Circular, sun synchronous	Circular, sun synchronous	Circular, sun synchronous
Global coverage	100% of Earth	80% of Earth[46]	100% of Earth
Distance from Earth	500 miles	Varies	438 miles and 570 miles
Color or black and white	Color	Color	Color
Ease of use	Relatively easy[47]	Relatively easy	Relatively easy[48]

understanding of semantics. Speech synthesis technology has been similarly problematic. One of the most well-known early systems invariably pronounces every word with a distinctly "Swedish" accent, and sounds like a computer.

Research being conducted in the 1990s may transform the world of computer speech into what was once only imagined in the realm of science fiction. Research at the Massachusetts Institute of Technology (MIT), AT&T Bell Labs, Carnegie Mellon, and SRI International may help speech recognition become a viable technology, not just for persons with disabilities, specialized applications, and limited needs, but for general-purpose computing. MIT's Victor W. Zue is designing a speech-recognition system that can understand spoken requests for street directions or for making airline reservations. If Zue tells his computer, "Show me the Chinese restaurant nearest MIT," the computer will show him a map of the area and highlight in blue a route from his office to Royal East on Main Street. The system is based on a technology that actually deciphers the spoken word. Sound waves are converted into a series of phonemes, the smallest units of speech, such as the *r* in restaurant. These phonemes are then combined into possible words ranked by the acoustical fit of each set of sounds, such as "rest I want" versus "restaurant." The words are then analyzed in the context of the surrounding words to determine the overall meaning of a phrase or sentence. Speech-recognition systems are also being developed for multiple languages. AT&T, for example, has licensed speech systems from Belgian-based Lernout and Haupsie Speech Products that function in German, French, and other languages. This application will allow for instantaneous long-distance voice communication across cultural divides. When this speech-recognition technology is perfected, Zue contends, it "will touch the lives of millions of people."[49] But the road to perfection is still far off. Even these latest generations of speech technology are slow and very expensive. Researchers at Bolt, Beranek, and Newman use $100,000 workstations with sophisticated microphones, not home PCs or telephones, to run their speech-recognition system.

In 1950, the first crude speech-recognition device was developed in the United States based on a stochastic method of pattern analysis. Although in 1926 Bell Laboratories had created a voice coder capable of analyzing certain features of speech (pitch, depth, and so on), in 1950 H. K. Davis of the United States created a system that could recognize specific spoken words (such as numbers). By 1971, the vocabularies of speech recognition devices had improved enough for deciphering of sentences.

The 1995 state of the art in speech-recognition in commercial systems is defined by the "big three" of large-vocabulary speech-recognition technology. These companies are IBM, with its IBM Personal Dictation System, Dragon Systems, with DragonDictate, and Kurzweil Applied Intelligence, with Kurzweil Voice. The *Seybold Report on Desktop Publishing* reviewed these systems in early 1994 and concluded that speech recognition is only now becoming feasible with desktop computers.[50] Although "voice typewriters" have impressed crowds at trade shows for some years, they have required hardware beyond the price range of most potential users. With both Dragon System's DragonDictate and IBM's Personal Dictation System now priced at less than $1,000 and running on a desktop computer (preferably at least a 486), the situation has now changed. Seybold reports that all three of the above systems have vocabularies of at least thirty thousand words and are increasingly reliable. The systems, however, still require each user to train the software to understand his or her voice and also require the speaker to learn to dictate, by pausing after pronouncing each word. Moreover, these dictation systems require careful attention to acoustics. These systems simply don't "hear" very well. Seybold identified some digital age phrases misunderstood by the Personal Dictation System. "Fiber to the home" became "either to the home," while "digital services" became "dental services." Seybold recommends, "Optimal mike position is at the corner of the mouth, not touching the face, with sensitive surface of the mike rotated toward the sound source" (that is, the user's mouth).[51] Nevertheless, these systems are particularly valuable for persons with disabilities or persons suffering from repetitive stress injury (RSI) who may find use of a standard QWERTY keyboard difficult or impossible. Seybold concludes that the next generation of these systems designed for a Windows interface is likely to be particularly powerful and without some of the significant limitations of the current models.

The New Transmission System: A Field of Dreams

Reminiscent of President John F. Kennedy's pledge three decades ago to make the United States the first country to put a man on the moon, President Clinton and Vice President Gore have written and spoken widely about the need to build a new national information infrastructure (NII), a new telecommunications system for transmission of all forms of data and information. In fact, some have claimed that if we had a dollar for every comment about the NII the administration has made since its successful presidential campaign, we could erase the national debt, or at least most of it. As others in Washington, on university campuses, in the media and industry, and in the general public have echoed and responded to this call, there has been much debate about who will build such an infrastructure and at what cost, who will have access to it, and what its traffic and benefits will be. Meanwhile, there has been little agreement about just what this infrastructure will be. From a technological point of view, there are at least four approaches to an electronic information infrastructure:

- over-the-air broadcasting, including radio and television, satellite and wireless communications, and other uses of the electromagnetic spectrum
- fully switched telecommunications network, including twisted pair, optical fiber, the switched telephone network, the advanced intelligent network (AIN), Integrated Services Digital Network (ISDN), asymmetrical digital subscriber line (ADSL)
- coaxial and optical fiber cable networks utilizing a one-way head-end system or file server (such as cable TV)
- electrical power lines

The following discussion examines these four broad technological approaches to transmitting data in digital form.

Over-the-Air Broadcasting

Since German scientist Heinrich Hertz first experimented with radio waves in 1888, over-the-air broadcasting has provided a technical basis for an electronic information highway. The electromagnetic spectrum has served a variety of information distribution and communication purposes, ranging from commercial broadcasting to secret military applications (see Figure 3-1 for details on these purposes). The development of compression technologies has improved the ability of over-the-air broadcasting to carry large amounts of information, including high-definition television. Interactivity has been one of the limits of over-the-air broadcasting, since it is designed for a single source to transmit its message to a large audience distributed over a defined geographic region. By linking to other media, such as the telephone or online computer communication networks, over-the-air broadcasters have been able to introduce greater interactivity into their broadcasts. For example, television networks NBC and ABC have both announced their Internet address on news broadcasts, soliciting thousands of e-mail responses from many countries around the world. Satellite communications, including C and Ku-band, mobile satellite communications, and direct-broadcast satellite (DBS), represent the area of broadcast spectrum use most likely to provide an interactive information infrastructure on a national or international basis.

Satellite—C and Ku Band.   Since its invention by Arthur C. Clarke in 1945, the communications satellite has rapidly become the foundation for the global communications network linking all the world's people and media. In 1962, AT&T launched Telstar, the first telecommunications satellite that could be used for both television and telephone signals. Partially financed by the U.S. government, Telstar featured 3,600 solar cells and provided the first satellite relay of black-and-white and color television. Also that year, the U.S. Congress passed the Communications Satellite Act, establishing Comsat, a communications satellite organization incorporated in 1963. The first satellite launched under Comsat's direction, Intelsat 1, was put into orbit in 1965. Referred to as Early Bird, Intelsat 1's television coverage included President Johnson's address to the United Nations, Pope Paul's visit to New York, and a Beatle's concert. Satellite transmission of television signals also transformed news coverage, with live coverage of news events delivered via satellite beginning in 1970. This had particularly important implications for coverage of the Vietnam War. The advent of the communications satellite

Radio	Microwave	Infrared	Visible light	Ultraviolet	X-ray	Gamma ray
500 MHz	1,000 MHz			2,000 MHz	3,000 MHz	4,000 MHz
2-way Radio	Cellular telephone	Air route surveillance radar		Frequencies to be auctioned by the FCC for personal communication services	Space tracking telemetry	Satellites
	Taxi and dispatch radio	Amateur radio			Instructional TV	
	Industrial, scientific, medical equipment		Flight testing telemetry		Radio astronomy	
UHF TV (channels 14–69)	Radio location				Storm-detection radar	
	Worldwide aeronautical radio navigation					Military bands—classified
←VHF TV (30–300 MHz)						

Note: Frequencies listed on the broadcast spectrum are in megahertz, a unit indicating how many million radio waves pass through an individual location each second. The spectrum is charted on a logarithmic scale, with frequencies at the end of the microwave band 1,000 times greater than those at the end of the radio band.

Source: The *New York Times*[52]

FIGURE 3-1   Use of the Broadcast Spectrum

also made possible the creation of so-called superstations. In 1973, Bob Wormington, the president of a Kansas City UHF TV station, developed a plan to transform an independent TV station into a national super-station if distributed via satellite to cable systems nationwide. Although Wormington spawned the idea, cable systems were not adequately able to receive satellite transmissions in the early 1970s and not until 1976 did the Turner Communications–owned WTCG-TV of Atlanta launch the first superstation using the RCA Satcom satellite. Newspapers also joined the satellite bandwagon in the 1970s. In 1973, a single page of the *Wall Street Journal's* Eastern Edition was transmitted for the first time from an earth station in Chicopee, Massachusetts, to South Brunswick, New Jersey, via satellite. This spawned a new era in distributed publishing, which eventually led media magnate Al Neuharth to employ satellite news-paper transmission in 1980 to launch *USA Today*, the first national newspaper in the United States. On June 1 of that same year, the Cable News Network (CNN) delivered via satellite the first 24-hour television newscast to 1.7 million American homes, introducing the first 24-hour news network. It was made possible through the convergence of satellite and cable technologies, delivering the signal nationally via satellite and locally via cable.

When first introduced, communications satellites used what is called the C-band, a low-frequency band, long wave-length transmission system. Still the most widely used in commercial satellite transmissions, the C-band satellite has been joined by a high-frequency, short wave-length technology called Ku-band. Because of its longer wave length, C-band requires a larger receiving dish than Ku-Band and is typically stationary. Ku-band use is growing, partly because the Ku-Band signal is shorter, requires a smaller dish—about 18 inches across, is portable, and can be placed on the roof of a truck. However, Ku-band signals are subject to greater absorption and, thus, interference during bad weather. Today, many media organizations use the C-band and Ku-band satellite technologies for different applications, relying more on the Ku-band for electronic news gathering transmissions from remote, mobile locations such as ENG trucks, and using C-band for program distribution to affiliated stations across the country.

The communications satellite mix has become even more complex with the introduction in the mid-1970s of direct-broadcast satellite (DBS), cellular communications, and other satellite services, as well. These are discussed later in this chapter.

Around the world, the satellite has proven to be an important tool for delivering a variety of television programming, including news and entertainment from many countries. Because of the transborder nature of satellite broadcasting, there has been a great deal of controversy about both the importation and exportation of televised culture, especially that of the West to the Far East and increasingly to Europe and the developing world. A number of countries have gone so far as to announce bans on the private ownership of satellite receiving dishes. The Chinese government announced its ban in the fall of 1993, and the government of Saudi Arabia announced its intention to ban private dish ownership in early 1994.[53, 54] Other Muslim countries in the Middle East are set to announce satellite dish bans as well, including Jordan, Bahrain, and Kuwait. The countries have agreed to back a Middle East Broadcasting Centre (MBC) scheme to install 20 MMDS (Microwave Multipoint Distribution System) networks across the entire Middle East region. BBC World Service Television had planned to deliver its service to the region via satellite, but those plans are now in doubt. Despite government attempts to ban satellite dishes in many countries, the proliferation of privately owned satellite dishes in many developing nations has been dramatic. The ability of governments to enforce a satellite dish ban will grow even more difficult with the advent of high-powered direct broadcast satellite technology that requires only an 18-inch dish mounted on an interior wall for digital television reception.

Emerging Satellite Systems.   Since the launch of the first communication satellite more than three decades ago, satellite services and products have flourished. In fact, the communication industry orbiting Earth has grown to rival the largest land-based industries, communication or not.

Recent years have witnessed the development of two proposed communication satellite systems with profound commercial and cultural implications. The Motorola Iridium system and the Teledesic Corporation's satellite system promise to redefine modern extraterrestrial relay technology. The Motorola Iridium system derives its name from the fact that the number of satellites featured in its system is 66, the atomic weight of the element Iridium, not as some might think from the historic route west from Chicago to Los Angeles. The Teledesic Corporation's satellite system, featuring an unprecedented 840 satellites all linked in low flying orbital paths, was proposed in early 1994 by Craig McCaw, who built McCaw Cellular Communications, and William Gates, who transformed Microsoft Corporation into the largest software company in the world. The nature of these systems is compared in Table 3-4. Both Iridium and Teledesic are years from completion and will require massive financial investment before a single satellite is ever launched. Motorola has raised $800 million of the needed $3.3 billion to create its system, while McCaw and Gates have not yet raised any of the necessary $6.5 billion for the Teledesic network. Neither system is likely to be in operation before 2000, and both will require permission from the FCC before any satellites are launched. In late March 1994, a fourth satellite network, called Globalstar network, was announced by the Loral Corporation and Qualcomm, Inc.[55] The companies reportedly have already lined up a dozen corporate partners and $275 million in capital for the $1.8 billion satellite phone system. Globalstar, which includes 48 satellites and is scheduled for operation in 1998, will compete with Inmarsat in the mobile global satellite communications industry.

Mobile Satellite Communications.   Mobile satellite communications refer to mobile technologies for uplinking to communication satellites.[56] The mobile satellite phone is one of the most widely used devices for mobile satellite communications among media organizations. Inmarsat is the principle provider of global mobile satellite communications, although other competing systems are under development.

TABLE 3-4   Satellite Footprints in the Sand

	Traditional communication satellite in geo-stationary orbit	Motorola's proposed Iridium satellite network	Teledesic's proposed satellite network
Number of satellites	One or a few	66	840
Orbit	22,300 miles above equator; expensive to launch	483 miles; pole to pole; 11 routes; cheap launch	440 miles; polar orbit; 21 routes; cheap launch
Ground footprint	Massive, entire hemisphere	2,800 miles across	440 miles across
Power requirements	Great power—requires large earth stations, large dishes	Low power—Earth stations small and mobile like cellular phones	Low power—small Earth stations, but not mobile
Signal capacity	Very broad; handles voice, high-speed data, and video transmissions up to broadcast quality	Narrow; handles voice, data, similar to cellular phone	Broad; can handle medium- to high-quality voice, data, and video, but *not* broadcast quality

Sources: Teledesic, Motorola, *New York Times*

Inmarsat.   The state of the art in mobile satellite communications is currently offered by Inmarsat, an international cooperative of 71 countries that provides global mobile satellite communications; it has been widely used by news organizations, especially broadcasters, such as during the war in the Persian Gulf, as well as engineering and petrochemical companies who usually rent equipment for specific projects.[57] Created in 1979, Inmarsat was the first global mobile satellite system and is still the only one, although domestic, regional, and other global systems are beginning to emerge.[58] Inmarsat operates a network of eleven satellites in geostationary orbit, meaning each satellite maintains its footprint over a specific geographic region. It provides commercial services in more than 140 countries. Originally established to provide services to the maritime community, Inmarsat has expanded its services to a variety of aeronautical and land mobile applications. Headquartered in London, Inmarsat offers a wide range of telecommunications services, including telephony, telex, fax, data communications, and some limited video services via a variety of standards of mobile Earth stations.

Direct-Broadcast Satellite (DBS). Deep in the tropical rain forest of French Guiana, a French Ariane rocket soared out of the jungle on Friday, December 17, 1993.[59] Its payload was DBS-1, the first of two 6,000-pound satellites being delivered to an orbit 22,300 miles above the Equator. These satellites signal the beginning of the direct-broadcast satellite (DBS) system in the United States. DBS uses the same technology as traditional C-band and Ku-band satellite transmissions. It is essentially a high-powered version of the existing technology that will allow for direct-to-home (DTH) transmission to small dishes.

DBS expert Mickey Alpert writes:

The (DBS) satellites will utilize 120–240 watt tubes in order to provide a strong enough signal that can be received by a small dish. This compares with satellites utilizing 5–20 watt tubes that today distribute network programs to their affiliates or programs to those households that have installed 10–12 foot C-band backyard dishes. Recently, it has become clear that advances in video compression will significantly impact DBS. Whereas in the 1980s one satellite transponder could deliver one program, video compression will transmit ten movies over that same transponder. Each DBS receiver in the home will be individually addressed and will unscramble signals from the satellite. The small dish will either be parabolic or flat. The small dish size solves installation problems and the flat plate model can be placed discretely on a wall and will overcome potential zoning difficulties. Finally, this small dish can be connected to a VCR, stereo system, and personal computer in addition to the television. In fact, with some receivers, data transmission direct from the satellite to the PC will not require an additional modem since all the electronics will be built in the receiver itself.[60]

NASA began experimenting in 1976 with direct-broadcast satellites (DBS) using its sixth Applications Technology Satellite, ATS-6. Educational programs were transmitted to remote regions of Alaska, Appalachia, and the Rocky Mountains. Since then, DBS systems have been developed around the world, with Murdoch's StarTV providing DBS service in Asia and his BSkyB providing DBS service in Europe. DBS is particularly strong in these regions because cable TV has been slow to develop, and existing telephony in those regions has not been able to deliver full-motion video service. DBS has developed more slowly in the United States, taking a back seat to cable TV. One of the limitations DBS systems face is that they cannot provide effective local coverage. In the emerging U.S. systems, for example, all programming will be national. Subscribers will be able to view local programming, such as local news, independent channels, or public television, by switching to over-the-air reception through a rabbit-ears antenna or a rooftop antenna, or to cable TV service. DBS receivers also will be proprietary devices, at least at the outset, with Sony providing the set-top box necessary to receive DBS service in the United States. Plans are to open up the platform for competing products in the future. DBS does have the needed bandwidth to deliver HDTV programming, and may provide channel capacity to provide special categories of programming for geographically dispersed ethnic groups not well served by a local provider.[61] The mid-1980s witnessed the failure of an earlier DBS venture in the United States.[62] In this costly venture, Prudential approached DBS as a wholesale business, approaching potential consumers from a central location with no local partners to provide the retail sales and service connection. But because DBS systems require substantial technology purchases by the consumer, a local retail partner is required, and Prudential took a financial bath. In the latest DBS venture in the United States, USSB and Hughes have aligned with retailers, such as Sears, to provide the local sales and service needed to support a technology-intensive business like DBS. Early results from the DBS roll-out in the summer of 1994 indicate brisk sales, with demand exceeding supply.

Rising from the Ashes.   Although direct-broadcast satellite (DBS) technology has existed for decades, it has only recently emerged as a viable competitor in the U.S. television market, with the 1994 launch of the DBS-1 satellite and the introduction of the DirecTV service offered by Hughes Communications, Inc. Hughes has at least eight cable companies signed on as partners to provide programming for the DBS system. Hughes expects that DirecTV will have ten million subscribers by 2000 and will generate $1 billion in annual revenues. DBS won't replace other forms of TV transmission, but it does lower the cost for creating a national TV network by eliminating the need for local station affiliates. It also makes specialized TV programming more viable on a national basis, since a program with a rating of 0.1 means more than 200,000 viewers nationwide. Depending on the demographics of the audience, such programming might also attract significant advertising support. DBS also provides limited interactive TV services, such as movies on demand or computer games.[63]

DBS-1 has thirty-two transponders, or satellite-based transmitters. Half the transponders transmit regularly, and half serve as backups. Sharing space on the DBS satellite is DBS hopeful Hubbard Communications, headed by Stanley Hubbard II. Hubbard's DBS operation, USSB, owns five of the active and backup transponders and provides an alternative DBS service to DirecTV, which owns the remaining eleven active and backup transponders. Both companies funded the DBS satellite launch and maintenance. From its position above western Kansas, DBS-1 extends its footprint, or coverage area, to all of the lower forty-eight states and parts of Canada and Mexico. DBS-2 was launched in the summer of 1994, and is devoted to DirecTV applications. A snapshot of USSB and DirecTV is provided in Table 3-5.[64] Programming on USSB reflects more of the traditional premium channels available on cable, while DirecTV includes more news, weather, and information, as well as entertainment programming.

TABLE 3-5   USSB and DirecTV: DBS Service in North America

	DirecTV	USSB
Headquarters	El Segundo, California	St. Paul/Minneapolis, Minnesota
Ownership	Subsidiary of GM Hughes Electronics	Subsidiary of Hubbard Broadcasting
Executives	Eddy Hartenstein, president; James Remo, senior vice president	Stanley S. Hubbard, chairman/chief executive officer; Stanley E. Hubbard, president and chief operating officer
Programming	The Cartoon Network CMT: Country Music TV CNN CNN International Courtroom TV Network C-SPAN, C-SPAN-2 The Discovery Channel The Disney Channel E! Entertainment TV The Family Channel Headline News All News Channel Playboy TV The Golf Channel The Learning Channel The Travel Channel The Weather Channel TBS superstation TNN: The Nashville Network Turner Classic Movies Turner Network Television (TNT) USA Network Newsworld International Northstar	HBO Cinemax Showtime The Movie Channel Flix MTV VH-1 Nickelodeon Nick at Nite Comedy Central Lifetime Headline News

Following is a summary of how DirecTV works.

- Two high-powered $200 million DBS satellites beam several digital signals directly to earth receivers.
- One $100 million earth station in Castle Rock, Colorado, compresses digital TV signals, putting eight channels in the space of one, fed by cable programmers such as CNN and ESPN.
- Subscribers buy a $699 system including an 18-inch satellite dish that can be mounted on an interior wall in a living room, a VCR-sized receiver, signal decompressor and decoder box, and a remote control.
- A package of thirty-eight channels runs $29.95 per month, with pay-per-view movies and sports events about $3 each.

DirecTV president Eddy Hartenstein estimates his business may grow to $3 billion in revenue by 2000, with as many as ten million subscribers paying $30 a month. One of the disadvantages the company faces is the lack of local programming available on DBS systems, but that is offset by the fact that DBS presents the first real multichannel alternative to cable TV in many markets. The high cost of the receiver is a second major drawback to the DBS concept. Initially, European consumer electronics company Thompson has exclusive rights to manufacture the box, but companies like Sony and other manufacturers are likely to enter the picture shortly thereafter, driving the price of the box down to $300–$400 estimates Jimmy Schaeffer, an independent analyst working for Paul Kagan Associates.[65] DirecTV offers viewers selections from the following four types of programming:

- **Cable networks,** with up to forty channels devoted to basic and premium cable networks. A host of programmers have signed up with DirecTV, including the Cartoon Network, CNN, CNN International, Country Music Television, C-SPAN and C-SPAN 2, the Discovery Channel, the Disney Channel, E!, Entertainment Television, the Family Channel, Headline News, the Nashville Network, the Learning Channel, the Sci-Fi Channel, TBS Superstation, Turner Classic Movies, Turner Network Television, and USA Network.
- **Pay-per-view movies,** with fifty to sixty channels devoted to movies on demand, and charges ranging from $1.00 to $4.00 per selection. DirecTV broadcasts popular movies every 30 minutes, allowing viewers to select movies on impulse from either an on-screen program guide or from a preview channel showing movie trailers. A number of Hollywood studios have signed on with DirecTV, including Columbia/TriStar, Paramount Pictures, Sony Pictures Entertainment, Turner MGM, and Universal Studios.

- **Sports,** with thirty channels devoted to sporting events; DirecTV has not yet signed agreements with any programmers or producers for sports, however.
- **Special interest,** with the remaining thirty to forty channels devoted to cultural, international, and educational programming.

Both DirecTV and USSB rely on a common receiver system, DSS, the Digital Satellite System. DSS has two main parts, an 18-inch receiving dish and a TV set-top box to descramble the signal and convert the digital DBS transmission to an analog format for display on a regular TV set. The basic DSS unit sells for $699, with a deluxe package from RCA starting at $899. DirecTV and USSB expect the price of the receiving unit to fall dramatically over the next few years as more units are purchased, just as the cost of the VCR fell after its initial introduction. They expect the price to fall to a few hundred dollars by 2000.

DBS also presents an opportunity for independent producers to develop original, special-interest programming to appeal to a national audience. One leading producer considering pioneering programming for the DBS frontier is former NBC chairman Grant Tinker, who produced some of the most successful television programming of the 1970s, such as the *Mary Tyler Moore Show.* Tinker, who established a reputation for producing creative, quality programming that helped lead NBC from last place to first in network audience ratings, left the network and its parent, RCA, after they were acquired by General Electric. Tinker, in coordination with former NBC executive Bud Rukyser, has planned a new enterprise to create quality television programming for distribution to a national audience via DBS. Through independent production, the cost of producing programming for DBS would be much less than that produced for the networks, which must support a large and heavily unionized workforce.

Primestar Partners, a small, medium-powered direct-to-home satellite service begun prior to the high-powered DirecTV venture launched in 1994, upgraded its system from analog to digital technology in 1994. Primestar replaced analog set-top boxes with digital boxes made by General Instrument Corp., allowing the company to increase its TV channel delivery from ten to seventy-seven TV channels for each of the system's 77,000 subscribers.

DBS is also seen as an important technology in Canada, where the television world is largely dominated by American broadcasters. A major Canadian broadcaster and Canada's largest telecommunications company are planning a direct-to-home satellite-television service as a "Canadian alternative" to U.S. television. The service will be owned by a consortium including Western International Communications (WIC),

Canadian Satellite Communications, and BCE, Inc., the parent of Bell Canada.[66, 67]

Cellular Communications.   Cellular communications is an over-the-air delivery medium currently used for telephone services, including voice, data transmission, and fax communications. Through convergence, cellular technologies are now built into portable computers, making nomadic computing, or mobile computer communications, a reality.

A February 1993 study by Response Analysis suggests that cellular, paging and voice, and "data fleet dispatch" services are likely to grow to more than ninety million users by 2002 from an estimated forty million today. Users say the major attractions to wireless services are: 1) communications to anyone, anywhere, anytime (90 percent), 2) emergency communications (85 percent), and landline backup (62 percent).[68]

One of the threats to the future growth of the cellular telephone industry is the possible harmful health effects of the cellular phone. Although no conclusive evidence has shown there to be harmful effects, there is no clear evidence proving the phones to be safe. A number of lawsuits have been filed against cellular telephone manufacturers alleging that heavy use of the phones, which produce an electromagnetic field because of their cellular transmission, causes cancer. In one case, a senior-level scientist at Motorola, one of the leading manufacturers of cellular telephones, claims that the testing of a cellular phone that he conducted in 1984 caused him to develop an inoperable and incurable brain tumor.

Personal Communication Networks and Services (PCNs).   In 1993, the FCC approved and allocated 120 megahertz of spectrum for the creation of personal communications services. Prospective providers will bid for the frequencies. The FCC expects to generate as much as $10 billion through the bidding, with the projected industry revenues reaching $40 billion within ten years. Pocket phones will be among the first services to compete with phone companies for house-to-house wireless service, as well as cellular communications, which have just 40 megahertz of spectrum. The *Kiplinger Washington Letter* predicts that wireless office computer networks will be available within three to five years.[69]

Calling the Future: Fully Switched Telecommunications Network

"Mr. Watson, come here, I want you," spoken by Alexander Graham Bell on March 10, 1876, was the first proof that Bell's invention of the telephone could serve as the infrastructure for an information highway, although no one at the time was using the term so much in vogue in

1995. Today, few would argue that the twentieth century's fully switched telecommunications infrastructure is an important part of the so-called information superhighway. The dimensions of the modern telecommunications network architecture are complex and include many different technologies. The most important from a communications perspective are discussed below.

Over the past twenty years, the telecommunications network has undergone nothing less than a revolution.[70] In 1975, narrowband circuit-switched networks were the state of the art in telecommunications. These networks were designed to accommodate voice traffic very efficiently. When a caller in New York placed a call to Los Angeles, the network would create a single circuit devoted to carrying that call. The network did not require great bandwidth because each call had its own devoted circuit, and there was no demand to send video, data, or other information that might require large bandwidth for transmission.

As technology has advanced, however, demand has grown for data transmission, video transmission by landlines rather than over the air or by satellite. Telephone companies have widely deployed optical fiber throughout not just the United States but internationally, making it feasible to send large amounts of information in digital form efficiently over the telephone network. In addition, engineers developed the technology of packet switching. Unlike circuit switching, packet switching works on the concept of shared networks. In a packet-switched network, all information, whether voice, video, or data, is converted into digital format, 1s and 0s. These digital data are then transmitted in bunches, packets, over the network, wherever the network finds space. Despite a variety of technical challenges, especially in creating protocols for providing seamless interconnections between networks of different types—such as local versus wide area networks, fiber optic versus twisted pair versus coaxial, landline versus wireless communications—the technology of packet switching has taken hold and become increasingly the law of the telecommunications land. Moreover, with the coming merger of telephone networks and cable systems, and the combination of the phone companies' packet switching and extensive optical fiber and the cable systems' high-capacity coaxial cabling, broadband packet-switched networks will even more rapidly emerge as the national standard.[71]

As the U.S. economy emerged from the doldrums, 1994 saw a dramatic and continual rise in telephone traffic. In the 1st quarter of the year, long-distance use rose 10 percent versus a year earlier, the largest wire use in four years. Although analysts suggest several factors that contributed to the rise, one of the most important is the boom in fax, e-mail, and online services. The average Fortune 500 facility has nineteen fax machines, up some 8 percent from the previous year. Roughly 15 percent of 135 million U.S. phone lines are for faxes, and online use is growing by an astounding 40 percent a year.

Copper Wire Twisted Pair.   The current telecommunications network is a combination of optical fiber and copper wire twisted pair, with fiber used generally in the network "backbone," or main trunk lines, and twisted pair serving each individual home or customer. Replacing all copper with fiber is extremely costly, with some estimates running as high as one trillion dollars. As a result, the telephone companies have conducted extensive experiments in running full-motion video over twisted-pair wiring. Using advances in compression technology, the telcos have achieved much success in this regard. Several tests by Bellcore, the research arm of the regional Bell telephone operating companies, have demonstrated that near-VCR quality video can be delivered over existing copper wire. When combined with fiber backbone and advanced switching technologies, some field trials have even successfully provided limited video on demand. In these trials, a central file server stores a variety of video offerings, such as a movie library, and fiber delivers these offerings to the neighborhood or curb. Only the selected movie is then delivered over the short length of copper running from where the fiber line ends. In these trials, the consumer does not have a full range of video options, such as reverse, forward, or pause.

Advanced Intelligent Network (AIN).   The advanced intelligent network—AIN—is a network architecture or design currently in development at Bellcore laboratories on behalf of the Regional Bell Operating Companies. Bellcore president George Heilmeier, inventor of the liquid-crystal display and former head of the federal agency that helped develop Stealth airplanes, reports that AIN represents "a fundamental paradigm shift" for telecommunications.[72] "It used to be," he explains, "if you wanted to create a new service, the only people that could do it were the telephone companies. AIN changes all that. It means that third parties are going to be able to customize their own services."

Heilmeier notes that AIN is different from the Integrated Services Digital Network (ISDN), which is essentially a transport architecture providing a data dial tone. ISDN lets people interested in transporting data move those data more efficiently over the existing phone system. "That's a lot different from giving people the ability to actually invoke switch features and customize services," Heilmeier adds. AIN will allow companies to provide a national service but on a local level. For example, a company could advertise a national phone number, but use AIN to route each call to a local office.

Asymmetrical Digital Subscriber Line (ADSL). Using this new digital telecommunications networking service (utilizing advances in packet switching), telephone companies have entered the video age. By compressing the video signal, telcos are able to use ADSL to provide near-VCR-quality video over existing telephone lines, the traditional copper wire twisted pair that we have used for decades to make voice calls. ADSL, in combination with compression and packet switching, have helped transform the narrowband telecommunications infrastructure into an information highway capable of providing the one service many claim will drive the development of the new broadband infrastructure: video on demand.

Asynchronous Transfer Mode (ATM). ATM is a new type of packet-switching technology for use in the telecommunications network. Many see it as a breakthrough technology because it enables the existing infrastructure to act as a broadband network, providing advanced telecommunications services such as video on demand. Demonstrating the commercial application of ATM technology, First Virtual, a virtual corporation recently founded in Silicon Valley, is using ATM technology to move full-motion video, sound, and graphics files over the public telecommunications network.[73] Applications might include live video-conferences, telemedicine, and interactive video training and distance learning.

Integrated Services Digital Network (ISDN). ISDN is a new telecommunications networking technology that brings together traditionally separate forms of communication, including voice and data transmission in a single delivery medium. ISDN transmits at a rate of up to 64 kilobits per second (kbps). The Regional Bell Operating Companies (RBOCs) have touted ISDN for many years, but have only recently begun aggressively deploying it in their service areas.[74] Bell Atlantic is expanding its ISDN implementation from 900 to all 1,400 switching stations within its service area, while Southwestern Bell is making ISDN available throughout Austin, Texas. It will charge $50 a month for its basic ISDN transmission rate of 56 kbps and will use a more complicated and costly pricing structure for its primary service, depending on the number of 64 kbps ISDN lines a customer orders. Although most ISDNs cannot transmit full-motion video, Southwestern Bell plans to offer SelectVideo, an advanced ISDN service capable of transmitting video. SelectVideo allows customers to configure their transmission system for between 64 kbps to 1,536 kbps in 64 kbps increments.

Optical Fiber.   Optical fiber was created by Corning Glass in the 1960s. Its potential as a medium of information transmission was immediately recognized, but was not feasible for more than twenty years until switch technologies were developed that could connect one fiber to another. Optical fiber is made out of silicon, the same material that is used in creating the transistor chip. Information is distributed via optical fiber in digital form through pulses of light at 186,000 miles per second, the speed of light. Perhaps even more important than the speed of the transmission, however, is the capacity of optical fiber. Optical fiber has vastly more bandwidth—or transmission capacity—than traditional telephone wire—twisted pairs of copper wire. With the latest compression technologies, optical fiber becomes an almost limitless capacity medium of transmission capable of 155 megabytes per second. For example, the contents of the entire *Oxford English Dictionary* or an entire feature-length motion picture can be can be sent via optical fiber in just seconds. It is the transmission capability of optical fiber that leads many to call it the basic infrastructure of the information highway. The transmission capacity of optical fiber makes possible a variety of video services, such as video on demand, or the video dial tone, as well as many applications for interactive video services, such as in medicine or other fields.

When first developed, optical fiber was much more expensive than copper wire. Advances in the technology as well as mass production have combined to bring down the price of fiber optics to less than the cost of copper wire. By early 1995, many thousands of miles of optical fiber had been laid in the United States. Although most of this has been laid by the phone companies, many cable companies have also laid considerable fiber miles as well, as have other communications companies. Most of this fiber has been installed in what is called the backbone, or the main trunk lines connecting major switching centers. In fact, fiber to the home is largely unnecessary. Optical fiber has another important advantage: unlike traditional twisted pair or coaxial cable, optical fiber is impervious to the massive electromagnetic fields created during nuclear explosions. This is one reason all nuclear submarines and many navy carriers are equipped with optical fiber for their onboard communications.

Despite the decreasing cost of fiber, connecting the entire nation, even if stopping at the curb or neighborhood and not the home, will still be very expensive. Some estimates are that the cost of fiber to the curb will exceed $300 billion. That's more than $1,000 for every person living in the United States. It is unclear where the funds will come from to pay for this cost, although some project that even if fiber is used only as a replacement for copper, the country will be connected by fiber by 2020.

If a more aggressive approach is taken, perhaps at the encouragement of the federal government or through competition between cable and phone companies and long-distance carriers, we could see most of the country connected by fiber by 2000.

But is all this fiber necessary? Telecommunications scholar Michael Noll says no.[75] Noll, dean of the Annenberg School for Communication at USC, is an expert on telecommunications technology and pioneered the development of the first "virtual reality" technology at the AT&T Bell Labs in the late 1960s, although his patent was for a sensory technology device never actually created. Noll conducted an analysis of the information traffic on the U.S. public telecommunications network. He found that even combining all the voice, data, and transactional communications, we would not near the capacity of the existing twisted-pair network. Even with video on demand, the capacity is not neared with today's compression technology. So why all the fuss about fiber optics? Fiber optics is really needed only if we were to develop a system in which every user began transmitting full-motion video messages the same way we use today's phone for voice messages.

Noll raises a bigger question about new media technologies. Are these new technologies being developed to meet real needs, or are they the result of technology push? Many would argue the latter, not the former. Professors Herbert Dordick and Dale Lehman argue just such a process may be driving much of the push for the development of a national information infrastructure, or information highway, in the United States.[76]

As telecommunications cables traverse thousands of miles of ocean, many of these coaxial cables are rapidly being linked or replaced by fiber optic cables. This conversion to optical fiber means the information superhighway stretches across the entire globe. Importantly, these transoceanic optical fiber lines are not equally distributed throughout all continents, regions, and countries of the world. The United States, for example, is the most well connected country in the world by optical fiber, with four transoceanic cables linking it to Asia, Australia, New Zealand, and Russia, and five optical fiber lines to countries in Europe and South America. By contrast, all of Africa is served by just two fiber optic connections, one of those links stretching from Europe to South Africa. The vast majority of countries have no transoceanic fiber optic connections with other countries. Similarly, only information societies such as the United States, Australia, Japan, or France have international fiber optic lines at all. Most third world or developing nations have no on-ramps to the world's information highway and are thus excluded from the globe' information grid.

High-Speed Data.   High-speed data (HSD) link refers to a telecommunications connection capable of transmitting data at relatively high rates of speed, generally at least 14.4 thousand bits per second, or a 14.4 K Baud rate. An HSD link is generally needed to transmit graphics or other visual information, such as full-motion video.

Local Area Network.   The term *local area network* (LAN) refers to a network of computers limited to a specific geographic location, such as an office or university campus. LANs allow file sharing, electronic mail communications, and systemwide applications, such as access to central databases and software or file backup procedures. LANs are made up of multiple workstations, personal computers, or terminals with a central processor or file server where computerized exchanges occur.

Wide Area Networks.   LANs can be connected to wide area networks, or WANs. A WAN is analogous to a LAN, except it is not limited to a specific geographic location. A WAN may cover the entire planet Earth and typically makes use of the public telecommunications network for communications, file sharing, and other network transactions. A WAN consists of many LANs, computers, and central processors, perhaps even a super-computer.

Modem.   Central to all these technologies is the computer modem, which is an acronym for MOdulate-DEModulate. A modem is a device that allows a computer to connect to a telephone line or wireless network and communicate with any computer also connected to that network. The modem acts as a translator of the digital information.

Cable TV
The Wired Nation.   About two-thirds of all American households receive television by cable television using a combination of coaxial and optical fiber cabling in a one-way head-end system. The term *head-end* refers to the fact that a central file server distributes full-motion video downstream, or one-way, from the head-end to the home. Interactive cable TV systems increasingly incorporate two-way or upstream capacity into their systems.

Coaxial Cable.   Coaxial cable is the delivery medium traditionally used for delivering cable television to the home. It provides broadband transmission capabilities for the delivery of full-motion video. Most cable TV systems are based on either coaxial cable or a combination of coax and optical fiber, all networked in a one-way head-end system. In 1971, freelance writer Ralph Lee Smith dubbed cable TV, delivered via coaxial cable, tomorrow's information highway, because of its broadband capability as well as the public-access potential promised in many cable franchises of the time.

Coaxial cable was invented in 1928 by Lloyd Espenschied, an electrical engineer for AT&T, and Herman Affel. The first use of coaxial cable was for undersea telephone transmission and later for television transmission.

CATV is an acronym for Community Antenna Television Systems. Using coaxial cable connections, CATV systems are established to improve television reception in areas where it was weak or blocked by geographic terrain or other interference. The first systems were built noncommercially in Mahoney City, Pennsylvania, in June 1948 and in Astoria, Oregon, on November 25, 1948. "Four television networks were launched that May 1 (1948), three by the established radio networks, ABC, CBS, and NBC, and one, DuMont, by a maker of television receivers," writes Rueven Frank, former NBC News president.[77] The television networks were made possible by AT&T's introduction on May 1 of "regular, commercial intercity transmission of television pictures. . . ." using coaxial cable connecting "only nine cities from Boston in the north to Richmond, Virginia, in the south," Frank adds.

Importantly, from a technical point of view, coaxial cable can be used effectively to provide telephone service and is in fact used in this fashion in various international venues, such as in the United Kingdom, where traditional telephone service provided by the PTT is notoriously poor quality and short on modern features, such as call waiting or caller ID. American telephone companies have built coaxial cable networks in the United Kingdom, and British residents have then used them not so much for their television offerings but for their improved telephone service. In the United States, cable TV providers have generally not used their coaxial cable networks to provide telephone service even though the broadband-width medium could easily accommodate the extra traffic, because they do not wish to become an even more heavily regulated industry, which they would be under current telecommunications law.

MMDS.   MMDS is an acronym for multichannel multipoint distribution service. Also known as wireless cable, MMDS is a terrestrial broadcast service that can transmit as many as thirty-three TV channels over the air via microwave transmission, although many more channels are possible with compression. MMDS systems are particularly effective in regions with flat terrain, especially in sparsely populated areas where wired cable systems are expensive to install and maintain, such as the rural plains areas of the Midwest. MMDS was made possible in 1983 by an FCC frequency reallocation that allowed broadcasters to use as many as thirty-three high-frequency 6-megahertz channels for an MMDS service.

Digital Radio (DAR).   Digital radio (DAR) refers to radio tranmissions in digital, or computerized format. Because of its bandwidth requirements, digital radio is delivered primarily via cable TV coaxial lines, although advances in compression technology have made it possible to deliver digital audio over the air. Its importance is profound for the radio industry because, unlike traditional analog radio transmission, digital radio suffers no signal degradation between the source and the radio listener's receiver. As a result, the consumer can not only listen to CD-quality music delivered via the radio but can also record it. And if recorded on a digital medium such as digital audio tape, the consumer can make unlimited digital recordings, each as perfect as the signal originally transmitted. This digital recording has enormous implications for the recording industry, which is concerned about potential audio piracy.

The National Association of Broadcasters has agreed on a standard for transmitting a new Radio Broadcast Data System, called CouponRadio, which could also emerge as an important force in radio's digital future. CouponRadio is part of a technology that allows radio listeners to save at the touch of a button a coupon transmitted electronically by an advertiser during a radio broadcast.

Electrical Power Lines
Although it may seem an unlikely idea to many, a growing number of utilities around the United States are conducting experiments to deliver information over electrical power lines. Since virtually every home is wired for electricity, the power grid would greatly increase the potential for universal access to the information superhighway. Although electrical lines have been used on a limited basis for delivering media content, such as providing radio service in college dormitories, they have not been used on a wide-scale basis. The latest generation of the technology is far advanced over earlier efforts. Several large utilities in California, Texas, Ohio, and Louisiana have already set up or planned experiments to give their customers more control in running their home appliances, such as the dishwasher or air conditioner, during off-peak hours when rates are lower, potentially saving consumers hundreds of dollars a year and possibly delaying the need to build new power plants.[78] Future designs may enable power companies to deliver movies on demand and other media content to home consumers. Noting that these developments may soon enable television viewers to use their remote controls to tell the microwave what they want to eat and when, Jens Carsten Nielsen, vice president of Marketing, Politiken, Denmark, observes tongue in cheek: "This will literally enable people to stay in front of their television sets for days."[79]

The American Electric Power Company of Columbus, Ohio, conducted a pilot project in which consumers using the system in Ohio, West

Virginia, and Indiana cut their energy consumption by 50–60 percent during peak hours.[80] The company plans to install the communication system in 25,000 homes out of its two million customer base. The system connects to an electronic box called an energy management unit, which is then wired to the customer's television set for display or displayed on a special screen the utility provides. Customers can then program their appliances to run during off-peak hours or at preset temperatures. Appliances require a special plug to run on the system and a special thermostat is needed to communicate with the energy management system. Other utilities testing similar systems include the Entergy Corporation, the parent company of Louisiana Power and Light and New Orleans Public Service, the Central and South West Corporation, the parent of Central Power and Light, Pacific Gas and Electric Company (PG&E), a large California utility, and the Glasgow, Kentucky, municipal utility. PG&E has found that customers are reluctant to expend much energy programming their appliances, and therefore require a system that is simple to use. As a result, PG&E has joined with the Microsoft Corporation to create a simple control system based on Microsoft Windows computer software. PG&E plans to install the system in Walnut Creek, California. Installation will initially cost about $1,000, which the company will pay, but in the long run will fall to about $200, which the customer would then pay. In addition, a monthly fee for the service would run about $10, says American Electric in Ohio.

To provide television service, movies on demand, or other types of information, these utility-based systems will provide a fiber optic link running alongside their electrical lines. Many utilities already have such fiber cables in place, using them to monitor their electrical transmission system and for internal communications, and only rarely using a significant portion of the optical fiber's information carrying capacity. The municipal utility in Glasgow, Kentucky, in fact, already offers two thousand of its customers such service.[81] Since 1989 the utility has offered its customers cable television service and a connection with databanks at schools and libraries. Unlike private utilities, the Glasgow public utility is not restricted by federal law prohibiting utilities from providing such additional services. See Chapter 8 for a further discussion of the laws pertaining to private utilities and media services.

Windows on the Electronic World: On-Ramps to the Superhighway

Technologies that allow us to access and display take many forms. They are computer-based and include a wide range of devices, such as personal digital appliances, flat panel screens, HDTV, interactive television, and virtual reality. In general, the trends in these technologies are toward smaller, lighter, more powerful devices capable of displaying multimedia information and receiving digital input from a variety of media, both cable and wireless.

Personal Digital Appliances (PDAs)

PDA's are essentially handheld computers that act as electronic pocket notebooks, organizers, address books, record keepers, and language translators.[82] In contrast to the first generation of pocket organizers, such as the Wizard from Sharpe, PDAs have no keyboard. You use a special pen to enter information directly on the screen. Most PDAs can be plugged in to other devices to transfer or receive digital information. As the technology develops and screen size increases and resolution improves, other applications are foreseen, such as electronic news products. Some companies are already experimenting with such products in Japan.

Among the first PDAs are Apple's Newton Message Pad, AT&T's Eo 440, Sharp's Expert Pad, and Casio's Z-7000. The Apple Newton is equipped with optical character recognition technology for hand-written input, although the technology is still rather primitive and unreliable, requiring considerable training to use effectively and verification of each word read by the Newton for accuracy. The Newton and other PDAs have not fared well in the U.S. market, but have proven immensely popular in Japan, where preteenage girls are enjoying not only the utilitarian functions of digital calendars and phone directories, but kids' games such as fortune-telling, computer-animated virtual pets, and electronic messaging across rooms via infrared light beams.[83]

Liquid Crystal Display (LCD). LCD technologies are based upon the principles of light-emitting diodes (LEDs), which are devices used to light up displays in electronic products. Originally researched by a British duo in the late 1950s, the first practical LED display was produced in 1962 by Nick Holonyak, Jr. Liquid crystals are organic substances whose properties and behavior lie somewhere between liquids and crystals.

While working in RCA's research laboratory in Princeton, New Jersey, in 1964, then twenty-four-year-old scientist and inventor George Heilmeier, today president of Bellcore, discovered that LCDs have the ability to change color instantly when an electric current is applied. His discovery led directly to the creation of digital watches, color portable computers, and soon, wall-hanging television sets. RCA did not successfully pursue the commercial application of the LCD. "People who were asked to commercialize (the technology) saw it as a distraction," recalls Heilmeier. "They tried, but they never unlocked the key to making this a commercial success."

The Japanese succeeded in 1975, when Sharp Corporation and other Japanese companies introduced liquid crystal displays (LCDs) to the market in consumer electronics products such as watches, calculators, and video games. The low resolution of LCDs is balanced by the reduced bulkiness of the picture tube. By the early 1980s small, flat screen TVs employed LCDs.

Figure 3-2 outlines projected growth for the liquid crystal display market through 2000.

Flat Panel Displays. The flat panel is an electronic tablet about 1–2 pounds in weight and the size and thickness of a notepad, utilizing LCD and other technologies to provide a flat computer display screen. Flat panels offer the potential to transform the computer from a tool for calculation to a portal of communication. This transformation, says Roger Fidler, director of the Knight-Ridder Information Design Laboratory in Boulder, Colorado, will lead to a "mediamorphosis" of the newspaper into an electronic news medium that not only delivers electronic text, but incorporates full-motion video and audio, interactivity, and information on demand.

Flat Screen Market. Japanese manufacturers currently dominate the flat screen market. As the flat screen market grows from today's $10 billion worldwide to $20 billion by 2000, a growing number of countries will challenge Japan's lock on the market. Among those eager to challenge the Japanese, who own 95 percent of the global market, are the United States and South Korea. In the United States, the Clinton administration

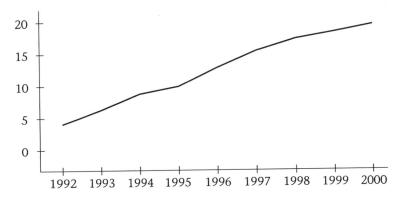

Sources: Stanford resources, *Video Technology News,* 1994[84]

FIGURE 3-2   Worldwide Liquid Crystal Display Component Market Forecast (billions of dollars)

and the Pentagon have announced a $1 billion "national flat panel display initiative."[85] Behind the initiative is Pentagon and White House investment in expanding U.S. manufacturing of flat panel displays. Not everyone agrees that making this kind of investment makes sense. Among those who question the wisdom of this investment is Charles T. Maxwell, a financial analyst specializing in new technologies and managing director of C. J. Lawrence/Deutsche Bank Securities Corporation.[86] Maxwell argues that although the LCD was invented by an American twenty-eight years ago, no American manufacturer has produced a competitive LCD.

South Korea has also announced an ambitious plan to challenge the Japanese. Having successfully broken Japan's manufacturing grip on the computer memory-chip market, South Korea has a proven track record in entering high-tech markets. In 1995, Samsung Electronics and the Goldstar Company both began mass manufacturing active-liquid LCDs, which are used in portable televisions and advanced color notebook computers.[87] Goldstar anticipates producing 500,000 flat panels in its first year production, a little more the world leader Sony expects to produce in a month at that time. This level of production is likely to create a glut in the market, eventually bringing down the price for LCDs.

The global $10 billion flat panel market is broken down by product applications in Table 3-6.

Current projections are that the market for flat panel displays will continue to grow throughout the remainder of the decade. The data suggest that while the U.S. market will continue to grow, it will not be a major competitor in the international marketplace with the more experienced Japanese manufacturers.[88] The next generation of flat panel displays are expected to have improved image resolution and by the end of the decade will approach that of ink on paper. Moreover, a team of French researchers has developed a paper-thin plastic transistor containing no metal parts, which may lead to flexible electronics, including flat panel screens that roll up like window shades.[89]

Diamond-Coated Displays.   While many in the flat-panel display industry are pinning their hopes on active-matrix, liquid crystal display (AMLCD) designs, a new technology is emerging that may bypass the AMLCD in the flat screen market. "A consortium of American companies and the nation's main nuclear weapons laboratory have joined forces to develop and market a revolutionary new type of computer and television display screen based on synthetic diamond," writes Pulitzer Prize–winning journalist Malcolm W. Browne.[90] SI Diamond Technology, Inc. (SIDT), and Microelectronics and Computer Technology Corporation (MCC) signed an agreement in 1993 to manufacture flat panel displays

TABLE 3-6 **Flat Panel Display Market: A Global Breakdown for 1994**

Market	Value in millions
Computers, including workstations, word processors, notebooks, and pen computers	$4,634
Consumer Products, including color, portable, projection TVs, handheld games, organizers, viewfinders, portable VCRs	$ 768
Industrial Uses, including medical and analytical equipment, machines to control factory processes	$ 585
Business and Commercial Applications, including copiers, projector plates, video and screen telephones, financial terminals	$ 430
Transportation, including automobile dashboards, marine, navigational aircraft instruments	$ 431

Source: Stanford resources[91]

using the electron-emitting qualities of diamonds.[92] The consortium contends the diamond technology can provide better brightness, contrast, and response time than active-matrix designs. It also expects that the diamond technology will lower power consumption and ease manufacturing, and at a lower cost. The consortium cites predictions that the flat panel display market will grow from about $10 billion in 1995 to more than $19 billion by 2000.

High-Definition Television
High-definition television (HDTV) represents the next generation of television technology, eventually expected to replace the existing generation of NTSC television. Developed in 1964 by the Japanese public broadcaster, NHK, the NHK system is called Hi-Vision. High definition, however, is really a misnomer, says broadcast pioneer Joe Flaherty, senior vice president of technology at CBS, because its connotation is merely improved resolution, sharper pictures.[93] Flaherty, who introduced HDTV to the United States in the 1980s, says that high-definition television actually has at least four important characteristics. First, of course, is improved image sharpness and resolution capability. While the U.S. standard is currently 525 lines and 60 frames per second, and in Europe

it is 625 lines at 50 frames per second, high-definition systems now being considered in the United States have about 1,125 scanning lines at 60 pictures a second, about twice the existing image resolution.

Second is substantially improved color rendition. "When my predecessors in this industry developed the present NTSC color system," Flaherty reflects, "great compromises in quality were taken in order to squeeze the color information into the already existing black-and-white picture. Little vacant spots in the spectrum were used to fit the color information in." In the early days of television, those compromises were not visible, largely because the screens on television sets were so small, 16 to 21 inches at best. But on today's large-screen television sets, "the warts of this system begin to show," Flaherty points out. High definition brings to today's television the color fidelity of 35-millimeter film. Third, and probably the most noticeable quality of high definition, says Flaherty, is the new aspect ratio. In today's television, the aspect ratio is four units of width to three units of height, or 1.33:1. HDTV will have a much wider aspect ratio at 1.78:1. This strange number was arrived at, Flaherty explains, as an approximation of the cinema. In most of the world, the cinematic aspect ratio is 1.66:1, while in the United States it varies, but is generally 1.85:1. 1.78:1 was arrived at as a compromise. The new aspect ratio of HDTV is better suited to the human eye, which sees a wider-angle view horizontally than vertically. Therefore, viewers get a more natural feeling watching images on a wide screen. The fourth important characteristic of HDTV is the introduction of digital multichannel sound, in both recording and transmission.

A final important development in the world of HDTV is the digital transmission standard for HDTV in the United States agreed on on November 8, 1993. "The things that are decided for HDTV will cast a long shadow," says Walt Cicciora, Time Warner vice president of technology and a member of the FCC's Advisory Committee on Advanced Television.[94] "This is going to be the first new standard (in television) in fifty years," says Dick Wiley, former FCC chairman and current chairman of the FCC's Advisory Committee on Advanced Television. The standards agreed on by the Digital HDTV Alliance and approved by the FCC's Advisory Committee on Advanced Television must still be tested and receive final approval by the FCC before they go into effect. The standards focus on several crucial issues, including the scanning approach, compression schemes, and sound quality. The standards combine both interlaced and progressive scanning. Interlaced scanning simultaneously refreshes every other line of pixels (dots) that make up a TV image; this is what is currently used in TV sets. Progressive scanning provides a picture more free of flicker and more suitable for reading; it's what computer screens use. The progressive scan approach is seen as providing the best hope for the future, especially if TV sets and computers merge to form the home entertainment center of the future. In this scenario, HDTV may be more than a new generation of television. It may become the living room access ramp to the information highway. Compression will be based on MPEG-2 (MPEG stands for Motion Picture Experts Group, which is made up of engineers working since 1988 to achieve world standards for the digital coding of moving pictures with sound; MPEG-2 are standards agreed on in 1993 designed primarily for decoding television signals), which is also the basis for compression employed in the cable industry.[95] HDTV sound will be transmitted at compact-disc-quality surround sound using Dolby audio technology.[96] Critics of the standards are concerned that there might be a lot more hype than reality in the proposed HDTV platform. One critic is Russell Neuman, Tufts University professor of communications and associate of the MIT Media Lab. Neuman worries that industry leaders may be selling a technology that may not deliver the goods. "This man wants to sell you a next generation of technology. Caveat emptor," Neuman says.[97]

Although HDTV ultimately represents an advanced device for displaying improved television images and sound, its current applications are primarily in production. A number of feature-length movies have been produced using HDTV both for theatrical release and for broadcast television. The first feature-length movie shot using HDTV cameras was *Julia, Julia,* a production by RAI, the Italian public broadcaster. The first made-for-television movie shot in HDTV in the United States was *The Littlest Victims,* a movie produced by CBS about babies with AIDS. HDTV cameras have been used to produce a number of other productions, including a large number of television commercials. HDTV technology is also used widely to produce Hollywood special effects for feature-length movies shot generally in film. In these cases, the film images are transferred to HDTV where the special effects are done by computer, and then the finished product is transferred back to 35-mm film for theatrical release. To date, HDTV productions shown on television in the United States are broadcast in regular NSTC format, since stations do not have the technology or available bandwidth needed to deliver HDTV signals over the air, nor do consumers have the required HDTV sets to watch in HDTV format. In Japan, where the analog MUSE HDTV system is in use, NHK, the public broadcaster, does air six hours of HDTV content a day to those few Japanese consumers and businesses with HDTV receivers. There are several major incentives to shoot movies and other content using HDTV, among them the improved image quality over NSTC cameras—even after transferring HDTV images to NSTC format the image is still improved. Also, with HDTV cameras, it is possible to immediately view the "rushes"—the term used by filmmakers to describe the initial film produced immediately after shooting.

Holography

Holography refers to a three-dimensional form of photography developed in the late 1940s by American scientist Dennis Gabor. Using laser cameras, multiple images of an object are recorded and reproduced in three-dimensional format. The result is an image that is far more complex and information-rich than conventional images. For the viewer, the three-dimensional holographic images can appear totally lifelike, in full color and even in full motion, all without the aid of special viewing glasses or other devices, unlike other forms of three-dimensional photography. Regardless of angle—front, back, top, or bottom—holographic images can maintain their full three-dimensional appearance. Taking the laser-based images required for holography is time consuming and expensive, and the resulting demands for holographic display are prohibitive. Thus, most holographic images are small or limited in scope. Still, a variety of holography applications have been developed, such as imprinting holographic images on credit cards. These images, because of their complexity and the amount of information stored within them, make counterfeiting extremely difficult. With advances in digital printing technologies making counterfeiting a growing concern for the U.S. Treasury Department, as well as many other treasury departments around the world, the U.S. government is considering creating a new form of paper money imprinted with holographic images.

Some scientists anticipate a future in which holographic images could be displayed in life-size proportions in everyday spaces. This is the basis for the notion of the so-called holodeck featured on the television science-fiction series, *Star Trek: The Next Generation.* Imagine the potential for learning, entertainment, or training experiences in which you participate in a completely synthetic environment, but one that looks totally real, seamlessly three-dimensional, one in which the real could not be distinguished by visual inspection from illusions. It might become addictive!

For those interested in the ultimate display of holographic imagery, you can visit the Museum of Holography located in the SoHo region of New York City, or you can visit the Haunted House at The Magic Kingdom in Walt Disney World in Orlando, Florida, both of which feature impressive examples of this remarkable technology of the image.

Interactive Television (ITV)

Interactive technology is one of the hottest topics in television. A number of companies are developing competing interactive television (TV) technologies, and the exact form that ultimately will emerge is anyone's guess, although it is almost certain to be digital in format.

Interactive TV, of course, has existed for decades, with the first ITV research being conducted in the 1920s and interactive programming seen as early as 1953 when the CBS children's series *Winky Dink and You* was introduced, reports telecommunications scholar and interactivity expert John Carey, director of Greystone Communications, Dobbs Ferry, New York.[98] *Winky Dink* invited children to use a crayon to draw a bridge on a special plastic sheet placed on their TV set screen in order to help Winky Dink escape from some calamity. Unfortunately, many children neglected to use the special paper, Carey notes, and the response from disgruntled parents quickly led the network to pull the plug on the *Winky Dink* show. Although he traces the modern origins of interactive media to the AT&T picture telephone demonstration at the New York World's Fair in 1964, Carey notes there was a flurry of interactive media research in the 1970s. Perhaps most well known was the Warner Amex Qube experiment in Columbus, Ohio, which brought interactivity to cable TV. Efforts there spawned the eventual development of Nickelodeon and MTV but demonstrated that interactive TV would work only when production values were up to the industry standard—which meant expensive production costs. Qube eventually shut down, but many of its lessons are not forgotten.

Today's interest in interactive TV comes from several sources. Much of it comes from private industry and new technological developments. The emergence of the information highway, fiber optics, digitization, video compression, and the convergence of computers, television, and telecommunications make interactive TV more feasible as a commercial enterprise.

ITV Field Trials. A number of industry-sponsored research experiments are now underway in the United States and Canada, as well as elsewhere around the world. Most are sponsored by cable TV and telephone companies. The early results have been mixed. One of the earliest of these second-generation experiments in providing an interactive TV service network is phone company GTE's trial in Cerritos, California. Launched in 1989, the Cerritos trial has met with limited success in the marketplace. The system provides fiber optic lines directly to 7,000 homes and gives subscribers access to a variety of services, including educational resources, stock quotes, and other interactive services. Some of the services, however, have been offered to a limited number of homes. For example, video-on-demand has been offered to just 2 homes, and home banking, home shopping, educational tools, games, and sports were offered to only 350 homes. While the technology seems to be working well enough, public interest has been almost nonexistent. One part of the test, called Main Street, was rolled out in Carlsbad, California, in December 1992 and in Boston in the spring of 1993. But all told, only 3,000 households have subscribed to Main Street, which costs just $9.95 a month. One of the problems is that Main Street does not incorporate full-motion video, relying instead on text, still images, and sound. Moreover, Main Street's games, including blackjack, poker, and a trivia contest, are somewhat low-tech for players used to the high-tech of Sega or Nintendo. GTE officials say the real goal of the Cerritos trial was to test the technology, not consumer interest, and in that sense, the trial has been moderately successful. "We weren't servicing this test to make a profit, but to learn from it," said Donald Bache, general manager of the Cerritos test. "You're changing the way people act, and that happens slowly," adds Thomas Greib, GTE Main Street's director. Company officials say future trials will be designed to test the marketability of the services. Others doubt the viability of the service as currently conceived. "People don't need it," says Michael Noll, dean of the Annenberg School for Communications at USC. "You pay your bills sitting at your table, not on a living room couch."[99]

A Full Service Network.   One of the most talked about interactive TV field trials is the Full Service Network (FSN) announced in 1994 by Time Warner for the Orlando, Florida, market.[100] The Full Service Network will put media control into the hands of the consumer, say Time Warner's leaders. The FSN will eventually provide all residents of Orlando with not only traditional television, but also interactive TV offerings such as movies on demand, personal communication services, video conferencing, home shopping, and many other enticing services. The heart of the system is interactive television, defined as full-service video on demand, with subscribers able to dial in for movies and other video offerings on demand, any time of the day or night, with the full range of video functions of a videocassette recorder, such as pause, fast forward, or rewind. Time Warner launched its first test of the FSN in Orlando the week before Christmas in 1994, installing the service in 5 homes. It expects to roll out the service to several hundred homes in early 1995 and up to 4,000 by the end of the year.[101] Time Warner had originally set April 1, 1994, as its target date for system deployment, but had to move back that date because of technical difficulties. "Writing one million lines of brand new software," was also a factor in the delay, says Jim Chiddix, senior vice president at Time Warner Cable.[102] The proposed network would include fiber optic wiring of the entire community, advanced computer set-top devices in every home that would give consumers access to a wide range of television and communications services, a central video server providing access to a vast digital movie library and other on-demand video services, such as on-demand news, a printer in every home, and eventually, personal communication services. Thus, the system would provide a full range of advanced information and communication services. The test is scheduled to last eighteen months, and costs are expected to be in the tens of millions of dollars, making it by far the costliest of interactive TV trials.

The research on interactive TV is still in the preliminary stage, although EON and one or two other companies do have working prototypes, such as Interactive Network in California and Illinois and Videoway, Montreal's interactive cable system that allows viewers to select camera angles during sporting events and different stories during the newscast. It even lets sports fans use their remote to call up baseball players batting averages, even their salaries. Others allow viewers to play along during game shows, such as *Jeopardy!* or blackjack. These prototypes raise the question as to what interactivity means. Some of these experiments are really examples of selectivity, not interactivity as we experience it in a telephone call. One of the most often mentioned interactive services of the future is video on demand. Some cable services, such as Time Warner's system in Queens, offer a version of video on demand, but it is relatively primitive, allowing viewers to select from a limited menu of movies starting at preset times (for example, a movie might be available every fifteen minutes). The future promises a video dial tone, which will allow viewers to select from a menu of thousands of movies and have them instantly available for a small charge, comparable to renting a video from a video rental store. The EON interactive TV system received approval from the FCC on March 3, 1994.[103]

A number of telephone companies are also investing heavily in field trials of interactive television systems. In May of 1994 Bell Atlantic Corporation, for example, announced plans to create within eighteen months an interactive video network in six metropolitan areas, including Philadelphia, Pittsburgh, Baltimore, Washington, D.C., Virginia Beach, Virginia., and northern New Jersey.[104] The system will offer a variety of video programming on demand, including entertainment, news, and information and provide two-way services, such as interactive multimedia television. Telephone company trials outside the United States are popular as well, with British Telecommunications offering a video-service to 2,500 homes in the United Kingdom.[105] The results of such field trials will help determine the future of interactive television.

Companies from other fields are also getting their interactive TV feet wet, including some banks, such as Chase Manhattan which is interested in the transactional capabilities of the technology, and computer software providers, such as Microsoft, whose interests also lie in the transactional services area.[106, 107]

Despite millions of dollars of investment in testing broadband and interactive television applications ranging from video on demand to interactive poker, no company or person has any definite answer to whether consumers will spend money on the expected applications of today's new media technologies. The field trials currently underway and those scheduled to begin in 1994 and to continue for the next twenty-four months and beyond will begin to provide some answers. But the bottom line is that most of the current generation of emerging media technologies were developed because they could be. Software applications and content are now being created for those technologies to see whether enough consumers will spend enough of their disposable income on them to let their developers turn a reasonable profit and attract advertising dollars. Table 3-7 presents a summary of the services being tested in the major interactive field trials scheduled in the United States in the coming months.

In addition to the dozens of video-on-demand trials set for the United States, trials are set in at least seven other countries around the world, including Australia, Canada, Germany, Hong Kong, Italy, Japan, Singapore, and the United Kingdom.[108]

News on Demand.   Content is a critical issue for interactive TV in general. As part of Time Warner's interactive TV trial known as the Full Service Network (FSN), Time will provide material from its thirty-seven magazines as part of the news-on-demand service. Cable News Network (CNN) will also be part of the news-on-demand service. CNN, the worldwide all-news cable network owned by Turner Broadcasting System, Inc., is the first outside news organization to sign onto the new service. The Time/CNN deal runs through mid-1996 and is nonexclusive, meaning CNN is free to make its programs available on other systems. The news-on-demand service will give subscribers a chance to obtain news, sports, weather, personal finance, health, and feature material whenever they . want it via their TV screens. The participation of CNN greatly increases the amount of material that will be available to subscribers to Time Warner's FSN.[109]

EON and Beyond.   One of the most eagerly anticipated interactive TV systems has been announced by EON Corporation (formerly TV Answer). EON is based on two-way radio technology.[110] Similarly, a growing number of regional Bell telephone companies have announced interactive TV and video dial tone field trials, as well. BellSouth Corporation has announced plans to test a two-way television system that would allow viewers to shop, play video games, and send computer messages as well as watch cable programming. In filing for permission from the Federal Communications Commission (FCC), the Atlanta-based regional phone

**TABLE 3-7   Major Field Trials of Interactive Services
in the United States**

Television field trials	Personal computer and cable TV field trials
Alexandria, Virginia Bell Atlantic Interactive TV delivered via phone lines	*Cambridge, Massachusettes* Continental Cablevision, Performance Systems Internet connection via cable
Castro Valley, California Viacom, AT&T Movies on demand, home shopping, banking, phone services via cable	*Castro Valley, California* Intel, Viacom, AT&T Video to PC via cable at high speed
Denver, Colorado TCI, AT&T, US West Movies on demand, home shopping, PC option	*Cupertino, California* TCI, Hybrid Communications Internet connection via cable providing PC network for Silicon Valley
Orlando, Florida Time Warner, Silicon Graphics, Scientific Atlanta Full Service Network, including movies on demand, home shopping, video games, personal communication services	*San Diego, California* Prodigy, Cox Cable Online services via cable serving twelve communities
Queens, New York Time Warner Limited movies on demand	*Seattle, Washington* Microsoft, TCI Microsoft software to allow access to databases via cable
Omaha, Nebraska (two trials) Cox Cable Movies on demand initially, later home shopping, music videos, arcade games, interactive multimedia, electronic classifieds	*Exeter, New Hampshire* CompuServe, Continental Cablevision, Teleport Online services via cable
US West, 3DO Movies on demand, interactive games via phone lines	

Sources: Company reports, the *New York Times*[111]

company said it wants to test the system in about twelve thousand homes in Chamblee, Georgia, a suburb of Atlanta. The system would provide sixty channels of traditional cable TV and three hundred two-way channels for home shopping, movies on demand, electronic mail, home banking, and other services.[112]

Lost in Hyperspace: Navigating in Cyberspace.   To those who have spent much time exploring any of the growing number of interactive TV trials, the Internet, or any other part of the online world, there is little need to explain the dangers of getting lost in cyberspace. With an increasingly polluted sea of options and a plethora of uniquely designed user interfaces, it is increasingly difficult to find one's way through this digital world. Sometimes, it is even hard to retrace one's electronic footsteps to exit an online system or a multimedia service. "Is the command 'exit' or 'quit'? Or is it 'logout'?" are all too familiar questions for even the savviest computer maven.

And all I ask is a tall ship and a star to steer her by.
                                                          —*JOHN MASEFIELD*[113]

As a result, a growing number of programmers, computer companies, and new media entrepreneurs are investing substantial resources to create cyberspace navigational tools. One interesting commercial entrant is Bell Atlantic's new navigational tool called Stargazer. Designed as a front-end system for interactive TV, Stargazer is based on the familiar American cultural icon the shopping mall. Though many may object to the commercial spirit of the shopping mall (that is, where does one find the library, school, or public health center at the shopping mall), there is no questioning the relevance of the metaphor to the American consumer experience. Witness the ubiquitousness nature and commercial success of the shopping mall in most American communities, or the Mall of America, the Minnesota landmark created as the largest shopping mall in the United States and a community in and of itself, with everything from restaurants to video arcades to discos to department stores. Stargazer brings the interactive TV viewer into an electronic mall and lets him or her visit any of the available shops or stores, such as the video store, where movies on demand are available, or a department store, where home shopping is done via remote control. Although some are concerned that Stargazer may do to interactive TV what Walmart has done for America, how much damage is there left to do to television's already "vast wasteland"?

Consumer Views.   Interactive TV is fast approaching, and consumers want it, reports Len Matthews, chairman of Next Century Media (NCM). He points to a variety of compelling evidence, particularly the experience of Videoway in Canada. "After three years, over 220,000 homes are paying an average of about $15 Canadian per month to interact with Videoway's interactive services for nearly two hours per day," Matthews reports.[114] The evidence will grow substantially during the next two years, he adds. Next Century Media reports that at least 103 interactive TV test-beds are planned for 1994–95. A number of RBOCs and MSOs are committed to rolling out interactive services at a minimum upfront cost to the consumer in order to maximize penetration of the service before competitors can do the same. Based on its data, NCM projects rapid growth of interactive TV during the next decade, with two of every three U.S. households subscribing to interactive TV by 2003.

Videophone.   Introduced at the 1964 New York World's fair, the videophone allowed caller and callee to see each other. At that time, color images were not possible and black-and-white moving images were blurry, although black-and-white stills were in sharp focus. Consumers using the videophone often felt embarrassed using the device, and were concerned about looking unpresentable, ultimately rendering this well-intentioned innovation a veritable failure. It was a classic example of technology push rather than market pull, and as such, was doomed. The development of video conferencing applications in business in the late 1980s rekindled interest in the videophone, and in the early 1990s AT&T, MCI, PictureTel, and other companies introduced a new generation of desktop videophones costing less than $1,000. Although business interest has grown, consumer response has been tepid, but improvements in image quality may improve the videophone's chances of success. Still, consumer attitudes are slow to change, and most express little interest in the device.

Other interesting telephone receivers include the Satellite Phone (Inmarsat-A satellite phone or satphone), which provides a high-speed data link via satellite communications. The Satellite Phone can transmit still video images, and advances in the technology may soon make it possible to transmit motion video.

Similarly, the Screen Phone is the latest generation in telephones for displaying text and data on a small liquid crystal screen. The screen phone is one possible on-ramp to the information superhighway. Although the first generation of consumer Screen Phones hit the market in late 1994, it is unclear how quickly they will be adopted. The initial price tag is likely to be several hundred dollars, although competition will quickly bring down the price to less than two hundred dollars.

Virtual Reality
Snap on your visor or head-mounted display helmet, slip on a data glove and slide into your sensorized body suit, and you're ready for the ultimate virtual experience. At least that is the promise of virtual reality. The reality may be something less, at least in today's marketplace. Called by some a technological LSD, virtual reality may be the ultimate information

technology. As Howard Rheingold puts it, "Virtual Reality (VR) is a magical window onto other worlds, from molecules to minds. . . . At the heart of VR is an experience—the experience of being in a virtual world or a remote location. . . ."[115]

Rheingold explains that two main concepts underline the virtual reality experience: *immersion* through computer-based technologies to "create the illusion of being inside a computer-generated scene," and *navigation* by "creating a computer model of a molecule or a city and enabling the user to move around, as if inside it."

From the Eyes of the Creator.   Widely recognized as the leading virtual reality (VR) visionary, Jaron Lanier coined the term *virtual reality* and is the founder of VPL (Virtual Programming Languages) Research of Foster City, California. His work led to the invention of the DataGlove™, the DataSuit™, and Swivel 3D™. He has recently developed the RB2™ system, the first commercially available VR development system and first multiple-user VR system. Lanier is now developing an application of the multiuser VR system to run in a Hollywood theater for consumer use. His other advanced VR products include a system for physicians to use in conducting microsurgery. Other interesting VR products have been developed by professor Myron Krueger, whose work has led to the development of an artificial reality product for education and research. Commercial VR products for arcade use have also been developed, although these VR products are currently little more than sophisticated video games with three-dimensional imaging, and do not offer the true level of interactivity developed by Lanier for his pioneering VR technology. VR products fall into six main areas:

- training and simulation
- entertainment
- scientific visualization
- communication
- computer-aided design (CAD) and modeling
- information

Research leading up to today's generation of virtual reality technology dates back to 1971, when technologist Michael Noll, now dean of the Annenberg School for Communications at USC, invented and patented a multisensory technology while a researcher for the AT&T Bell Labs. Myron Krueger, president of Artificial Reality Corporation, Vernon, Connecticut, has studied VR and its related technologies since 1972, when he wrote his doctoral dissertation on the subject.

The Optical Revolution: Storage Technologies

As the information society has unfolded, the need to store increasingly vast amounts of digital information has soared. Anyone who has ever bought a computer with 150 megabytes of hard-disk storage has seen how quickly a seemingly limitless storage device can fill up. Computer-based storage technologies have evolved through many stages in recent decades. As recently as the mid-1970s, magnetic storage on nine-track magnetic tape was the predominant form of large volume storage, although many users saved their data files and programs on paper computer key-punch cards. The PC era ushered in much more wide-scale magnetic storage devices, especially the hard and floppy disks, and witnessed the end of the punch-card era. Today, storage is based increasingly on optical technologies capable of much greater volumes of storage. Because of the slowness of the devices for reading many optical media, such as CD-ROM or optical tape, magnetic devices are still heavily relied on for a variety of desktop, mainframe, and supercomputing applications, especially when high-speed access is essential. One optical storage technology under development by Matsushita Electric Industrial Company, Japan's largest consumer electronics company, uses an atomic force microscope to pack as much as a trillion bits of information into a single square centimeter.[116]

Whether optical or magnetic, one shortcoming of electronic storage media is their relatively short life span and speed of obsolescence. Unlike ancient writing media, including stone tablets such as the Rosetta Stone, magnetic tape, videotape, magnetic, and optical disks are likely to become obsolete because of changes in technology within five to ten years, and even if not obsolete, face a short physical lifespan of less than ten years, with the exception of the optical disk which has a life span of about thirty years.[117]

Computer memory comes in several forms, including random-access and read-only memory, as well as readable and writeable storage media. Random-access memory, or RAM, refers to information stored by the computer in a way that allows the user instant access to any part of the stored information. This type of storage is relatively expensive, both in dollars and in computing power. Most desktop computers have 2 to 4 megabytes of RAM, with 8 megabytes of RAM needed for most multimedia desktop computing applications. Multitasking, or when a computer is running more than one application simultaneously in its random access memory, requires greater amounts of RAM, as well. Because it is based on the use of capacitors, current technology allows computers to store information in resident memory or RAM only while power is turned on. Recent advances in the field of supermagnetic storage may eliminate this storage limitation, making it possible to keep information in resident memory even when the computer is turned off. This same form of memory is also promising to greatly increase the amount of storage capacity in magnetic discs.

Read-only memory, or ROM, is a less expensive form of memory that refers to information stored in a way that can be read only, and not written to. A third type of memory is information stored on read and write storage media, such as computer hard drives, floppy disks, magnetic tape, or certain forms of optical media. Computers use and store information, such as computer applications or files, on these media, retrieve information from them, and erase or write over existing data.

CD-ROM

Compact disc–read only memory (CD-ROM) refers to an optical storage medium that can be read only, once data are initially recorded. Essentially the same technology as audio CDs used for music recording, CD-ROM is used to store computer data of all types. Like the laserdisc, CD-ROMs store data optically, as opposed to the magnetic storage technology of the well-known floppy disk. Because they are optical, CD-ROMs can store massive amounts of data, with the current standard being more than 600 megabytes. This means that a single CD-ROM can store more than 330,000 pages of text or, with advances in digital compression, nearly an entire feature-length movie. Sony-Philips has announced that in 1996 it will release a new CD-ROM that can store five times as much data, approximately 3.7 gigabytes (a billion bytes).[118] On the down side, CD-ROMs require a special player, and as the name implies, can only be read once the data have been recorded on the disc. Unlike a magnetic floppy disc, they cannot be written to by the user. For anyone who has ever accidentally erased an important file, this may be viewed as an advantage. CD-ROM drives tend to read data more slowly than hard drives, however, which is a disadvantage from any point of view, especially from a computing perspective. The technology is improving, but slowly. The lasercard may emerge as an attractive alternative, since lasercard readers have no moving parts and are lightning fast. CD-ROMs are also fairly expensive, with most titles in the $40–$60 price range.

IBM scientists have recently developed an advanced laser technology for storing up to ten times the amount of data on a single compact disc.[119] Although the technology is still in the laboratory, it may soon serve as a viable replacement for VCRs or other media for storing feature-length movies. The technology works by stacking data on multiple surfaces on the CD, as opposed to the traditional method, which stores data on a single layer. The laser then is instructed to read data on each individual layer "much as a person can look at the raindrops on a window or focus through them to see the view outside."[120]

Lasercard
Nevertheless, some are already proclaiming the CD-ROM to be obsolete, having been supplanted technologically by the much smaller lasercard. The lasercard, which is an optical storage device about the size, weight, and thickness of a credit card, can store a gigabyte of information, enough to record the entire twenty-volume set of the *Oxford English Dictionary* and then some, including full-motion video and audio. Perhaps most importantly, unlike a CD-ROM reader, devices to read a lasercard have no moving parts, leaving little possibility of a malfunction or wearing out. Moreover, it means a lasercard can be read and accessed much faster.

Compact Disk–Interactive (CD-I)
CD-I is a cousin of the CD-ROM. Also optically based, this medium provides much greater capacity for interactivity with the user. As a result, CD-I is often preferred for fast-paced game software. Moreover, CD-I is the only format currently with the storage capacity to show entire feature-length films. The leading manufacturer of the CD-I format is Holland's Philips, the pioneering consumer electronics company credited with introducing the first cassette-type video recorder in 1971 and the first laserdisc in 1972.

Digital Audio Tape (DAT)
DAT is a recording medium that stores incoming audio signals in digital format. With DAT, there is no signal degradation on any subsequent copies. It means that for the first time, digital audio recording technology is available to the consumer at a low cost. Although it is possible to store audio in digital format on a magnetic drive or even on an optical storage or WORM (write-once, read-many) device, these alternatives are either expensive or inefficient, because audio information in digital format requires large amounts of storage and would quickly consume large quantities of a hard disk, as would digital images or video. Importantly, DAT will make perfect digital recordings not only of analog transmissions but also digital ones [see the section Digital Radio (DAR), earlier in this chapter]. In 1971, Oki of Japan introduced the first professional digital audio tape studio. The 4-mm digital audio tape recorded data in long tracks that stretched from one end of the tape to the other.

Laserdisc or Videodisc
The precursor to the compact disc, the first optical videodisc or laserdisc was demonstrated in 1962 at SRI International.[121] Subsequently, Dutch scientist Dr. Pieter Kramer produced the first commercially viable laserdisc in 1968 for the Dutch consumer electronics firm Philips. During its initial commercial introduction, few consumers showed interest in the

high-priced products or players, and with few titles and a lackluster marketing effort by Dutch company Philips, the laserdisc quickly disappeared. In the late 1980s, improvements in laserdisc technology allowed producers to store up to an hour of full-motion video on a single side of the laserdisc, making it possible to put entire feature-length films on both sides of a single laserdisc. Movie companies and television networks as well as electronics consumer manufacturers took a renewed interest, and consumers responded more favorably. Today, the laserdisc market embraces not only entertainment products, but also educational and training materials. Although not as large as the VCR market, the digital quality of the laserdisc, which also offers CD-quality sound, has become a viable one. Still, few expect the laserdisc market to be an important one in the future, as advances in CD-ROM and CD-I, as well as the lasercard, may make the larger optical medium of the laserdisc obsolete.

Videocassette Recorder (VCR)

Although Sony demonstrated the first VCR in 1969, the technology of magnetic tape recording is much older. As early as 1951 singer Bing Crosby demonstrated the magnetic videotape recorder, and Ampex introduced the first videotape recorder for television use in 1956.[122] The technology became widely adopted in the consumer marketplace in the 1980s as prices fell dramatically from about $1,000 to less than $200. A digital VCR is likely to hit the consumer market in 1995, offering better picture quality, the ability to make repeated tape copies without loss of picture detail, and a better ability to match future television sets, which will likely process signals in digital format.[123] The digital VCR would also be able to store large amounts of computer data. One of the obstacles in creating the digital VCR has been establishing international standards for the technology. Some fifty American, European, and Asian companies recently agreed to a set of three standards for digital home videocassette recorders. These standards include one for NTSC TV, the TV system currently in use in North America, Japan, and some other countries; a second for Hi-Vision, the Japanese high-definition TV system; and a third for the digital HDTV system being developed in the United States.

The autocut VCR is an electronic device available in Japan, but not in the United States, which edits out commercials while recording from television. "The device distinguishes between the stereo sound of commercials and the monaural sound of programs," reports Sid Lerner.[124] Given the strength of the commercial sector in the United States, it is little surprise that advertisers have been able to resist the introduction of the autocut VCR in the United States.

THE TECHNOLOGY MAP: A SUMMARY

The conceptual framework developed for this chapter emphasized digital, computer-based technologies and how they change the way media content is

- gathered, processed and produced
- transmitted
- stored
- received and displayed

Technologies used in the gathering, producing, and processing of media and communications content fall into two main areas: information processing devices, primarily computers and related technologies, and devices for gathering and producing content, such as electronic photography, optical scanning, remote sensing, and speech recognition. Transmission technologies embrace four main types of technologies:

- over-the-air broadcasting, including radio and television, satellite and wireless communications, and other uses of the electromagnetic spectrum
- fully switched telecommunications network, including twisted pair, optical fiber, the switched telephone network, the advanced intelligent network (AIN), Integrated Services Digital Network (ISDN), asymmetrical digital subscriber line (ADSL)
- coaxial and optical fiber cable networks utilizing a one-way head-end system or file server (that is, cable TV)
- electrical power lines

Display technologies are largely computer-based and include a variety of devices, including personal digital appliances, flat panel screens, HDTV, and interactive television. Advances in these technologies signal improved access to information in digital format, emphasizing greater speed, higher image resolution and better color rendition, lighter weight, enhanced portability and battery life, multiple computing functions including wireless communications, and the enhanced status of the computer as an interactive, multimedia communications device.

Electronic storage technologies are primarily magnetic and optical and include magnetic forms of random-access and read-only memory, as well as optical disc storage media in increasingly miniaturized, compact disc formats.

NOTES

1. Daniel Tynan, "PC meets TV," *PC World,* February 1994:139.

2. Frederick Williams and John V. Pavlik, *The People's Right to Know: Media, Democracy, and the Information Highway.* Hillsdale, NJ: Lawrence Erlbaum Associates, 1994.

3. "Global Competitiveness of US Computer Industry," *Transnational Data and Communications Report,* March/April 1994:46.

4. U.S. International Trade Commission, 1993. "Global Competitiveness of US Advanced-Technology Industries: Computers." Washington, DC:USITC, Pub. no. 2705, December 1992.

5. Jim Seymour, "Pentium PCs: Pentium: The Second Wave," *PC Magazine,* 25 January 1994:110

6. John Markoff, "Chip Makers' Competing Creed," *New York Times, 11* March 1994:D1, D2.

7. Otis Port, "Wonder Chips: How They'll Make Computing Power Ultrafast and Ultracheap," *Business Week,* 4 July 1994:86–92.

8. John Markoff, "Intel's Crash Course on Consumers," *New York Times,* 21 December 1994:C1.

9. John Clyman, "PowerPC: Your Next CPU?" *PC Magazine,* 22 February 1994.

10. Markoff, op. cit., 1994.

11. Ibid.

12. David L. Wilson, "Compatible at Last? Alliance of Apple and IBM Leads to New Machines, but Differences Remain," *The Chronicle of Higher Education,* 16 March 1994:A19.

13. Markoff, op.cit., 1994.

14. Steven Levy, *Insanely Great: The Life and Times of Macintosh, the Computer that Changed Everything.* New York: Viking, 1994.

15. John Pavlik, *Media Technology Chronology.* Software published by Wayne Danielson Software, 1992.

16. Adam Clayton Powell III, "Getting the Picture" in John V. Pavlik and Everette E. Dennis, eds., *Demystifying Media Technology,* Mountain View, CA: Mayfield Publishing, 1993.

17. Tim Weiner, "C.I.A. Considers Allowing Sale of Spy Technology," *New York Times,* 13 November 1993:A8.

18. Ibid.

19. Edward B. Espanshade, Jr., ed., *Goode's Rand McNally World Atlas,* 18th ed. Skokie, IL: Rand McNally, 1990.

20. John H. Gibbons, ed., *U.S. Congress Office of Technology Assessment, Commercial Newsgathering from Space: A Technical Memorandum.* Washington, DC: Government Printing Office, 1987, pp. 39–44.

21. Tom Glasco, Information Director, interview, EOSAT/NASA, Washington, DC, 1992.

22. Landsat Spacecraft Data Sheet, EOSAT, January 1991.

23. Stanley A. Morain, "Remote Sensing: Instrumentation for Nondestructive Exploration of Cultural Resources," No. 2 in *Remote Sensing: A Handbook for*

Archaeologists and Cultural Resource Managers. Washington, DC: Cultural Resources Management Division, National Park Service, U.S. Department of the Interior, 1978.

24. Multispectral Imagery report, EOSAT, January, 1991.

25. Hilton Paris, NASA Teacher Resource Center, City College of New York, 17 June 1992.

26. *The Great Geographical Atlas.* Skokie, IL:Rand McNally, 1991, pp. 8–9.

27. *The Great World Atlas.* Maspeth, NY:American Map Corporation, pp. 12–39, 1992.

28. Henry Sheehan, "Philip Noyce Plays 'Patriot Games' with the CIA," Satellite TV Pre-Vue, June 28–July 4, 1992:5, 25.

29. William J. Broad, "Spy Data Now Open for Studies of Climate," *New York Times,* 23 June 1992:C1, C10.

30. Bernard Kalb, speech to the Freedom Forum Trustees, February 1993.

31. "The Mysterious Case of the Missing Troops," *St. Petersburg Times,* 30 November 1990.

32. Sandra Braman, "Contradictions in Brilliant Eyes," *Gazette* 47, 1991:177–194.

33. Allen W. Palmer, "On the Limits of a Free Press: Remote Imaging and Commercial News Gathering," *Gazette* 49, 1992:159–176.

34. Mark E. Brender, "High Resolution in Remote Sensing by the News Media," *Technology in Society* 22, 1989:89–98.

35. Clark Nelson, Director for Corporate Communication, interview, SPOT Image, Reston, VA, 1992.

36. SPOT Image refers to the French remote-sensing satellite system, Systeme Probatoire d'Observation de la Terre, launched in 1984.

37. Landsat refers to the satellite system set up by NASA. It was originally called ERTS, for Earth Resource Technology Satellite. NASA launched Landsat 1 in 1972 and now has six Landsat satellites orbiting the earth that produce remote-sensing images for civilian use.

38. EOSAT is the company established by NASA to administer its Landsat operations. The acronym refers to Earth Observation Satellite Company, 4300 Forbes Blvd., Lanham, MD 20706, (301) 562-0537.

39. Multispectral Scanner.

40. SPOT satellites have twin sensors with pointable mirrors that can produce stereo images for three-dimensional modeling.

41. Deciphering objects such as cities is relatively simple, while data such as crops, geological formations, and weather patterns require advanced technical skill.

42. Legislation before the Senate would allow anyone to buy a Landsat image for a price equal to the government cost of the image, about $500.

43. Flexibility refers to the ability of a news organization to request a specific image that is not in the satellite company's archive.

44. Soyuzkarta satellites have a life of only 3–6 weeks, and there is no Soyuzkarta satellite now orbiting the Earth. In most cases, news organizations are limited to archive images only, although it is possible to "buy" a mission for a specific purpose.

45. No extra charge for specific requests.

46. All of the earth except the polar caps.

47. A number of software packages that make television and newspaper and magazine use relatively easy.

48. The European Space Agency recently launched a competing remote-sensing satellite, ERS-1. Japan is also planning to launch a remote-sensing satellite soon.

49. Gary McWilliams, "Computers Are Finally Learning to Listen," *Business Week*, 1 November 1993.

50. *The Seybold Report on Desktop Publishing*, 7 March 1994.

51. Ibid.:1.

52. "Rabbit Is Naked," *New York Times Magazine*, 27 March 1994:22.

53. Jonathan Karp, "Prime Time Police: China Tries to Pull the Plug on Satellite TV," *Far Eastern Economic Review*, 21 October 1993:72–73.

54. *Cable and Satellite Europe* (C&SEu), "Top 50 Cable and Satellite Companies," 1994.

55. Edmund L. Andrews, "A Satellite System Is Planned to Link Most of the Globe," *New York Times*, 21 March 1994:A1, D2.

56. Ruth Ling, "Try Before You Buy," *Satellite Communications*, November 1993:25.

57. Ibid.

58. David Wright, "Mobile Satellite Communications in Developing Countries," *Telecommunications Policy*, January/February 1994.

59. Edmund L. Andrews, "Betting on Small-Dish TV," *New York Times*, 15 December 1993:D1, D7..

60. Mickey Alpert, "DBS," in John Pavlik and Everette E. Dennis, eds., 1993, *Demystifying Media Technology: Disk Edition*. Mountain View, CA: Mayfield Publishing, 1993.

61. *Via Satellite*, 4 April 1994.

62. Les Brown, *Les Brown's Encyclopedia of Televison*, ed 3. Detroit, MI: Gale Research Inc., 1992.

63. Hartenstein, 1993: 84–88.

64. *Broadcasting & Cable*, "The ABC's of DBS," 6 December 1993:38.

65. Kevin Marey, "High Price May Create Initial Static," *USA Today*, 4 May 1994:10B.

66. *Executive News Summary*, 6 May 1994:4.

67. *Wall Street Journal*, 6 May 1994:B10

68. "Study Suggests Wireless Could Transform Communications Industry," *The Sampler*, Response Analysis Corp., Princeton, NJ, pp. 1, 4.

69. *Kiplinger Washington Letter*, 24 September 1993.

70. Mischa Schwartz, "Telecommunications Networks and Multimedia," fellows seminar, the Freedom Forum Media Studies Center, 2 February 1994.

71. Julie Schmit, "High Tech Has Phones Humming," *USA Today*, 23 April 1994.

72. John V. Pavlik, and Frederick Williams, op. cit., 1994.

73. Laurie Flynn, "A Multimedia Networking Challenge," *New York Times*, 14 December 1994.

74. Gary H. Arlen, "RBOCs Finally Deploy ISDN" *Information & Interactive Services Report,* 25 February 1994:11.

75. Michael Noll, "Is All That Fiber Necessary?" *New York Times,* 1993.

76. Herbert S. Dordick and Dale E. Lehman, "Information Highways: 'Trickle Down' Infrastructure' " in Fred Williams and John V. Pavlik, eds., *The People's Right to Know: Media, Democracy and the Information Highway.* Hillsdale, NJ: Lawrence Erlbaum Associates, 1993.

77. Reuven Frank, *Out of Thin Air: The Brief Wonderful Life of Network News.* New York: Simon and Schuster, 1991, p. 7.

78. Agis Salpukas, "Big Hopes Put on Electric Wires," *New York Times,* 6 July 1994:D1, D4.

79. Tom Fenton, Freedom Forum report on a speech by Charles Brumback at the 47th World Newspaper Congress and FIEJ Annual General Meeting 29 May–1 June 1994, Vienna, Austria.

80. Salpukas, op. cit., 1994.

81. Ibid.

82. Amy Dunkin, *Business Week,* 4 October 1993:124–5.

83. Andrew Pollack, "Organizers Captivate Japanese Girls," *New York Times,* 22 December 1994:C1.

84. "Active-Matrix LCD Will Stay a Flat Panel Technology with Large Markets," *Video Technology News,* 3 January 1994.

85. John Carey, "Thinking Flat in Washington," *Business Week,* 9 May 1994:36.

86. Charles T. Maxwell, "U.S. Blunders on Computer Screen Subsidy," letter to the editor, *New York Times,* 11 May 1994.

87. Andrew Pollack, "From Korea, A Challenge to Japan," *New York Times,* 12 May 1994:D1, D5.

88. "Motif Unveils New Flat-Panel Technology, Largest Manufacturing Plant in U.S.," *Video Technology News,* 11 October 1993:8.

89. Warren E. Leary, "French Team Develops Flexible, Electronic Transistor Made of Plastic," *New York Times,* 16 September 1994.

90. Malcolm W. Browne, *New York Times,* 28 September 1993:C1

91. Stanford Resources, San Jose, California, 1994; *New York Times,* 12 May 1994.

92. "SI Diamond Plans Flat-Panel Display Project Using Diamond-Based Technology," *HDTV Report,* 13 October 1993.

93. Joseph Flaherty, "High-Definition Television: Technical and Political Issues." in John V. Pavlik and Everette E. Dennis, eds., *Demystifying Media Technology,* Mountain View, CA: Mayfield Publishing, 1993.

94. Chris Nolan, "Does HDTV Compute?" *Cablevision,* 6 December 1993:94.

95. "The World's Top AV Companies: The IDATE 100," *Screen Digest,* August 1993.

96. Nolan, op. cit., 1993.

97. Ibid.

98. John Carey, "Field Testing the Information Superhighway," speech, the Freedom Forum Media Studies Center, 5 April 1994.

99. Iris Cohen Selinger, "Cerritos Test Shows There's More to Learn About Interactive Television," *Advertising Age,* 25 October 1993:25.

100. Evan Ramstad, "Interactive TV gets Another Moment in the Sun," the Associated Press, 11 December 1994.

101. Edmund L. Andrews, "Time Warner's 'Time Machine,' " *New York Times,* 12 December 1994:C1, C7.

102. Harry A. Jessell, "For Time Warner, Software Is Hard Part." *Broadcasting & Cable,* 28 March 1994:42.

103. M. Gipson, *Information & Interactive Services Report,* 8 October 1994.

104. Mark Thalhimer, ed., *Media Industry News Roundup,* compiled from the Associated Press, the Freedom Forum Media Studies Center, 24 May 1994.

105. James Kim, "British Pioneer Launches Interactive Network," *USA Today,* 15 November 1994:7B.

106. Saul Hansell, "Banks Go Interactive to Beat the Rush of Services," *New York Times,* 19 October 1994:C1, C6.

107. John Markoff, "Microsoft Organizes Its Interactive TV Team," *New York Times,* 2 November 1994.

108. Paul Kempton, "Who in the World Wants VOD?" *Cable and Satellite Europe,* 19 April 1994:26–34.

109. Mark Thalhimer and Joanna Campbell, *Media Industry News Roundup,* the Freedom Forum Media Studies Center, 19 April 1994.

110. Leslie Regan Shade, "Computer Networking in Canada: From CA*net to CANARIE," *Canadian Journal of Communication,* Vol. 19, 1994:61, 53–69.

111. John Markoff, "'I Wonder What's on the PC Tonight,'" *New York Times,* 8 May 1994:F1, F8.

112. Mark Thalhimer, ed., *Media Industry News Roundup,* compiled from the Associated Press, the Freedom Forum Media Studies Center, 6 July 1994.

113. John Masefield, "Sea Fever" in *Salt Water Ballads and Poems.* New York: Macmillan, 1923:18.

114. Len Matthews, Special Report, Next Century Media, 1994:6.

115. Howard Rheingold, *The Virtual Community: Homesteading on the Electronic Frontier.* New York: Simon and Schuster, 1993, pp. 19, 26.

116. Andrew Pollack, "Matsushita, in Lab Test, Reduces Disk to a Dot," *New York Times,* 19 September 1994:C2.

117. Jeff Rothenberg, "Ensuring the Longevity of Digital Documents," *Scientific American,* January 1995:42–47.

118. "Sony and Philips Design CD's for Movies," *New York Times,* 17 December 1994.

119. John Markoff, "New I.B.M. Laser Method Stacks Data on Disks," *New York Times,* 12 May 1994.

120. Ibid.: D1.

121. Bruce C. Klopfenstein, "The Diffusion of the VCR in the United States," in Mark Levy, ed., *The VCR Age: Home Video and Mass Communication.* Newbury Park, CA: Sage Publications, 1989.

122. Ibid.

123. "Talks Set on Digital VCR," *New York Times,* 12 April 1994.

124. Sid Lerner, "Lexicon for the Auto-Maga-Video Age," *New York Times,* 5 December 1993.

4

CONCEPTS AND APPLICATIONS
IN CYBERSPACE

With digitization, all of the media becomes translat-
able into each other—computer bits migrate merrily—
and they escape from their traditional means of
transmission.

—STEWART BRAND[1]

Central to any understanding of new media technologies are a number
of important concepts and technological applications. These concepts
refer to various new media notions and ideas, whereas the applications
refer to the software products developed to perform specific functions in
the world of digital communications. Not all technological concepts and
applications are included in this chapter. Many have already been examined in earlier chapters, and some are largely settled issues. Rather,
included here are concepts and applications that represent some of the
great unsettled and evolving issues of the digital communication age.

KEY CONCEPTS: THE UNSETTLED ISSUES

The number of terms and concepts littering the road to tomorrow's media
technology is virtually limitless, but there are several concepts that serve
as keys to understanding the contours of the new media terrain. These
terms are used widely in discussions of new media technology, but are
often ill-defined, or defined in inconsistent, sometimes contradictory

fashion. Collectively, they represent some of the vital energizing forces driving the development of new media technologies, their applications, and consequences and are at the crux of much public debate about those technologies. The key concepts examined here fall into three main groups:

- overarching trends in the transformation of media technology, including convergence, compression, and digitization
- new media qualities and attributes, including hypertext and inter-activity
- computer network concepts, including the information superhighway, the Internet, and online communications

We begin the discussion with an examination of the overarching trends transforming the media technology landscape.

Convergence

Convergence is the coming together of all forms of mediated communications in an electronic, digital form, driven by computers. Convergence presents profound challenges for the existing media order and has paved the way for the development of multimedia products blending text, data, graphics, full-motion video, and sound.

Compression

Compression is a technical process through which large amounts of data are condensed, or compressed, by removing the redundant information in one video frame to the next, for example, faster transmission or easier storage. Many multimedia products would not be feasible today if not for advances in compression technology that reduce the digital information needed to replicate an image on a video monitor.[2] This process has important implications for the creation of a video dial tone and for the storage of video signals, especially full-motion video, on CD-ROM or laserdisc devices. Engineers have systematically improved compression algorithms so that today entire feature-length movies can be stored on a single CD-ROM, or VCR-quality movies can be transmitted in a matter of minutes over existing telephone wires. Compression also has important implications for the transmission of television signals in a multichannel environment, whether via coaxial cable, over the air, or via direct broadcast satellite. Although traditionally each television channel required a single channel on a cable system, for example, compression now can be used to deliver ten or more NTSC TV signals over a single cable channel,

TABLE 4-1 Compression

	Number of Channels	
	Standard Television	Compression 10:1
NTSC television	50	500
HDTV	5	50

Source: John Carey, Greystone Communications, 1994[3]

thus making the five hundred channel environment a possibility on existing coaxial cable systems. Moreover, an HDTV signal, which contains many times the information in a regular NTSC signal, can be compressed and delivered over a single channel, thereby offering the possibility of an HDTV system using existing delivery media. Using compression in a fiber optic system creates even greater opportunities for signal transmission. Telecommunications expert John Carey has developed the following analysis of compression's impact on television distribution (see Table 4-1).

Compression of video and audio information often involves coder-decoder (CODEC) technology, which translates analog information into digital format, which is then compressed for storage, processing, or transmission.

Digitization

Digitization refers to the conversion of analog information into the computer-readable format of 1s and 0s. In digital format, all audio, visual, or textual information blends together in the process of convergence.

James Beniger writes:

The progressive digitalization of mass media and telecommunications content begins to blur earlier distinctions between the communication of information and its processing (as implied by the term compunications *coined by Anthony Oettinger), as well as between people and machines. Digitalization makes communication from persons to machines, between machines, and even from machines to persons as easy as it is between persons. Also blurred are the distinctions among information types: numbers, words, pictures, and sounds, and eventually tastes, odors, and possibly even sensations, all might one day be stored, processed, and communicated in the same digital form.*[4]

This view of new media technology resonates with other technology forecasters, who foresee the importance of the digital revolution and optical technologies in the future of media and society. Daniel Burrus, president of Burrus Research Associates and author of *Technotrends*, identifies twenty core technologies that will shape the future.[5] Although heading the list are genetic engineering (1) and advanced biochemistry (2), third on the list is digital electronics. Also high on Burrus's list are optical data storage (4), advanced video displays (5), advanced computers (6), distributed computing (7), artificial intelligence (8), fiber optics (10), microwaves (11), and advanced satellites (12). In fact, seven of Burrus's top ten technologies are media and communications based.

The second area of new media concepts deals with some of the qualities and attributes transforming the communication landscape, including hypertext and interactivity.

Hypertext

Technologist Ted Nelson coined the term *hypertext* in 1962. He defined the term quite simply as nonlinear text, or text that does not flow sequentially from start to finish. Rather, there may be many pathways through a body of text, even a narrative, with many words, phrases, or passages linked to others anywhere in the total document or body of text. Although hypertext is a simple idea, its implications are enormous and have served as the foundation for much subsequent work in multimedia computing in which digital data, text, audio, and video are linked in spiderweb fashion in an *n*-dimensional space rather than linearly as they are in conventional media such as newspapers or television. For example, a term in this text might be "linked" electronically to an image or any other part of a document. The reader might journey through this hypertext document in a free-form pattern, creating her or his own meaning or story in the process. For example, in many hypertext documents, a term, such as cyberspace, might be underlined or highlighted (for example, *cyberspace*), thus signaling to the reader that the highlighted term is "hot" or linked to something else. By double-clicking the mouse when the cursor is positioned over the highlighted word, the origin and meaning of *cyberspace* (see the passage from Gibson on page 136) might appear on the screen. Hypertext has been applied in a variety of fields, especially in education, where students are encouraged to explore a document following their own interests rather than via a preset path.

Many wonder what the future of writing and authorship may be in a world of hypertext and hypermedia. Will writing continue as we know it in a nonlinear communication environment? What will it mean to be an author when the story changes depending on who is doing the reading?

What does authorship mean when hundreds, perhaps thousands, of people collaborate electronically on a continually unfolding story each day? Canadian scholar Jesse Hunter suggests an optimistic view of that future.

> *Hypermedia and multimedia authoring systems come on the cusp of an apparent upheaval in communications technology. New structures of literacy are falling into place that call into question the defining paradigms of our current assumptions. In the post-Modern condition, the problems of heterogeneity are easily attended to by hypermedia. Whether this technology of accountability is incident with, or answers to, the needs of an age caught in a deluge of information is not at issue. Nor do we need to worry that this technology threatens to make obsolete comfortable categories such as "author." Just as there remained Herculean heroism in the age of print, a place will be found for authors in the digital age.*[6]

Interactivity

Interactivity has been one of the most sought-after goals of the new media age. With roots going back to at least the 1950s, efforts to develop truly interactive television have generally met with failure, often either for technical reasons or because of prohibitive expense. Nevertheless, interactivity has been relentlessly pursued and is one of the cornerstones of the new media age movement to create an information superhighway. Still, there is little agreement about just what constitutes true interactivity. Many in television have presented interactive TV models in which interaction is essentially defined as the ability to select from a menu of choices or to choose movies on demand. With the convergence of telecommunications, television, and the computer, however, others argue for a more complete view of interactivity in which everyone on the superhighway can be both a source and receiver, just as anyone using a telephone can place or receive a call. In a telecommunications context, interactivity means two-way communication between source and receiver, or more broadly, multidirectional communication between any number of sources and receivers. In a broadest sense, interactivity simply means a process of reciprocal influence. Regardless of the prevailing definition of interactivity, the new media age will present media consumers with opportunities to become more active participants in the world of mediated communications. Whether their level of interaction is limited to pushing buttons on the next-generation remote control may depend not only on industry innovation and initiative, but on the strength and momentum of the couch potato legacy.

The third major area of technology concepts deals with notions of computer networks and networked communications, including the information superhighway, the Internet, and online communications.

Cyberspace

Science fiction writer William Gibson coined the term *cyberspace* in his 1984 award winning novel *Neuromancer*, writing:

> *Cyberspace. A consensual hallucination experienced daily by billions of legitimate operators, in every nation. . . . A graphic representation of data abstracted from the banks of every computer in the human system. Unthinkable complexity. Lines of light ranged in the non-space of the mind, clusters and constellations of data. Like city lights, receding. . . .* [7]

In writing that definition, Gibson suggests cyberspace is similar to what many now loosely describe as virtual reality. Since Gibson wrote those words, cyberspace has often been used to describe any form of online communication that exists in the global web of computer networks. Communication ethicist John Phelan, the director of the McGannon Center for Communication Research at Fordham University, traces the origins of cyberspace to the world of cybernetics conceived by Norbert Weiner.[8] From its Greek roots, cybernetics denotes the use of technology for control and interactivity, both of which are concepts central to contemporary applications of new media technologies in modern society.

Information Superhighway

Just what exactly the information superhighway means, no one really knows. When legendary CBS Evening News anchor Walter ("And that's the way it is") Cronkite in early 1994 appeared as a guest on the *Late Show*, David Letterman asked Cronkite if he could tell the viewers just what the information highway is. "Well, I know," replied the sage news veteran, "but I'm not telling you."[9] Letterman has since described his show as an information highway, "without the information."[10]

The information superhighway is perhaps best thought of as a metaphor for the emerging digital data networks that are rapidly covering the globe and have important implications not only for journalism and the First Amendment, but for all of society and democracy itself. It is a mistake to think there will be just one information superhighway; there will be many, including the global web of computer networks known as the Internet, the broadband packet-switched telecommunications network of optical fiber, coaxial cable, and twisted pair capable of delivering video on demand, and emerging technologies such as wireless communications and direct-broadcast satellite that will utilize compression techniques to provide digital interactive television and other new information services.

Phillip Elmer-DeWitt, associate editor at *Time* magazine, identifies three distinct views of the information superhighway, each with its own constituency as well as varying implications for public policy, media coverage, and the consumer.[11] These three views can be summed up as:

- the telephone company view
- the cable and broadcast view
- the Al Gore/computer user view

The telephone companies, the RBOCs, see the information superhighway as a new information infrastructure based on broadband switched network technology. This view sees the highway as a new way to rack up billable message units for the phone companies. The particular content on the highway is irrelevant, as long as the message flow increases.

Cable companies and broadcasters see the information superhighway as a new way to deliver television, regardless of its form. In this view, interactive television, video on demand, or transaction services are all improved ways to bring the advertiser or seller together with the viewer or buyer.

Those involved in computer networking define the information superhighway in online terms, invoking a somewhat more metaphorical notion of the information superhighway as a new democratic medium of communication in which everyone can participate in a global cyberspace. The model they look to is the Internet, the global web of computer networks, in which electronic messages are sent and received by the millions every day, files are transferred and research is conducted. Depending on one's view, the notion of an information highway takes on decidedly different meaning and significance.

In 1835, American Samuel Morse of Charleston, Massachusetts, invented the arguably first generation of the electronic information superhighway, the telegraph. The telegraph, the first electromagnetic signaling system, was first used on May 24, 1844, for a communication from Samuel Morse in Washington, D.C. to newspaper colleagues at the *Baltimore* (Maryland) *Patriot*. Using a code of dots and dashes that still bears his name, Morse transmitted the first message by wire: "One o'clock—There has just been made a motion in the House to go into committee of the whole on the Oregon question. Rejected—ayes, 79; nays, 86. What hath God wrought?" The Associated Press news wire service began employing the telegraph device in 1913. Legend has it that when asked to explain the difference between the telegraph and wireless telegraphy, what is now called radio, Samuel Morse replied that the function of the telegraph is like pinching a dog's tail: it barks on the other end. Wireless telegraphy, Morse explained, operates in the same fashion, only there's no dog.

Many object to the term *information superhighway,* arguing that it has been used to describe many different technologies and has become so vague as to be not only meaningless but even misleading. "It's not only a scientifically wrong term. It's a counterproductive term," says Andrew Grove, chief executive officer of Intel Corporation, the world's largest manufacturer of computer chips.[12] In agreement is John Naisbitt, author of *Megatrends.* "It's a huge step backward because it gets people in the mindset there's going to be a beginning, a middle, and an end," he contends.[13] Naisbitt also criticizes the term in his new book, *Global Paradox,* arguing that it leaves people with the impression that a single entity, not the marketplace, is controlling technological advances.[14] Many have offered alternative terms. It's the "information railroad," says labor activist Rand Wilson[15]; "the electronic ocean," counters Tom Henry, partner in a small software firm. "I would call it the Information Environment," suggests Esther Dyson, a member of a White House advisory council.[16] "Infobahn" is the Germanic term offered by Mark Stahlman, president of New York–based New Media Associates. Despite all these dueling metaphors, writer Laurent Belsie concludes that although many deplore the information superhighway imagery, the term is here to stay. In fact, it's already set in concrete, Belsie argues. "The metaphor is so fixed in public consciousness that it won't go away," he writes.[17]

The notion of an information superhighway is made even cloudier by the fact that the media have used a variety of synonymous terms in their coverage. In a study of media coverage of the information superhighway, Pavlik and Szanto report identifying nine terms that have been used almost interchangeably in referring to the superhighway.[18] The terms are *information superhighway, information highway, data highway, data superhighway, electronic superhighway, electronic highway, info-superhighway, info-highway,* and *national information infrastructure,* or *NII,* the official term used by the Clinton-Gore administration. The study looked at coverage between January 1992 and February 1994 and included a dozen major newspapers, six news magazines and three network TV programs. Although the greatest number of stories refer to *information superhighway* (1,208) or *highway* (965), other terms have received significant attention, such as *data highway* (199), *electronic superhighway* (182), and *national information infrastructure* (126). This same study shows that the information superhighway is most often linked to some specific technologies. Among those technologies mentioned in information superhighway stories, the greatest number include the Internet (306), e-mail (185), video on demand (184), and interactive TV (167). The study also shows that the information superhighway is linked in the press with certain political and industry leaders. Vice President Al Gore tops the list, with 347 stories mentioning his name in the context of the information superhighway or any of its synonyms. John Malone, CEO of TCI, is second on the list (241 stories), followed by President Bill Clinton (232), Home Shopping Network CEO Barry Diller (140), and Bell Atlantic CEO Raymond W. Smith (107).

The exact origins of the term *information highway,* or *superhighway,* are unclear, although Vice President Al Gore claims credit for inventing the term in the late 1970s. Gore used the term often in the 1992 presidential campaign, and has since promoted the information highway for its economic and educational potential both in the United States and internationally. Gore has even joked about the highway metaphors that have recently sprung up. "One businessman told me recently that he was accelerating his investment in new technology to avoid ending up as roadkill on the information superhighway," Gore quipped at the "superhighway summit" in Los Angeles in January 1994.[19]

The term *information highway* has roots going back nearly a quarter of a century, however, with one author having used the term in a book published in 1972. In *The Wired Nation: Cable TV: The Coming Information Highway,* Ralph Lee Smith caused something of a public and media sensation when he described the future of an electronically connected society that might provide a broad spectrum of the public with greater access to the media system.[20] Smith's book was published as an entire issue of *The Nation* opinion magazine, and the author toured the talk-show circuit discussing his revolutionary view. Since the publication of his landmark book, however, the term *information highway* disappeared from vogue, and resurfaced only recently in the public discourse. Smith recently admitted that the public potential of cable TV was never fully realized.[21] Although cable TV did achieve a great deal of commercial success, public access channels, once touted as an important medium for public participation in local cable systems, rarely became an integral part of cable programming in most communities. Whether the information superhighway of today will achieve its full public potential, or become little more than a potentially profitable commercial venture, is one of the intriguing questions of the coming decade. The democratic nature of electronic mail and online communications suggests the potential is there for public participation in the new medium. The realization of this potential may depend on both the shape of public policy affecting the superhighway, as well as the commitment shown by corporate interests in supporting a new public communication system.

Despite all the media hoopla about the information superhighway, most members of the public know little or nothing about it, at least according to a poll taken in the spring of 1994.[22] Louis Harris and Associates report that two-thirds (66 percent) of the public have not seen, read, or heard anything about the information superhighway. Among those who had (34 percent), less than half said they understood what it is. Nevertheless, a quarter (27 percent) thought building an information superhighway was an excellent idea, and another third (34 percent) said it sounded pretty good. The poll was based on telephone interviews with a national probability sample of 1,255 adults conducted April 4–7, 1994, with a margin of sampling error of plus or minus three percent.

Internet

Although it is often referred to as if it were a specific entity, the Internet is really a vast interconnection of some 45,000 computer networks around the world. Many have called it the prototype for the information superhighway. No one owns the Internet, and no one specifically controls it. Its origins are to be found in the Department of Defense's Advanced Research Projects Agency network (ARPAnet) created in 1969 as the first national computer network. The Internet was born officially in 1983, when ARPAnet divided into military and civilian components, with the civilian component giving rise to the Internet. At that time, the National Science Foundation (NSF) established the NSFnet as the research backbone network for scholarly investigators at U.S. universities.[23] For more than a decade NSFnet served as the backbone of the Internet, but in October 1994, the NSF began converting its network to private hands.

The concepts that gave birth to the Internet are credited to Vinton G. Cerf, currently the president of The Internet Society and senior vice president in the Data Service Division of MCI Telecommunications Corporation.[24] With the privatization of the Internet, institutions and private individuals seeking to use the Internet will provide full support for the Internet through access fees based largely on their level of usage. A growing number of commercial online services such as America Online provide an Internet connection as part of their service. Because of the structure of the Internet, users pay only local telecommunications charges for accessing the Internet, regardless of whether their messages go across town or across the planet, and regardless of the amount of data transmitted in their messages. This fee structure may change with the privatization of the Internet.

Until recently, this global web of computer networks had been "an underground movement of sorts—a cyberspace hangout where researchers, students, and techies spend hours tapping into databases and discussing the most esoteric of subjects in electronic forums," reports Evan I. Schwartz.[25] Navigating the Internet is still pretty challenging. "You have to learn a rather arcane language of commands," says Howard Fund, associate of the Internet Society, a users group headquartered in Reston, Virginia.

Internet is now reaching beyond the realm of computer nerds and enthusiasts, scholars and researchers, to the ordinary consumer. For much of the history of the Internet, most users could access the Internet exclusively through universities, companies, or research labs that paid an average of $40,000 a year in service fees. Now, many consumers may access the Internet through online computer services such as Prodigy, CompuServe, America Online, GEnie, and Delphi, at a typical rate of about $10 a month.

The Internet is also transforming the ways in which journalists gather information. Reporting in the *Quill*, a trade journal for journalists, John S. Makulowich writes, "The Internet allows you to use resources better, use better resources, and use fewer person hours to produce your product."[26] John Battelle, managing editor of *Wired*, a new magazine reporting on the digital age of communication, agrees, adding, "I do about 70 percent of my editing and communications with writers over the Internet. Our publication certainly would not exist in its current form without it." Major metropolitan daily newspapers are also being transformed by the Internet. Steve Doig, associate editor/researcher for the *Miami Herald* says the Internet has helped him do his job "faster, better, and cheaper." He explains, "I also use the Internet to access via anonymous FTP (file transfer protocol, which allows you to get files such as text, programs, pictures, from other computers) to thousands of lines of SAS (a statistical package) code dealing with census analysis. And I have access via Telnet to a giant database of 1990 and 1980 census data." Tom Regan, columnist/editorial writer for *The Daily News*, Halifax, Nova Scotia, Canada, says the Internet has completely changed the nature of his work. "The research tools possible with Internet have allowed me to create much more substantive articles." Regan used the Internet to research an article on the debt/deficit crisis in Canada, and gathered evidence that the crisis was "more fancy than fact. I used the Internet to gather most of the facts and quotes used for the articles."

Some major newspapers are even publishing news products on the Internet. The *Electronic Trib,* an electronic edition of the *Albuquerque* (New Mexico) *Tribune,* went online via the Internet in the fall of 1993. Similarly, *New York Newsday* published in July 1993 a special series on the "Battle for the Information Highway" that was made available via the Internet. The series was available to "anyone with a personal computer and modem. In addition, readers can communicate directly with writers, by electronic mail and by participating in a live 'chat' period—a group conversation conducted online through personal computers."[27] During a recent newspaper strike in San Francisco both striking reporters and newspaper management immediately began publishing online news products on the Internet. Although total online daily readership reached about 100,000—only a fraction of the 600,000 printed newspapers' normal daily circulation—it far exceeded the estimated 10,000 people in the Bay Area with the electronic access to the Internet.[28] The lessons here are many for publishers, including the need to envision audiences well beyond the traditional local geographic markets most newspapers are tailored to serve.

Some news organizations have begun experimenting with Internet applications as means to increase viewer involvement and interactivity. One fascinating example comes from network television, a news medium some have given up for dead. During the final week of 1993, *NBC Nightly News* ran a series entitled "Almost 2001." As part of the series NBC gave out on Monday, December 27, an Internet address: NBC.COM.

As of noon on Thursday, December 30, NBC had received more than 4,000 replies from all corners of the world. Within a few weeks, the number of responses had topped 10,000. Joe Harris, former director of information technology at NBC-TV, says the phenomenon has triggered a great deal of discussion of the subject of television and the new media. He believes the NBC-TV effort has given birth to Marshall McLuhan's global village. "Last message I read last night was from CROATIA!" noted Harris in an Internet message to the author. Among the other 4,000 messages:

- About time you saw us. Show more.
- Nice story on the I-net I certainly thought it was interesting that I was ON internet while your show just came on talking about it! How about more news from cyberspace?
- Could you blow up more trucks. That was cool.
- We're all just crash dummies in the information highway.

One message was particularly moving, Harris says, reflecting on the political changes of Eastern Europe and the end of the Cold War.

From: Arcady G. Khotin
Date: Tue, 28 Dec 93
Subject: From Russia, with love

Dear Americans,
my warmest season greetings from St. Petersburg, Russia. Please, keep
up your great work helping us out of the deep hole we got into about
70 years ago! I'm sure it will be rewardable for both nations!
Cheers,
Arcady Khotin
software developer

Veteran news executive Adam Clayton Powell III provided this e-mail response to the author's electronic query about the blossoming network news use of the Internet.

I had not heard about the NBC Internet address, but it makes all the
sense in the world (no pun intended), since all three U.S. evening news-
casts are now seen worldwide. In Johannesburg, Rather/Chung runs as
a morning show, Jennings is in late morning, and I have seen Brokaw
pop up unpredictably, all three coming in via Murdoch's, the BBC's,
and USIA's various satellite services. If CNN were to publicize an Inter-
net address, I suspect they would be swamped.
Cheers :-)
Adam

Still, the Internet is not a panacea for the electronic journalist, nor for the information consumer. Much information is not available in the online world, and many sources cannot be reached through cyberspace. Some online searches can produce massive amounts of information, but little usable knowledge. Explains Frederick Williams, professor at the University of Texas at Austin and an expert in networked communications: "Going into the worldwide web is like going through someone else's trash."[29]

As usage of the Internet has swelled (see Figures 4-1 and 4-2), so have problems of heavy demand. "Call it a cautionary tale for the information age: The nation's increasingly popular data highway is beginning to groan under the load of rush-hour traffic," writes John Markoff.[30] Once the exclusive domain of computer scientists, programmers, and engineers, usage of the Internet has grown into the millions as anyone with a computer and modem can access the Internet easily and cheaply. Consequently, much highly valued information that has been available freely to anyone on the Internet has often become inaccessible to

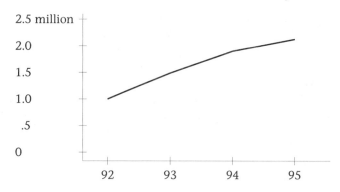

FIGURE 4-1   Number of Host Computers Serving as On-Ramps for the Internet

Source: The Internet Society, Reston, VA, 1995.

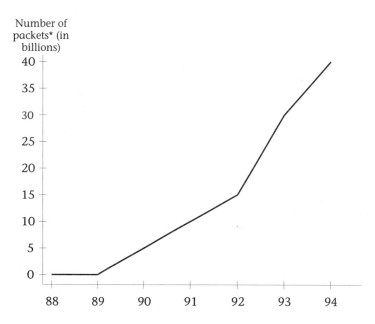

FIGURE 4-2 Number of Packets of Data Transmitted Monthly on the National Science Foundation's Backbone Network for the Internet.

*A packet is approximately equal to 200 typewritten characters.
Source: The Internet Society, Reston, VA, 1995.

everyone as "a clamoring horde overwhelms the computer databases."[31] Traffic jams on the Internet are severely limiting access to a variety of databases and online services, including National Weather Service satellite photos, computer software, online searches of the catalog of the Library of Congress, and free access to filings with the Securities and Exchange Commission.[32] Examples of the growth in usage and the resulting traffic jams include demand for the National Center for Supercomputer Applications' World Wide Web home page, a service that responds to inquiries to an electronic library. The number of daily requests has grown from 100,000 in June, 1993 to almost 400,000 in October. Similarly, the amount of information retrieved using a popular search program called Gopher increased in 1993 by more than 400 percent, to nearly 200 billion bytes per month, the equivalent of some seven million newspaper pages. MSEN Inc., an Ann Arbor, Michigan, company made information on career counseling available free through the Internet and usage skyrocketed from 1,000 inquiries a day in June when the service began to 12,000 a day on Monday, November 1, 1993. Without a more powerful computer, MSEN says it will have to deny access to the system to any additional requests. Internet traffic is even subject to rubbernecking delays. When word got out in October 1993 that a computer intruder had broken into the Panix Public Access Network intent on stealing passwords, "thousands of curiosity seekers decided to take a look at the Panix network—the digital equivalent of driving by the scene of an accident."[33] Those "driving by" used a program on the Panix system called in computer jargon a "finger demon," a program that lets hundreds of users remotely determine everyone currently on the system. But when thousands called up the program, the system crashed and Panix ground to a halt. "It was a traffic jam caused by rubberneckers on the nation's data highway," said Marc Rotenberg of the Computer Professionals for Social Responsibility, a Washington, D.C.–based public interest group.

Flamed on the Internet

As the virtual community of the Internet has grown, so has it developed its own rules for self-governance. Like any other community, it has developed its own mores and norms, and those who violate proper "netiquette" are promptly and resoundingly chastised, what netters call "flamed." Getting flamed on the Internet can range from a mild verbal reprimand from other netters, to having your computer subjected to a digital assault, the equivalent of an electronic mob or a virtual lynch mob. Tactics range from receiving thousands of e-mail messages clogging your mail box to electronic-mail bombs.

One case of flaming whose implications stretched far beyond the boundaries of cyberspace involved a law firm that used the Internet Usenet as an advertising medium—a purpose in violation of traditional guidelines of netiquette. In April 1994, Laurence A. Canter and Martha S. Siegel flooded the Internet Usenet with advertisements for their Phoenix law firm, Canter and Siegel, which specializes in immigration law. Such random posting of ads or other messages on the Internet is known as "spamming," (for the brand of canned meat that splatters messily if thrown at an object) and is frowned upon, although not prohibited by any law. The ad offered help in entering the government's so-called Green Card Lottery, for a fee of $95 for individuals and $145 for couples.

Usenet is one of the biggest users groups on the Internet, with some ten million users out of the twenty million or so Internet users worldwide. The response to the ad was overwhelming, especially at first when most people who replied to the message expressed their outrage at using the Internet for such blatant commercial services. Many were upset that the limited bandwidth of the Internet might become clogged with commercial messages, at the expense of more substantive dialogue. "Unsolicited advertising on the global Internet is as acceptable as junk fax is in the real world," notes Robert Raisch, president of the Internet Company and chairman of the Electronic Newsstand, a joint effort of the Internet Company and the *New Republic* magazine.[34] Raisch and others would prefer to group advertising channels under a broad "market" directory on Usenet, with a variety of subdirectories for different categories of products and services. Advertising and other commercial enterprises on the Internet are in fact common and widely accepted, as long as they are done within established rules.

Flaming responses to the Canter and Seigel spam attack included electronic-mail bombs designed to knock out targeted computers, or robotic callers, such as the Phantom Phone Beeper, who programmed a robot to automatically call the Canter and Siegel office forty times a night, stuffing their voice-mailbox with electronic trash.[35] Other negative responses included a flood of critical faxes and the posting of digitized photos of the couple on computer bulletin boards throughout the world, "like 'Wanted' posters on the electronic frontier."[36] In one case, a twenty-five-year-old Norwegian programmer named Arnt Gulbrandsen used his computer from half way around the world to "launch the electronic equivalent of a Patriot missile: each time the law firm sent out an electronic advertisement, his computer automatically sent out a message ordering that the firm's transmission be intercepted and destroyed," reports technology writer Peter H. Lewis.[37]

Canter and Siegel are unfazed by the negative backlash and attention their efforts have drawn and have vowed not only to continue their efforts online but to expand them. "In the beginning there were more negative than positive responses," admits Ms. Siegel.[38] "That is shifting. Now almost every response we're getting is positive." And the responses have come in rapidly and in great volume. The couple received some 20,000 responses by the middle of May 1994 and were receiving messages at a rate of nearly 1,000 a day. Canter and Siegel are now collaborating on a book explaining how others can use the Internet as an advertising medium. The couple is also considering filing a lawsuit against some of the flamers for defamation of character. They have even started a firm called Cybersell to advertise other companies' products on Usenet. The new company's first product: superoxygenated water. "You drink it, and the fact that it has additional oxygen gives you additional energy and promotes the healing process," Siegel says.[39] What all this means for the future of the Internet culture and its spirit of frontier freedom is uncertain, but sellers of snake oil, hair tonics, and X-ray glasses may have reason to smile.

Some industry analysts see the 1990s as a period of sharp growth in the business usage of the Internet. The *Kiplinger Washington Letter* reports that large firms will find many uses as the Internet becomes easier to learn and navigate with emerging services such as Mosaic. "Electronic mail . . . cheaper than phones, especially for overseas business. Exchanging computer files. Transmitting software from office to office. And finding information . . . gov't rules, bids, and grants, SEC filings."[40] Kiplinger sees fewer opportunities for smaller firms, at least in the short run, although the development of electronic supermarkets where a smorgasbord of marketing information from the census department and other federal agencies will soon make the Internet valuable even for small businesses.

One man who is confident about the future of the information superhighway is James H. Clark, the former Stanford University professor who founded Silicon Graphics, Inc., and led it to the forefront of the computer workstation market. "I believe that the Internet is the information highway," Clark says.[41] "I'm religious about this. I don't think it's cable television."

World Wide Web

An important and growing part of the Internet is the World Wide Web, an interconnected set of computer servers on the Internet that conform to a set of network interface protocols created by Tim Berners-Lee of CERN, the European high-energy physics laboratory in Geneva,

Switzerland.[42] The Web began as an electronic library for physicists and grew into an "international bazaar."[43] Any individual or organization with Internet access can create what is called a "home page" on the Web, as long as that individual or organization uses the programming protocols established at CERN. These protocols include assigning the home page a universal resource locator (url), its Internet address, and using what is known as hypertext transport protocol (http), which enables the standardized transfer of e-mail and other text, audio, and video files. In addition, each Web document tagged with hypertext markup language, or HTML, allows automatic routing from one electronic document to another, whether elsewhere in the same Web document or anywhere else in the entire World Wide Web, simply by clicking the mouse on highlighted text. Web applications grew rapidly in 1994, with thousands of home pages sprouting up in a variety of places and venues all around the world, ranging from the city of Palo Alto, California, to the White House in Washington, D.C. One of the most remarkable home pages was created by Navy physicist Richard Bocker, whose Planet Earth Home Page for the City of San Diego has become the nineteenth most popular home page anywhere on the Internet, with users accessing nearly a billion bytes of information about San Diego each day. "Webmaster" Bocker created his home page as a tool for organizing information he needed for his own online work, but worldwide interest grew as fellow network mavens "surfed the net" and found their electronic way to southern California.

Online Communications

Online communications refers to communication that occurs between users at two or more computers connected over a local or wide area network. It is now estimated that the online community, or cyberspace as it is sometimes called, is populated by as many as thirty-five million users.[44] This estimate includes every computer network in offices, commercial networks such as CompuServe and Prodigy and Minitel in France, thousands of privately run electronic bulletin board services, and the Internet. As a publishing medium, online communications is one of the two hottest forms of electronic publication, with CD-ROM publishing being the other. Many see online communications and electronic publishing as a huge growth industry. Noted cable and new media industry analyst Paul Kagan is one of them. "The world is populated by a growing number of information hunters, roaming electronic libraries around the globe in search of a competitive edge," says Kagan, founder of Paul Kagan Associates, Inc., whose industry forecasts have become a mainstay in the cable and multimedia industries. "It's a market that has no foreseeable end, because the theoretical limit is retrieving and sorting all the information in the world. That's like finding the digital Holy Grail," he says.[45]

One leading industry newsletter reported that the online audience reached record levels during the fourth quarter of 1993, with 713,450 new users coming online, bringing the commercial online audience to 4,585,000 customers, an 18.4 percent growth since the last quarter.[46]

The Expanding Online World

Although online communications have existed for more than a quarter of a century, they have flourished in the 1990s. With the growth of the Internet and commercial online services, the increased capacity of the public telecommunications network, and the increased speed of communications modems and personal computers, online communications have become an increasingly effective communication medium worldwide. This section examines leading online services and products, paying particular attention to the emerging range of consumer information services and specialized information services. It should be noted here that the organizational structure presented here suggests a division between multimedia products discussed earlier and online products discussed below. This distinction is largely a technological artifact of the current limitations of the personal computer and the state and economics of public telecommunications. We are rapidly moving into an era of multimedia products distributed via online communications. Some limited examples of such products will be discussed below. Nevertheless, the vast majority of multimedia products are not currently delivered electronically, although the next five years may see that change dramatically, as optical fiber and the information superhighway come into the mainstream.

Consumer Online Services

Consumer online services provide PC users with an electronic commercial link to a growing network of computer users. By subscribing to an online service, such as Prodigy, America Online, or CompuServe, users of PCs equipped with a modem, appropriate communications software, and a connection to Touch-Tone telephone service can dial into a broad array of electronic services, such as sending and receiving electronic mail, making plane reservations, and paying bills electronically. Perhaps most importantly, these services are increasingly providing easy access to the Internet, the global web of computer networks, through graphical user interfaces. The potential market for online services has grown significantly in the past decade. In the early 1980s only two to three million homes were equipped with PCs, while in 1994 the number had risen to some thirty-five million, with roughly 62 percent of those homes equipped with a modem.

Prodigy, the number one online service, offered its two million members a simple electronic mail "gateway" to the Internet in November of 1993.[47] Vienna, Virginia–based America Online, Inc. (AOL), the fastest-growing service with some 550,000 members (as of January 28, 1994)—more than double its size in 1992, will soon offer its members some of the Internet's more advanced features, such as wide area information searching (WAIS), a menu-based gopher service, and file transfer protocol (FTP).[48] "That will put the generally well-heeled suburbanites on these services in touch with folks they might not meet otherwise," writes Schwartz.[49] America Online also serves up the online versions of *Time, Omni, Compute, Wired, Disney Adventures,* the *Chicago Tribune,* and the *San Jose Mercury News.*[50] America Online is poised for even more growth. "1993 has been an extraordinary year for America Online," says Steve Chase, president of AOL.[51] The company's growth rate for 1993 was 130 percent, with 150,000 new members signing up in the last ninety days of the year. Much of AOL's growth, Case says, can be attributed to the graphical user interface and integration of services and information providers. "Most importantly, we understand this new interactive medium can change the way we communicate, inform, educate, work, and play, and we are excited about its potential," Case adds.

The 1.6 million member CompuServe, which offers online versions of *Florida Today,* the *Detroit Free Press,* and Gannett Suburban Newspapers in White Plains, New York, and 400,000 member GEnie also offer Internet e-mail gateways. America Online will also soon let members access Internet's 4,000 bulletin boards. These commercial online services stand to benefit financially from providing Internet gateway services. Prodigy, for example, the joint Sears–IBM venture, allows its two million members (about 1.1 million homes) thirty free messages per month, and charges 15 cents for each Internet message thereafter. The only major service to allow users to "roam freely" on the Internet has been Delphi Internet Services, Inc., recently acquired by Rupert Murdoch's NewsCorp.

Among the popular offerings available on commercial online services as well as on the Internet are news groups. News groups are electronic bulletin boards where users share information about a subject, such as computer programming, health care, or the environment. Thousands of such news groups have been started, primarily as grassroots exercises in online communications communities. Perhaps the most widely used news group is called Newsnet, available on the Internet. Some estimates put as many as ten million users on the Newsnet group worldwide.

Online services, particularly commercial online services, are a medium of the well off. Users tend to have a higher than average level of income, are well educated, have a professional occupation or operate their own businesses, and are largely male. These patterns hold true for all three major commercial services, although Prodigy tends to attract a slightly lower socioeconomic group, while AOL draws the most well-educated group. CompuServe's users tend to be male (90 percent), with just 10 percent female. The median age is 41.4. Most (55 percent) have no children living at home and have an average household income of $93,000. The vast majority (91 percent) are employed in professional or business occupations. Nearly half (45 percent) operate a home-based business.[52]

The Taxman Cometh

The financial success of these information services has not gone unnoticed by state tax commissioners. The Massachusetts Department of Revenue, for example, has told information service firms, computer bulletin boards, and the people using those services of its plans to add a 5 percent sales tax to their bills.[53, 54] In New York, a scarcely noticed 5 percent sales tax on online services was passed by the State Assembly in 1993. Only a handful of newspapers considered strictly entertainment, however, such as bulletin boards, crossword puzzles, and rotisserie baseball, would be subject to the tax.[55, 56]

Early Online Services

The 1970s was a historic decade in the history of online communications. In 1973, Mead Data Central of Columbus, Ohio, developed Lexis, the first online full-text database. Lexis featured case law, judicial rulings, and other information for the legal profession. Five years later, Mead Data Central debuted Nexis, the first online database containing national news publications including the *New York Times*, the *Washington Post*, *U.S. News and World Report*, and Associated Press (AP) News Service information. Dialog, a major commercial database network distributor, opened for business in 1972 and, by 1979, had made available its National Newspaper Index, a bibliographic database later converted into a full-text service. CompuServe, a major online consumer service, also began selling access to its network to computer hobbyists as well as professionals in 1979.

New Kids on the Block

Catching the wave of new online products from traditional news organizations, *Time* magazine went online in the fall of 1993 and quickly amassed a devoted online following. After only its first three weeks of online availability through America Online, *Time Online* was accessed 126,563 times.[57] Since then, *Time Online* has become a popular destination in the growing online universe. From September to December, the number of visitors to *Time Online* has risen steadily from 40,000 a week to 60,000 a week, "a trend that shows no sign of stopping."[58] *Time* logged its one millionth online visit on Thursday, January 24, 1994, and reached 1.5 million visits after six months of operation.[59] With total weekly usage reaching 100,000, *Time Online* generated some $350,000 in users fees by the end of its sixth month of operation. In response to the most common request *Time Online* receives, *Time's* professional futurist, Tom Mandel, who guided the magazine's online expedition, expects some of the photographs that appear in the magazine to be available by the spring of 1994 via AOL. *U.S. News and World Report* magazine offers a two-way interactive service similar to *Time Online.*

In an online collaboration between the *Atlanta Journal–Constitution* and Prodigy Services Company, Cox Newspapers, Inc., offers its readers a new electronic news service called *Access Atlanta.* The service provides a variety of information ranging from news stories and photographs to classified advertisements and current sports scores. *Access Atlanta* has signed up 11,500 subscribers in ten weeks, a rate David Easterly, the president of Cox Newspapers, Inc., told the Southern Newspaper Publishers Association conference is much faster than he expected.[60]

Even the staid New York Times Company and Washington Post Company have launched online news products. On June 9, 1994 the *New York Times* launched an interactive news service on America Online, called simply *@times.*[61] *@times* includes a variety of offerings, ranging from news stories, reviews, and information on cultural, arts, and leisure activities in New York City to an electronic bulletin board. The service is offered free to anyone subscribing to America Online, which costs $9.95 a month.

The *Washington Post's* new online product is called *Washington Post Online,* and it uses Ziff-Davis Interactive's Interchange online service (acquired in December 1994 by AT&T). The product maintains as much as possible in online form the look of the *Washington Post,* featuring the same typeface in its banner, with the term *EXTRA* added to *The Washington Post.* The left side of the on-screen menu lists major sections, such as news, arts, lifestyle, features, and displays lead stories in the main part of screen. Ads and computer functions are on the lower part of the frame, in the same fashion as Prodigy.[62] Of course, not everyone is a fan of such on-screen advertising. Prodigy users have been known to object so much to the ever-present commercial messages that they sometimes put tape over the lower part of the screen, permanently obscuring the electronic ads.

Although revenue has begun to flow in for many of these online information products, and some commercial online services such as AOL are turning a profit, few content providers are in the black. Most companies view online services as a low-cost opportunity to experiment with electronic products. One service that has made a profit in just its first year of operation is the *Electronic Trib* offering from the *Albuquerque* (New Mexico) *Tribune.* The *Electronic Trib* is available via Prodigy and offers readers access not only to the content of the day's paper but also to additional material that did not make it into the paper, live chat sessions with reporters, and transactional services such as online classifieds. Because the *Electronic Trib* has very little overhead and a very small staff (one editor), the revenue generated from advertising in the electronic product has exceeded the cost of producing the electronic product.

Real-Time News Services: Bloomberg Business News
In many ways outweighing consumer online news services is the class of online products known as real-time financial information services. Leading competitors include *Reuters PLC,* with 190,000 subscribers worldwide, *Dow Jones Telerate,* with 90,000, and *Bloomberg Business News,* with 38,000. Although it is the smallest of the three, *Bloomberg Business News* is a fascinating case study in the future of news. "We follow the dictum," says Matthew Winkler, editor in chief for *Bloomberg Business News,* "follow the money." Journalists reporting for *Bloomberg Business News* try to "make money stories transparent," Winkler explains.[63]

   Bloomberg Business News was founded in 1990, as a part of Bloomberg LP, a company created in 1982 by Michael Bloomberg, a Wall Street investment banker with a Ph.D. in physics. Bloomberg's entrepreneurial spirit led him to leave the confines of Merrill Lynch and apply his knowledge of the world of financial trading and technology to create a company devoted to real-time information services for financial traders and anyone interested in "following the money." His first client, and still his biggest, was Merrill Lynch. Although most clients are in the financial world, Bloomberg clients can be found in many other places around the world, including a growing number of news organizations and a few schools of journalism and communication. While about half of Bloomberg's clients are found throughout North and South America, many are located in Europe, and an increasing number are in the Pacific Rim. Bloomberg terminals can also be found in some unexpected places. "Bill Clinton has a Bloomberg," says Matt Winkler. "So does the Sultan of Brunei and the Vatican."

   Bloomberg Business News was started as a real-time news service for Bloomberg LP clients, many of whose investment decisions are greatly affected by news events. In three and a half years, *Bloomberg Business News* has grown to 225 journalists and 40 editors serving thousands of clients all around the world 24 hours a day, 365 days a week. Not all of *Bloomberg Business News* users are financial traders. Dozens of news organizations are online with *Bloomberg Business News.* Eighty are newspapers, mostly flagship papers, such as the *New York Times* and the *Washington Post*, although many smaller papers also use the service, ranging from the *Buffalo* (New York) *News* to the *Australian Financial Review*. A growing number of network television news divisions, radio news programs, and magazines are using the Bloomberg service.

From a technological point of view, the Bloomberg system is relatively straightforward. The Bloomberg terminal (simply called a Bloomberg) is little more than a Texas Instruments personal computer with some special software and hardware peripherals. What is remarkable is that Bloomberg has created a multimedia news product using all off-the-shelf technology. "We massage it, but anyone is capable of doing it," explains Winkler. "People talk about the electronic newspaper of the future," he adds. "We already have an electronic newspaper." The Bloomberg product includes text, graphic information, audio, and video, all delivered using the existing public telecommunications network. No devoted fiber optic lines are required to receive *Bloomberg Business News*. Although the video currently provided is still images only, technology will soon allow moving images, as well. In early 1994, Bloomberg introduced a television business news service that would initially serve the New York market. With the creation of this video product line, however, the next step to online delivery of full-motion video news is only a short digital step away.

Bloomberg clients are required to lease a Bloomberg terminal. The rationale for this approach is that it allows Bloomberg to regularly update its hardware and software, without having to worry about compatibility with a variety of hardware and software platforms. "We've gone through four generations of hardware already," says Winkler.

The cost for a Bloomberg terminal is expensive relative to the cost of a traditional printed newspaper, but no more expensive than other real-time information services, such as *Dow Jones Telerate* or *Reuters PLC*. A single terminal leases for $1,400 a month, while two or more lease for $1,000 each per month. Bloomberg is more than a thorn in the side of industry giants *Reuters PLC*, with 190,000 terminals worldwide, and *Dow Jones Telerate*, with 90,000 worldwide. With 38,000 terminals leased around the world—up from just 8,500 since the launch of *Bloomberg Business News* in 1990—Bloomberg generates some $38 million a month in revenues. Where is the biggest cost to Bloomberg? It's not in the technology. Easily the biggest cost is people. Well over two-thirds of Bloomberg's costs are salaries; Bloomberg's journalists tend to be relatively well paid. In most traditional newspapers, the biggest single cost is printing, production, and delivery, with journalists traditionally poorly paid.

Technology has also enabled Bloomberg's journalists to do their jobs in new, more efficient, and more flexible ways. Telecommuting has become increasingly common at Bloomberg. "Many of our people work at home," says Winkler. "Both our Detroit and Los Angeles bureaus are located in reporter's homes." In every case, the reporters have the same sophisticated hardware in their homes that they would have if they worked out of a central Bloomberg office. They have a Bloomberg terminal, modem, and phone that allow them to fully access the Bloomberg electronic library, send and receive communications over the Bloomberg messaging system, and file their stories electronically. Perhaps more important is the corporate culture that exists in the Bloomberg newsroom.

The best-laid plans of mice and men are still subject to the whims of human fancy. Bloomberg LP found this out the hard way in February 1994 during the Winter Olympics in Lillehammer, Norway. In the United States, the biggest news story of the 1994 Olympics revolved around the attack on U.S. skater Nancy Kerrigan, who was clubbed on the knee just weeks before the Olympics. Not only did the event cast doubt on whether Kerrigan could win a medal, but it was unclear whether she would even be able to compete. Kerrigan surprised many observers by not only performing in the Olympics, but heading into the final day of the figure-skating competition she was in first place. But what happened next even caught Bloomberg by surprise. When the results of the competition were in, a message was flashed on the Bloomberg screen. Suddenly, the system froze. The reason? Thousands of Bloomberg clients had simultaneously requested the story to find out if Kerrigan had won the gold medal and, in the process, caused a traffic jam so great it overloaded the system causing it to freeze. "But if you think that was something," notes Winkler, "you should have seen what happened when the word 'penis' flashed across the screen a few months earlier." Although the system froze for about sixty seconds at the time of the Kerrigan medal story, the Bloomberg system crashed for nearly half an hour when the story of Lorena Bobbitt broke.[64] The Bobbitt story revolved around a woman who cut off her husband's penis, which was subsequently reattached in microsurgery. The story captured the attention of much of the American public for months as the case unfolded. By the way, Kerrigan failed in her gold medal bid, capturing the silver instead.

Noncommercial Providers and Products
Much online activity is the result of noncommercial interests and organizations, including not-for-profit groups as well as governmental agencies. These organizations and their new media products often serve audiences unable to pay for commercial services or unattractive to advertisers, such as the urban poor, children, the homeless, the aged, and persons with disabilities.

Among the most well-known and widely available noncommercial services are the freenets, public-access computer systems designed for the free exchange of information among members of both local and global communities. The first freenet was created in 1986 at Case Western Reserve University Medical School in Cleveland, Ohio.[65] Originally a small bulletin-board service for doctors, the Case freenet quickly grew in response to public demand and now serves more than 22,000 registered users and processes some 5,000 logins a day. The freenet features more than 300 information and communication services, ranging from e-mail to medical information to Project Hermes, which contains the full text of U.S. Supreme Court decisions. The network also offers users free access to the online version of *USA Today* and Academy One, a K–12 electronic schoolhouse.[66] Since then, freenets have been established in dozens of communities around the United States and internationally. Illustrative is the National Capital FreeNet (NCF) in Ottawa, "created in 1992 as a non-commercial, cooperative, community project with the active participation of volunteers, institutions such as Carleton University, and organizations such as Gandalf Technologies (which donated modems and the communications equipment for connecting the freenet to the Ottawa Public Library) and Sun Microsystems (which donated a Sparc-Station 10)," writes Canadian scholar Leslie Shade. Freenets represent a much-needed alternative to the commercial online offerings.

APPLICATIONS

Although this book is about new media technologies, any discussion of the significance of those technologies for commerce or culture depends almost exclusively on what those technologies can do. In turn, what those technologies can do is defined largely by the applications they run or perform. This section of Chapter 4 complements the opening section on new media technology concepts by examining the unsettled and evolving applications being created for those technologies. The applications discussed here fall into four main areas:

- artificial life, including agents (that is, interface agents), artificial intelligence, and the computer virus
- commercial applications, such as computer-assisted investigative reporting, electronic newspapers, information graphics, teletext and videotex, the video dial tone, and video on demand, pay per view, transactional services, and video conferencing
- user services, including electronic mail, electronic bulletin boards, and multiuser domains (MUDs)
- network applications, including Mosaic

Artificial Life

Artificial life may seem an unlikely place to begin this discussion, but it represents one of the most potentially significant applications on the new media horizon. Included here are artificial intelligence, interface agents, and the computer virus.

Artificial Intelligence (AI)

Because it provides a window on the functioning of the human mind, artificial intelligence is what is for many the most exciting application of computing technology. It refers to computer processes of analysis and decision making that come closest to paralleling those of humans. "Can computers think?" is perhaps the most intriguing question central to the field of artificial intelligence. For some, the answer is easy. Among the major AI thinkers, such as MIT's Marvin Minsky, Stanford's Edward Feigenbaum, and Oxford's Roger Penrose, only Herbert A. Simon, a Nobel Prize–winning AI expert whose research in the field dates back to 1955, is convinced that machines can think. "I'm not claiming any magic for machines," says Simon.[67] "All I claim is that they can think." Simon says his computers think all the time. "They've been thinking since 1955 when we wrote the first program to get a computer to solve a problem by searching selectively through a mass of possibilities, which we think is the basis for human thinking." Others are much more skeptical, concluding that computers may mimic human thought and decision making, but they cannot actually "think" and lack self-awareness or consciousness.

Regardless of whether computers really think, however, scientists have developed a variety of AI applications, ranging from systems that understand the spoken word to robotic television cameras. These applications have been in primarily four areas: natural language processing, expert systems, vision, and robotics. Natural language processing refers to computer systems that can "understand" or process the word, either written or spoken. Expert systems are those that involve decision making based on the distilled knowledge of human experts and research. Vision refers to computer sight systems that can be used for navigation or recognition of objects. Robotics is the AI branch in which machines are able to replicate, and in some cases improve on, human actions. In 1948, Missouri mathematician Norbert Wiener established the science of cybernetics, which eventually formed the basis for the development of robotics. Cybernetics primarily concerns the management of controls and communications within automatic machines, organizations, and living beings.

Artificial intelligence, as opposed to natural, human intelligence, has been dramatized in popular culture for many years. One of the most powerful and believable portrayals of a thinking machine was HAL (derived by subtracting one letter from the alphabet from each letter in *IBM*) in Stanley Kubrick's classic science fiction film, *2001: A Space Odyssey,* based on Arthur C. Clarke's book, and released in 1968. HAL not only ran the ship's basic life-support systems and kept it on course, but engaged the astronauts in "intelligent" conversation and more. Science-fiction writer Isaac Asimov even wrote of the three laws of robotics, including, above all else, that a robot could never harm a human.[68]

Long before there was HAL, however, mathematicians, computer scientists, and philosophers had pondered the nature of human intelligence and that which is possible in a machine. British mathematician Alan Turing, called the father of the modern computer and famous for helping a British–American team at Bletchley Park break the German code during World War II (subsequently immortalized on Broadway in the award-winning play, *Breaking the Code*), developed the classic test of artificial intelligence.[69] Turing proposed that the ultimate test, now known as "The Turing Test," of artificial intelligence is whether a human being can distinguish between communication with a computer and with a human. If not, then the computer truly possesses artificial intelligence. Shortly after HAL was created in *2001,* an MIT professor wrote a remarkable program called Eliza. Eliza simulated a session with a psychologist using exclusively natural language prompts and responses. An Eliza session might go something like this: User: "Hello." Eliza: "Good morning. How are you?" User: "OK." Eliza: "Really?" User: "Well, I've been better." Eliza: "Tell me what's on your mind." User: "I haven't been getting along with my brother." Eliza: "Tell me about the problem you're having with your brother." Et cetera.

One day, a visitor to the professor's home encountered a computer prompt that caught his attention. The professor was not in the room, and the visitor thought it might be a message from the professor, so he answered it. The computer immediately responded, and the visitor began a dialogue. Eventually, the professor returned, surprising his visitor, who had thought he was busily engaged in a conversation with the professor by computer. Unknowingly, he had just administered the Turing Test, and Eliza had passed.

Testing the Outer (and Inner) Limits

Those in the field of artificial intelligence have succeeded in many significant applications to media and communication. Voice recognition and speech synthesis for speaking and listening to a computer are already in use in fields such as medicine. They are particularly effective for doctors in the operating room, who need to have both hands free and speak with a relatively specialized and limited vocabulary the computer can be taught to understand, persons suffering from carpal tunnel syndrome, such as journalists, who can write without a keyboard. Many who are disabled use Kurzweil voice recognition technology, which is among the most advanced in this area, though still relatively expensive. Even some automobiles are now equipped with voice recognition technology that will do everything from start the car to dial a cel phone on spoken command.

Compton's new encyclopedia on CD-ROM features AI applications that use fuzzy logic when searching text. For instance, if a student asks, "Do fish in the ocean sleep?", the computer will find all text that discusses fish in the ocean and highlight passages that discuss their sleeping habits. It's no longer necessary to be a database librarian to conduct efficient database searches, although when searching an expensive online service like Nexis, it helps.

Agents.   Agents, or interface agents, are computer programs that employ artificial intelligence to help users operate various computer applications. Acting much as a personal assistant, agents can learn by observation, make decisions, and filter incoming information, such as select news items based on personal preferences, search a database looking for selected pieces of information, or conduct transactions such as electronic banking or making an airline reservation. Heralded as a form of artificial life, agents operate autonomously on the network into which they are released. They are sometimes called know-bots, short for knowledge robots.

Such software agents are quickly transforming the media landscape into a "smart" environment. An increasing number of scholars and business investors are recognizing the need for smart agents that can travel the information superhighway conducting research, making decisions, and generally acting as our personal representatives and information filters to screen out unwanted messages from an increasingly cluttered information environment. Media mogul Rupert Murdoch, the owner of News Corp and Fox TV network, in fact, is building a business based on interface agents.[70] Murdoch's designated new media evangelist is John Evans, head of News Electronic Data (NED), the new media subsidiary of Murdoch's News Corp. Evans is designing a media software product called Taxi for traveling the information superhighway. Taxi will use interface agents dubbed Marilyn and Oliver to comb databases, fetch information, develop profiles, and even schedule airplane reservations. Reflecting the "Daily Me" philosophy of the MIT Media Lab, Evans rewrites the media future as MEdia, in which software like Taxi use agents to create our own personalized media products. "Eventually, [that] agent will go to the *Daily*

News and to the *Post* and will pick columnists for me, and TV guides for me, and maybe go for horoscopes," says Evans. "Now I've got my paper."[71]

One interesting media application of interface agents is underway at the University of Texas at Austin. Professor Wayne Danielson, a pioneer in computer applications for instruction and research in journalism who in 1964 developed a computer program for analyzing Associated Press news feeds, is leading a project to develop a news filter agent for the Newton Messagepad.[72] Calling it a "personal editor," Danielson's interface agent will let the Newton:

- sort newsfeeds into nine categories, including sports, entertainment, crime, accidents, business, protest, politics, war, and medicine
- decide which stories to display intact, which to shorten, and which to discard
- learn individual news preferences by observing a human editor make news decisions

Danielson believes the personal editor will serve an important role in helping news consumers sort through massive databases by automating certain decisions about news values and preferences. To some, the information superhighway is more analogous to turning on a fire hydrant and trying to get a drink. There's simply too much water flowing too fast to drink without getting hurt or drowned. A personal editor, or interface agent, can act as a filter to help reduce the flow of water, or information, and let the thirsty news consumer get a drink. Danielson's personal editor uses a keyword strategy to categorize stories and make decisions. For example, a story containing a dozen words dealing with politics, a half dozen on economics, and two or three on religion would be classified as a politics story. The personal editor would let the Newton offer the user three options in selecting stories:

- make preprogrammed decisions mimicking the decisions of real-world news editors
- specify subject preferences by setting percentages for each of the nine categories listed above
- infer the user's own preferences by monitoring the amount of time he or she spends reading different types of stories.

The personal editor edits stories not on a generic word count, but edits stories to fit each user's reading pattern based on observing the user's average reading speed. In a series of tests comparing human editors against the computer, the personal editor replicated human choices with about 85 percent reliability or agreement.

Virus

In a digital world where floppy disks are inserted in and out of a series of computer disk drives, files and messages are transmitted over online networks circumnavigating the globe, and stolen software is perhaps more common than that properly paid for, it was inevitable that some form of digital social diseases would emerge. The computer virus, in itself a metaphorical form of artificial life, has emerged as the first such disease to plague the world of cyberspace. In 1992, computer users around the world worried about system crashes as the calendar approached May 5th, the five-hundredth anniversary of the birth of Leonardo Da Vinci. An anonymous hacker had proclaimed that computer files and networks the world over were infected with a devastating computer virus dubbed Da Vinci, capable of wiping out the contents of entire hard drives and scheduled to take effect on May 5. The threatened damage loomed as large to computer systems managers as a nuclear mushroom cloud to ranchers living near the Nevada Proving Grounds. Ultimately, computer users took such extensive precautionary steps to minimize the danger of the Da Vinci virus that only a handful of documented cases of the "computer disease" actually occurred. Two earlier computer viruses, the Internet Worm and the Pakistani Brain Virus, actually wreaked much greater havoc in the computer world. The Internet Worm, ironically released in 1988 by Robert Morris, Jr., the son of one of the creators of the very first computer virus at AT&T Bells Labs in 1962, quickly shut down a network affecting millions of users.

The origin of the computer virus is not easily determined, but author Steven Levy has developed the most comprehensive family tree to date.[73] He traces the origin to the AT&T Bell Labs in 1962, where computer scientists Victor Vyssotsky, H. Douglas McIlroy, and Robert Morris, Sr., created "the first known predatory self-replicating" computer organisms. "These beasts were the digital warriors in a gladiatorial game called 'Darwin.'"[74] The term *computer virus* was first used by science-fiction writer David Gerrold in his 1972 book, *When Harley Was One*, to refer to a rogue computer creation. Gerrold, however, dropped any reference to the term in reprints of the novel, and the term failed to catch on. Finally, the computer virus was officially born in 1983 by then USC engineering and computer security doctoral student Fred Cohen, recognized today as the father of the computer virus, not a "career-enhancing distinction," notes Levy.[75] Although the term itself was coined by his professor Dr. Leonard Adleman, Cohen defined a computer virus as "a program that can 'infect' other programs by modifying them to include a possibly evolved copy of itself."[76] Cohen created and released into the university's UNIX system such a computer virus that enabled him to access the programs and files of any system user. "He could type commands as if he were that user."[77] The virus worked its magic with remarkable speed, penetrating the entire network in just a matter of minutes. Unfortunately for Cohen, the notion of a destructive computer virus did not appeal to most system administrators. Many, in fact, said that what he had created was not only unethical but even immoral. Computer virus scholar Eugene Spafford has outlined his concern:

> *Viruses created for malicious purposes are obviously bad: viruses constructed as experiments and released in the public domain are likewise unethical, and poor science besides. . . . Facetiously, I suggest that if computer viruses evolve into something with artificial consciousness, this might provide a doctrine of "original sin" for their theology.*[78]

Since the publication of Cohen's paper describing his research in 1987, computer scientists have begun to reconsider the implications of computer viruses, envisioning a form of antivirus that might serve a positive function in computer environments. Others have pursued notions of artificial life that might serve as computer agents to serve at a human user's bidding in the digital world. These agents would act as automatons roaming cyberspace under each user's control and command, gathering desired information, screening incoming messages, or otherwise acting as one's personal digital assistant. Nevertheless, many are still concerned about the evil prospects for computer viruses as a destructive form of artificial life. Some have conjectured about the horrifying possibilities of computer viruses invading military applications, "from battlefield robots to satellite warfare." "Once self-reproducing war machines are in place, even if we should change our mind and establish a consensus, dismantling them may become impossible—they may be literally out of our control." As Levy points out, this warning seems more plausible since in 1990 the United States government solicited contracts for the creation of computer viruses for military use. Forty years ago computer science pioneer Norbert Weiner issued this warning:

> *Again and again I have heard the statement that learning machines cannot subject us to any new dangers, because we can turn them off when we feel like it. But can we? To turn a machine off effectively, we must be in possession of information as to whether the danger point has come. The mere fact that we have made the machine does not guarantee that we shall have the proper information to do this.*[79]

Interestingly, the development of computer viruses by deviant computer hackers has spawned an entire subindustry, with many computers now running electronic virus detectors and treatment packages.

Computer viruses and their offspring have important implications for the future of the media. Clearly, all media organizations and all consumers of electronic media products need to take precautions to protect themselves from infections by computer viruses. Although there have been no documented cases to date of computer viruses invading and causing significant damage to a media network, there is no reason to doubt it can happen. Perhaps more importantly, imagine a time in the not-too-distant future when the majority of news, information, and entertainment are delivered to consumers via electronic means. What might happen on the eve of an important election or referendum if an invading computer virus sent false information to those preparing to vote? How might an unscrupulous corporate giant use a computer virus to attach itself to the communications of anyone on the network, allowing corporate spies to watch or even alter messages transmitted over the network? How might computerized transactions be affected? Not even the First Amendment can protect the media from these electronic marauders.

Commercial Applications

No doubt because of their value in the marketplace, the greatest number of new media applications are commercial in nature. They include interactive television services such as the video dial tone, video on demand, and pay-per-view TV, transactional services and video conferencing, as well as newsroom technologies, such as computer-assisted investigative reporting, electronic newspapers, information graphics, teletext, and videotex.

Attack of the Killer Applications

Denizens of the computer world like to talk about killer applications, software products that serve a vital function, meet a pressing need, or represent a sure-fire, can't miss commercial success. Most fall into the latter category. Microsoft Windows, for example, is a killer application that allows IBM compatibles to function like a Macintosh, simulating the graphical user interface pioneered by Apple Computer. It has sold millions of copies worldwide and is the standard for office computing.

On the information highway, there is already talk of the first of the killer applications. Bell Atlantic chief executive officer Ray Smith told reporters at the 1993 Western Cable Show that five killer applications will help finance the $15 billion construction cost of the advanced network bringing two-way video services to 1.25 million homes by 1995 and 8.75 million by 2000.[80] The five killer apps are:

- video on demand
- home shopping
- video games
- programming
- direct-response advertising

These services are "plums ripe to be picked," Smith noted.[81] Others, including Time Warner's Wendell Bailey, have identified three major applications driving his company's so-called Full Service Network targeted for Orlando, Florida:

- (near) video on demand
- transaction services, including home shopping, banking, airline reservations (with Microsoft's $1.5 billion acquisition of Quicken, the leading personal finance software, software pioneer and billionaire William H. Gates III demonstrated his belief in the moneymaking potential of the emerging transactional marketplace for writing checks, paying bills, and shopping electronically)
- games, such as Nintendo and Sega

Journalist and author Les Brown adds that there are two other killer applications lurking on the information superhighway horizon that may not have the redeeming social value of the other three.[82] As a result, they are not often mentioned in public discussions of the future of media technology, but they are likely to drive the consumer market, at least in the early years. They are gambling and pornography. Both already represent multibillion dollar industries and are guaranteed success stories, at least commercially, in the world of digitally delivered media technologies.

John Hillis, the president of Newschannel 8 in Washington, D.C., observes that much of the discussion of so-called "killer applications" is a lot like killer bees, however. "There's a lot of hype and hysteria, but somehow they never seem to arrive."[83]

Video Dial Tone. To many, the video dial tone is the driving force behind the construction of the information highway. Although many information services from online banking to home shopping face uncertain demand, most industry advocates hail the video dial tone, or video on demand, as a sure-fire hit. "Video on demand is expected to be the next big wave," writes Richard Lipkin.[84] "Rather than walking to the local video shop, customers will get films transmitted electronically to their homes just by dialing in their requests." Just as you can use any telephone to call anyone else with telephone service, the video dial tone would let anyone connected to the information highway access a broad array of video services on demand, from movies on demand to news information. These services are generally seen as being offered on a pay-per-view basis, although many say the fee will be modest, as little as 25 cents a movie. The technology necessary to provide a video dial tone ranges from advanced systems linking digital video file servers or juke-boxes, TV set-top decoders, and optical fiber lines to less expensive systems based on asymmetrical digital subscriber line (ADSL) services. Time Warner's Full Service Network in Orlando, Florida, is an example of the high-end approach, while Bell Atlantic's video-on-demand service in suburban Washington, D.C., is an example of an ADSL approach. The ADSL approach transmits compressed video signals over existing conventional telephone lines or twisted-pair cable made of copper wire, in combination with a video server, telephone switch, digital video switch, and ADSL terminal in a central office, along with a TV set-top decoder and ADSL unit in the home. With a $160 million price tag, the ADSL trial is still not cheap, but it is considerably less expensive than laying fiber to every home in suburban Washington. Assuming FCC approval, the trial will provide a video dial tone to 250,000 homes by the fall of 1994. Bell Atlantic anticipates a fee of about $7.50 per home per month for the service.[85]

Video on demand (VOD) refers to the ability to call up movies and other video services directly from the home or other location electronically from a central file server or digital video library. Video on demand gives the viewer access to a full range of video applications, including pause and resume, rewind, fast forward, and search within any video selected. Near video on demand is similar to full VOD, but does not offer the viewer instant access to any video selected and may not include a full range of video applications. A number of cable Multiple System Operators (MSOs) started offering near video on demand in the early 1990s, such as Time Warner's Quantum cable system in Queens, New York. Quantum, with a 150-channel capacity, offers viewers selected movies on demand, but is not full-fledged video dial tone, providing subscribers with the option to select movies started every few minutes and fed down alternative cable channels.

Pay-per-View (PPV) TV.   Pay per view (PPV) is a television service that invites viewers to pay to watch selected individual programs. PPV is available either via cable or satellite and has been widely used for boxing and other sporting events, such as professional wrestling. During the '80s, PPV grew in audience demand and total revenues but began to decline slightly in the '90s, although the all-time PPV record was set on New Year's Eve 1994 by "The Miss Howard Stern New Year's Eve Pageant." The controversial program grossed an estimated $16 million from 375,000 sales at $39.95 each. Stern's show drew the ire of critics for its sexually explicit content and exploitation of female contestants in the so-called "beauty pageant."[86]

Pay-per-view systems are based on a century-old approach to broadcasting. In 1894 the Electrophone Company of London established the world's first pay-broadcast system service which, for ten pounds a month, distributed concerts, lectures, and church services to subscribers over the telephone. The technology was underdeveloped, however, and poor service caused the system to close down after ten years.

Introduced in 1940, Skiatron was one of the earliest pay television systems attempted prior to World War II. Phonevision was an experimental pay TV service attempted by Zenith Corporation in 1947 that entailed the transmission of signals for unscrambling by a machine. The machine was connected to the television set of a subscriber and required a card to be inserted for activation.

In 1972, HBO (Home Box Office) began broadcasting in Wilkes-Barre, Pennsylvania. It was soon acquired by Time, Inc. HBO was among the first cable systems to offer recent feature movies and special entertainment not available through the regular television broadcasts—the pay-cable law allows it, in particular, to provide R-rated entertainment programs. In 1975, HBO began transmitting programs to cable TV systems via satellite, setting off the growth of the cable industry in the United States, and in the process became the premiere pay cable TV service.

STV or Subscription Television became widely popular when celebrated television producer Norman Lear (for example, *All in the Family,*) successfully established the first STV station (KSBC-TV in Los Angeles). STV required electronic "unscrambling" of cabled or satellite data on a pay-per-view basis. With an initial viewership of 800 subscribers in April 1977, KSBC grew to 100,000 subscribers within one year. Startup STV stations mushroomed on the East Coast and around metropolitan areas.

Not discussed at length here are a variety of other largely settled commercial applications, ranging from early technologies such as videotex, teletext, and audiotext, transactional services including online airline reservations, banking, and bill paying, and video conferencing and the videophone. Like the fax, video conferencing has existed for many years but has never really found a niche. Recently, advances in telecommunications networks and flat screen telephones are making videophone services increasingly affordable and more useful to end users, especially in business.

User Services

User services are applications in which the end user becomes the content provider and communications source. The discussion here includes a review of electronic mail, electronic bulletin boards, and multiuser domains (MUDs),

Electronic Mail (E-Mail).   Electronic mail (e-mail) is a form of computer-to-computer messaging that has existed since the first computer networks in the 1960s. It achieved widespread popularity in the 1990s, when the growth of the Internet made e-mail a rapid and easy replacement for traditional postal services. The users of e-mail have ranged from university professors to business communicators, private citizens connected to the online world to teenage computer hackers. Even the homeless have found an address in cyberspace where they can receive electronic mail.[87] Among the most well-known Americans who regularly use e-mail are Vice President Al Gore and former Associated Press foreign correspondent Terry Anderson, who spent seven long years as a hostage in Beirut. Since regaining his freedom, Anderson has become active in the public arena and has become a heavy user of electronic mail. Because of its ease of use, low cost, and universal reach, he sees e-mail as a potentially invaluable tool for linking and unifying a broad spectrum of public interest groups.

E-mail has emerged to serve a variety of functions, sometimes replacing traditional telephone-based voice communications among people weary of telephone tag. Moreover, since e-mail services on the Internet rely on local telephone calls connected to a national or international computer network, the user pays no long-distance telecommunications fees, thereby making e-mail a very cost-effective means of communications. Moreover, e-mail is transmitted via packet-switched telecommunications, rather than circuit-switched voice lines, and is highly reliable. As a result, e-mail has not only become a mainstay of domestic and international personal and business communications, but has been an important medium during international political crises and emergencies when rapid communications are critical but conventional media may be unavailable. For example, much of the early communications during the Russian coup attempt during the summer of 1992 was based on e-mail. During the massive earthquake of January 17, 1994, in Los Angeles, California, people in the stricken area who could not make a long-distance phone call learned they could dial local telephone numbers that gave them access to electronic-mail networks undisturbed by the quake.[88] Prodigy set up a special free area on its electronic bulletin board for users to post messages about the quake. Within the first six hours, users posted four thousand notes, says Prodigy spokeswoman Carol Wallace.[89, 90] In one case, a New Jersey resident sent out a plea over Prodigy at 11:34 A.M. Eastern time, asking, "If you have any information about conditions in Northridge, the epicenter of the quake, please write back. We cannot reach our relatives there and are extremely worried about them. They live on Olympia Road." Three minutes later he received a comforting message from another network user who wrote, "My aunt and uncle in Northridge report a lot of glass breakage etc. in the house but no real structural damage visible in the neighborhood." Prodigy set up similar computer bulletin boards following the 1989 San Francisco earthquake and after the World Trade Center bombing and hurricanes Hugo and Andrew. The other major consumer network, CompuServe, experienced a similar heavy flow of traffic in the "live chat" area of discussions in and about southern California. Many online night owls gave live reports of the earthquake and its aftermath on the Internet Relay Chat service, "the cyberspace equivalent of citizens' band radio."[91] On the IRC, as it is called, people gather for open discussions on a virtually limitless range of topics.

Electronic Vox Populi.   E-mail even reached the historically low-tech White House during the first year of the Clinton administration. The most exclusive address on the Internet is in the nation's capital: president@whitehouse.gov. Vice President Al Gore entered the e-mail hall of fame on January 13, 1994, when he became the first vice president to participate in a live news conference by computer network. "The Vice President strode into his office, took a seat at a Compac personal computer and briskly pecked out a confident greeting. 'Welcome to the White House,' Al Gore typed. 'Let's get started.'"[92] The first query scrolled onto the vice president's screen:

Mr VP. . .
I am from Hammond IN
What are your views on These
Virtual Communities . . . and
Are you currently involved
in iany [sic] *networks?*

After a brief technical interruption, Mr. Gore responded:

I'm back. Sorry.
Anyway, we have a
kind of "virtual community" here
in the White House
that gets a lot of work
done but we have not
yet established the myriad
links outside that we hope to soon.

A subsequent exchange reflected Gore's interest in developing the information highway to serve the needs and interests of all citizens.

Question:

Mr Vice-President
Alta Loma, Ca
I'm handicapped & spend a lot of time on the net
Do you envision home computer jobs
& how will that effect the economy?

Gore:

Yes. In fact you may be
interested in knowing
that the sysop of the White House
Forum, Georgia Griffith, is deaf and
blind.
There will be MANY opportunities
Thank you
for the disabled to use
their minds productively on
networks.

Although not profound on any policy matters pertaining to the national data highway, the administration's first official hands-on foray into cyberspace was nonetheless significant; before the Clinton–Gore team entered the Executive Office, the White House was so low-tech that the President couldn't even get a dial tone on his office phone. Vice President Gore, the administration's point man in building the national data highway, is now perhaps the world's leading advocate of providing universal access to a video dial tone.

Moreover, with the launching of the White House's own "Home Page" on the World Wide Web (WWW), the administration now receives many thousands of electronic inquiries each day. For those interested, the WWW address for the White House is http://www.whitehouse.gov/. By accessing this service, not only can the user send an e-mail message to the President, but he or she can listen to Socks the cat meow.

Electronic Bulletin Boards. Electronic bulletin boards (BBSs) are online counterparts of the cork-board bulletin boards long used in the offline world. BBSs are thematic and deal with a full range of human interests, from topics on health to gun control. Online travelers can access BBSs to see what messages have been posted or to post their own messages and await response. With the growth of the Internet and commercial online services, the number of computer or electronic bulletin boards has grown exponentially, with the estimated number of BBSs now exceeding 10,000.

1985 marked the beginning of the period of rapid growth of online bulletin boards throughout the United States, as low-cost modems and the general use of microcomputers made these community or trade-oriented information systems a practical and interesting communication and advertising option for many.

Multiuser Domains.   Multiuser domains, or MUDs (originally for multi-user dungeons), refers to a broad class of online adventure games in which at least two participants play in fantasy worlds they help create, ranging from medieval villages to science-fiction settings such as Frank Herbert's *Dune* or the universe of Gene Roddenberry's *Star Trek. Wired* magazine reports that MUDs have become the "addiction of the '90s" among cybernauts and other online mavens seeking real interactivity in a creative computing environment.[93] The allure of MUDs is not techno-logical; it has more to do with the nature and psychology of the MUD experience. MUDs offer real interaction between the participants, the opportunity for creative expression. Participants are by nature highly involved in any MUD experience. Ultimately, MUDs develop into com-plete virtual communities.[94] Many MUDs are short-lived, but current esti-mates are that some three hundred MUDs exist worldwide.

For a variety of reasons, MUDders frequently change or hide their gender. MIT MUD researcher Amy Bruckman says, "A lot of men pretend to be women so they can have more virtual sex." Conversely, "A lot of women pretend to be men so they'll be left alone."[95] Moreover, many MUDders find the experience addictive, spending as much as eighty hours a week playing in their virtual worlds. In response, Amherst Col-lege banned MUDs from its computer system in 1992, while Australia banned them from the entire continent.

The first MUD was invented by Roy Traubshaw in 1980, during his final year at Essex College in the United Kingdom. Traubshaw adapted the popular Dungeons and Dragons game to an electronic, computer for-mat. The next year, his classmate Richard Bartle named it a MUD, or multiuser dungeon, and placed it on the Internet.[96]

Since then, MUDs have grown widely in popularity and in the diver-sity of their format, ranging from MIT's Cyberion City, an electronic metropolis designed by elementary and high-school students, to Media-MOO, an electronic conference space created by Amy Bruckman and Michael Resnick. Many now define MUDs as multiuser domains, reflect-ing the broader use. Bruckman and Resnick are studying "MUDing as a serious form of scientific communication."[97] Cyberion City, an interactive text built through the collaborative writing of some five hundred participants a day, consists of more than 50,000 objects, rooms, and characters. As the number of participants in this MUD continues to grow, so too will the world they have created. Although a small story in the rapidly expanding world of MUDs, Cyberion City may contain a much larger lesson for the future of new media applications. Put simply: if they build it, they will come.

Playing in the MUD. MUDs, or multiuser domains, are among the most addictive and popular of online pursuits. Created mostly by computer hackers and mavens, most MUDs reflect the most creative side of the online world. To date, there are no commercially offered MUDs. Instead, most are fantasy, participatory, and educational in nature, and to many, represent many of the best qualities the online environment has to offer.

One of the more interesting MUDs is called LambdaMOO, a MUD established as an experiment in 1990 by Pavel Curtis at Xerox's Palo Alto Research Center (PARC). It has since evolved into a real community.[97] To put down roots in LambdaMOO, the first thing one must do is create a character. One such character is Johnny Manhattan, created by Josh Quittner, one of the latest addicts to the world of MUDs. By carefully typing, "@describe me as tall and thin, pale as string cheese, wearing a neighborhood hat," Johnny Manhattan had an identity. From then on, anyone typing "look at Johnny Manhattan," would see the above description. On one journey into LambdaMOO, Johnny Manhattan encountered Jongleur, "a wiry fellow in orange and black motley who carries a sack with juggling balls and a diabolo slung over his back." Jongleur, it turned out, could also perform magic. To experience his digital magic in an analog world, cover the following page (Figure 4-3) with a piece of paper and slowly pull it down, one line at a time, to simulate scrolling text on a screen.

Network Applications

Network applications, such as Mosaic, enable providers to develop their own online services and applications. Many such applications are just beginning to enter the mainstream, with new products such as Mosaic rapidly gaining a wide following, partly because of its graphical user interface and its free availability.

Mosaic

Observers are hailing Mosaic as the first killer application developed for network computing.[98] Created by a crack young team of programmers at the National Center for Supercomputing Applications (NCSA) at the

Jongleur says, "Want to see an example of programming, Johnny?"
Johnny Manhattan says, "Yes."
Jongleur says, "OK, silence and watchup."
Jongleur recites the incantation and invokes the snow storm. A chill wind
begins to whip around the towers and walkways . . .
```
     *

   *  *  *

   *  *  *  *  *  *  *  *

   *  *  *  *  *  *  *  *  *  *  *  *  ****  *  **  *****

   *  *  *  ****  *  *  *  *  *  *  *  *  *  *  *  *  *  *  *  *  *  *  *  *

Sparrows were feeding in a freezing drizzle *  *  *  *  *  *  *  *

   *  *  **  *  *  *  *  *  *  *  *  **  *  *  *  *  *  *  *  *  *  *  *  *  *

   *  *  *  *  That while you watched turned into pieces of snow  *  *

   *  *  **  *  *  *  *  *  *  *  *  **  *  *  *  *  *  *  *  *  *  *  *  *  *

   **  *  *  *  *  *  *  *  *  Riding a gradient invisible *  *  *  *  *

   *  *  ***  *  *  *  *  *  ******  ****  *  *  *  *  *  *  *  *  *  *  *

   *  *  *  *  *  From silver aslant to random, white, and slow *  *  *

   *  *  **  *  *  *  *  *  *  *  **  *  *  *  *  *  *  *  *  *  *  *  *  *

   *  *  *  *  *  *  *  There came a moment that you couldn't tell.  *  *

   *  *  *  *  *  *  *  *  *  *  *  *  *  *  *  *  *  *  **  *  *  *  *  *  *

   *  *  *  *  And then they clearly flew instead of fell *  *  *  *

   *  *  *  *  *  *  *  *  *  *  *  *  *  *  *  *  *  *  *  *

   *     *

   *        *

      *

   *     /<Finis>
```

FIGURE 4-3   Scenario on the LamdaMOO MUD[99]

University of Illinois in Champagne-Urbana, Mosaic is a new software
program free to anyone interested in finding their way around the global
Internet. "Mosaic is the first window into cyberspace," says Larry Smarr,
NCSA director.[100] Mosaic serves as a powerful search tool, or browser, as
such tools are called on the Internet.[101]

Before Mosaic, finding one's way around the Internet required mastery of a variety of arcane commands and addresses, such as "Telnet
192.100.81.100." Based on the World Wide Web protocols developed at
CERN, Mosaic provides a graphical user interface that lets users simply
click a mouse on images or words to select text, images, or sounds from
the many databases available on the Internet. In its first year of

existence, hundreds of thousands of Internet users have downloaded copies of Mosaic, making it one of the most widely used applications in network computing. Many think that the widespread adoption of Mosaic may influence the shape of the national information infrastructure now under debate in Washington, D.C. Among those convinced of the program's value is Mitchell D. Kapor, founder of the Lotus Development Corporation and creator of the revolutionary spreadsheet package, Lotus 1-2-3, as well as founder of the Electronic Frontier Foundation, a public interest group devoted to freedom of expression and access in the information age. "For me Mosaic was a turning point," said Kapor.[102] "It's like C-Span for everyone."

Jim Clark, the former Stanford professor who founded Silicon Graphics, Inc., is convinced that Mosaic is one of the keys to unlocking the riches of the Internet. So committed to his vision is Clark that he has started a new company called Mosaic Communications Corporation in Mountain View, California.[103] Cofounder of the company with Clark is Marc Andreessen, a twenty-two year-old computer designer who helped create Mosiac as part of the original Mosaic design team at the National Center for Supercomputing Applications. Clark and Andreessen have included on their staff six other former members of the design team, as well.

EPILOGUE: WHAT'S MISSING—THE RACE FOR CONTENT

Despite all the hype about exciting new technologies like virtual reality, personal communication devices, and flat panel newspapers, none of it really means anything without quality content. Although messaging, or person-to-person communications from the old fashioned (a phone call) to the new fangled (e-mail) will make up a significant portion of the traffic on the information highway, a large portion of the remaining traffic will be content created by commercial providers, ranging from newspaper publishers to new media entrepreneurs. Of course, even in a 500-channel viewing environment, there is no guarantee there will be anything on worth watching, tuning in to, or downloading. Bruce Springsteen, the boss of rock and roll, once summed things up, "Fifty-seven channels and nothing on." The big issue will still boil down to content.

Peter Kann, chairman and publisher of Dow Jones and Company, Inc., and the *Wall Street Journal*, echoes this view, emphasizing that it's what's inside a medium that really counts. At Dow Jones half the company's revenue now comes from electronic delivery, he says, but Dow Jones remains a "content company." Rejecting Marshall McLuhan, Kann declares, "The form of delivery is not the most important thing. Content is king."[104]

NOTES

1. Stewart Brand, *The Media Lab: Inventing the Future at MIT.* New York: Viking, 1987.

2. Frederick Williams, *The New Telecommunications.* Free Press: New York, 1991.

3. John Carey, "Field Testing the Information Superhighway," speech, the Freedom Forum Media Studies Center, 5 April 1994.

4. James R. Beniger, *The Control Revolution: Technological and Economic Origins of the Information Society.* Cambridge, MA: Harvard University Press, 1986.

5. Daniel Burrus with Roger Gittines, *Technotrends: How to Use Technology to Go Beyond Your Competition.* New York: Harper Business, 1993.

6. Jesse Hunter, "Authoring Literacy: From Index to Hypermedia," *Canadian Journal of Communication,* vol. 19, 1994:41–52.

7. William Gibson, *Neuromancer.* New York: Ace Books, 1984.

8. John M. Phelan, "The Inner Face of Interface," unpublished essay, June 1994.

9. The *Late Show* with David Letterman, 7 February 1994.

10. Evan Ramstad, "Whoa, Slow Down! Metaphor Abuse Causing Whiplash on Information Highway," the Associated Press, 3 February 1994.

11. Phillip Elmer-DeWitt, "Traveling the Information Superhighway," speaking at a press briefing hosted by the Freedom Forum Media Studies Center on 1 February 1994.

12. Evan Ramstad, "Whoa, Slow Down! Metaphor Abuse Causing Whiplash on the Information Highway," the Associated Press, 3 February 1994.

13. Ibid.

14. John Naisbitt, *Global Paradox.* New York: William Morrow, 1994.

15. Laurent Belsie, "Info Superhighway: Metaphor in Concrete," *Christian Science Monitor,* 23 February 1994:A1.

16. Ibid.

17. Ibid.

18. John Pavlik and Andras Szanto, "Coverage of the Information Superhighway," in 'Separating Fact from Fiction on the Information Superhighway' the Research Group, the Freedom Forum Media Studies Center, May, 1994.

19. Ramstad, op. cit.

20. Ralph Lee Smith, *The Wired Nation: Cable TV: The Coming Information Highway.* New York: Harper and Row, 1972.

21. Mark Thalhimer, "Origins of the Information Superhighway Metaphor," in 'Separating Fact from Fiction on the Information Superhighway,' the Research Group, the Freedom Forum Media Studies Center, May 1994.

22. "Information Highway Still a Mystery," *USA Today,* 8 May 1994:5B.

23. Peter H. Lewis, "U.S. Begins Privatizing of Internet Operations," *New York Times,* 24 October 1994:A10.

24. David L. Wilson, "Threats to Internet Security," *Chronicle of Higher Education,* 30 March 1994:A22.

25. Evan I. Schwartz, "The Cleavers Enter Cyberspace," *Business Week,* 11 October 1993:142.

26. John S. Makulowich, "Internet: Explore the 'network of networks,'" *Quill,* September 1993:28.

27. Kinsey Wilson, "Your Life as an Open Book," *New York Newsday,* 21 July 1993:46.

28. Peter H. Lewis, *New York Times,* 13 December 1994.

29. Frederick Williams, the Freedom Forum Media Studies Center Leadership Institute, 22 June 1994.

30. John Markoff, "Traffic Jams Already on the Information Highway," *New York Times,* 3 November 1993.

31. Ibid.

32. Peter H. Lewis, "Internet Users Get Access to S.E.C. Filings Fee-Free," *New York Times,* 17 January 1994.

33. John Markoff, "An Electronic Salon," *New York Times,* 27 March 1994:F10.

34. Peter H. Lewis, "Companies Rush to Set Up Shop in Cyberspace," *New York Times,* 2 November 1994:C1, C6.

35. Peter H. Lewis, "Sneering at a Virtual Lynch Mob," *New York Times,* 11 May 1994:D7.

36. Ibid.

37. Peter H. Lewis, "Censors Become a Force on Cyberspace Frontier," *New York Times,* 29 June 1994:A1, D5.

38. Lewis, op. cit., 11 May 1994.

39. Ibid.: 51.

40. *Kiplinger Washington Letter,* October 1994:2.

41. John Markoff, "New Venture in Cyberspace by Silicon Graphics Founder," *New York Times,* 7 May 1994:B1.

42. David Miller, "The Many Faces of the Internet," *Internet World,* October, 1994:34–38.

43. John Markoff, *New York Times,* 8 October 1994:47.

44. Peter H. Lewis, "Strangers, Not Their Computers, Build a Network in Time of Grief," *New York Times,* 8 March 1994.

45. Curtis Lang, "The Pied Piper of Convergence," *Advertising Age,* 6 December 1993:16.

46. Gary H. Arlen, "Who Uses CompuServe?" *Information & Interactive Services Report,* 11 February 1994:4.

47. Evan I. Schwartz, "The Cleavers Enter Cyberspace," *Business Week,* 11 October 1993:142.

48. Gary H. Arlen, "America OnLine Continues Meteoric Growth, Signs Consumer Magazine Publisher," *Information & Interactive Services Report,* 19 November 1993.

49. Schwartz, op. cit.

50. Hanna Liebman, "About Time for On-Line," *MEDIAWEEK,* 27 September 1993:32, 36–7.

51. Gary H. Arlen, *Information & Interactive Services Report,* 17 December 1993:5.

52. Gary H. Arlen, *Information & Interactive Services Report,* 11 February 1994:4.

53. *Gannett Executive News Summary,* 5 October 1993.

54. *Financial World,* 12 October 1994:56.

55. *Gannett Executive News Summary,* 7 October 1993.

56. *News, Inc.,* 4 October 1993:1.

57. Deirdre Carmody, "For Magazines, a Multimedia Wonderland," *New York Times,* 11 October 1993.

58. Elizabeth Valle Long, "To Our Readers," *Time,* 1 January 1994.

59. Phillip Elmer-DeWitt, Space Technology Studies Seminar, the Freedom Forum Media Studies Center, 5 April 1994.

60. Mark Thalhimer, ed., *Media Industry News Roundup,* compiled from the Associated Press, the Freedom Forum Media Studies Center, 31 May 1994.

61. Ibid.

62. Gary H. Arlen, "Washington Post Picks Ziff Interactive to Publish Its Online Newspaper," *Information & Interactive Services Report,* 25 March 1994.

63. Matthew Winkler, Technology Studies Seminar, the Freedom Forum Media Studies Center, 6 April 1994.

64. Ibid.

65. Leslie Regan Shade, "Computer Networking in Canada: From CA*net to CANARIE," *Canadian Journal of Communication,* vol. 19, 1994.

66. Thomas Grundner, "Free-Nets: Networking Meets Middle America." *Link Letter,* September/October 1991.

67. "Herbert A. Simon," *Omni,* November 1994:71, 72.

68. Isaac Asimov, *I, Robot.* London: Dobson, 1967.

69. Walter Goodman, "Code Breaking and the Good It Does," *New York Times,* 18 January 1994.

70. "Bulletins from the Information Highway: John Evans on New Media, Roadkill and More," *T Leaves,* vol. 3, no. 2, March 1994. Published by the Newspaper Association of America.

71. Ibid.: 6.

72. Mike Maher, "Electronic Gatekeeper for News," *Editor & Publisher,* 25 June 1994:70, 72.

73. Steven Levy, *Artificial Life: The Quest for a New Creation.* London: Penguin Books, 1993.

74. Ibid.: 316.

75. Ibid.: 317.

76. Ibid.: 312.

77. Ibid.: 314.

78. Ibid.: 330.

79. Ibid.: 339.

80. Harry A. Jessell, "VOD, Gaming to Help Pave Superhighway," *Broadcasting & Cable,* 6 December 1993.

81. Ibid.: 6.

82. Les Brown, Technology Studies Seminar, the Freedom Forum Media Studies Center, 6 April 1994.

83. John Hillis, Technology Studies Seminar, the Freedom Forum Media Studies Center, 15 May 1994.

84. Richard Lipkin, "Making the Calls in a New Era of Communication," *Insight,* 12 July 1993:9.

85. Harry A. Jessell, "VOD, Gaming to Help Pave Superhighway," *Broadcasting & Cable,* 6 December 1993.

86. Wayne Walley, "Grossing Out at New Levels: Stern PPV Event Posts Strong Buy Rates." *Electronic Media,* 10 January 1994.

87. William Dutton, 1994. "Lessons from Public and Nonprofit Services," in *The People's Right to Know,* Frederick Williams and John Pavlik, eds. Hillsdale, NY: Lawrence Erlbaum Associates, 1994:105–129.

88. John Schwartz and Tracy Thompson, "The On-Line Link to a Natural Disaster," *Washington Post,* 19 January 1994.

89. "With Phones Out, Computer Networks Provide Key Link," Reporter dispatch, Gannett Suburban Newspapers, 18 January 1994.

90. Anthony Ramirez, "Computers Reach Out and Touch," *New York Times,* 18 January 1994:A20.

91. Peter H. Lewis, "Strangers, Not Their Computers, Build a Network in Time of Grief," *New York Times,* 8 March 1994:D4.

92. Peter H. Lewis, "Preaching the Techno-Gospel, Al Gore Version" *New York Times,* 17 January 1994:D1.

93. Josh Quittner, "Johnny Manhattan Meets the FurryMuckers," *Wired,* March 1994:92.

94. Howard Rheingold, *The Virtual Community: Homesteading on the Electronic Frontier.* New York: Simon and Schuster, 1993:19, 26.

95. Ellen Germain, *Time,* 13 September 1993:61.

96. Jesse Hunter, "Authoring Literacy: From Index to Hypermedia," *Canadian Journal of Communication,* vol. 19, 1994:41–52.

97. Quittner, op. cit., 1994.

98. Richard W. Wiggins, "Examining Mosaic," *Internet World,* October 1994:48–51.

99. Ibid.

100. John Markoff, "A Free and Simple Computer Link," *New York Times,* 8 December 1993:D1, D7.

101. Peter H. Lewis, "Companies Rush to Set Up Shop in Cyberspace," *New York Times,* 2 November 1994:C1, C6.

102. Markoff, op. cit., 8 December 1993:D7.

103. John Markoff, "New Venture in Cyberspace by Silicon Graphics Founder," *New York Times,* 7 May 1994:B1.

104. Tom Fenton, Freedom Forum report on a speech by Charles Brumback at the 47th World Newspaper Congress and FIEJ Annual General Meeting, 29 May–1 June 1994, Vienna, Austria.

5

MASTERS OF THE UNIVERSE

We are in the midst of a technological storm.
—RUPERT MURDOCH[1]

GLOBAL AND DOMESTIC PLAYERS

Vying for control of the new media world is a remarkable cast of characters, including players from a variety of traditional media companies, telecommunications, computer and consumer electronic companies, and a variety of new media entrepreneurs from across the United States and internationally. A few years ago, most of these companies would never have imagined they would one day be competing head-to-head for control of the media universe. Convergence of technologies, regulation, and business have brought these companies into an unprecedented era of global competition. Many new media players are large behemoths determined to maintain their position in the unfolding landscape. Others are racing to stake a claim of any size or shape on the new media frontier in what can be compared only to the land stampedes of the 1800s West, where cutthroats, outlaws, and legitimate business people all struggled for control of the same terrain. Only this time the stage is global and the stakes are profound both commercially and culturally.

Telecommunications: The Big Investors

Leading the commercial charge into the electronic frontier are the telecommunications giants, including the seven U.S. Regional Bell Operating Companies, telephone company GTE, long-distance companies AT&T, MCI, a smattering of smaller companies, and a growing number of recently or soon-to-be privatized international firms (for example, Singapore Tel). Most of these firms have invested billions of dollars in constructing a new information infrastructure, in large part the advanced packet-switched telecommunications network based on optical fiber wiring; smart, computer-based technologies; and integrated systems linking wireless and wired networks.

Driving much of the construction of the information superhighway has been the entry of the telephone companies into the cable television business. Although government regulations presently prohibit telephone companies from providing cable TV service in their telephone franchise areas, many telephone companies are lobbying vigorously to change that law and may soon succeed, as lawmakers are swayed by arguments of economic growth and improved services.

Table 5-1 summarizes the telephone company entrants into the cable TV business as of December 1993.[2]

AT&T has emerged as one of the principal architects of the new information infrastructure. Joining in alliances with several of the RBOCs, including Bell Atlantic, Bell South, and New England Bell, AT&T has agreed to build much of the hardware necessary for the delivery of interactive, full-motion video, or the video dial tone, over the switched telephone network.

Because of its interest and stake in the information superhighway, AT&T has developed a specific set of policies on the development of the national information infrastructure (NII). In the view of AT&T, the NII is made up of four integrated elements:

- computing and information appliances
- communications networks

TABLE 5-1   U.S. Telco Investment in Cable TV Systems

Telco	Price/Terms	Cable company
Southwestern Bell	$4.9 billion partnership	Cox Cable
Bell Atlantic	$30 billion merger	TCI
Southwestern Bell	$675 million purchase	Hauser cable systems in Washington D.C. area
US West	$2 billion investment	25% of Time Warner
Nynex	$1.6 billion investment	Viacom
Bell South	$1.5 billion investment	QVC
Bell South	$1 billion investment	Prime Cable
BCE Telecom	$400 million investment	30% of Jones Intercable

- information and computing resources
- skilled, well-trained people[3]

Multimedia Producers

While the telephone companies are leading the charge to create the information superhighway, multimedia producers are leading the race for content. The leading producers of multimedia software are ranked in Table 5-2 by total revenues for 1993. Heading the list is Electronic Arts, Inc./Broderbund Software, Inc., who in 1994 agreed to merge and thus form the largest multimedia production company. Broderbund is well known for its highly popular education children's multimedia software, including Where in the World is Carmen Sandiego? The ranking is likely to change soon as more mergers are announced. In fact, at the time of this writing, Pearson P.L.C., one of Britain's largest publishers, had recently announced it would pay $462 million to buy Software Toolkits, Inc., the Silicon Valley multimedia software company that has successfully produced *Star Wars* characters to Marvel Comics' Captain America in video games and personal computer programs.[4] Others high on the list include Acclaim Entertainment, well known for its popular but controversial video game, Mortal Kombat, and Microsoft Multimedia, a division of Bill Gates's powerful Microsoft Corporation.

TABLE 5-2   Leading Multimedia Producers*

Company	Revenue in millions
Electronic Arts/ Broderbund (agreed to merge)	$493.2
Acclaim Entertainment	$375.7
Microsoft Multimedia	$200
Software Toolworks	$129.7
Spectrum Holobyte	$ 66.1
Sierra On-Line	$ 61.3
Davidson Associates	$ 58.6
Learning Company	$ 32.9

* Total revenues of leading multimedia software companies for 1993

Source: The *New York Times*[5]; Company reports; Lehman Brothers' estimates.

The Supporting Cast

Also sharing the new media spotlight are a variety of major computer companies, including recently down-sized but still large IBM and Apple Computer, more specialized computer manufacturers such as Silicon Graphics, chip manufacturers such as Intel Corporation, and a host of smaller but fast-charging companies, with both domestic and foreign interests. Also taking a leading position on the new media stage is Microsoft, the dominant computer software company founded by Bill Gates, who has recently turned his attention to writing a book on the information superhighway and was named the 1994 CEO of the Year by *Chief Executive Magazine*. Silicon Graphics, Inc. (SGI), merits special note, as well, with its more than $1 billion in sales and $100 million in profits in 1993. Headed by Chief Executive Edward R. McCracken, SGI is widely recognized for its state-of-the-art computer graphics and animation, as seen in the dinosaurs of *Jurassic Park* or the lifelike meeting of President John F. Kennedy and actor Tom Hanks in the 1994 blockbuster *Forrest Gump*. Consumer electronics companies play a major role, as well, with foreign companies being especially important, such as Dutch company Philips and Japanese company Sony. Video game player and game manufacturers such as leading Japanese companies Nintendo and Sega are in the forefront also.

In a strong supporting role are a number of American newspaper companies, such as Knight-Ridder, Times Mirror, Cox Enterprises, and the Gannett Company, each of which is conducting important trials in the new media realm, especially in the area of online and electronic newspapers and news products. A number of these companies were involved in videotex trials a decade ago and lost considerable sums. As a result, most are taking a somewhat less risky approach this time around, investing smaller amounts in more limited trials.

The Appendix provides a more complete listing of the top companies in eight major subindustries, ranked by gross revenues or sales, each competing for control of the new media landscape. These subindustries are:

- media companies
- cable operators
- telecommunications equipment and services companies
- telephone companies
- computer and communications firms
- computer software companies
- leading newspaper companies
- television programming

Because of the convergence of these once-distinct fields, a number of companies appear on more than one list. Moreover, the distinctions implied by such separate listings are not really very sharp and will become increasingly clouded as these industries all merge in the digital future. Moreover, there are many small but important companies not included on any top ten or twenty lists. Their significance should not be underestimated, especially during a time when adaptability, risk taking, and entrepreneurial experimentation are all at a premium and may be greatest in smaller, newer companies. What these companies lack in capital, they may make up in creativity.

Rising Stars

Other important media companies include firms from Latin America, such as Grupo Televisa in Mexico, whose owner, Emilio Azcarraga Milmo is the wealthiest man in Latin America, amassing a media-based fortune valued at $3.7 billion as well as the nick-name "El Tigre," for his aggressive style. Globo Television in Brazil (Rede Globo) owns the largest TV network in that country as well as one of the leading newspapers (*O Globo do Brasil*), magazines, and radio stations and is one of the largest television networks in the world. It is a major exporter of TV programming throughout the Western Hemisphere, especially TV soap operas, or *novellas*. Important telecommunications companies include Singapore Telecommunications, which first issued public stock in October 1993. Rupert Murdoch's holdings include the satellite systems BSkyB in the United Kingdom and the Hong Kong–based StarTV, which provides television programming to China, India, and much of Southeast Asia. In Japan, Nippon TV is an important content provider, and in France, Canal+ is an important player in the television industry. In the West, Black Entertainment Television (BET), led by president Robert Johnson, experienced rapid growth of 24 percent in 1992.

It's also worth noting some small entrepreneurial companies that may not rewrite the future of new media technologies but do reflect a grassroots movement in new technology. Some industry analysts, in fact, have suggested that it is small innovative companies that are cumulatively investing the most heavily in new media technologies and taking the boldest steps and the greatest relative risks. Because they are small, however, they have the advantage of quick adaptability. Many large technology companies, such as IBM, AT&T, and others, have downsized in recent years to increase their adaptability. One interesting new company is Gateway Computers, a small firm building powerful IBM clones at very affordable prices. Founded in a garage in South Dakota, Gateway has introduced a lightweight portable computer weighing less than three pounds, running on a 486 chip, and costing less than $2,000. Another entrepreneurial spirit has emerged in the online world of New York City. Stacy Horn, a graduate of New York University's interactive telecommunications master's program, has created the East Coast Hang-Out, or Echo, an online virtual community of more than two thousand men and women, who pay about $19.95 to connect to the service. Horn started her business with the severance pay she received from her previous employer when the company relocated and she opted to stay in New York. The entire system runs via two 486 computers, about three dozen phone lines, and a couple of part-time employees.

As corporate leaders in these diverse fields have recognized the growing convergence of telecommunications, computers, and communications, there has been growing interest in developing collaborative efforts between and among companies in different fields. Although much early interest and media reporting have emphasized major merger announcements and activity, there have actually been a variety of corporate alliances. The headlines have gone to mergers and acquisitions, both friendly and unfriendly, but many other strategies have been announced to bring together companies with complementary skills, talents, and resources, ranging from contractual agreements to transcorporate investments and resource sharing. Not all of the antitrust considerations have been played out in the regulatory and judicial arenas, but these types of alliances are increasingly likely in a future dominated by global market interests, complex technological infrastructures, and high-level demand for high-quality multimedia content. The majority of these collaborative ventures involve interactive TV trials and the video dial tone, especially via cable and telephone systems, with a smaller number dealing in online news and information services. At stake is a potentially huge, multibillion dollar business. Arthur Bushkin, an executive at Bell Atlantic Corporation, says hundreds of billions of dollars are at stake, far more than the $25 billion cable market or the $12 billion video rental market. Some of the significant announced corporate collaborations in 1994 include:

- TCI (Tele-Communications, Inc.), Liberty Cable (part of TCI), QVC (the home shopping network) in an interactive TV, home shopping experiment
- 3DO (a company designing a new interactive disc player), MCA (entertainment company), AT&T (long-distance telecommunications giant), and Time Warner (huge entertainment, cable and news conglomerate) in a video-on-demand and interactive TV trial

- Hauser Communications and Southwestern Bell (one of the Regional Bell Operating Companies—RBOC—formed after the divestiture of AT&T in 1984) in an interactive TV trial
- Microsoft, Intel, and General Instrument (three companies involved in computer hardware and software) in an effort to develop software to drive interactive services to the PC
- AT&T and TCI in an interactive TV trial
- US West (another RBOC) and Time Warner in another interactive TV trial
- Capital Cities/ABC Corporation and EON Corporation, who are joining forces to offer interactive television programming by combining current ABC shows with EON's interactive video and data service (IVDS) system[6]
- Newspaper companies are also interested in testing the interactive multimedia waters on a collaborative basis, but many are moving cautiously after losing millions in the failed videotex trials a decade earlier.

Some of the companies in the vanguard include Copley Press, owners of the *San Diego Union Tribune* and forty-five other newspapers, which has announced an ambitious joint venture with Linkatel to lay 3,700 miles of optical fiber throughout San Diego County[7]; Cox newspapers (in a joint venture with an RBOC); New York *Newsday;* Times Mirror Group, including the *Los Angeles Times* and *Baltimore Sun* now developing a joint project with Prodigy. Multimedia, Inc., a company with newspaper holdings as well as interests in broadcasting, cable TV, and entertainment programming, has agreed to join a consortium with BellSouth Enterprises, Inc., and Cox Enterprises, Inc. The consortium will include Multimedia's largest newspapers, located in Greenville, South Carolina, Asheville, North Carolina, and Montgomery, Alabama, and will market telephonic classified and Yellow Page advertising throughout all of BellSouth's operating area.[8] The Washington Post Company has established Digital Ink as its electronic publishing operation. In March 1994, Ziff Communications Company and Digital Ink agreed to put the Washington Post on Ziff's new online service. The offering is now available on Ziff Interchange online service.[9, 10] The Washington Post Company has also acquired an 80 percent stake in Mammoth Micro Productions, a Golden, Colorado–based publisher of multimedia CD-ROM titles.[11] Dow Jones and Company, Inc., and West Publishing Company have agreed to provide a combined online legal and business information service. West Publishing's legal database Westlaw will be the only online service to have access to the Dow Jones News-Retrieval service, which provides full text of the *Wall Street Journal, Barron's,* and some 1,500 other publications.

Collaborative interests are also growing on the international front. Among such joint ventures are:

- U.S. cable companies TCI, Comcast Corporation, Continental Cablevision Corporation, NewChannel Corporation, and Landmark Communications, Inc., in a collaborative effort with Japanese communications company Mitsui Comtek Corporation, in a joint venture to create interactive cable TV
- Sega (a leading Japanese video game company) and U.S. entertainment and cable company Time Warner and U.S. cable company TCI in an experiment to deliver video games and other multimedia products electronically to the home consumer over cable systems
- Bell Atlantic Corporation and the Italian state telecommunications company (STET) in an agreement to develop interactive TV in Italy and other markets.[12]

The Bell Atlantic–STET deal gives Philadelphia-based Bell Atlantic a foothold in the growing European interactive television business. Meanwhile, STET gains a powerful partner in creating services linking phones and televisions. In the project, customers will use a telephone line and TV to order movies and conduct transactions such as buying airline tickets or paying bills. November 1994 is the scheduled start date for a test among two thousand Italian households. The deal gives Bell Atlantic an option to purchase up to a 49 percent stake in STET's interactive multimedia services group, while Bell Atlantic must provide consulting services, technology, and software to develop interactive services for STET.

THE FINANCIAL EQUATION

Driving much of the decision making behind the development of new media technologies and corporate collaboration are bottom-line financial data. Who will pay, how much will they pay, and what will be the profits are all essential questions. Much of the hype surrounding the development of the information superhighway has assumed a great consumer interest in new information services such as interactive TV, PCNs, and movies on demand. Many suggest that much of the cost of these new technologies will be absorbed by the consumer. A growing amount of financial data, however, suggests otherwise. Next Century Media released a report in January 1994, indicating that consumers will not be able to afford the twelve-figure cost of interactive TV. Rather, they suggest, only advertisers have the incentive and the means to make it happen.[13] Figure 5-1 summarizes these data. Clearly, the amount consumers

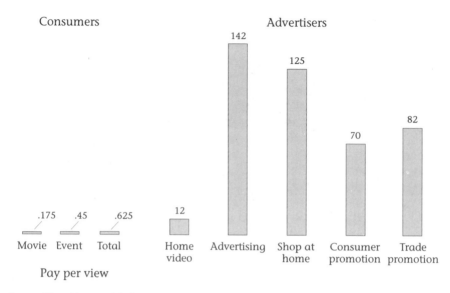

Consumers

Advertisers

Source: Next Century Media

**FIGURE 5-1   Advertising Expenditures in 1992
(in billions of dollars)**

currently spend on pay-per-view, which has seen a relatively flat growth curve in recent years, does not bode well for the future of the pay-per-view society.

Also troubling is the financial math underlying the construction of the broadband, switched network to the home. Bringing to mind the mystery of Foucault's pendulum or the long-standing mathematical puzzle of Fermat's proof, many promoters of the information superhighway have ignored, denied, or simply been unaware of the likely cost of building the necessary infrastructure to provide video on demand to every home currently served by telephony or cable TV. These highwaymen may soon awake to the real costs involved. Sobering data are provided by Next . Century Media.[14] See Table 5-3.

These data show that even a low-tech approach to interactivity, one without switching capabilities to allow consumers a full range of services including true video on demand, will be expensive. Even in a best-case scenario, it will take half a year just to recoup the cost of laying the infrastructure. More likely, it will take two to three years, assuming most homes sign up for the service. If the high-tech path is chosen, one with full switching capabilities to create a full-service network, the best-case scenario takes a minimum of three years to break even on the infrastructure costs. In worst-case scenario, with slow consumer adoption and use of the interactive TV services, which early evidence from field trials suggests is probable, it could take more than eight years. Further, these are just the costs for the hardware. The costs for software are likely to be much greater.

Still many media and telecommunications companies have invested millions in building a new information infrastructure, laying millions of miles of optical fiber, installing new advanced switches, and designing field trials to test new communication technologies ranging from interactive TV to wireless communications. Multimedia, Inc., a company involved in newspaper publishing, broadcasting, entertainment programming, and cable television, is placing its bet on the information superhighway. Mr. Walter Bartlett, Multimedia's chairman, president, and chief executive officer, says the company has planned a number of strategic initiatives to strengthen its competitive position and to provide greater access to the information superhighway. These initiatives include a $150 million technical upgrade of Multimedia's cable operations, $90 million of which will be to replace coaxial cable with fiber. "The strategic investment we're making in our cable systems between now and the end of 1997 will enable us to fully participate in the additional revenue streams resulting from potentially hundreds of new cable channels."[15]

ENTREPRENEURIAL SPIRIT

Vision and inspiration have always been important ingredients in the development and successful marketing of new products. Never have these qualities been in greater demand than in the era of the informa-

TABLE 5-3   Cost per Home for Interactive TV Infrastructure

	Cost per home without switching	With switching
One-time-only cost	$150–$1,000	$1,500–$4,500
Revenue per month		
VOD	$2.50	$4.00
Games	$5.00	$6.00
Advertisers	$18.00	$36.00
Months to break even (excluding marketing cost)	6–39	33–98

tion superhighway, where all bets are off and the frontier is virtually unknown. One media magnate who has great plans for the communications future is Rupert Murdoch, founder and chief executive officer of News Corp, his global media corporation. Murdoch, in delivering the keynote address at the Center for Communications' annual luncheon honoring Ted Turner as 1993 communicator of the year, underscored the importance of courageous leadership in introducing new information services and products around the world. "We are in the midst of a technological storm," Murdoch declared.[16] "Eventually, there will be smooth sailing, but we have to get there first." To get there, Murdoch added, will require "less fear and more flexibility" by media and communication innovators.

Media Entrepreneurs

The history of media industry and new media technology is based not only on corporate agreements and the financial bottom line. It is a story written in the personalities and genius, failures and foibles, vision and sometimes greed of entrepreneurs whose legacies sometimes last far beyond their lifetime. From Gutenberg to William Randolph Hearst, the history of journalism often has been defined in terms of the figures who controlled the presses and printing technology. Telecommunications history is writ large in the names of Samuel Morse, Alexander Bain, and Alexander Graham Bell. The early history of computing rests largely on the shoulders of giants such as Charles Babbage, Lord Kelvin, Vannevar Bush, and Grace Hopper.

In today's global media environment, media entrepreneurs are no less important. Much has been written about media entrepreneurs, with much attention being paid to identifying the critical factors that explain the entrepreneurs' success or failure. Theories range from the sublime to the ridiculous, with one author proposing that it is the "Big T" factor—high levels of testosterone—that explain why some media entrepreneurs have made it to the top.

First Boston's distinguished media analyst Richard MacDonald spent a year as a fellow at the Freedom Forum Media Studies Center analyzing patterns of media entrepreneurship. At his final fellows presentation, MacDonald outlined his findings.[17] He based his analysis on three media entrepreneurs who have had perhaps the greatest impact on media in the United States in the twentieth century. The three entrepreneurs he identified: Walt Disney, founder of the Walt Disney Company, with total assets of $10.861 billion in 1992; Ted Turner, founder of Turner Broadcasting System, Inc., with total assets of $2.523 billion in 1992; and, Rupert Murdoch, founder of News Corporation Limited, with total assets of $26.221 billion in 1992.

MacDonald identified six special attributes that explain the success of these media entrepreneurs. First, they usually began with a media inheritance (with the exception of Disney). Second, they had no particularly overarching skill; just a total commitment to their enterprise. Third, they could galvanize those around them. Fourth, they had an absolute personal identification with their company. Fifth, they knew how to fully exploit the intellectual capital of their workforce and even set up formal schools to develop their potential. Finally, and most importantly from the point of view of this book, they had a stunning and immediate grasp of technological change, they knew its significance, and could act on it quickly.

Creator of the Enchanted Kingdom: Walt Disney
In the case of Walt Disney, his grasp of technological change first demonstrated itself during the production of *Steamboat Willie*, the Disney classic cartoon featuring Mickey Mouse, produced in 1929. *Steamboat Willie* was in midproduction when sound was introduced to the film industry. Disney immediately realized its importance, used his own voice as that of Mickey for the film, and *Steamboat Willie*—with sound—became a smash hit.

The Swashbuckler: Ted Turner
For Ted Turner, the key technology moment came in 1976, the same year he won America's Cup in yachting. Turner saw the potential of satellite distribution as a driving force in the cable television business and in 1976 bought transponder space on a satellite serving the continental United States. Although the subscriber base was only five million homes, Turner realized he could use the system to build a nationwide cable television network with programming distributed to cable head-ends via satellite. He used his Atlanta, Georgia, television station, merged with the technologies of satellites and cable TV, to create the first superstation, WTBS. Turner also used satellite technology to launch the Cable News Network, his globally successful news effort. Reflecting his well-known confidence, Turner boldly announced in early 1980 his plans for the CNN launch: "We'll be signing on June 1, and barring any satellite problems, we won't be signing off 'till the world ends."

Media Mogul Down Under: Rupert Murdoch
Australian-born Rupert Murdoch perhaps has used technology to come the farthest of these three entrepreneurs. Murdoch inherited from his father a small newspaper in Adelaide, Australia, in the mid-1950s. Shortly thereafter, he won a license to start a television station in Adelaide. Over the next four decades, Murdoch combined his business savvy and his understanding of new technology to create a global media

empire serving most of the world's population. He has been particularly adept at utilizing direct broadcast satellite in Europe and Asia, pioneering BSkyB in the United Kingdom and Star TV in Asia. Although beyond the scope of MacDonald's analysis, many other media entrepreneurs have demonstrated similar skill with the management and application of new technology, such as Al Neuharth, who founded *USA Today* using satellite distribution technology, and Michael Bloomberg, who founded Bloomberg LP using the convergence of telecommunications, computers, and media to create a global multimedia information service. Neuharth and Bloomberg are discussed in detail elsewhere in the book.

Masters of the Universe

One writer, Kathryn Harris, a reporter who covers media industry developments for the *Los Angeles Times,* contends that seven American men from seven traditional media companies are uniquely positioned to wield extraordinary power in shaping the content of the information superhighway. Borrowing from Tom Wolfe, she calls these "stupendous seven" the "new masters of the universe."[18] Among the masters are Murdoch, who became a U.S. citizen to buy American television stations, and Turner, both from MacDonald's list, as well as Sumner Redstone, chairman of Viacom, Inc., Gerald Levin, chairman of Time Warner, Inc., Michael Eisner, chairman of Walt Disney Company, John Malone, chairman of Tele-Communications, Inc., and Barry Diller, chairman of QVC Network, Inc. See the Appendix for a financial breakdown of their corporate holdings.

Sumner Redstone is the most tenacious of the big seven, having once survived a hotel fire by hanging from the window ledge. His company, Viacom, is the largest of the "big seven," with $9.3 billion in total revenues in 1994. Its holdings include Blockbuster Corporation, Paramount Communications, Simon and Schuster, MTV, and Nickelodeon, making Viacom perhaps uniquely suited to shape the emerging information superhighway. Although he is relatively unknown and new to his position at Time Warner, Gerald Levin is a strong leader and a technology visionary. His company, Time Warner, has extensive cable holdings and a broad array of content production companies. Michael Eisner has been tightfisted with his investment dollars at Disney but since joining the company in 1984 has brought it eightfold growth. Eisner has taken a less aggressive approach to developing new media applications but has strong content-production and distribution capabilities. Rupert Murdoch has ambitiously pursued a multifaceted global media empire, with diverse holdings ranging from newspapers to broadcast television to direct broadcast satellite TV. News Corp has extensive content production capabilities and extensive holdings in television, print, and satellite technologies. John Malone, holder of a Ph.D. in operations research, is perhaps the most well educated in new media technologies and brings an aggressive style of management, tempered by a "methodical calm," to the new media business.[19] His Tele-Communications, Inc. (TCI), is a major cable company in the United States and is conducting extensive field trials in interactive television. Barry Diller is an experienced studio executive and understands creating programming for the viewing audience. QVC is the king of home shopping and is poised to enter the interactive TV fray. Turner is easily the most flamboyant of these new media moguls, having captured America's Cup sailing championship in 1976 and built a media empire through energy, vision, and wit. Turner Broadcasting is the smallest of the big seven but is strong domestically and internationally, with CNN enjoying a prominent global presence.

Although these seven may represent the most important players from the traditional media industries, any analysis of the key players in the new media mix would be remiss without mentioning one other individual: Bill Gates, the founder and CEO of Microsoft Corporation. The thirty-eight-year-old Gates, a college dropout who went on to found the largest software company in the world, Microsoft, has engineered or is engineering many projects to shape the future of the information superhighway. His company occupies the dominant position in virtually every major software market, whether consumer or business. His plans to create a global communication satellite system may be just the beginning of a global new media empire headquartered in Seattle.

The Magnificent Seven

Although media analysts such as Harris and MacDonald may have accurately surveyed and studied the universe of media players likely to control the realm of new media content, a number of other players from competing fields are also likely to have a similarly profound impact on the nature of the new media system. Profiled here are what we might call "the magnificent seven" of the new media world—players representing diverse fields, some of whom are either not well known outside the communication field, have not been widely discussed as important figures in the shape of media things to come, or do not represent the highest levels of corporate leadership in the media and communication field. Discussed here are:

- Lawrence Ellison, founder of Oracle Systems
- Bill Ziff, Jr., chairman of Ziff Communications
- global financier George Soros

- Anne Wells Branscomb of the Harvard Program on Information Resources Policy
- Adam Clayton Powell, III, of the Freedom Forum Media Studies Center
- Vivian Horner of Bell Atlantic Video Services
- Roger Fidler, of the Knight-Ridder Information Design Laboratory

Oracle of the Computer Age: Lawrence Ellison

One corporate player who has kept a relatively low profile is Oracle Systems CEO Lawrence Ellison, Silicon Valley's latest superbillionaire. He has emerged as a computing guru as an outsider, not from the world of the personal computer, but from mainframe computing. In contrast to many of his counterparts such as Bill Gates of Microsoft, he "actually looks and acts superrich."[20] He dresses in elegant style, wearing "double-breasted suits of black silk, Japanese sports shirts,"[21] and lives in a Japanese-style mansion "fit for a warlord." Ellison sees the information highway as ultimately rewriting the nature of all mediated communication. Ellison says that all media, including books, magazines, music, TV shows, movies, and catalogs, will one day be digitized and readily available to everyone via computer-driven networks.[22] Oracle, with $1.6 billion in annual sales, is the leading producer of software for corporate databases. Building on this foundation, Ellison's company has embarked on the Alexandria Project, whose mission is to use computers to change the way human knowledge is amassed and stored. Just as the ancient Greeks built their famous library in Alexandria as a storehouse for all the world's books, ultimately assembling more than 500,000 volumes before the Christians burned the site in 391 A.D., Ellison envisions the Alexandria Project as the ultimate multimedia database. The Alexandria Project will encompass unfathomably more in its digital collection than even a great analog library such as the New York Public Library with its collection of eleven million books. Oracle envisions creating multimedia databases encompassing in digital form not merely texts and illustrations of the world's books and periodicals, but also the film and TV libraries of Hollywood, endless streams of news coverage, and much more. Ellison wants to create a global consumer electronic bazaar where shoppers will find everything from bronze vases made in Korea to hand-loomed silk pants from Japan.

The Quiet Man: Bill Ziff, Jr.

Unknown to most of the American public is William B. Ziff, Jr., retired chairman of Ziff Communications, one of the least prominent leaders of the new media world, but among its greatest pioneers. Recently sold, his family-owned new media empire included Ziff-Davis Publishing Co., whose seven magazines pull in $700 million a year in annual advertising and reach more than three million readers in the United States alone.[23] Global revenues are estimated at nearly $1 billion. The flagship publication is *PC Magazine*, a thirteen-year-old bimonthly with more than one million circulation and annual revenue of $281 million, making it the largest computer magazine in the world and the ninth largest magazine overall in the United States. In 1994, Ziff won the Magazine Publishers of America's distinguished Henry Johnson Fisher Award as executive of the year. Under Ziff's leadership, Ziff Communications entered the rapidly growing field of online communications. David Armstrong, media critic at the *San Francisco Examiner* and the author of three books describes 63-year-old Ziff as "second perhaps only to Bill Gates as a prime mover in the $70 billion personal computer industry that has changed the way we work, think, and communicate."[24] Ziff's personal wealth is estimated by *Fortune* magazine at $1.5 billion. His influence derived not only from his wealth and his media reach but because his prosperous and powerful computer magazines impact heavily on which new products live and die in the digital age. Ziff is said to have run his company in a ruthless and manipulative style, striking fear into the hearts of many employees, both current and former.[25] Still, despite his aggressive business style, Ziff is highly respected and admonishes the publishing industry to strive to recapture the honor, quality, and ethics of the golden era of publishing that lasted through the 1970s, not just the bottom-line mentality that emerged in the 1980s. "From the cynical point of view of a modern Wall Street analyst," Ziff says, "our industry was then run by eccentric amateurs engaged in their lives' work for the uneconomic reason that they enjoyed it."[26] Ziff has been a quiet, major player in the media business for decades, assuming the corporate reins at Ziff-Davis in 1953. He steered the course for some three decades, when in 1982 crisis struck and he was diagnosed with prostate cancer. Ziff sold most of his company's 24 magazines in 1984 for some $712.5 million to Rupert Murdoch and CBS. Ziff held onto only a few weak computer magazines, but struck gold with the rise of the desktop computer industry in the 1980s. Ziff recently retired from Ziff Communications and sold off his company, but he's far from through in writing the history of new media technology. The online publishing world beckons, and Bill Ziff, Jr., may find its allure irresistible.

Global Financier: George Soros
A relatively new player in the competition for control of the information highway is legendary investor George Soros, the Hungarian financier whose Quantum Fund is valued at $800 million. Soros, who single-handedly triggered a European currency crisis in 1992 and in mid-1993

sparked a rally in gold prices, invested in two companies in the telephone industry in early November 1993. Soros bought into Viatel, a privately owned New York company that runs international telephone services, and invested $40 million in Geotek, a New Jersey mobile radio company. "George believes that the international telecommunications environment is one that is going to experience a lot of growth in the '90s," said Viatel's chief executive, Martin Varsavsky. "Soros's move into the market is likely to add to the rush by institutional investors to get a position in the industry," wrote Martin Peers in the *New York Post.*[27]

The Legal Scholar's View: Anne Wells Branscomb

Anne Wells Branscomb is a communications lawyer at the Harvard University Program on Information Resources Policy where she is conducting research on the impact of new information technologies on intellectual property rights. Branscomb was an inaugural senior fellow of the Freedom Forum Media Studies Center at Columbia University, and has served as an Adjunct Professor of International Law at the Fletcher School of Law and Diplomacy and as Professor of Telecommunications Law and Public Policy at the Polytechnic Institute of New York. In addition, she has been a consultant to the World Bank and the U.S. Office of Technology Assessment. She has been the chairman of the board of Kalba-Bowen Associates of Cambridge, Massachusetts, and a visiting scholar at the Yale Law School. Branscomb is the editor of *Toward a Law of Global Communications Networks* and the author of the book *Teletribes and Telecommunities.* She has written more than fifty monographs, reports, and articles in law reviews and communication journals. Her work revolves around the principles of the ownership of information, especially the individual and corporate rights to ownership of facts about individuals. In her latest book, she asks the fundamental question of the digital age, Who owns information? The answer may be not only surprising, but to some even shocking. In many cases, the owner of information, including one's name, address, phone number, financial record or even medical record, may not be you!

Technology's Sense Maker: Adam Clayton Powell, III

A veteran of the broadcast newsroom, Adam Clayton Powell, III, is director of Technology Studies and Programs at the Freedom Forum Media Studies Center, where he was previously a fellow. Powell directed the introduction of new technology in several news organizations and has conducted extensive research on the unexpected and unintended consequences of new technology in the newsroom, ranging from the impact of videotape on TV news to the implications of fiber optics for newsroom management. Powell has been a producer for Quincy Jones Entertainment and consultant to KMTP-TV in San Francisco. Formerly, he was executive producer of the Jesse Jackson Show and vice president of news and information programming for National Public Radio. A former director of news at the Satellite News Channel, he has also served as news manager and broadcast producer at CBS News and as head of the Metroplex Broadcasting Company, Inc. Powell served on the National Advisory Panel to the U.S. Congress' Office of Technology Assessment. In 1979 he was the recipient of the Overseas Press Club Award for the best interpretation of foreign news for a series of specials he produced on Iran, and in 1989 he organized and supervised a reporting project that won many major awards, including the Peabody, the Columbia-duPont, the Ohio State, and the Armstrong awards. His work has taken him to many international venues, including extensive work on the emerging media system in postapartheid South Africa and in converging technologies in Japan. Widely respected in the news and entertainment industries and government, as well as in journalism education, Powell's analysis of the consequences of new technology on the media are likely to shape views in industry, government, and higher education. His strong reputation internationally is also likely to give him an increasing voice as media technology sense maker around the world, from South Africa to Japan.

A Telecommunications Perspective: Dr. Vivian Horner

Vivian M. Horner is director of Video Services for Bell Atlantic. A pioneer in the development of new and interactive programming for children's television, Dr. Horner was vice president for program development at Warner Amex Cable Communications, where she conceptualized and then served as executive producer of Nickelodeon, the leading satellite-delivered young people's cable channel. Horner also was vice president of educational and children's programming for Qube, a two-way cable system in Columbus, Ohio. She was also director of research of The Electric Company, for the Children's Television Workshop. Horner was an associate professor of psycholinguistics and education in the Department of Educational Psychology of the Ferkauf Graduate School of Humanities and Social Sciences at Yeshiva University in New York. She has written extensively on children and television, her publications appearing in *Journal of Communications, Journal of Consulting and Clinical Psychology,* and *Videography.* She has also been an electronic media consultant since 1983, helping develop product applications, marketing, and business plans for communications and marketing firms entering new media areas. Her work at Bell Atlantic will help define the nature of video services on the information superhighway.

From the Newspaper World: Roger Fidler

Roger Fidler, founding director of Knight-Ridder's Information Design Laboratory, is a veteran newspaper designer and graphic artist with a knack for new technology and information navigation. Fidler has considerable experience in developing interactive, electronic news products, including several years as a founding member of the design team for Knight-Ridder's Viewtron experiment in videotext. During a 1991–1992 fellowship at the Freedom Forum Media Studies Center he created the first electronic prototype for a flat panel newspaper. His pioneering work on the electronic flat panel newspaper has been reported in a variety of media, ranging from the *New York Times* to *Forbes ASAP.* Current versions include a "mediamorphosis" combining the navigational system, reporting, and depth of newspapers with the audiovisual, full-motion video of television news, along with the advertising central to today's media system.

NOTES

1. Rupert Murdoch, keynote address, Center for Communication, Communicator of the Year Award Luncheon, 11 April 1994.
2. Rich Brown, "BellSouth Makes Another Move into Cable," *Broadcasting & Cable,* 13 December 1993.
3. AT&T, "The National Information Infrastructure: A Key to America's Economic Growth and Global Competitiveness," a report from AT&T, August 1993.
4. Steve Lohr, "Pearson Enters Multimedia Software Arena," *New York Times,* 1 April , 1994.
5. *New York Times,* 14 March 1994.
6. "Cap Cities/ABC TV Selects EON for Interactive Television Services," *Information & Interactive Services Report,* 8 October 1993:4.
7. Pam Kragen, "Copley Press Jumping on Info Superhighway," *Times Advocate,* November 1994.
8. *SNPA Bulletin,* "Multimedia Announces Strategic Initiatives to Strengthen Competitive Position and Give Access to Superhighway," 1 March 1994.
9. *Washington Post,* 17 March 1994:B14.
10. *Wall Street Journal,* 17 March 1994:B5.
11. Mark Thalhimer, ed., *Media Industry News Roundup,* compiled from the Associated Press, the Freedom Forum Media Studies Center, 24 May 1994.
12. Ibid., 31 May 1994.
13. "Superhypeway Backlash," *The Marketing Pulse,* Vol. XIV, Issue 5, 31 January 1994.
14. Ibid.
15. *SNPA Bulletin,* op. cit., 1994:5.
16. Rupert Murdoch, op. cit.

17. Richard MacDonald, "Patterns of Media Entrepreneurship," fellows presentation, the Freedom Forum Media Studies Center, 15 December 1993.

18. Kathryn Harris, "The Stupendous Seven—The New Masters of the Universe," *Media Studies Journal*, Winter 1994:81–93.

19. Ibid.

20. J. Deutschman, feature story on Larry Ellison, *Broadcasting & Cable*, 17 January 1994:3.

21. Ibid.

22. *Broadcasting & Cable*, feature story on Larry Ellison, 17 January 1994:3.

23. David Amstrong, "Ziff Happens," *Wired*, June 1994.

24. Ibid.: 87.

25. Ibid.

26. Ibid.

27. Martin Peers, *New York Post*, 5 November 1993:23.

6

REWRITING THE EDITORIAL
AND CREATIVE PROCESS

I've worked for all the mediums of communication.
—*MAYOR RICHARD M. DALEY* [1]

ONCE UPON A TIME

When the Brothers Grimm wrote their fairy tales, the quill pen was the writing tool of choice and the words were intended to be read in a linear fashion, from start to finish. Every story had a single plot, a beginning, middle, and end, and every reader, even twentieth-century ones, read the same story.

Although the technology of writing changed significantly from the days of the Brothers Grimm to the middle of the twentieth century, the notion of story telling evolved very little until relatively recently. By and large, stories still had a beginning, middle, and end, and readers still digested a single plot or set of facts. Even the "new" electronic media of radio and television did little to change the editorial process, although the written word became the spoken word and images only imagined, drawn, or in still form became animated and lifelike. Nevertheless, facts or narration still unfolded in linear fashion, from start to finish.

The advent of the computer, the convergence of all media, and Ted Nelson's creation in 1961 of hypertext, or nonlinear text, forever changed all that. Nonlinear text, the basis for interactive, multimedia communications, represents an entirely new approach to the editorial process. Its implications are profound but are only now beginning to be recognized and studied, much less understood. Rather than telling a single story with a beginning and end, narrations in hypertext let the reader or consumer develop her or his own story, sometimes doing so by participating in a multiuser networked environment distributed around the world. In this world, individuals, whether reader or storyteller, are linked in a communication environment somewhat analogous to a three-dimensional spider web. Communication flows in an *n*-directional space. Digital information takes on a highly fluid form, and communication undergoes an almost continual evolution. Some even contend that in this digital publishing environment, there is no longer a defined moment when a communication product exists in its final form. In this sense, digital communication comes alive in a continual dialogue.

Some have now dubbed the latest generation of hypertext as hyperfiction. "Hyperfiction is a new narrative art form, readable only on the computer, and made possible by the developing technology of hypertext and hypermedia," writes Robert Coover.[2] Hyperfiction has evolved from these notions to open new worlds of interactivity and create a new fiction art form. The *New York Times Book Review* has included reviews of at least a dozen hyperfiction books, including Stuart Moulthrop's *Victory Garden* and Judy Mallow's *Its Name was Penelope*, suggesting we have seen "only the beginning: Watch out!"[3] An even more unusual offering in the realm of hyperfiction art is *Myst*, a surrealistic video game published on CD-ROM. Players of *Myst* enter a dreamlike landscape where sights, sounds, and narrative guide them through a compelling adventure without any clear rules, goals, or outcome other than exploration and experience.

DESIGNING THE ELECTRONIC PRODUCT

New media executives are daily confronted by the dilemma of designing a multimedia product that will both take advantage of the capabilities of new technology yet at the same time be familiar enough to allow audience members easy access. This is not a simple task, as the increasingly long list of new media failures attests. Nevertheless, there are important principles and lessons to be learned from experience and research. Roger Fidler, director of the Knight-Ridder Information Design Laboratory in Boulder, Colorado, has been a new media pioneer since the days of Viewtron, the ill-fated Knight-Ridder videotex trial of the early 1980s. As he heads into the brave new world of multimedia, he offers this advice to newspaper barons of the digital age: "Only those newspapers that can blend credible, high-quality information with compelling, interactive presentations will have an opportunity to live long and prosper," says Fidler.[4] Although Fidler's words are targeted at newspaper publishers, the principles are really much broader and apply equally well to any new media entrepreneur. Quality content, compelling multimedia presentations, and full interactivity are three keys to the successful design of new media product.

Defining the Rules

One of the greatest debates in the field of electronic publishing revolves around the issue of editorial quality. "So much of what's being produced today is what we call 'shovel-ware,'" says Bruce Page, president of Magnetic Press, a small firm in Soho, New York.[5] "Shovel-ware" refers to electronic products that are nothing more than their paper products converted to electronic form, especially text-only products, notes Mark Thalhimer, director of the News of the Future project for the Radio and Television News Directors Association.[6] For example, when *Time* magazine produced its *Desert Storm* CD-ROM only months after the end of the war in the Persian Gulf, it simply poured in everything it had, including not just stories from the magazine, but correspondents' files, some audio clips, and some still images, into CD-ROM format. Beyond its novelty and potential as a research tool, this example of shovel-ware produced little consumer interest.

Linear and Nonlinear Editing and Scripting Models

As media companies and other creative entrepreneurs have attempted to design new media products, one important unsettled issue they have confronted is how to conceptualize the process of creating content for a new medium. Much as Hollywood entrepreneurs of the early part of the twentieth century developed new models for producing motion pictures, new media visionaries must invent their own creative systems for designing multimedia and online products.

As expected, some of the earliest creative approaches borrow heavily from existing media. In the multimedia realm, much has been borrowed from the world of television and film production. At Warner New Media a hybrid approach has been developed, incorporating elements from motion picture and documentary production, musical recording, and weekly magazine journalism. In this approach, multimedia production teams operate under the leadership of a director, who has responsibility for the overall project vision and execution, and producers, who are responsible for product quality and cost control.

Seven Days in August

Illustrative of the above is one of Warner New Media's most interesting early efforts to create an interactive documentary titled, *Seven Days in August*, examining the week in 1961 when the Berlin Wall was constructed. The multimedia product combines news footage from 1961, additional historical data and information, eyewitness accounts, original video, including interviews with survivors from the week of crisis, a game set in the Cold War climate of August 1961, a look at life in the Wisconsin town of Berlin, the residents of which actually changed the pronunciation of the town's name to put the accent on the first syllable so it would not sound as much like Berlin, Germany, and images and sounds from popular culture of 1961, such as hit songs like "The Lion Sleeps Tonight." Created on a platform combining both CD-ROM and laserdisc, *Seven Days in August* was produced by a team consisting of magazine journalists and producers in Time Warner headquarters at Rockefeller Center in New York and a Hollywood creative team at Warner New Media offices in Burbank, California. Originally titled *The Berlin Wall,* the title was changed to *Seven Days in August* both to avoid potential confusion with the falling of the Berlin Wall and to better reflect the weekly concept underlying *Time* magazine.

Early efforts to create multimedia, or hypermedia, products were often based on the encyclopedia model, as well. Products like Grolier's CD-ROM *Encyclopedia,* Microsoft's *Encarta,* or IBM's *Columbus Encounter* are good examples of this process and the nature of works derived from a combination of the encyclopedia and film models. The encyclopedia model emphasizes a structured approach to information, providing easy user access to concepts and ideas, supported by detailed information and data provided by subject experts and supplemented by images. Multimedia products derived from this model add motion video and sound and may add interactivity by providing greater search engines such as Boolean search procedures, as well as feedback from an expert system, a note-taking feature, and even a system to allow the user to create her or his own multimedia products based on the original software. An excellent example of this type of product is the series of multimedia offerings from ABC Interactive, launched with *The '88 Vote,* and including educational products ranging from *The Holyland* to *Martin Luther King, Jr.* These videodisc offerings combine historical data with news footage from the ABC News archives, allowing the user, typically a high school student, to search for information as they would in an encyclopedia, according to topics, key people and events, or chronologically. Users can call up video or audio and get feedback and analysis from the laserdisc. Ultimately, student users can create their own documentaries by editing video and audio to tell their own stories based on the video contained on the laserdisc.

From Silver Screen to Silver Disc

Like the videocassette a decade earlier, CD-ROM technologies are beginning to transform Hollywood.[7] Filmmakers are looking to the optical medium as a new vehicle for reaching the increasingly fragmented viewing audience. Hollywood's high-tech guru, George Lucas, has already pioneered CD-ROM applications in moving image software. One of the most popular CD-ROM titles on the market in 1994 is LucasArts's *Rebel Assault*, a CD-ROM game that has sold 400,000 copies since its market introduction in 1993. Movie director Dwight Little has created a CD adventure game for Sega called *Ground Zero Texas*. "Hollywood and Silicon Valley are about to get into bed together because of this technology," quips Mark Waldrep of Pacific Coast Sound Works in West Hollywood, and a specialist in audio tracks for multimedia products.[8]

When he helped create the *Star Wars* trilogy, George Lucas transformed the Hollywood moviemaking process, bringing about a special-effects renaissance. The Lucas companies, including Industrial Light and Magic (ILM), LucasArts Entertainment Company, and LucasFilm, Ltd., have ushered in the digital age of special effects, and in the process have won numerous Academy Awards for their technical brilliance.[9] Beyond introducing high-tech special effects in film, Lucas has changed the nature of the relationship between film and other media. His companies produced the first link between a home video game and a film (*Indiana Jones and the Temple of Doom*) and the first game with fully interactive music (LOOM). In many ways, Lucas has become the Walt Disney of the digital age. If his high-tech movie wizardry does not convince you of Lucas's ability to create compelling fantasy, a visit to his production facilities near San Francisco certainly will. On arrival at the Industrial Light and Magic (ILM) facilities, all one sees is a quaint Victorian home and a plush green yard. Closer inspection, however, reveals that the house is merely a front end for the super high-tech facilities housed in the immense state-of-the-art underground complex where Lucas and his technical staff work their movie magic.[10] The digital creative process is so meticulous at Lucas Arts that one studio technician admits that a single second of audio from a movie sound track might require an entire day of digital processing, selecting each microscopic snippet of sound one at a time from a digital pallet. Digitally processing images takes even greater care. ILM is not alone in this arduous process of digital editing. As part of a test, a Sony HDTV production facility at the Kaufman-Astoria Studio in Queens, New York, spent three years creating about three minutes of computer-generated animation of dinosaurs walking through a primeval forest.

Clearly, the process of linking film and interactive multimedia is a slow and painful process, fraught with many technical and cultural difficulties. "Ultimately, the problem with video is that it's simply not very interactive," says Randy Komisar, president and chief executive officer of LucasArts.[11] "We watch movies and we play games. And therein lies the obvious crux of the difference between film and interactive entertainment today." Lucas agrees but does see market promise in the development of networked, interactive entertainment. "I think ultimately the home-delivered, so-called information superhighway and black box will be the big player, but I think that's quite a few years down the road," Lucas says. "I think once the technology is in place, it's really going to open up into a very big picture."

The New Creative Process

Many in Hollywood are enthralled by the opportunities presented by new media applications. But at the same time, most are frightened by the undefined nature of the creative process in creating interactive multimedia products. Some are already proclaiming interactive development "the new hell."[12] In the past, Hollywood's development system for moviemaking featured a predictable scenario, with pitch meetings, story conferences, talent deals, and uniform 120-page scripts. Any departure from this model was a major test of the system's flexibility. Today, the development of interactive multimedia products and games has produced no generally agreed on production process. Consider the following recent examples from high-tech games under development.

- Road Scholar, an interactive multimedia game produced by Media Vision, features a 1,000 page script, "keeping blurry-eyed executives at that company up many a night."[13]
- Shock Wave, a science fiction title about an alien invasion, under development by Electronic Arts is based on a script in excess of 500 pages.
- Loadstar, a sci-fi title about space truckers, now in production at Rocket Science Game, features a "design document" of more than 500 pages.

These "scripts," or more appropriately "design documents," follow no standard form or length, have no single ending, and cannot be completed until all technical details and problems are worked out. In "Catch-22" fashion, technical directors cannot design scenes that haven't been written, either. Not surprisingly, all this confusion has left Hollywood moguls feeling more than a little anxiety and creative types uncertain about how to break into the business.

"Because it's fairly new, nobody knows exactly how to do this," says Steven Blank, president and CEO for Rocket Science Games.[14] Still, the principle of team design has emerged as perhaps even more important in the creation of interactive multimedia products than in traditional film production. Although in film projects a single screenwriter will typically be hired and work alone for several months to turn out the screenplay, the interactive media project is itself more likely to be interactive. "There's no job that can avoid the technical side of developing a game," notes Doug Barnett, the designer of the hit game, Return to Zork.

With most interactive games being written for the CD-ROM platform, which can store ever-greater amounts of data, text, and video, creators are writing increasing amounts of information for each game. A typical CD-ROM game might include twenty-five minutes of full-motion video integrated into the rest of the computer-generated graphics, extensive dialogue, and hundreds of pages of computer programming. Each part might require different writers and designers, with the complete package combined into a single, massive design document or script. A typical design document might have "elements of a script, elements of a novel, computer elements, mathematical elements, and even financial elements," notes Strauss Zelnick, president and CEO of Crystal Dynamics and former president and chief operating officer at 20th Century Fox.[15] "All of these areas are just as important. We don't just operate from scripts. The execution is terribly important."

Another important difference between creating an interactive game and writing a traditional film script is the importance of narrative structure. In films, the narrative structure is fundamentally important, while in multimedia, place and character are at least as important. "Up to now, the environment has been more important than the narrative," observes Michael Backes, coscreenwriter of Fox's *Rising Sun* and cofounder of Rocket Science Games. "There's no equivalent to that in the movie world. The development process is much more intense in the game world at the beginning."[16] In addition, player's actions also drive story development in interactive games. Choices by the user can lead a story in a variety of directions. "An author's opinion about the choices made in the game is less important," says Backes.[17] "What is more important is making sure that the environment is rich enough." Also unlike most Hollywood movies, interactive multimedia games and adventures lack a predetermined beginning, middle, and end. Rather, they follow a tree-and-branch structure that allows the users, primarily children and young adults, to follow different paths each time they play. "In Silicon Valley they give a story 183 endings," says Peter Black, president of Xiphias, a Los Angeles multimedia software production company.[18]

The Studio System
Still, some Hollywood leaders see parallels between the studio system and the multimedia production process. "We're seeing a funnel develop, like the studios," says Zelnick, "where there are a lot of ideas at the top given some creative development but not that many actually getting greenlit."[19]

In agreement is Robert Kotick, chair and CEO of Activision. "It's just like a movie studio," Kotick says.[20] "We get two or three submissions a day. We have thirty or forty projects in development that would result in about twelve or fifteen projects being made."

Multimedia Design and User Interfaces
One of the hottest pioneers in the creation of multimedia software for the information highway is Trip Hawkins, founder and president of the 3DO Company, a Silicon Valley startup. Dubbed the "guru of interactivity" by *Billboard Magazine,* Hawkins is leading the drive to create interactive television. His just-released system, Interactive Multiplayer, was designed by 3DO and manufactured by Panasonic. It connects to existing television sets and allows the user to enter the realm of interactivity through the use of a joy stick. One of 3DO's earliest interactive TV products is Twisted, a game show spoof. With sophisticated, arcade-quality graphics, 3DO hopes to capture the next generation of TV viewers. "Yet, given the choice, do viewers really want to interact with their entertainment?" asks Trip Gabriel.[21] "Watching, say *Jurassic Park,* wouldn't they prefer to have Steven Spielberg spin the tale of dinosaurs munching on their keepers in an island theme park?"

Some viewers might, but not Mr. Hawkins. "I want to be on the island," says Hawkins. "I want to show that I could have done better than those idiots did. I could have gotten out of that situation."[22]

Graphics and Design

Any sufficiently advanced technology is indistinguishable from magic.
—ARTHUR C. CLARKE[23]

Improving graphics and design has been one of the continuing challenges and struggles in products created for the computer and online world. In the early days of online communications, there was little concern about design, as most applications were text-only, and few of the developers were concerned about typeface, much less graphical design. This was partly a result of the dominance of the IBM platform, which emphasized function over form, and the primary function had been the processing of numbers. With the development of the Macintosh computer and with it a new emphasis on design, all this began to change.[24]

Today, state-of-the-art online design sports a new look and enhanced status. Increasingly, online products are being created by people whose background is in design or at least features expertise in design. Unfortunately, most online products are still constrained by relatively low band width on most telecommunications networks serving the general public requiring most services to rely on transmission rates of 9,600 baud or slower. As a result, complex graphics and high-resolution images and photographs are very slow to draw on most services. Thus, few online commercial services place great emphasis on images and complex graphics, and those that try are often plagued by slow, even lethargic, page creation. This is often a source of frustration for users, who now generally expect the rapid graphics possible when running directly off the hard drive of a 486 computer or a Macintosh Quadra. This slow transmission rate doesn't explain some other aspects of screen design in many online products. Prodigy, for example, uses a sans serif type face (for example, this Helvetica font is a sans serif typeface). Sans serif fonts such as Helvetica may look modern, but they are harder to read than serif typefaces. CompuServe, by contrast, uses a serif typeface. Moreover, most online products are relatively indistinguishable in terms of overall design. Most are reminiscent of a multiple choice test, says leading newspaper designer Roger Fidler, "And I don't want to take a multiple choice test when I come home at the end of the day," Fidler observes.[25] Most services are menu driven, require the reader or user to select from a set of choices laid out on the screen, and follow a tree and branch structure. Fidler, who has designed and redesigned dozens of newspapers around the world, has created an online news product that takes a different approach to design. Rather than requiring the user to take a test, it presents information in a familiar, intuitive format that takes him or her easily through the electronic product. The design is based on principles some three hundred years in the making: principles of newspaper design. Using headlines, layout, and other graphical design features to direct attention, Fidler's *New York Current* prototype is as enjoyable to read as a well-designed newspaper.

Digital Design

Since Johannes Gutenberg's invention of the printing press some five hundred years ago, typography and technology often have been interwoven. Counter to this trend until recently was the work of avant-garde typography artist Neville Brody, a thirty-six-year-old graphics guru whose home base is London. Known for his design of magazines like *The Face, Arena,* and *City Limits,* until 1988 Brody designed every typeface by hand. Then, overcoming his confessed "technophobia," he bought his first Apple Macintosh and became obsessed with its potential.[26] Describing his experience with the Macintosh, Brody says, "People think of computers as if they were replicate brains. But the Mac is more like a saxophone. You don't learn to use it, you begin to play it. You learn a whole technology so that you can improvise."[27] Not only is Brody convinced the Macintosh is an enabling technology, but he believes the digitization of information has fundamentally transformed the graphics arts. To him, digital design has become very fluid. "It's like I'm doing a painting where the paint refuses to dry. I hand it on to someone else, who pushes that paint around. And the process is continuous."

Digital Production: Not a Matter of Choice

The year 1994 saw the first HDTV production of a made-for-TV miniseries in the United States. *World War II: When Lions Roared* was shot using digital HDTV cameras, which not only improved the quality of the visual image, but was necessary to create the complex production. "In this case, shooting high definition was not a matter of choice, but of necessity," says Joseph Sargent, director of the miniseries.[28] The series is about the collaboration of the three Allied leaders, Franklin D. Roosevelt (played by John Lithgow), Winston Churchill (Bob Hoskins), and Joseph Stalin (Michael Caine). Since the leaders spent most of their time in three different parts of the world, the director wanted to show his three actors interacting from those same three locations: Washington, London, and Moscow. Using digital HDTV, the actors were brought together seamlessly, showing Roosevelt moving about the Oval Office in a wheelchair, Churchill issuing orders from his command bunker, and Stalin brooding in the Hall of the People. HDTV allows the cinematographer to blend images together softly, curving edges and smoothing and matching colors in an elegant fashion. "Instead of twelve crayons, you have forty-eight," says John Alonzo, the cinematographer for *World War II*, whose screen credits include *Chinatown*.

Although most are moving cautiously, an increasing number of major Hollywood studios are becoming involved in multimedia production and CD-ROM products in particular. Taking a leading position in the race for multimedia content is Paramount Home Video, which has agreed to distribute a CD-ROM product from an independent Los Angeles computer software publisher. Xiphias has released on CD-ROM the *Mighty Morphin Power Rangers*, a popular interactive multimedia adventure based on the popular Fox television show, which sold more than 113,000 copies in 1994. Unlike many video game products which tend to appeal primarily to teenage boys, the *Mighty Morphin Power Rangers* appeals to a broad cross-section of children. Paramount is bullish on CD-ROMs because, "We think that over time the VCR cassette will give way to the 5-inch disk," says Eric Doctorow, president of Paramount Home Video.[29]

***Reanimator*, Digital Style.**   Digital technology also has the potential to bring the dead to life, or to at least reanimate deceased Hollywood stars.

The first computer-synthesized performances were offered in 1987 when two Swiss scientists created the short film, *Rendezvous à Montréal,* featuring Humphrey Bogart and Marilyn Monroe in a role neither actor could have imagined during life.[30] Not to be confused with H. P. Lovecraft's horror classic, *Reanimator, Rendezvous'* reanimation of Bogie and Marilyn was not very convincing, as the characters blended together in a not-too-seamless style. But in the years since the film's release, the technology of computer animation has advanced significantly. *Jurassic Park* in 1993 is just one example of how far the technology has come. It is now possible to use computer animation to transform raw data into images that look, sound, and act on screen like real, recognizable people—or creatures. In the past, it had been possible to bring dead actors together with their living counterparts by splicing together film footage of each performer or by blending actual footage of each performer using digital image processors. In either case, no actor could be shown doing something he or she had never done on film. Now, however, computer reanimation technology can take original footage, digitize it, and then create completely seamless full-motion video sequences of an actor doing something he or she never actually did. Still, the process of creating synthetic images is very expensive, especially when involving the subtlety of human behavior. "The software exists, but it takes a lot of handwork," says Jim Morris, vice president and general manager of Industrial Light and Magic, the firm that animated the dinosaurs for *Jurassic Park.* Because of the complexity and subtlety of human movement and speech, Morris estimates it would take 10–15 times the work to animate a scene with a human character as it would take with a Tyrannosaurus Rex. Still, the cost of reanimating human actors will decline, and technical ease and speed will increase, and it is just a matter of time till Hollywood may not need live actors at all!

Pacific Data International (PDI). Creating movie magic via digital technology has become the hallmark of one pioneering company called Pacific Data International (PDI). PDI has used state-of-the-art imaging technology to create the special effects for some of the most commercially successful movies ever produced, such as Arnold Schwartzenegger's *Terminator II* and *Heart and Souls.* The process involves digitally scanning the images originally captured on film, processing them digitally by computer, and then transferring them back to film. The digital format means each film image has been reduced to a mathematical series of 1s and 0s. The changes are made at the "atomic" level called the pixel in digital vernacular. A *pixel* refers to a picture element and is the smallest point of light represented on a computer screen. When viewed together, thousands of pixels make up a single image, much as French surrealist Georges Seurat created impressionistic paintings dot by dot.

Altering the Digital Design

Alterations to digital images generally take one of three forms: addition, subtraction, and manipulation (for example, enhancement, merger). Digital addition means adding something to a picture that wasn't originally there, such as a crowd at a baseball stadium. Digital subtraction refers to deleting something from a picture, such as removing someone or something like a cable supporting a character magically "flying." Digital manipulation refers to transforming an image, such as making it lighter or darker, blending two things into one, or distorting one face into another (called a *morph* in the industry vernacular). In *Terminator II,* one memorable scene involved Arnold Schwarzenegger in cyborg form driving a motorcycle atop a wall. When the wall ends abruptly, he lands safely and continues riding along unaffected in the bottom of a drainage ditch. The stunt would have been extremely dangerous without certain safety precautions, so a special pulley and cable system was rigged up to carry Mr. Schwarzenegger and his motorcycle safely from atop the wall to the bottom of the ditch. The pulley and cable, however, were clearly visible on the original film. Then, in came digital image processing to the rescue. After transferring the film to digital format, the cable and pulley were deleted, pixel by pixel, frame by frame. Then, through digital addition, the missing slices of background were filled in where the cable and pulley had been, and a complete scene was created. Finally, when the special effects were complete, the digital images were transferred back to film, and the movie was released for theatrical distribution.

Digital Darkroom

The rise of the digital image has important implications for the practice of photojournalism, where the credibility of the news has eroded considerably since the journalistic heyday of the Watergate era. Since images captured by a digital camera can be easily manipulated and consequently provide no negative to verify the original image, seeing is no longer believing, at least as far of digital cameras are concerned. Moreover, the use of a digital darkroom can erode the credibility of images captured originally on film. Witness the case of a 1994 *Newsweek* cover featuring a sinister looking O.J. Simpson, shortly after his arrest in the slaying of his ex-wife. *Time* ran the same image on its cover, but O.J.'s face was much lighter looking. In the resulting controversy surrounding the contrasting portrayals, *Newsweek* admitted that it had used a digital darkroom to darken O.J.'s face. The public is left wondering whom to trust in the media.

Because digital darkrooms are now available for processing full-motion video, the issues raised above are as relevant to television, multimedia, or any moving-image media as they are for print media such as newspapers and magazines.

New Creative Avenues. Conversely, the digital darkroom has been a boon to the creative side of media support institutions such as advertising and public relations, and other commercial and aesthetic areas of communication, such as entertainment television and film. The digital darkroom has enabled advertising creative directors to produce magazine ads that look completely real, but are totally synthetic or have only a slight connection to any real photographic image. For instance, one advertiser has created a magazine ad campaign for the makers of a gourmet coffee in which full-color images of each coffee flavor are shown together on a single page. The six coffee flavors appear to be resting on an elegant satin cloth. To the viewer, it appears that the six coffees were placed on the cloth and photographed, with text superimposed later to further describe the nature of the product. The reality, however, is somewhat different. Although there are in fact six different coffee flavors, they were never placed together on the satin cloth. In fact, there is no satin cloth. The satin cloth was created synthetically in the digital paintbox, and images of each coffee flavor—photographed separately—are then electronically cut and pasted against the digital satiny-looking cloth background. Similar techniques are used to create alluring images of a variety of products and services and are not limited to inanimate objects. Human models are often photographed in a studio and then placed digitally into an exotic location, such as the Caribbean or the Mediterranean, or a model's face or body might be digitally altered to make it appear even more perfect. All of this is completely invisible and undetectable to the viewer.

These techniques were used in the well-known "Hey, you never know" advertising campaign for the New York State Lotto in 1994.[31] The DDB Needham Worldwide advertising agency used a computer to combine three images: a photograph of a classic chateau at Sceaux, France, featuring an elegant garden and reflecting pool; Frederick W. Vanderbilt's palatial estate on the Hudson River, near Hyde Park, New York; and a picture of a swimmer, which was actually shot indoors in Manhattan. The swimmer, a heavyset middle aged man floating in a rubber inner tube, was inserted electronically into the reflecting pool. Finally, the Vanderbilt estate was inserted into the composite image, and the New York fantasy scene was complete. Desktop video has made this production technique the growing standard in television commercials, as well. Pepsi used such technology to produce its commercial featuring Paula Abdul dancing, singing, and interacting with legendary actor Cary Grant and comedian Groucho Marx.

Digital Effects in the Workplace
Desktop video has rapidly transformed the media work environment, with television stations widely adopting and warmly embracing the tech-

nology. As Table 6-1 reveals, nearly two-thirds of broadcast facilities now have at least one digital editing machine. Desktop computers include Apple Macintosh, IBM PC compatibles, and Amiga, notes Douglas Shear, president of S C Research International, a firm that conducts annual surveys of industry technology trends. Graphics and effects workstations include Silicon Graphics, Dynatech, and Quantel.[32] No longer do video editors rely on the linear editing principles required by analog tape machines that have prevailed throughout the history of taped broadcasting. Nonlinear editing and thinking are presenting an entirely new approach to video production, much as the word processor redefined how words are edited.

BREAKING THE RULES: EROTICA AND PORNOGRAPHY IN CYBERSPACE

Sex is a virus that infects new technology first.
—*GERARD VAN DER LEUN*[33]

Driving much of the early development of new media products has been demand for erotic content and software. The earliest adopters of the VCR were heavy purchasers and renters of adult movies. It was in large part the insatiable demand of this early user group that helped bring down the cost of the VCR and make the VCR affordable to a wider general audience. It also helped open the market to a much wider variety of video products, ranging from feature-length Hollywood films to how-to videos such as *Hometime* house repair.

Similarly, much of the usage of France's successful videotex service, Minitel, has been the so-called blue forums, or adult-oriented discussion groups. "Sometimes the erotic has been a force driving technological innovation; virtually always, from Stone Age sculpture to computer bulletin boards, it has been one of the first uses for a new medium," writes *New York Times'* technology reporter John Tierney.[34]

TABLE 6-1 Adoption of Desktop Video and High-End Workstations at U.S. TV Stations

	1992	1993
Desktop video/ multimedia PCs	29.9%	31.4%
Graphics and effects workstations	63.6%	64.6%

Source: S C Research International; *Video Technology News*, 1994

Since the first days of erotic e-mail more than a decade ago, usage of consumer-oriented online communications in the United States has reflected an insatiable interest in adult-oriented content. Scores of online forums have adult themes. On the Internet, for example, the alt.sex.news groups are "definitely among the higher traffic areas," says Jack Rickard, editor and publisher of *Boardwatch* magazine.[35] Moreover, "the number of electronic pen pals exchanging bawdy bytes is impossible to track," writes technology reporter Suzanne Stefanac.[36] Countless adult-oriented private bulletin boards have also emerged, specializing in erotic chat and graphic exchanges. Event Horizons, the largest of these, brought in $3 million in 1992, with sixty-four chat lines and 35,000 customers internationally. Although the board has family-oriented chat lines, 85 percent of the traffic is in the "restricted-access adult areas."[37] Playboy Enterprises, which recently won a $500,000 copyright infringement lawsuit against Event Horizons for distributing digitized photos that originally appeared in *Playboy* magazine, also is planning to introduce an adult electronic bulletin board.

Moreover, sex has helped transform the very nature of the online communications industry. Says one observer, "As a communications industry, sex has transmogrified itself from the province of a few large companies and individuals into a massive cottage industry."[38] Hundreds of adult bulletin boards now offer a plethora of erotic services, from chat lines to picture file exchanges, and many of them make a tidy profit for their providers. Even mainstream providers such as CompuServe are players. "CompuServe can fill your nights at $12.00 an hour with more fantasies behind the green screen than ever lurked behind the green door," says Van Der Leun.[39] As the Internet expands its capabilities to deliver video, the next development is likely to be "amateur" erotic home videos, which are already the hottest new category in pornography shops.

Many of the commercially successful CD-ROM products are erotic in nature, as well. One of the hottest products is Reactor's *Virtual Valerie,* an adult-oriented game on CD-ROM. "It's a moving target, but it looks like *Virtual Valerie* has captured about 25 percent of the erotic sector, selling about 25,000 a year for a total of 100,000 units," says Chris Andrews, president of Unidisc, publisher of *The CD-ROM Directory 1993.*[40]

Increased interactivity and improved graphics are at the core of these CD-ROMs. "The ability to choose your virtual partners, scenarios, and pace, plus the fact that you can 'converse' with your cybermate, all lend a degree of personal involvement that no XXX movie or magazine can hope to match."[41] *Nightwatch,* Interotica's 1993 release, allows the user to play voyeur at a plush singles resort by way of a bank of security monitors. The company's *Dream Machine* provides even greater interactivity, with an on-screen female guide to help the player choose from among various fantasy portals.

Uncovering a Disney Classic

The award for most unconventional adult multimedia product will undoubtedly go to the creators of an innovative product that doesn't even feature real human actors. The *Who Framed Roger Rabbit* laserdisc, based on the hit movie of the same name released in 1990, appears to feature a brief risqué video segment of a popular cartoon character. Unbeknownst to the Disney studio executives in charge of the product's release, artists or programmers apparently inserted adult-oriented footage of Jessica Rabbit, the voluptuous, animated star of the laserdisc, à la Sharon Stone in *Basic Instinct*. Jessica is riding in an animated cab through Toon Town with real-life Bob Hoskins driving. The taxi careens into a lightpost, and Hoskins and Jessica are thrown from the cab. Jessica, who is wearing her trademark dress slit to the hip, spins around and on her first rotation, her white panties are briefly visible. But on her second spin, Jessica's panties disappear, and Jessica appears to be wearing nothing under her dress.

Legend has it that Disney animators have for years inserted bawdy frames into Disney classics such as *Snow White*, but they were always undetectable to the viewer because of the frame speed of film. But with the advent of the digital age, it is now a simple matter to advance the image one frame at a time and see exactly what is there on each razor-shape picture. One animator suggests, however, that Jessica may not really be bottomless. Mark Kausler, an animator for *Roger Rabbit*, says it is more likely that with the thousands of frames that need to be drawn and painted, it is possible that an animator simply forgot to paint her panties white in those infamous three frames.[42] Nevertheless, the genie is out of the bottle, and the rumor has been reported that Jessica can be seen sans panties. When *Roger* was first released, producer Frank Marshall admitted that a prank frame showed Betty Boop dropping her top, but the film's producers, Steven Spielberg's Amblin Entertainment and Disney airbrushed her breasts for the video and laserdisc release. Michael Fleming, reporting in Variety, the entertainment industry's leading newspaper, writes that the *Roger Rabbit* product also may contain a telephone number for the fictional brothel, Madam Allyson Wonderland; the number is in fact the home number of Michael Eisner, Disney's chairman and CEO.[43] When the public learned of the unexpected product features, sales of the laserdisc became quite brisk at most retail outlets. At this writing, it is unclear whether Disney will eventually pull the disk from retail shelves, but if you happen across an uncensored version of the product, keep it. It will likely be worth a lot of money some day as a rare collector's item in the software hall of fame or shame. In any event, the story has given new meaning to Jessica's classic line, "I'm not bad, I'm just drawn that way."

Improved Graphics

The quality of the graphics have greatly improved since the early days of digital erotica. Enabled by inexpensive scanners and GIF format graphics transmission, users began uploading and downloading low-resolution erotic images on major bulletin boards in the mid-1980s. The advent of QuickTime and other software for image handling has brought the adult software industry to new highs (or lows) in technical quality. An ad for Space Coast Software's *Bare Assets* CD-ROM issues this siren call, "How about a QuickieTime?" *Penthouse Interactive* CD-ROM, soon to be released by ICFX, features state-of-the-art graphics and video. ICFX was founded by president David Biedny, a veteran of the Industrial Light and Magic school of special effects, and executive producer James Ehrlich, formerly with CBS records. The product places the user at a "Penthouse Pet" photo shoot, and lets the player choose the model and select her poses. During video segments, the player can snap still shots for storage or printing. "You are the photographer while three Penthouse Pets cavort and pose in thirty different situations. No question about it—it's astounding," says *Forbes F.Y.I.* Some are not sure this is a good thing. "What will they think of next?" questions Dan Rather, anchor, *CBS Evening News.*[44]

New Content Providers: The Audience

New media technology, especially the intersection of the online world and multimedia computing, are redefining the notion of sources of media content. In the traditional publishing environment, commercial publishers have tended to dominate the creation of media content, whether in the form of books, newspapers, magazines, radio, or television. In the digital environment, traditional content providers will continue to play a role, as will new forms of commercial content providers. But perhaps the greatest amount of content will be created by what is traditionally thought of as the media audience. In online communications, everyone is a content provider as well as an audience member.

JOURNALISTS: AN ENDANGERED SPECIES

Implications of new media technology also present a profound challenge to the future of journalism and communication professions as we know them. In addition to the ability of information consumers to use new information technologies to go directly to information sources, circumventing traditional journalistic sources, journalism itself is being rewritten by new computer software. As a natural outgrowth of advances in artificial intelligence, word processing, grammar, spelling and style-checker software packages, software is now available to actually write news stories. In fact, a growing number of newspapers and other news organizations have purchased such software packages and are using them to write stories for publication. Some have even fired reporters who were made obsolete by the technology. In the areas of sports and financial reporting, many stories are written using basic formulae derived from specific statistical data, such as scores, stock changes, and other routine data.

Software packages are now available that will write stories automatically based on electronic data feeds transmitted directly by various news sources. There is no need for a human, journalistic filter at all. One such software package is called SportsWriter, a program published by Zybrainics Software, Inc., and created by Roger Helms, a forty-two-year-old freelance writer from Rochester, Minnesota. The program grew out of Helms's initial efforts to improve the sports coverage of a weekly newspaper he was considering buying. Using an Apple Macintosh computer, he developed a HyperCard™ stack to train reporters in better newswriting style, but found the approach ineffective. "I decided the only thing my program was good at was making its own decisions," Helms says.[45] And it turned out to be a pretty decent writer, at least for routine sports stories, such as the results of high school basketball and football games. Critics say SportsWriter's biggest drawback is that the stories are dry and full of clichés and lack the perspective only a human observer can provide.[46] The program bases its decisions and writing on input received from the coaches of the games, who are asked by the newspaper to fill out a form requesting various results, such as the score by period and to describe key plays. The coaches phone or fax in the data, and they are entered into the program, which then spits out a story. Consider this sample lead written by SportsWriter: "The Humphrey Bulldogs fell victim to a second-half rally and dropped a close decision to the Leigh Lady Panthers 27–24 in girls basketball at Clarkson in the first round of the Cornhusker Conference Tournament."[47] This lead ran in the *Humphrey Democrat* in Humphrey, Nebraska, one of some eighty small newspapers in the Midwest that have already bought SportsWriter. Dean Backes used to cover high school sports for the *Humphrey Democrat,* but two years ago was replaced by SportsWriter. The decision to replace a reporter with software was an easy one financially. SportsWriter costs $100, while "we were laying out $1,500 a month for the sports reporter," says Donald Zavadil, editor and owner of the 1,800 circulation weekly. These economics apply to other areas of news coverage, as well. Computers at the Bloomberg LP financial news service write hourly stock market reports and foreign-market trends. Computers at Individual, Inc., Cambridge, Massachusetts, sort thousands of wire service, newspaper, and magazine articles and summarize them into customized newsletters faxed daily to three thousand subscribers.[48] In the future, there may be no need for a news organization at all. By merging the notions of direct access media and news writing software, there is no need for a newspaper or other news product. It's perfectly feasible for a news source to provide data directly to the news consumer, who, using a news writing software package, will see a story written based upon the latest sports scores or stock market fluctuations.

What are the implications of this technology for journalism? "It's scary," says Don Skwar, sports editor at the *Boston Globe*.[49] "In forty or fifty years a computer might be sports editor." It may not take that long. Interface agents already have been developed that can act as an information gatekeeper or editor. Some are concerned that computer programmed writing takes out the creative element added by human writers. But others argue that by using software to write routine stories, human writers are free to spend more time writing creative feature and analytical pieces. On a more profound level, the implications of technological applications such as SportsWriter may reflect a fundamental shift in the function of journalism in society. Enshrined in the First Amendment, the press has served a vital role in democratic society as a fourth branch of government. Intelligent applications that automate the journalistic function and begin to link news sources more directly to news consumers may represent the declining role of journalism as filter, or gatekeeper, in interpreting information in society and the rising role of commercial forces in the newsroom.

Online Communications and the Transformation of Journalism

One journalistic practice that has long been taken for granted is whether to let a source preview a story before publication. The answer has always been no, with few exceptions, such as on highly technical stories, such as science or health reporting, where a source might be asked to preview a quote for accuracy. Reporters and their news organizations have had many reasons for not allowing sources to preview stories, such as not wanting to alert a source to a negative story before it is published, avoiding leaking an exclusive to a competing news organization, and general principles about standing by the quality of a reporter's work. One practical reason that has probably played a bigger reason than many in the newsroom would admit is that there hasn't generally been time to let a source preview a story. Reporters working under deadline pressure have enjoyed little opportunity to send a story to a source, let them review it, and then return the edited copy to the reporter. This might work for a monthly magazine, but not for an investigative reporter working on a five o'clock deadline for tomorrow's newspaper. But in today's world of online communications and the ubiquitous fax machine, time delays have little meaning. It takes but a few keystrokes to e-mail a draft of a story or a quotation to a source, and even receive the source's response electronically in a matter of minutes.

Media and technology reporters debated some of these issues at an April 5–6, 1994, Freedom Forum Media Studies Center Technology Studies seminar. The discussion lead to a lively forum on the popular electronic bulletin board service known as The WELL. An edited version of the discussion is reprinted here, courtesy of Tom Valovic, a technology reporter who attended the Freedom Forum seminar and hosted the online discussion on The WELL on April 18–19, 1994.

Excerpts from an Electronic Bulletin Board Discussion

> *Topic 761 [media]: Should Sources Be Allowed to Preview*
> *Copy Via E-mail? Started by: Tom Valovic (tvacorn) on Mon, Apr 18,*
> *'94*
> *202 responses so far*
>
> *<linked topic>*
>
> *This picks up on a thread discussed in topic 737 . . .*
>
> *At a recent seminar at Columbia on how the press has covered the "info superhighway," an interesting question surfaced: should reporters and journalists let a source for and/or subject of an article see (via e-mail of course) prepublication drafts of the story in order to be allowed a chance to make "corrections." . . . Is it something that will ultimately change journalistic standards and practices? If so, positively or negatively? Has it done so already?*
> *For the reporters in the house, have you done it? Do you do it routinely? Why or why not?*
>
> *202 responses total.*
>
> *PR hacks always do it. Don't want to offend the client.*

Reporters should *never* do it. If they are unclear on the technology, they can ask the source questions to clear it up.

Giving the source the whole article just lets them buff it up. And they will. Every time.

I posted about this above. I used to disapprove entirely; now I don't. There are situations in which the reporter is essentially trying to get a complicated set of facts before his readers; there is no controversy, only explanation. (Reporting on the results of astronomical research could be an example). In that case, I see no problem at all.

As the excerpts from this two-day exchange reveal, the online world is as full of rich and varied points of view as the real world. Issues of journalistic practice and their technological influences may not be resolved in a single electronic forum. But, a glimpse inside the process does reveal the popularity of online chat sessions, with more than two hundred responses to a single electronic query. Moreover, even if new technology has not transformed the practice of journalism, it has at least provided a new and effective forum for examining it. One innovative magazine, *Hotwired,* a spinoff from the popular *Wired* magazine, is attempting to create a new style of journalism based on the use of the interactive capabilities of online publishing.[50] Louis Rossetto, *Hotwired's* editor in chief, designed the groundbreaking magazine as a blend of electronic publishing, the interactive capacity of the personal computer, and a style of participatory journalism his editors call "way new journalism." *Hotwired* is available free but requires users to sign up as members and combines short articles on technology and society with a variety of interactive features, such as a textual report on a musical group linked with audio samples and video clips. Rossetto sees his nearest competitor as broadcast and cable television, not conventional print publications.

DIGITAL CONTENT MANUFACTURING

As this chapter suggests, new media technologies have led to a virtual reinvention of the process of manufacturing media content. Nearly all content production is done in a digital environment where nonlinear text, images, and sound are manipulable on a digital palette. The relationship between events and objects observed in the so-called real world and their depiction or re-creation in the digital media is increasingly tenuous and abstract. No longer are content creators constrained by the limits of the so-called real world, if they ever were. In an increasingly interactive, online communication system, "audience members" are rapidly becoming cocreators of media content. Narrative structure is in flux, as hyperfiction and virtual reality become mainstream media products. Has the transformation of the creative process reached its ultimate state? Probably not. Rather, the evolution of new media products and how they are created has only just begun. It is likely that in the next millennium, entirely new forms of media content will emerge, and the process by which they are created will continue to evolve in an unexpected and startling fashion.

NOTES

1. Richard J. Daley, speech, Chicago, IL, 15 October 1993.
2. Robert Coover, *New York Times Book Review*, 29 August 1993.
3. Ibid.
4. Roger Fidler, "Mediamorphosis," in Frederick Williams and John V. Pavlik, eds., *The People's Right to Know: Media, Democracy and the Information Highway*. Hillsdale, NJ: Lawrence Erlbaum Associates, 1994.
5. Bruce Page, meeting, 12 February 1994.
6. Mark Thalhimer, "Online News Services," 'The Race for Content,' *The Media Studies Journal*, Winter 1994.
7. Steve Lohr, "The Silver Disk May Soon Eclipse the Silver Screen," *New York Times*, 1 March 1994.
8. Ibid.: D6.
9. Gary H. Arlen, "LucasArts Charts Digital Path Between Film, Interactivity," *Information & Interactive Services Report*, 11 March 1994:11.
10. Adam Clayton Powell, III, meeting, 6 May 1994.
11. Arlen, op. cit.
12. Andy Marx, "Interactive Development: The New Hell," *Variety*, March 1994:1.
13. Ibid: 78.
14. Ibid.
15. Ibid.
16. Ibid.
17. Ibid.
18. Peter M. Nichols, "Home Video: What Exactly Is 'Multimedia'?" *New York Times*, 1 April 1994:D17.
19. Andy Marx, "Interactive Development: The New Hell," *Variety*, March 1994:78.
20. Ibid.
21. Trip Gabriel, "A Visionary on the Border of Movies and Microchips," *New York Times*, 27 October 1993.
22. Ibid.
23. Arthur C. Clarke, *The Lost Worlds of 2001*. Boston: Gregg Press, 1979.

24. Steven Levy, *Insanely Great: The Life and Times of Macintosh, the Computer that Changed Everything.* New York: Viking, 1994.

25. Fidler, op. cit., 1994.

26. Cynthia Rose, "Neville Brody: How to Be a Graphics Guru," *The International Herald Tribune,* 8 July 1994:24.

27. Ibid.

28. Peter M. Nichols, "Mini-Series Blazes Trail in High-Definition TV," *New York Times,* 19 April 1994:D10.

29. Nichols, Ibid.:D17.

30. Bruce Weber, "Why Marilyn and Bogie Still Need a Lawyer," *New York Times,* 11 March 1994.

31. Deitz, Paula, "All It Takes Is a Computer and Photos," *New York Times,* 31 March 1994.

32. S C Research International, "Professional Video Marketplace," cited in *Video Technology News,* 14 March 1994.

33. Gerard Van Der Leun, "'This Is a Naked Lady,'" *Wired,* Premiere Issue 1993:74.

34. John Tierney, "Porn, the Low-Slung Engine of Progress," *New York Times,* 9 January 1994.

35. Suzanne Stefanac, "Sex and the New Media," *NewMedia,* April 1993:39.

36. Ibid.: 39.

37. Ibid.: 40.

38. Van Der Leun, op. cit.:109.

39. Ibid.

40. Stefanac, op. cit.

41. Ibid.

42. Leonard Maltin, *Entertainment Tonight,* 29 March 1994.

43. Michael Fleming, "Freeze Frame: Who Undressed Jessica Rabbit?" *Variety,* March 14–20, 1994.

44. *Omni,* advertisement, January 1994: 75.

45. William M. Bulkeley, "Semi-Prose, Perhaps, But Sportswriting By Software Is a Hit," *Wall Street Journal,* 29 March 1994:1.

46. Mark Thalhimer, ed., *Media Industry News Roundup,* compiled from the Associated Press, the Freedom Forum Media Studies Center, 24 May 1994.

47. Bulkeley, op. cit.

48. Ibid.

49. Ibid.

50. John Markoff, "A Magazine Seeks to Push the On-Line Envelope," *New York Times,* 31 October 1994:C6.

7

MARKETING ELECTRONIC PUBLICATIONS

TV will become a mere PC peripheral.
—ANDY GROVE[1]

SHOOT FIRST, ASK QUESTIONS LATER

One of the most intractable problems in marketing new media technologies is determining their most likely use in the consumer marketplace. Predicting the successful application of a new media technology may be just as well done using a crystal ball or by reading tea leaves as by any more systematic or scientific technique. History is replete with failed predictions by some of the most noted figures of the past, as well as some more obscure ones. Consider, for example, the case of Thomas Alva Edison, one of America's greatest inventors. In 1877, in his New Jersey laboratory near Princeton, Edison invented the phonograph, using a combination of tinfoil and wax cylinders to record sound. Of the thousand patents for which he is credited, it is the invention he is said to have been most proud of. Edison expected great things from his invention but was completely wrong in the predicted application. He thought the phonograph would be used for recording speeches. Edison never imagined that his invention would give birth to the music recording industry, now a multibillion dollar industry worldwide.

Publishing Multimedia

Perhaps the most well-traveled terrain on the new media landscape is multimedia publishing, with a growing number of companies offering a

221

rapidly expanding set of products for the consumer marketplace. The consumer multimedia market consists of primarily two types of products: packaged products and networked or transmitted products.[2] Packaged products fall into three broad categories based on the type of platform:

- desktop products, largely PCs equipped with CD-ROM drives
- TV-based systems, generally dedicated devices that plug into television sets
- portable, self-contained devices used primarily outside the home

Networked or transmitted products will be examined in the section on online services and products.

Consumer CD-ROM Products

In-home desktop multimedia systems consist primarily of IBM and Macintosh PCs equipped with CD-ROM drives and sound capability. Some systems are based on laserdisc technology, although most products in this area are limited to movies and training. CD-ROM titles fall into three main areas:

- training or education,
- entertainment
- information and databases

Because of the sheer number of new media products—there were more than 7,000 CD-ROM titles alone available in 1994, with more than 1,700 available for the home market—this discussion will focus on products that represent either the cutting edge, tell-tale patterns and trends, or hidden but important issues on the new media frontier. Among the leading CD-ROM titles in the United States are Broderbund's *Myst*, Virgin's *The 7th Guest*, LucasArts's *Star Wars Rebel Assault*, Sierra On-Line's *Kings Quest VI*, Microsoft's *Encarta*, Compton's *Interactive Encyclopedia*, and Activision's *Return to Zork*. Of these titles, all are entertainment game formats, with the exceptions of *Encarta* and Compton's *Interactive Encyclopedia*, which are educational. Another leading educational CD-ROM title is Grolier's *CD-ROM Encyclopedia*, although it is not among the top ten bestsellers.

Video Games and Game Players

Video games are electronic games played on a video game player, arcade machine, or a personal computer. In fact, both video game players and arcade machines are actually specialized computers. Although many think of them as mere toys, video game players are among the most powerful home computing devices in existence, largely because they are designed to process full-motion video and high-quality graphics in real time and, thus, have extremely powerful and fast microprocessors. Because of their low price (generally only a few hundred dollars), videogame players have become more ubiquitous in U.S. households than are personal computers, with some thirty million homes equipped with game players, while only about twenty million homes have PCs. Some envision a future in which the videogame player becomes the principal information superhighway on-ramp of the future, rather than the personal computer or the television set alone. Although some may scoff at this seemingly far-fetched notion, many industry analysts a decade ago doubted the personal computer could ever replace or supplant a mainframe or even midsized computer in business or educational settings, and many skeptics wrote off the Apple Macintosh as a toy.

Nintendo established its early dominance in the video game market with its 8-bit player, which it sold at near cost and that provides superior graphics and color over Atari, taking its profits from software sales. Sega caught Nintendo by surprise in 1989 by introducing a 16-bit player, offering superior game performance. This pattern of "technological leapfrog" has continued through today, with each generation of the technology offering more powerful graphics processing ability to "render realistic computer-generated 3D images in real time."[3] At the same time, video game player technology has offered improved ability to decompress motion video and provide broadcast-quality TV pictures to the viewer.

Sega is now building on its large 16-bit installed base (more than thirteen million in the United States alone) by introducing in 1992 a CD-ROM drive to plug into its existing console. More than one million of the drives have been sold worldwide. Sega has also launched a 149 British pound add-on device that includes 32-bit RISC chips, more RAM, and a video processor. The significance of this addition is that it will enable the upgraded Sega console to play games with 256-plus colors and 3D processing. Called Super 32X in the United States and Mars in the United Kingdom, Sega expects to sell more than 2.5 million units in its first year of release, with less expensive and more powerful systems planned for subsequent years.

Nintendo's Project Reality is designed to leap-frog Sega by offering 64-bit capacity, based on a processing technology developed by Silicon Graphics. Nintendo will stick with the cartridge format rather than the CD, but it has increased its capacity to 12.5 MB, about six times the current cartridge capacity. The cartridge offers faster access time than does a CD-ROM drive and allows Nintendo to maintain proprietary control over the cartridge manufacture.

Another new competitor receiving a great deal of attention in the trade and popular press is the Panasonic 3DO Interactive Multiplayer, featuring a state-of-the-art graphics interface that *Time* magazine says offers "jaw-dropping visuals."[4] With CD-quality sound and a 32-bit processor, the Multiplayer is the most powerful video game system on the market. The system uses a built-in CD-ROM drive, video-compression, and special graphics technology to create full-screen, full-motion video, digitized speech, and flicker-free animation.[5] With backing from AT&T, Time Warner, and MCA, the $399 product (originally offered at $699, a price at which it failed to sell well) was designed by Silicon Valley startup company 3DO.

Video Game Cartridges

The videogame cartridge is the principle product for the TV-based platform. Leading manufacturers are Nintendo and Sega. Among the most popular products are Sega's *Sonic the Hedgehog,* which has sold some fifty million units worldwide, and Acclaim's more-recent *Mortal Kombat,* which has enjoyed sales of more than six million units worldwide, although most sales of all video game products have been in the United States. Notably, contrary to popular opinion, not all leading video games are violent, although most of the very best sellers are. Many of the top video game titles are sports-related, such as *Super Kick Off, FIFA Soccer,* and *PGA Tour Golf 2.*

Placing the PC

Knowing the location of use of any new media technology is one of the most important factors in successfully marketing that technology. Where people use a technology often reveals who will use it, as well as how and when and how often. Most personal computers, including multimedia platforms, are usually found on a desktop in an office or den. TV sets, meanwhile, tend to be in the living room, bedroom, or sometimes in the kitchen. In contrast, most TV-based multimedia platforms are connected to a TV set in a child's bedroom. How these patterns evolve or solidify will determine much of the potential use of multimedia in the home. Moreover, who controls the on-ramp to in-home multimedia will be a critical issue in the decade ahead, with much of the power today resting in the hands of children and youth, especially for TV-based systems, which are generally in the form of video games. Witness the struggle for control of the TV set remote control, which has often pitted man against woman in an electronic battle of the sexes. *Screen Digest* reports that opinion is sharply divided over whether the desktop PC or the TV set will emerge as the principal multimedia device in the home.[6] Although Intel boss Andy Grove predicts, "TV will become a mere PC peripheral," many see a very different pattern emerging, with the TV set remaining dominant but absorbing more intelligence and "smart" processing abilities.[7] Technology reporter John Markoff similarly predicts that future generations will ask, "What's on the PC tonight?" in the same fashion that earlier couch potatoes pondered the evening's television schedule. To a certain degree, both trends are occurring and may coexist well into the future.

Desktop Market

Data for multimedia products are difficult to come by and often inconsistent. Figure 7-1 presents a reasonable estimate of the market given the best available data from TFPL, a leading company in the multimedia market research area. Although initial growth of the desktop market was slow, it took off in 1993 and 1994, and shows no sign of slowing in 1995 and beyond. The in-home market is rapidly reaching what industry analysts describe as a critical mass, the number of machines necessary to make marketing CD-ROM titles on a mass scale profitable. Many have

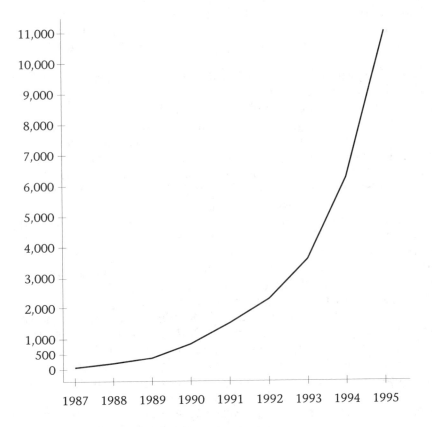

FIGURE 7-1   Number of CD-ROM Titles

Source: TFPL Publishing, Washington, D.C., The CD-ROM Directory, 1995.[8]

suggested the critical mass is approximately seven million multimedia devices. The total installed base reached this number in 1993, both world-wide and in the United States. One market research firm, Dataquest, is more conservative in its estimate, putting the number of in-home multi-media PCs in the United States at just 1.98 million in 1992, 3.6 million in 1993, and 5.6 million in 1995. Elsewhere in the world, growth of the installed multimedia base has been slower, but is reaching a critical mass there as well. Thus, 1995 is expected to be a banner year for CD-ROM software sales.

The market is primarily an American phenomenon, with some 80 percent of all devices located in the United States. In the United States, Inteco estimates that 60 percent of the installed base of multimedia devices are in homes, with the percentage increasing to 75 percent by the end of 1996. This means analysts expect much slower growth in the installed base outside the home, such as in schools and in the workplace. The marketing implication is that sales growth for multimedia products will likely be greatest in the home market, both in the United States and abroad.

Since its invention in 1982, the CD-ROM has emerged as the medium of choice for not just storage of digital information, but as a multimedia delivery and publishing system. CD-ROM publishing has grown so rapidly that it now even boasts its own annual CD-ROM exposition. The worldwide CD-ROM business is large and growing fast (see Figure 7-2) with total worldwide revenues expected to reach $18.1 billion by the end of 1995.[9] In 1992, the number of installed CD-ROM readers was just four million worldwide across all hardware platforms—desktop, TV set-top, and portable. It reached nearly 27 million in 1994, and is expected to reach nearly 50 million by the end of 1995, and more than 400 million by 2000 (Infotech, 1995). With CD-ROM drive prices falling to as low as $199, the installed base will continue to grow. One problem still plagu-ing the burgeoning industry is the continually evolving hardware and software standards, which have limited compatibility between systems, platforms, and discs. Likewise, there has been some debate about how big the industry really is, largely because of the difficulty in pinning down the exact number of titles and discs in circulation. One source, TFPL, pro-jects for 1995 nearly 11,000 CD-ROM titles and 15 million discs (com-mercial and in-house), and a $3 billion commercial CD-ROM publishing industry growing at more than 40 percent annually.[10] About one in five titles is multimedia, which could be text and images and possibly audio and motion video. Dataquest, Inc., an industry analyst headquartered in San Jose, California, estimates that consumer titles (shrink-wrapped and bundled titles) made up about a fifth of the market in 1992 or roughly $600 million. *PC Magazine* estimates more than 4,500 CD-ROM titles

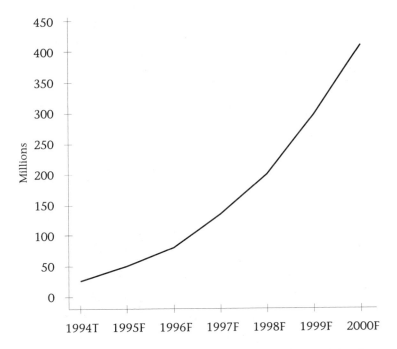

FIGURE 7-2   **Worldwide CD-ROM Installed Base Total Desktop and Set Top**

*T refers to total; F to forecast

Source: InfoTech Optical Publishing Industry Assessment 7th Edition, Woodstock: VT: InfoTech, April 28, 1995

© 1995 InfoTech.

were available as of January 1994.[11] Dataquest estimates that 2.7 million CD-ROM discs were purchased in 1993, up some 450 percent from 1992's total of 700,000 sales. "CD-ROM sales went through the roof this past Christmas (1993)" says one industry consultant, Joanna Tamer, and did so again in 1994.[12] Consumer electronics manufacturers are also convinced that CD-ROM is here to stay. Olaf Olafsson, president of Sony Electronic Publishing, believes CD-ROM has arrived as a mass market product, and Sony Electronic Publishing opened a new CD-ROM manufacturing plant in Eugene, Oregon, in late 1994.[13]

Leading video distributors also see the market potential of CD-ROM. Blockbuster Entertainment recently conducted a test of CD-ROM sales and rentals in its fifty-eight stores in the San Francisco Bay Area. "We don't have a business yet," says Michael van der Kieft, director of business development at Blockbuster, "but we think it will be one."[14]

Similarly, Tower Records will open twelve to eighteen multimedia stores in 1994–1997, reports Russ Solomon, Tower Record's president. MPI of Oak Forest, Illinois, a video distributor specializing in television shows and documentaries, released its first CD-ROM product in March 1994. The title *The Honeymooners' Funniest Moments*, features Jackie Gleason, Art Carney, and Audrey Meadows. The CD-ROM title will compete with some sixty *Honeymooners* videos already on the market. "It's entertainment, and that fits perfectly with us," says Michael van der Kieft.[15] MPI has formed a multimedia division charged with developing CD-ROM projects and has access to both a large video catalogue as well as rights to the WPA Film Library of nearly twenty thousand hours of material ranging from old Pathé newsreels to extensive collections of film on history, music, nature, and many other subjects.

Full-motion video on CD-ROM is played on a computer and appears as a somewhat "herky-jerky" image on a small portion of the screen, although improvements in the technology are likely to increase the image display size to fill the entire screen and to smooth out the image, as well. MPI's *Honeymooners* disc runs on both Macintosh and Windows platforms, displaying the image in a box in the center of the screen, surrounded by text and still images allowing viewers to select the clips they wish to see next.

TV-Based Market

The video-game market is now in its second phase of growth and finally seems here to stay. Introduced by the American firm Atari, the market eventually collapsed in 1985, and most people wrote it off as a fad. However, the unexpected rise of Nintendo and Sega after 1986 has infused the video-game market with new life. Although the video-game marketplace is dominated by Sega and Nintendo, competitors are lining up to challenge their leading position. Commodore's 32-bit CD32, Panasonic's 32-bit 3DO player, and Atari's 64-bit Jaguar are already in the market, and Sony has scheduled for release by the end of 1995 its 32-bit PSX console.[16]

Most analysts expect video games to be one of the first success stories on the information superhighway. Nintendo, Sega, Atari, and Genesis have already captured a large share of the lucrative $7 billion video-game market worldwide.[17] Nintendo holds more than 80 percent of the world's video game market, although Sega is rapidly gaining market share. In 1993, Sega posted earnings of ¥416 billion, up 68 percent from the previous year, compared to Nintendo's ¥635, up 13 percent.[18] Nintendo has an especially strong foothold in its native Japan, where a third of all households have a Nintendo game system and where there are two Nintendo machines for every personal computer sold for home use.

Nintendo machines even outnumber their home computer counterparts in the United States, where there are six million Macintosh computers and twenty million IBM compatibles in U.S. homes compared to thirty million Nintendo game systems. The growth of video game companies is particularly impressive in Japan, where the country is in a recession and consumer electronics companies experienced a 21 percent drop in operating income in 1991. Meanwhile, Nintendo grew by 19 percent that same year and Sega hired executives laid off by other cost-cutting electronics giants.[19]

The Wrong Kong?

The seminal Nintendo game, Donkey Kong, was produced in Japan and subsequently released in the United States in 1980. Ironically, technology had an unintended consequence on this pioneering video game, which introduced to the world Mario, the short, fat, cult figure star of Super Mario Bros. and Super Marioland 2: Six Golden Coins, all produced by Nintendo. Originally titled "Monkey Kong" by its Japanese inventors, the name became Donkey Kong because of a glitch in the fax transmission to New York.[20] After producing all the materials for marketing the game, it was cheaper to simply change the title screen, and the world now knows Donkey Kong.

The Video Game Generation

The users of video games are predominantly society's next generation: the vast majority of video game players are ages twelve through seventeen.[21] Not surprisingly, many youngsters have developed advanced game playing skills. After being thrashed at Pac-Man (a popular video game) by a five-year-old, Patricia Greenfield observed, "as a person socialized into the world of static visual information, I made the unconscious assumption that Pac-Man would not change visual form. Children socialized with television and film are more used to dealing with dynamic visual change."[22]

Some are even suggesting that video game players may do to computing what PCs did to mainframes a decade ago. Many in the early 1980s dismissed the PC, and especially the Macintosh computer, as a "hacker's toy unsuitable for business use—only to watch brash new personal computer makers win the hearts and desktops of Corporate America and a college dropout from Seattle named Bill Gates ascend to the industry summit."[23] The popularity of video game players and their rapidly increasing computing power have transformed them into serious computing contenders in the home and may even present a challenge in the business marketplace when economic efficiency rules the day. Nintendo, Sega, and Sony all plan to introduce next year consumer devices that will outstrip the processing speed and power of even the fastest desktop PCs. Howard Lincoln, president of Nintendo of America, says his company will introduce the Project Reality video game player next year. The player will outperform everything from the Pentium PC to the PowerPC Macintosh with even the fastest Intel and Motorola computer chips and at a much lower cost: the Project Reality player will cost just $250. In addition to offering interactive TV-quality video and audio, the player will serve as a communications device operating over cable TV networks. If these trends continue, the future may belong not to the video generation, but to the video game generation.

CD-I

Another small but potentially important platform is the Philips CD-I player, or compact-disc interactive. CD-I supports a variety of software types, including "edutainment" titles, as well as games. Philips estimates an installed base of some three hundred thousand CD-I players worldwide, and expects to reach more than one million by the end of 1995. Until then, however, developers are likely largely to continue to ignore producing products for the CD-I format.

Portable Market

Led by sales of Nintendo's Game Boy and Sega's Game Gear, the handheld video game market has expanded rapidly since 1989 and now has an installed base in the United States of about twenty million units. Unlike the console market, however, the pace of technological change for portable devices has been much slower and depends largely on the development of low-cost color flat displays.

Electronic Books (EB)

Electronic books represent another major format for portable devices. The market leader is Sony's Data Discman, introduced in 1990 and based on a smaller version of the company's 3-inch CD-ROM disc. In 1991, Sony introduced an upgraded system, CD-ROM XA, with faster access time and sound capability. Competitors in the EB market include Matsushita, Sanyo, and Sharp. Sony has also begun selling portable CD-I players, aimed at the professional market, offering niche applications for specialized fields and at a much higher price.

EB formats are now evolving in important directions, including discs that will no longer need to be encased in a plastic caddy, and will be sold like typical CD-ROMs. This reduces packaging costs and lets users insert discs into conventional CD-ROM drives. These forces may help the market expand beyond the five hundred thousand installed base worldwide.

STRATEGIC CONSIDERATIONS

Although a vast array of ever-changing forces influence the economics of successfully marketing multimedia products, several factors emerge as essential in any strategic plan.[24] Among them are:

- a substantial installed base of the selected platform(s) that defines the market potential for any new product
- production costs, as defined by the value of the intellectual property at stake, the choice of platform, size and talents of production team, software complexity, and necessary development time
- strength of competing companies offering comparable multimedia products
- availability of finance for production, comparable to that for film and television
- pricing structure for the product and development of revenue stream (*Screen Digest* defines this as the proportion of the price per unit returned to the developer or publisher.)

Choosing the right platform depends largely on the nature of the software. Electronic books on CD-ROM lend themselves naturally to reference or encyclopedic material, while state-of-the-art games may require high-powered console platforms. Companies increasingly maximize market potential by releasing products designed for multiple platforms, although *Screen Digest* estimates that engineering costs may add 40 percent to the production budget.

Pricing

Estimating prices and possible returns on multimedia products is still hazardous terrain, since the business itself is unstable and small variations in any of the key variables can greatly affect outcomes. *Screen Digest* provides several examples to help outline some typical cases.[25]

Electronic Books (EB)

Sony and its affiliate companies Columbia/Tri-Star and Sony Electronic Publishing dominate the EB market, especially outside Japan.[26] Sony offers attractive pre-sales agreements to developers to help support the EB platform and take most of the risk out of EB publishing. Typically, Sony agrees to purchase a guaranteed minimum of 2,000–3,000 units and pay approximately 50 percent of the retail price to the developer or publisher, collecting only a marginal distribution fee for itself. With an average EB title priced at $40, the return might be $13 per unit sold.

As this scenario suggests, the EB publishing market is at present potentially highly profitable and with little risk. The necessary investment capital is relatively low, as well. *Screen Digest* reports that an acceptable quality disc can be produced for $5,000–$35,000, although some developers have spent up to $100,000. Moreover, even an expensive title can return a profit on sales of less than 2 percent (ten thousand) of the installed base of five hundred thousand. An average EB title might sell five thousand units in a year.

CD-I

Philips Media dominates the CD-I market, and obtaining a contract from Philips is a key factor in successfully marketing a CD-I title. Philips has identified more than a dozen ways it can participate in product development, from production financing to finished title distribution. As the example presented below suggests, the return on CD-I titles is attractive, but not as strong as for EB products. Sales per CD-I player are high, however, with *Screen Digest* reporting an average of ten titles per player.

CD-I Price/Return Formula:
Return = (Price – Retail Margin) – Distributor Margin – (Royalty)
Where:
Price = $45
Retail Margin (40 percent) = $17
Distributor Margin (55 percent) = $14.85
Royalty to underlying rights holder (10 percent of wholesale price) = $2.70
Or,
$10.45 = $45 – $17 – $14.85 – $2.70

Breakeven is about ten thousand units for products produced inexpensively, while high-end products may require sales of one hundred thousand.[27] Best-selling CD-I titles that have shipped more than one hundred thousand units include *ABC Sports Presents: The Palm Springs Open,* Compton's *Interactive Encyclopedia,* and CapDisc's *Battleship.* Other titles have not performed as well, such as CapDisc's *Amparo Museum,* which has sold about five thousand titles. Two-thirds of the CD-I sales are game titles (65 percent), with children's titles accounting for another 20 percent of sales and the remaining 15 percent including a range of products.

CD-ROM

The CD-ROM market involves many more players and distributors and is, as a result, harder to define. Heightened competition means deals can be struck, but effective sales may depend on a much more complex distribution arrangement. The installed base is much larger for CD-ROM products, and retail sales averaged ten thousand to fifteen thousand in 1993, with a hit reaching sales of more than thirty thousand. *Screen Digest* predicts average sales will increase to some fifteen thousand units in 1994, with hits reaching fifty thousand in unit sales. Microsoft reports that its *Encarta* is now returning a profit after selling more than three hundred thousand units of *Encarta* worldwide at retail as of May 1994 and selling at a rate of eighty thousand units a month. Worldwide, Grolier's *CD-ROM Encyclopedia* has sold more than one million units, primarily since the beginning of 1993. Production costs are similar to CD-I, with developers spending $500,000 to $1,000,000 on average (for example, MGM-UA's *Blown Away* CD-ROM cost about $900,000 to develop).[28] Typical returns are analyzed in the formula below.

CD-ROM Price/Return Formula:
Return = Price – (Retail Margin) – (Distributor Margin) – (Royalty) – (Pressing Costs)
Where:
Price = $50
Retail Margin (40 percent) = $20
Distributor Margin (50 percent) = $15
Royalty to underlying rights holder (10 percent of wholesale price) = $3
Pressing Costs = $2
Or,
$10 = $50 – $20 – $15 – $3 – $2

3DO has a pricing structure similar to that of CD-ROM, except that because the platform is entirely controlled by the 3DO company, an additional $3 royalty is payable to 3DO, reducing the return to $7 per unit sold. Production costs are similar for 3DO products, with one developer, Crystal Dynamics, spending about $500,000 on each 3DO title.

Increasingly, developers are looking toward more sure-fire product development strategies, such as licensing rights to a story or character with a ready-made following, rather than creating an entirely new story and audience. Examples include the *Mighty Morphin' Power Rangers* CD-ROM from Xiphias and a title based on the children's book *Where's Waldo* under development by Warner Music Group.

Video Game Cartridge

Compared to the other multimedia formats, the video game cartridge platform presents considerably tighter profit margins, largely because market leaders Nintendo and Sega control the publishing of games for their proprietary systems. Third-party developers must submit to

Nintendo or Sega all game proposals for advance approval and release date guidance. Moreover, Nintendo and Sega carry out manufacturing for a royalty payment, as well as distribution in most cases, with a royalty on sales paid to the developer. Inventory risk is also high, since both manufacturers require minimum initial orders of ten thousand to twenty thousand units, and Nintendo requires a letter of credit or full payment prior to manufacture. Because of the tighter margins in this field, many developers have turned increasingly to other platforms, where returns are higher. Of course, the installed base for video game players is much greater, and sales potential is thus much higher. Sega, for example, has sold more than five million units of *Sonic the Hedgehog,* generating more than $225 million in revenues on a production budget of less than $1 million. Acclaim's popular *Mortal Kombat* reached six million unit sales on the 16-bit platform, backed by a $10 million marketing campaign, and has generated more than $150 million in revenues. Sales per player have dropped off, however, from a high of seven units per player in 1989 to about 2 per player in 1994. The average title for the 16-bit platform is selling about twenty thousand yearly in Europe, with a hot title reaching sixty thousand sales. A pricing model is presented below.

Video Game Cartridge Price/Return Formula:

Return = Price – (Retail Margin) – (Distributor Margin) – (Royalty) – (Manufacturing Costs)
Where:
Price = $50 (pounds)
Retail Margin (20 percent) = $10
Distributor Margin (50 percent) = $20
Royalty to underlying rights holder (10 percent of wholesale price) = $4
Manufacturing Costs = $8
Or,
$8 = $50 – $10 – $20 – $4 – $8

Pricing New Information Services

Pricing new information services is one of the great unknowns of electronic publishing. Because the product does not yet exist and there may be no market to use as a reference point, pricing is often a guessing game. Sometimes prices are based on estimates derived from consumer responses in field trials. Similarly, estimates for some digital services, such as movies on demand, have been derived from the established price for comparable analog service, such as videocassette rentals. In some instances, introductory prices have been set low relative to the cost of the service in order to facilitate initial demand, with prices subsequently increased. This strategy has backfired on occasion, producing consumer resentment. In the case of cable television rates, the consumer backlash to price increases was so great that it produced reregulation of cable TV prices. It may even be accounting for the strong sales of DBS receiver dishes in 1994.

Online Services
Pricing for online services has presented a special case to the new media industry. In the early 1980s, many videotext services were priced too high and produced few adopters. Many of the next generation of consumer online services in the 1990s were priced much lower, such as Prodigy or CompuServe, which have attracted much greater subscriber bases. Unfortunately, although the low subscription prices have generated large numbers of subscribers, they have not produced enough revenue. Accompanied by somewhat limited advertising support, the financial well-being of some of the commercial online services is in some doubt. Prodigy, a joint IBM-Sears effort, has lost millions of dollars in its several years of operation.

In the nonconsumer commercial online services, pricing has been designed somewhat differently. Because users have tended to be corporate organizations, services such as Dialog or Reed Elsevier, which markets the Nexis/Lexis service, prices have been much higher. Dialog has recently introduced a new approach to pricing based on the number of people in a corporation who are authorized to read documents downloaded from the computerized database service Dialog Information Systems.[29] Using a formula of "multipliers," it will be cheaper for a Dialog client to allow many of its users to share computer access to a single electronic document than to make multiple copies and distribute them electronically to each user. Table 7-1 outlines the new Dialog pricing structure.

Finding the Real in Virtual Reality
Separating the fact from fiction is always a challenge in new technology, and it is especially so for virtual reality (VR). Hollywood depictions of metallic bodies having cybersex in Stephen King's *Lawnmower Man,* or virtual vacations like the one Arnold Schwarzenegger took to Mars in *Total Recall* are a far cry from the capabilities of virtual reality today. "Some of that stuff might be possible in 50 to 100 years," says Harvey Newquist, CEO of the Relayer Group. Today's VR graphics are slow and look cartoonish. Moreover, VR technology is expensive. W Industries of Leicester, England, produces and markets VR games to arcades in seventeen countries. It has sold ninety of its $55,000 Virtuality machines in the United States, mostly to sports bars and arcades. World Entertainment of

TABLE 7-1   Dialog Pricing Structure

Archival storage

Price	Multiplier	Total	Number of people authorized to read a single copy of document
$2	3	$ 6	up to 25
$2	6	$12	26–200
$2	10	$20	201–500

Redistribution rights

Price	Multiplier	Total	Number of additional authorized copies of document
$2	1	$ 2	2
$2	3	$ 6	3–15
$2	4	$ 8	16–50
$2	5	$10	51–99
$2	6	$12	100–200
$2	10	$20	201–500

Sources: Dialog Information Systems; the *New York Times*.

Chicago is a competitor, with machines in the United States and Japan. Sega announced a $200 display helmet for delivery in 1994 but has experienced a number of delays and promises to be little more than a "novel projection system for standard video games."[30] It is rumored that one of the reasons for the delay has to do with health concerns. Sony, which manufactures an important chip in the helmet, is concerned about preliminary data that show a link between wearing the helmet and eye strain. As a result, Sony has delayed delivery of the chip to Sega.

Virtual Markets.   A report by Find/SVP of New York and the Relayer Group of Scottsdale, Arizona, says the virtual reality industry is on the brink of rapid growth, estimating that the virtual reality market could reach $575 million by 1999 (see Table 7-2).[31] Nevertheless, sales of the data glove for 1991 were a disappointing $5 million, the report says. The report also predicts sales of entertainment and training/simulation VR products will reach $150 million by the end of the decade. The surprising growth area for virtual reality products will be information services, which the report expects to grow from $0 sales in 1991 to $10 million by the end of 1993 and $75 million by the end of the decade.

TABLE 7-2 **Estimated and Projected Sales (in millions of dollars) of Virtual Reality Products by Application, 1991–1999**

VR application	1991	1993	1995	1997	1999
Training and simulation	$1.5	$7.5	$15.0	$60.0	$150.0
Entertainment	1.5	7.5	15.0	60.0	150.0
Scientific visualization	1.0	5.0	10.0	40.0	100.0
Communication	0.5	2.5	5.0	20.0	50.0
CAD and modeling	0.5	2.5	5.0	20.0	50.0
Information	0.0	10.0	35.0	55.0	75.0

Hollywood Delivered Digitally

One optical fiber application with potentially profound implications for both American culture and industry is the digital delivery of movies directly from Hollywood studios to movie theaters. In March of 1994, Pacific Bell announced the first test of technology for delivering in digital format movies, high-definition video, and live events directly from Hollywood studios or other locations to movie theaters.[32] The technology, which will send compressed video over high-speed fiber optic networks, has been developed jointly with Alcatel Network Systems, providers of video transmission and switching equipment. This new delivery system could produce a significant shift in theater revenue trends that began with the mass introduction of an earlier technology, the videocassette, in the 1980s. In 1980, the vast majority of Hollywood revenues, nearly 80 percent, came from theatrical film releases. Only a few percent of Hollywood's total revenues came from videocassette sales and rentals. By 1987, total revenue derived from videocassette sales and rentals of Hollywood movies had surpassed the total revenues from theatrical release of those movies, and the gap in revenues has only widened since then.[33] The digital transmission of Hollywood productions directly to movie theaters by optical fiber might give theaters a significant advantage over videocassette sales and rentals by providing instant access to digitally perfect video products on a first-run basis. As a result, revenues for theatrical releases could begin to climb again, possibly reversing a decade-long slide.

Digital Video/Audio via Fiber. An alternative type of network service is being promoted by Pacific Bell, one of the Regional Bell Operating Companies. Pac Bell, as it is known locally, is offering TV stations and post-production houses a new digital video and audio delivery service over its fiber optic lines. The Advanced Broadcast Video Service received its first real-time test during Superbowl XXVII in January 1993 and was rolled out to the general market in December of that year. The site-to-site transmission system is offered as a competitive alternative to satellite video transmission. "One key advantage over satellites is that it is digital, while satellites are still largely analog," says Rich Mizer, Pacific Bell product engineer for ABVS.[34] Because it is delivered via fiber, ABVS is also impervious to piracy and weather disturbances. The service costs $850 a month, or $212.50 a day. It may save many times over that in distribution costs.

Maintaining the Film "Look."   An important part of the debate about digital movie delivery revolves around the issue of the film "look" or aesthetic, as opposed to video. Many film auteurs and critics argue that 35 mm film has intrinsic qualities that set it apart as an art form from video, including high-definition television. They point out that video, even high-definition television, has lower resolution than 35 mm film. Moreover, video has a different texture than film, somewhat harsher and flatter in appearance. As a result, many in the film industry frown on the notion that film products could be shown on any medium other than film.

However valid this argument, there is a major problem. What most people see in the average movie theater in America, or anywhere else in the world, does not even come close to what is the potential of 35 mm film. The process of making film dubs or copies for distribution, the variability of film projectors, dust in the air or on the projector lens, imperfections in film screens, and other shortcomings of most movie theaters significantly degrade the theatrical movie-watching experience. One study commissioned by CBS television has shown that the actual resolution obtained in even the best movie theaters is only 1,000 lines of resolution, only half the potential of HDTV.[35] Moreover, many Hollywood movies, although shot on 35 mm film, are transferred to digital video format for special effects processing, and then transferred back to film for theatrical release. Thus, any inherent qualities of film stock have been eroded by the transference to video in many existing Hollywood movies. To most viewers, however, the subtleties of film stock are not apparent, at least in most movie theaters. Thus, the new technology for delivering digital movies directly to movie theaters holds much promise. Still, it remains to be seen whether the compression technology developed by Alcatel and Pacific Bell for the delivery test will produce moving-image picture quality comparable to that of physically distributed 35 mm film. Nevertheless, Michael Fitzpatrick, executive vice president of Pacific Bell, remains optimistic. "The current method of copying and shipping movies to theaters is outdated," Fitzpatrick declares.[36] "The imminent shift from 35 mm film to the delivery of movies in digital form is as momentous as the change from black and white to color." This may be overstating the case, but the point is valid.

It is unclear whether electronic delivery of movies to theaters will have any effect on the price the consumer pays to see those movies. In New York City, for example, where consumers now pay $8 a ticket to see a movie at Loew's Theaters, it is unlikely that even electronically delivered movies, though more efficiently delivered than those on 35 mm film, would bring about a lower cost. It is likely, however, that such a distribution system, by increasing efficiency and possibly reducing piracy, would increase profits for movie distributors.

International Distribution

The global information grid has profound implications for news and entertainment programming. Rupert Murdoch, whose media empire encompasses News Corp, BSkyB, the Fox Network, and a controlling interest in the Hong Kong–based StarTV satellite network, bases his programming decisions on how those programs will fare not just domestically, but in the international market. An example, Adam Powell notes, is the television show *Studs,* created in the early 1990s for Murdoch's Fox Network. "Murdoch isn't making *Studs* anymore, even though it was successful in the U.S. market," Powell explains, "because it doesn't travel well. You can't show *Studs* in India."[37] A spin-off from *The Dating Game,* *Studs* featured single young women competing for dates with eligible bachelors equipped with high volumes of testosterone.

Although it is not unique to the international arena, one important issue that is especially apparent in developing societies is data quality. Regardless of technological advances and sophistication, the information superhighway is only valuable if the information it carries is reliable. As Oxford's Anthony Smith observes, the credibility of any nation-state, or any institution or individual, rests on the accuracy of the information it produces.[38] If information cannot be trusted, it loses all value.

ADOPTERS OF NEW TECHNOLOGY: WHAT RESEARCH TELLS US

Although uncertainty abounds in the new technology marketplace, recent research does tell us some interesting things about how new media technologies enter U.S. households. Many lessons come from the past, both its technological successes and failures. Some of the most revealing

research in this area has been conducted by telecommunications authority John Carey, director of Greystone Communications.[39] Figure 7-3
shows the relationship between price and consumer purchases of new
technologies. But rather than looking at simple dollar amounts, Carey
has translated the price of each technology into the number of weeks of
average income. This is a means of standardizing the price of each technology and facilitating comparisons across time and technology. The
final number in each column represents the point at which each technology entered at least 50 percent of U.S. households.

The data reveal several interesting trends in the adoption of new technology. First, they show that the price of each new media technology has
fallen dramatically over time, and with that drop, each technology has
been adopted by a widening group of households. Second, for radio,
black-and-white and color television, 50 percent adoption was reached

Year	Radio set	Black-and-white TV	Color TV	VCR	CD player
1929	1.8*				
1947		5.3			
1950		3.3			
1955		1.8*	6.6		
1960			4.1		
1965			3.1		
1970			1.9*		
1975				6.2	
1980				3.3	
1983				1.4	1.8
1985				1.1	.7
1987				.8	.4
1989				.7*	.4
1992					.3
1993					.2
1994					.8*

*Year product entered 50 percent of U.S. households.
Source: John Carey, U.S. Department of Commerce.

FIGURE 7-3   **Price of Selected Electronic Products in Terms of
Weekly Household Income—Number of Weeks'
Income to Pay for Product**

when the cost of the technology was slightly less than two weeks' income. For more recent technologies, however, the price has had to drop even further for penetration to reach 50 percent. The VCR's price had to reach less than one week's income and the CD player less than one-half week's. This pattern suggests that it is becoming harder to introduce new media technologies in the United States. The U.S. household is becoming saturated with media technologies.

Table 7-3 confirms this conclusion. These data show that a variety of media technologies have entered the vast majority of U.S. households, including the television, telephone, remote control, and VCR, with several others reaching about half of all U.S. households, such as basic cable television, the telephone answering machine, and the compact disk player. Other data Carey has compiled further show that many households have multiple units of a variety of these technologies. For example, nearly three-quarters (73 percent) of households with telephone service have at least two phones, with more than a third (38 percent) having at least three phones. An increasing number have two or more lines. Similarly, two-thirds (65 percent) of U.S. households have two or more television sets.

TABLE 7-3   Penetration of New Media Technologies—Percentage of U.S. Households with Technology or Service, January 1993

Television	98%
Telephone service	95%
Remote control	90%
VCR	91%
Basic cable	63%
Answering machine	55%
Stereo TV	44%
Compact disk player	43%
Video game player	43%
Home computer	37%
Camcorder	21%
Projection TV	9%
Satellite dish	4%
Videotex	4%
Home fax	4%
Laserdisc player	1%

Source: John Carey, Electronic Industry Association; A. C. Neilsen.

Business Users and Technophiles

Carey also points out that historically the adoption of new technology tends to go through several stages, almost in a stair-step fashion.[40] The first step, which must be taken before adoption will proceed, is generally taken by business users. Business users typically have greater resources to pay the high initial price of the technology and can often justify the cost in terms of their expected return on investment and capitalization.

As adoption begins to move into the consumer realm, the second step involves those heavy technology users aptly called technophiles. One *New Yorker* cartoon depicts a typical technophile who enters a consumer electronics store and tells the clerk. "All my gadgets are old. What new gadgets do you have?" Susan Mitchell of *American Demographics* magazine describes the difference between technophiles and technophobes in these words:

> *Your personal communicator beeps to alert you to an incoming message. Its palm-sized screen tells you that your "smart home" needs instructions. You tell your portable computer to dial your home-control center, which relays an image of the problem. You left the rice cooking. Inserting your hand into a virtual reality glove, you control the movements of a home robot to turn off the stovetop.*
>
> *When you read the above, do you: (a) abstractly ponder what it would be like to live in such a world; (b) jump up from your chair and begin making animated hand gestures while screaming, "Yeah, yeah! That's great"; or (c) feel the need to lie down? If you answered (a), you're a regular Jane or Joe. If you answered (b) or (c), you are probably a technophile or a technophobe.*
>
> —SUSAN MITCHELL[41]

It is also worth noting that many new technologies may never reach the mass market stage but may find a profitable niche market instead. This has proven to be the case with videotex and teletext. Some 20 percent of farmers in Iowa, for example, now subscribe to a Ku-band satellite agricultural teletext service providing weather, market information, agricultural news, and other information.

Generational, Gender, and Socioeconomic Issues

Although men have tended to dominate the world of new media technology, one exception to this trend is *The Women's Forum*, set up by *U.S. News and World Report* as part of that magazine's online service. Kathy Bushkin of *U.S. News and World Report* says the service was developed in response to women's requests for just such a service devoted to issues of concern to women.[42] Although men are welcome to participate in the forum, only a few have done so.

The implications of gender, race, and other demographic factors on the media world were a major concern of the late Bob Maynard, former publisher of the *Oakland Tribune,* for many years the only Black-owned daily newspaper in a major U.S. market. Maynard argued that we cannot weave together the fault lines of race, gender, age, geography, and class, but we can build bridges. He concluded that the process of building such bridges can open important markets for niche information products and new media products appealing to communities of interest that cut across these fault lines.

Views of the Consumer

As the Time Warners, TCIs, and Bell Atlantics vie for control of the information highway, it is clear that the corporate titans of the information business are convinced of the importance of the new media technologies. But what do consumers make of these emerging technologies? After all, it is their spending decisions that will determine the ultimate success or failure of these devices.

Listening to the Polls

Consumers are relatively cool to the promise of the new media technologies, reveals a 1993 public opinion poll commissioned by the Institute of Electrical and Electronics Engineers. The survey of one thousand residents of four U.S. cities, including Edison, New Jersey, Appleton, Wisconsin, Fort Worth, Texas, and Stockton, California, shows that only a small percentage of Americans think advanced electronics and computer developments will greatly affect their lives during the next decade.[43] Just 15 percent say the new technology of the data superhighway, interactive television, video on demand (VOD), and virtual reality will greatly affect their personal and business communications, and only 7 percent say these technologies will greatly influence their entertainment and leisure time. The largest number (42 percent) say the greatest effect in their lives will be in health and medical care, where fiber optics, virtual reality, and other technologies are already being used in medical diagnosis.

Other surveys have confirmed a technical reluctance of many Americans and the necessity of technical simplicity in new media products. A nationwide poll of one thousand adults and five hundred teenagers found that a quarter of adults have never programmed a VCR to record a television show or set the buttons on their radio.[44] Sponsored by Dell Computer Corporation, of Austin, Texas, the survey also showed that a quarter lamented the passing of the typewriter and that technophobia was especially prevalent among the elderly. Similarly, few elderly Americans are willing to pay more than a few dollars for new media products and services. Another thousand-person survey sponsored by the New York Telephone Company showed that only one in five (22 percent) of those surveyed over the age of 65 would pay as much as $5 to $15 a month for new media services, such as movies on demand, home shopping, or picture phones. In contrast, two-thirds (64 percent) of men under 45 would pay at least that much a month for such services. A Gallup survey commissioned by MCI Telecommunications likewise found that nearly a third (32 percent) of 605 white-collar workers are cyberphobic, and nearly two-thirds (59 percent) will try technology only after it is proven effective.[45] Nearly as many (58 percent) have never heard of the Internet.

Two other studies present a more optimistic scenario.[46] AT&T, TCI, and US West found in the first phase of their Viewer Controlled TV (VCTV) marketing test in Littleton, Colorado, that customers used VOD services more than the national averages for traditional pay-per-view services. Three hundred customers had access to either Hits at Home, a service offering twenty-four channels of entertainment, and Take One, offering 1,500 movies on demand. On average, customers ordered two and a half movies a month, nearly twelve times the average rate, said John Malone, TCI President, at the Cable TV Forum at the December 1993 Western Cable Show. National PPV services average about two and a half movies a year. Seventy percent used the VOD service at least once a month, with prices comparable to those available in video rental outlets, ranging from 99 cents to $3.99 a movie. The vast majority (90 percent) preferred the VOD services to renting videotapes, with most (60 percent) citing "ease of ordering" as a major advantage. Most placed their orders on impulse, with 5 percent using a "reservation" feature. A significant percentage (20 percent) opted to block certain programming from their children through the use of a personal identification code. Importantly, the TCI test offered viewers "full pause features," which allow the viewer to temporarily stop the movie at any time.[47] "That gives people the chance to get up and go to the bathroom," observed Turner Broadcasting founder Ted Turner, also speaking at the Cable Show.[48]

A survey conducted by Radnor, Pennsylvania–based Chilton Research Services found interest in interactive television services to be highest for video on demand.[49] In a survey of adults interested in media coverage of emerging media technologies, Chilton found that 86 percent are likely to use movie access services (see Figure 7-4). Somewhat surprisingly, the services next most likely to be used (68 percent) are educa-

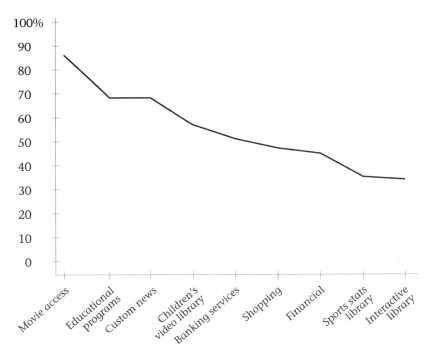

Figure 7-4   Percent Likely to Use Interactive TV Services

tion and do-it-yourself programs and a custom news channel. Interest is greatest among the younger generation, with three-quarters (75 percent) of eighteen to thirty year olds holding a favorable view of interactive television services, compared to 63 percent of thirty-one to forty-four year olds, 54 percent of forty-five to sixty year olds, and 35 percent of those over sixty. Table 7-4 presents data on the likely penetration of interactive TV in American households. "The twenty-something generation has grown up in a world filled with technological innovation, like computers and VCRs," says Majorie Michitti, vice president and general manager for Chilton.[50] "It seems only natural that those who are most comfortable with new computer technology see interactive TV as the next step in the evolution of information services." Gender also plays a role in interest in interactive services. More men than women (47 percent vs. 24 percent) said they would use sports information, while more women than men (51 percent vs. 41 percent) said they would be likely to use home shopping services. More men than women said they would use educational services (77 percent vs. 60 percent), as well as interactive banking services (58 percent vs. 44 percent).

TABLE 7-4   Projected Penetration of Interactive TV in U.S. Households

1994	455,000
1995	2,105,000
1996	5,705,000
1997	12,905,000
1998	21,605,000
1999	30,305,000
2000	39,005,000
2001	47,705,000
2002	56,405,000
2003	65,105,000

Source: Next Century Media, *The Marketing Pulse,* Volume XIV, Issue 3, 1994: 6.

A study reported by the Times Mirror Center for The People and The Press sheds further light on the nature of new media technology in the home. In a survey of more than four thousand people nationwide, Times Mirror found that most television sets are also plugged into a cable system, VCR, game machine, or satellite dish.[51] The survey confirmed many expectations about new technologies, including that young people are more comfortable with technology than old people and that the affluent and highly educated are more likely to own and use new media technologies than the poor and less educated. The survey also confirmed that more than half of all adults use a PC in their work and that one-third of all households have a PC.

A study reported by Link Resources adds an important twist to this finding. Link's study reveals that families with children younger than eighteen are especially likely to have a personal computer; 42 percent of these households have a home computer, compared to just 37 percent of those homes without children.[52] The Times Mirror study also shows that 47 percent of Americans have an ATM banking card, and at least 13 million pay at least some of their bills electronically. Eighty-five percent of all households have a VCR, and 64 percent are connected to a cable TV system.

Perhaps more unexpectedly, the Times Mirror survey found that PCs are not replacing the traditional ways people get their information or conduct their personal business. For example, the study showed that the 12 percent of Americans with a PC with a modem in their home use it primarily for business. They frequently use their modem-equipped PC for electronic mail, but only one-fifth say they use the technological combination to receive news, participate in "chat" groups, get travel information, or play games. The survey also suggested that introducing new technology may contribute to a knowledge gap between the information rich and poor. Results show that people who are most comfortable with PCs, VCRs, and fax machines track the news more closely, read more generally, and know more about the world than those who use fewer technologies.

IMPLICATIONS FOR ADVERTISING

Although innovative advertisers have always been intrigued by new media for marketing their products, today's digital technologies have particularly energized the industry. From the Ad Council to the Sci-Fi Channel, new media are transforming the methods and means of advertising. Advertisers are especially interested in two aspects of the new media technologies: interactivity and multimedia. Interactivity offers advertisers an unprecedented ability to involve the buyer in the marketing process. Multimedia technologies enable advertisers to simultaneously take advantage of the impact of video, audio, and text in the communication and persuasion process.

Online services and CD-ROM are the principal tools in the new media mix currently being used by these groundbreaking advertisers. Online services, especially via major consumer services such as AOL, CompuServe, and Prodigy, offer advertisers the ability to reach potential buyers through highly targeted messages. For example, online consumers interested in a particular type of product or ad message might select additional information available online or might even engage a live online sales representative in a conversation about the product. Such a direct-response mechanism provides the advertiser with the greatest potential for obtaining a sale.

CD-ROM messages offer the potential to provide a highly sophisticated multimedia experience tailored to the consumer's particular interest. CD-ROM messages, however, cannot allow the consumer to interact without a live company representative, since there is no online connection. Because of these qualities, CD-ROM technology has been used more often as a special sales tool for sales representatives going into the field to talk directly to clients. For example, a new multimedia CD-ROM presentation has taken the Sci-Fi Channel's sales pitch "from the age of flip charts to the era of cyberspace."[53]

Perhaps the most important new media development for the advertising world will be found in the next generation of interactive television. Because it is still in its infancy, today's interactive TV is still in the early trial phase as an advertising and marketing tool. Its potential is great because it combines all the advantages of online communications and CD-ROM multimedia communications plus the potential for mass audience reach. Like online services, interactive TV also offers sellers the opportunity to develop a detailed database on consumer preferences and tastes, thus tailoring messages in a highly efficient, and it is hoped, effective fashion. Privacy remains a major concern here, and advertisers will need to act early and consistently to communicate clearly their efforts to protect consumer privacy in the age of interactive media.

New media face a number of limitations such as their currently limited audience reach, uncertain impact, and cost. But advertisers are approaching digital media creatively, and many see them as an opportunity to experiment and position their product first on the electronic frontier before it becomes cluttered and congested like many of today's traditional media venues.[54, 55]

Some members of the nonprofit sector are also entering the digital marketing age. The Advertising Council, whose public service campaigns include such well-known efforts as Smokey Bear and McGruff the Crime Dog, has already begun examining new media forays with some of the field's leading players, including Time Warner, Sega of America, Interactive Network, and Prodigy Services.[56] The Ad Councils' first use of new media was an ad on Prodigy for Earth Share, an environmental group. The ad message quizzed users on their knowledge of the environment and helped the group receive during a 9-month period some $54,000 in pledges and more than 66,000 requests for a free poster offered in the on-screen ads. The council has since launched a second online campaign, and because of the response to both campaigns has planned an additional half-dozen online efforts. The council also has signed on as one of the Interactive Network's charter advertisers, along with Chrysler Corporation and American Airlines. The council also plans to join in the Full Service Network planned for Orlando, Florida. Moreover, the council is compiling a library of its new media campaigns, which will be available to programming executives through NATPE*NET, an online service that distributes information to radio and TV stations.

CPB Goes Online

In another new venture in the not-for-profit world, the Corporation for Public Broadcasting (CPB), the main funding organization for public TV and radio stations, in 1994 announced its plans to provide a dozen broadcasting companies with $1.4 million to create or expand various online computer services. The not-for-profit CPB receives its funding from Congress. CPB expects public broadcasters to work with local organizations and businesses to create or expand computer links to schools, libraries, museums, hospitals, and public organizations. Ten of the funded projects include cities and metropolitan areas, while two are statewide. CPB estimates that up to twenty-five million people could have access to the online services, scheduled for availability in April 1995. Larry Irving, chief of the Commerce Department's National Telecommunications and Information Administration (NTIA), says the Clinton administration hopes to see more of such community networks developed. In 1994, the NTIA provided $32 million for experimental projects proposed by local governments and nonprofit institutions. In 1995, another $32 million in grant money may become available for such projects.[57]

THE NEW BUSINESS ENVIRONMENT

Nancy Hicks Maynard, a media leader and new media entrepreneur who is president of Maynard Partners Incorporated, argues that media convergence has produced a rude awakening for many newspaper publishers, who only recently discovered they're not really in the news business. At least news is not how they make most of their money, notes Maynard, who has been the deputy publisher and senior vice president of the *Oakland Tribune,* a former correspondent for the *New York Times,* and former president and executive director of the Institute for Journalism Education, now known as the Robert C. Maynard Institute for Journalism. Advertisers provide about 80 percent of the revenue of traditional newspapers. Newspaper sales and subscriptions generate only about 18 percent of the revenues. "If you think about it," Maynard explains, "18 percent is also about what it costs to distribute the paper, in the marketplace."[58] Thus, newspapers are, essentially, a free product subsidized by advertisers for which readers pay for the delivery. "How many marketing schemes have you heard like that?" Maynard asks. She describes this traditional relationship between newspapers, readers, and advertisers as the media triangle, with newspapers at the top of the triangle, readers in one corner, and advertisers in the other. Convergence is bringing about the collapse of the triangle. As a result, media convergence and in particular online communications are creating a direct straight-line relationship between the supplier and the consumer. For newspapers, this increasingly direct relationship between buyer and seller has begun to seriously erode the newspaper advertising subsidy. Information technology is allowing sellers to seek more efficient distribution channels, channels more efficient than traditional newspapers.

Online communications have also begun to transform the entire environment for conducting business. On the Internet, not only are a growing number of companies exploring avenues for reaching consumers, but in April 1994 an online industrial park was opened. Commercenet, as it is called, has already attracted some of the biggest companies in the United States, including Sun Microsystems, Hewlett-Packard, Chase Manhattan, and many others. Commercenet allows these companies from a variety of fields, many outside the computer industry, to conduct all aspects of their businesses, including processing legal document fulfillment online, requesting proposals online, commodity bidding, and so forth. They conduct their online business in a secure environment using currently available encryption schemes, although regulatory battles now being waged in Washington, D.C., pose interesting questions about the future of online cryptography. Using Mosaic or MacWeb, participants log onto the Commercenet, an electronic location on the Internet that allows the transmission of not only text, but multimedia content and relatively secure transactional services. They will soon have access to a form of electronic money called *digital cash,* as well.

In addition to Commercenet, other interesting online business ventures for the new media world include MIDX Worldwide, Inc., the first online media information data exchange system. Created by Joe C. Harris, Jr., the former director of information technology at NBC TV, the system allows media companies, both new and old, to work with advertisers and advertising agencies in an online environment to access information on audience delivery and impact. Users can access the MIDX system at MIDX@aol.com or CSERVE"INTERNET:midx@aol.com":MAIL. Another new media online startup is the Online Ad Agency, founded in January 1994 by advertising veteran Larry Chase. With no central office, the Online Ad Agency goes well beyond conventional notions of telecommuting and exists entirely in cyberspace. Prospective clients dial in to the agency via modem at compuserve: 70700,616, and can download work samples and talk online to creative directors, account executives, or copy writers who come from all over the United States. All business is conducted online, and production costs are significantly reduced. Moreover, the agency can contract specialists on an as-needed basis to work on individual accounts and need not maintain a high level of costly overhead. The Online Ad Agency may not completely redefine the world of advertising, but had it existed half a century ago, Mr. Blandings may have had a lot less trouble building his dream house. (If Mr. Blandings is an unfamiliar name, tune in to American Movie Classics and watch Cary Grant and Myrna Loy in the cinema classic *Mr. Blandings Builds His Dream House.* Mr. Blandings, played by Cary Grant, may have saved a lot of time commuting and come up with "If it ain't *Wham*, you ain't eatin' ham," with a lot less stress had he been able to work for the Online Ad Agency.)

NOTES

1. "The Consumer Multimedia Marketplace 2: Software," *Screen Digest*, May 1994:1.
2. Ibid.
3. Ibid., 106.
4. "The Best Products of 1993," *Time*, 3 January 1994:76.
5. Gregg Keizer, "Debbie Does Silicon Valley: In Search of Sophisticated Electronic Entertainment," *Omni*, February 1994:24.
6. "Consumer Multimedia," op. cit.
7. Ibid.:1.
8. TFPL Publishing, Washington, DC, 1994.
9. *Seybold Report on Desktop Publishing*, 1993.
10. TFPL, The CD-ROM Directory, 1995. TFPL, Washington, DC, 1995.
11. Robin Raskin, "Inside," *PC Magazine*, 22 February 1994:4.
12. Charles Paikert, "CD-ROM Next Best Hope," *Variety*, 28 February–6 March 1994.
13. Ibid.
14. Ibid.
15. Nichols, op. cit., D17.
16. Ibid.:107.
17. G. Eisenstadt, "That's Where the Money Is," *Forbes* 151 (2), 18 January 1993:56–57.
18. McKenzie Wark, "The Video Game as an Emergent Media Form," *Media Information Australia*, February 1994.
19. "Poached by Sonic the Hedgehog," *Economist*, 20 February 1993:326.
20. Wark, op. cit.
21. B. Johnstone, "True Believers," *Far Eastern Economic Review*, 155 (51), 24 December 1993:70–71.
22. P. M. Greenfield, *Mind and Media: the Effects of Television, Video Games, and Computers.* Harvard University Press, 1984, p. 108.
23. John Markoff, "Toys Now, Computers Tomorrow," *New York Times*, 20 April 1994:D1, D6.
24. *Screen Digest*, op.cit.:109.
25. Ibid.
26. "Consumer Multimedia," op. cit.

27. Ibid.

28. Laurie Flynn, "Thrills and Chills of Marketing a CD-ROM Adventure," *New York Times,* 27 November 1994:F3.

29. "A New Fee Structure to Share On-Line Data," *New York Times,* 6 April 1994:D1, D6.

30. Jennifer Piirto, *American Demographics,* November 1993:6.

31. Kim Long, "The Year Ahead," *American Demographics,* December 1993.

32. *New York Times,* "Test Set for Digital Movies," 21 March 1994:D2.

33. Joseph Flaherty, "High-Definition Television: Technical and Political Issues," in *Demystifying Media Technology,* John V. Pavlik and Everette E. Dennis, eds., 1993.

34. Russell Shaw, "Pac Bell Offering Video, Audio Over Phone Lines," *Electronic Media,* 22 November 1993:10.

35. Flaherty, op. cit.

36. *New York Times,* 21 March 1994:D2.

37. Adam Clayton Powell, III, Technology Studies Seminar, the Freedom Forum Media Studies Center, 6 April 1994.

38. Anthony Smith, "New Communication Technology and Changing Political Boundaries," Technology Paper, the Freedom Forum Media Studies Center, 1993.

39. John Carey, "Back to the Future: How New Communication Technologies Enter American Homes," Technology Studies Seminar, the Freedom Forum Media Studies Center, 26 October 1993.

40. Ibid.

41. Susan Mitchell, "Technophiles and Technophobes," *American Demographics,* February 1994:36.

42. Kathy Bushkin, interview, 13 April 1994.

43. Steve Lohr, "Americans See Future and Say, 'So What?'" *New York Times,* 7 October 1993.

44. "Technophobia Emerging as the Malady of the '90s for Half of Americans," Knight-Ridder Newspapers, 12 June 1994.

45. Paul Wiseman and Dottie Enrico, "Techno Terror Slows Info Highway Traffic," *USA Today,* 14 November 1994.

46. Rod W. Kuckro, "Studies Show Growing Demand for Interactive TV Services," *Information & Interactive Services Report,* 3 December 1993.

47. John Malone, speaking at the 1993 Cable TV Show.

48. Ted Turner, speaking at the 1993 Cable TV Show.

49. Kuckro, op. cit.

50. Ibid.:3.

51. Mark Thalhimer and Marcella Steingart, eds., *Media Industry News Roundup,* compiled from the Associated Press, the Freedom Forum Media Studies Center, 31 May 1994.

52. Laurie Flynn, "For Children, a Gift of Software," *New York Times,* 16 December 1994:C1.

53. Joe Mardese, "Sci-Fi's Futuristic Sales Pitch," *Advertising Age,* 11 April 1995:18.

54. Scott Dovaton, "Ad Council Finds a Niche in New Media, *Advertising Age,* 11 April 1995:18.

55. Scott Dovaton, "While Other Agencies Talk, Bozell Acts," *Advertising Age,* 4 April 1995:20.

56. Dovaton, op. cit.:18.

57. Thalhimer, op. cit.

58. Nancy Hicks Maynard, speech, Technology Studies Seminar, the Freedom Forum Media Studies Center, 5 April 1994.

8

THE LEGAL AND REGULATORY ENVIRONMENT

Those who would expect to reap the blessings of freedom, must undergo the fatigue of supporting it.
—*THOMAS PAINE*[1]

In a perfect world, the development of new media technologies might rest exclusively on the genius of technological wizards, the capital investment of corporate players, and the communication needs of a diverse public. Instead, a variety of institutional frameworks converge to control, regulate, and monitor the technological development process as well, sometimes enhancing the process of invention, discovery, and diffusion, and other times hindering it. One should note that no single institution or branch of government acts as an all-powerful body to control new media technologies in the United States. Rather, the office of the President, the Congress, the FCC and other federal agencies, and the Courts all exert influence at the federal level, and a variety of state and local regulatory agencies, including the public utility commissions (PUCs) and state courts, set state and local regulations and laws over the development of new media technologies in the United States. Various international bodies set standards and policies affecting the development of new media technologies around the world.

The following chapter examines the legal and regulatory framework that exists in the United States, especially at the federal level, and internationally to control and monitor new media technologies. The discussion begins with a look at policies, laws, and court rulings that have set the stage for the development of the so-called information superhighway by establishing a climate of deregulation of and increased competition

254

in the telecommunications industry. Included here is a special look at the increasingly contentious debate over communications security and encryption of online communications, pitting the right to privacy against the government's mandate to battle crime in cyberspace. The second part of the discussion examines the status of freedom of expression and civil liberties in the new media environment, including intellectual property rights, piracy, censorship, and libel.

DEREGULATING COMMUNICATIONS

Since Federal Judge Harold Greene handed down the Modified Final Judgment (MFA) in 1984 divesting AT&T from the Regional Bell Operating Companies (RBOCs), the regulatory barriers prohibiting telephone companies from entering the information business have been steadily coming down. More recent decisions have almost fully opened the doors for telephone company entry into the information business as content providers. Coupled with the convergence of telecommunications, computing, and media, these regulatory changes have opened the way for a "united state of media" described by media studies scholar Everette E. Dennis.[2]

THE COURTS

As Judge Greene's decision suggests, it would be impossible to overstate the importance of the courts in shaping public policy in the arena of communications. From rulings on the First Amendment to intellectual property rights, the U.S. Supreme Court, federal courts, and even state courts have helped define the nature of public and private communication in an era of advanced information technology. The primary role of the courts in shaping public policy on communications technology has been as an important check against the administration and the Congress.

THE CLINTON ADMINISTRATION

The Clinton administration has made clear its intentions to support the removal of most of the remaining legal obstacles limiting the actions of all telecommunications companies. Vice President Al Gore says the administration will encourage removal, "over time, under appropriate conditions, of judicial and legislative restrictions on all types of telecommunications companies."[3]

At the core of the administration's vision are five principles:

- encourage private investment
- promote competition
- create a flexible regulatory framework that can keep pace with rapid technological and market changes
- provide open access to the network for all information providers
- ensure universal access (to end users)[4]

To nurture the development of new technologies, the administration must undertake a delicate balancing act. The government must set standards whereby all information can flow seamlessly and securely from one network to another, but these standards must be flexible to allow adaptation. The government needs to further deregulate the communications industries, encouraging greater competition among telephone, cable, and computer companies, as well as traditional media companies, yet must take care not to give any particular industry an unfair edge in the marketplace. To avoid the development of an information "underclass," the government must mandate a universal service goal, at least providing access to certain essential services, such as emergency information or information about government services. But, should this access include information essential to the effective functioning of the democracy? Should it include information about controversial public services such as reproductive choice or abortion? The administration needs to guarantee freedom of expression, privacy, and data security on the electronic frontier but at the same time must balance those values against the need for law enforcement on the information superhighway, such as providing federal agencies an avenue to conduct "wire taps."[5]

The Field of Dreams Model: If You Build It, They Will Come

Many business leaders agree that the federal government should not get involved in actually building the new information superhighway. Big corporate mergers, such as the one proposed by Bell Atlantic and TCI, will spur the global communication revolution more than government programs, former Apple Computer chairman John Sculley has said.[6] "This megadeal is the most definitive evidence yet that the digital communications revolution can and should be implemented by the private sector, not built and paid for by the U.S. government," Sculley told an industry conference on the National Information Infrastructure, or the information superhighway. Although the Bell Atlantic/TCI deal ultimately failed, many are still convinced that the private sector should be in the driver's seat for the construction of the information highway. Conversely, however, some say a more accurate model should be, "If you build it, will they come?"

THE CONGRESS

Congress has outlined its desire to deregulate the communications industry and to establish rules to treat telephone, cable, and broadcasters in much the same regulatory light.[7] In 1994, a variety of Congressional representatives introduced proposals to modify the legislative restrictions of the telecommunications industry, including telephone and cable TV companies. Although the proposals received strong initial support in the House of Representatives, they ultimately failed in the Senate. Despite this failure, however, and in light of the new Republican majority in Congress, many anticipate a new round of legislative proposals aimed at rewriting the 1934 Communications Act.

Senator Larry Pressler (R-South Dakota) introduced one bill in 1995 designed to:

- lift some restrictions on the telephone companies to allow them to begin providing cable service within their own service areas
- open the door for telephone company provision of their own information services
- place cable TV and telephone companies under the same rules, requiring both to serve as common carriers—and granting both industries permission to deliver telephone and cable TV services[8]

One issue not likely to be included in this legislation is whether private utilities will be permitted to provide additional information services to their customers. The Public Utility Holding Company Act of 1935 restricts utilities from providing services outside the domain of their core business.[9] Utilities have appealed repeatedly to the Securities and Exchange Commission (SEC), which enforces the act, but in most cases have been refused permission to offer services such as cable television.

Emerging Public Policy Principles

Emerging from Congressional hearings in 1993 and 1994 are four general principles guiding emerging federal policy on the development of a national information infrastructure (NII), or information highway. Although there is not universal agreement on these principles, many think they represent a starting point. These principles suggest that public communications policy should:

- let private industry build the NII
- remove most regulatory barriers blocking the development of the NII
- insure open, universal access to the NII
- create a level playing field that allows every firm, large and small, to compete in the new media field

Endorsing these principles is Representative Jack Fields (R-Texas), who feels government's best policy is to simply get out of the way. "If Congress wants the information superhighway to be built," he contends, "then it must refrain from imposing any speed limits or erecting any road blocks."[10] Larry Irving, communications and information chief for the Commerce Department, agrees that the information highway promises many benefits, but adds that government must take certain steps to make sure those benefits reach every segment of society. He suggests that getting the necessary on-ramps built in inner cities and getting the information superhighway into every neighborhood will insure equitable access to this twenty-first-century resource. Representative Dan Schaefer (R-Colorado) sees similar potential benefits in the emerging digital highway, but is concerned that without a clear policy to insure it, there will be no real competition in the marketplace, where telephone companies still dwarf cable providers in most markets. Others are concerned about insuring other long-valued principles, such as diversity and localism in any communications infrastructure, digital or otherwise. Some are also concerned about the government's continued role in insuring universal access to new media technology. One strategy for providing universal access to the information superhighway has come from cable TV tycoon Ted Turner. Turner proposes that the government issue "cable stamps," the telecommunications equivalent of food stamps, to poor people to ensure universal access to cable television.

The government's interests in promoting new media technologies are wide ranging. The Clinton-Gore administration sees the creation of a national information infrastructure (NII) as the cornerstone of the U.S. economy in a global marketplace dominated by information industries. The administration also sees the NII as fundamental to achieving excellence in education and lifelong learning in America. "Today, we have a dream for a different kind of superhighway that can save lives, create jobs, and give every American young and old the chance for the best education available to anyone, anywhere," said Vice President Al Gore, speaking to communications industry leaders January 11, 1994.[11]

At the same time, many in Congress are concerned about the social consequences of the information highway. Former House Telecommunications Subcommittee Chairman Ed Markey (D-Massachusetts) believes that the role of the government should be to insure that the telecommunications marketplace of tomorrow is not monopoly dominated. "Our goal should be to construct a marketplace where every home has access to not one, but two wires and a myriad of wireless services, as well," he says.[12] True competition will be the foundation of this marketplace, he suggests. "Unfortunately," he explains, "competition is not necessarily the company watchword at either Bell Atlantic or TCI, both of which grow out of monopoly traditions." Moreover, he wants to guarantee that people in every social stratum and geographic region have full access to the tools and knowledge of the information age. It is essential, he argues, that we do not foster an "information apartheid" divided into the information haves and have-nots.

An industry group known as the Computer Systems Policy Project (CSPP), consisting of representatives from thirteen high-tech corporations, such as AT&T, has proposed its own principles for a national information infrastructure. The eleven principles are:

- Access—Universal access is required.
- First Amendment—Freedom of expression should be guaranteed.
- Privacy—The right to privacy is essential.
- Security—All communications should be secure against unauthorized access and tampering.
- Confidentiality—NII users should have access to industry-developed encryption.
- Affordability—Reasonable prices are a prerequisite to universal access.
- Intellectual property—Copyright must be protected.
- New technologies—Government policies should encourage the development of appropriate new technologies.
- Interoperability—Interconnectivity and interoperability between networks both domestically and internationally is critical.
- Competition—Service providers need fair and open access to the NII to assure effective competition.
- Carrier liability—Common carriers should not be liable for the content they distribute since they have no editorial control over that content.[13]

The Evolution of Policy

The Aspen Institute's Charles Firestone writes that the regulation of communication has evolved through three distinct stages.[14] Stage one, he suggests, was based on notions of the regulation of scarcity in the broadcast spectrum. Regulators required broadcasters to act in the public interest and tried to break any bottlenecks in the system. The high priests of this first stage were lawyers. This stage formally began with the 1934 Communications Act, establishing among other things the Federal Communications Commission, but was based on 1890 legislation devised to regulate transportation via the railroad. An important principle derived from this nineteenth-century era was the concept of common carriage, which Title One of the 1934 Communications Act defines in terms of providing open nondiscriminatory access. This has meant that telephone companies must provide access at a fair price, as defined by federal government and state public utility commissions (PUCs).

Stage two regulations were based on principles of abundance that evolved with the growth of cable TV in the 1980s. Here there was a move to deregulate communication industries. The high priests of this stage were the economists, who based their decisions on efficiency.

Each regulatory stage thus far has emphasized different values. Stage one placed great emphasis on equal access, or equitable access to telecommunications services, as reflected in the fundamental notion of universal service. Stage one also emphasized the value of community or localism defined in terms of geographic considerations. Stage two, in contrast, emphasized not only efficiency but also personal liberty including the First Amendment guarantee of freedom of speech, diversity, as reflected in ownership, and personal privacy. Common to both stages has been the notion of universal access, which today means providing service for all members of society, including urban poor and rural residents.

Today, Firestone argues, society is ready for the development of a third regulatory stage, a new paradigm of communication regulation. It is unclear what form this new stage will take, but several factors will pay a part, Firestone suggests. One important factor is the decentralization of the communications infrastructure, which could allow every end user to have a voice. This system will be much more complex than before and will require a new set of regulatory assumptions.

One important attribute all agree on in the current legislative debate is that any new policy or law needs to be flexible to ensure applicability to the future.

The NREN

An important piece of legislation that has set the stage for this new regulatory paradigm is the High-Performance Computing Act of 1991. Introduced by then Senator and now Vice President Al Gore, the act established the National Research and Educational Network (NREN), a fiber optic telecommunications network linking research sites at many American universities around the United States, which has served an important part of the Internet backbone.

The Federal Communications Commission

Established under the 1934 Communications Act, the Federal Communications Commission (FCC) was charged with policing the public airwaves. Its responsibilities included licensing broadcasters initially for radio spectrum use and later for television. Its mission was to ensure that every broadcaster serve "in the public interest, convenience, and necessity."[15] Just what that means has been a continuing subject of debate.

Many today feel that the 1934 Communications Act is obsolete. One fundamental reason is technology. A primary reason for regulating the public airwaves was the principle of spectrum scarcity. That is, because airwaves are limited, or scarce, they should be regulated and controlled as a public resource. Digital technology, however, has made spectrum, or channel scarcity little more than a quaint relic of the past. Compression, broadband telecommunications, and advanced techniques for using the radio spectrum more efficiently have transformed the communication environment into one of channel abundance. As a result, the FCC now spends much of its time regulating pricing structures for cable television, allocating radio spectrum for new information services such as wireless and personal communication services, and monitoring the activities of such over-the-air broadcast personalities as shock-jock Howard Stern, the outlandish radio disc jockey known for his frequently "obscene" comments on air.

As a result, a number of groups have lobbied for a complete rewriting of the act. Charles M. Firestone, director of the Aspen Institute's Communication and Society Program, is leading a current effort to rewrite the act, and has recently offered up a series of drafts. Based on a meeting in January 1992, the Aspen Institute released a report titled, *A Preliminary Review of the Communications Act,* and subsequently released *Towards a Reformulation of the Communications Act,* published in late 1993.[16] Working with Congressional representatives, media telecommunications and cable industry leaders, communication scholars, and others, Firestone has reformulated the Communications Act to incorporate the notion of a new information infrastructure based on today's multichannel communication environment. This reformulation sets out a principal goal of "maximizing the contribution of communications and information technologies and services to economic welfare and enhancing the overall quality of democracy in America."[17] Although the notion of common carriage is questioned in the reformulation, certain principles remain, especially the notion of universal service, with an emphasis on affordability and availability, as well as interconnection and interoperability.

Deconstructing the FCC
The FCC consists of a chairperson and five commissioners, each of whom is appointed to a five-year term by the president, although the appointments are scheduled on an alternating basis so that a president elected to a single term cannot appoint an entire commission. Moreover, by law,

no more than three commissioners may be of the same political party, and each appointment must be approved by Congress. The current chairman, Reed Hundt, was appointed by President Bill Clinton.

The FCC may not be the most important communication policy-making body in the United States, but it does act as a lightning rod on communication issues, often drawing attention for its decisions, sometimes credited for gains made in industry, but more often attracting criticism. For example, following the 1994 failure of the proposed Bell Atlantic–TCI merger, the FCC was widely criticized by telecommunications and cable industry leaders and in the trade press for having caused the failure because of its decision to roll back cable TV rates by 17 percent in response to the 1992 Cable TV Act. Many subsequently admitted that the rate rollback may have had less to do with the failure than a clash of cultures between the two companies in traditionally distinct industries, or perhaps a clash in the personal styles or personalities of Raymond Smith and John Malone.

On occasion, FCC chairmen have been particularly visible in their vision or leadership of the commission. Perhaps the most notable example was John F. Kennedy's appointee, Newton Minow. Minow served from 1960–64, and made history in his first major communication policy address, delivered at the 1961 meeting of the National Association of Broadcasters. In what has come to be known as the "vast wasteland" speech, Minow sought to reinvigorate the *public interest* spirit of the broadcast industry. After all, he argued, the 1934 Communications Act specifies that broadcasters should act in the public interest or face the prospect of losing their television or radio station license to use the public airwaves. Broadcasters, however, were struck not by Minow's reference to the public interest, but by two other words: vast wasteland. Minow had characterized the landscape of television programming as a "vast wasteland," suggesting that there was too little of redeeming social value to be found in the television fare of the day. Thirty years later in 1991, Minow delivered the reprise to his famous speech, and found that little had really changed.[18] One thing that did happen as a result of Minow's earlier speech was the chairman was immortalized in one of television's most enduring programs, the long-running situation comedy, *Gilligan's Island*. *The Minow*, the ship that ran aground on a deserted island in the show, is named for the legendary FCC chairman.

The FCC's Role: Choosing Winners or Promoting Technologies?
FCC Chairman Reed Hundt, appointed in late 1993, has promised to promote the economic development of new media technologies while insuring equitable access, both to the end user and to a diverse array of content and information service providers. This will prove to be a very difficult

balancing act, especially as major transnational organizations lobby to ensure a regulatory framework that supports their position and competitiveness in the international marketplace. Hundt has outlined three principles as central to the FCC's policy on the information superhighway:

- providing universal service at a reasonable cost
- ensuring the presence of the broadband interactive network in every classroom
- providing universal access to the digital technologies and services

Pioneer Preference Policy

One controversial FCC policy that exemplifies the notion of choosing winners is called the pioneer preference policy. Instituted in 1991, this policy allows the FCC to award multimillion dollar licenses to companies of any size that have met criteria of originality and social value. On December 23, 1993, the FCC used this policy to award a license conservatively valued at $250 million to a tiny Colorado corporation to sell enhanced wireless voice, video, and data services to the twenty-seven million people in metropolitan New York.[19] In awarding the highly valued license, the FCC cited the Omnipoint Corporation for its early development of handheld phones that operate in high frequencies set aside for personal communication services (PCNs). The FCC also used its pioneer policy to award other multimillion dollar licenses for wireless communications to Cox Enterprises for linking mobile phones to a cable television system in southern California, and American Personal Communications for research on how PCNs can share the radio spectrum with existing microwave users in the Washington-Baltimore area.

Many industry groups and even some independent observers have criticized the FCC policy, suggesting that it is unfair and reflects lobbying intensity rather than innovative technology. Pacific Telesis has challenged the fairness of the FCC policy, citing a rule that prohibits informal contact between interested parties and commission members of staff during licensing proceedings. In the two months preceding the awards, FCC commissioners and staff logged twenty-six contacts with representatives from the three license winners.[20] These contacts were not illegal, however, unless there was discussion of whether any of these companies deserved pioneer preference. "We did everything by the book," says Douglas Smith, president of Omnipoint. An independent critic of the FCC pioneer preference policy is Henry Geller, a former general counsel to the commission who "crusaded for pioneer preferences."[21] Admitting he "made a mistake," Geller now says the "auctions make pioneer preferences unnecessary," since applicants demonstrate their convictions with their checkbooks.[22]

ITV and the FCC

Shaping the future of interactive TV is a recent ruling from the Federal Communications Commission (FCC) that allows for the auction of certain radio frequencies to be used for over-the-air interactive TV. Called the Interactive Video Data Services (IVDS) auction, this could allow traditional broadcasters to get involved in interactive TV.[23] The National Association of Broadcasters (NAB) has taken an interest in this technology. Although there is no single agreed-on format for interactive TV, a number of companies have put forward different approaches based on alternative technologies, including some that use the television vertical blanking interval (VBI) and others that use radio frequencies, including one called EON (originally named TV Answer).[24] The FCC embraces the concept of interactive TV and supports a radio-based approach to interactivity. In contrast, some broadcasters have already begun plans to produce interactive television using online services. For example, Capital Cities/ABC has entered an exclusive agreement with America Online to develop an interactive TV service offering interactive news, sports, and entertainment.[25]

The Federal Communications Commission gave permission on July 6, 1994 to Bell Atlantic–New Jersey to become the first telephone company to deliver commercial video services to consumers.[26] The company's proposed system would carry television programs over its telephone network to 38,000 residents of Dover Township in central New Jersey. Under the FCC's rules adopted in 1992, local telephone companies may deliver over their telecommunications networks programs created by others, who pay a regulated fee to access the phone company's network.

Sex, Lies, and the Telephone

As public policy experts debate the ethics of the latest advances in telephone technologies such as Caller-ID, here comes one they may not be ready for: the Truth Phone. Available for a cool $2,500 at Manhattan's Counter Spy Store, the Truth Phone "is the world's first telephone that can discern between truth and deception."[27] The phone analyzes the stress of lying, which theoretically shows up in microtremors in the voice, and unknown to the speaker, displays the verdict on a digital display for the listener. Does the device really work? Probably not, say the experts. Regardless, "I'll be working late tonight, sweetheart," may be uttered a lot less often—or at least less confidently—in the future.

Other Federal NII Involvement

A variety of other federal agencies and departments have taken an active role in shaping the development of a national information infrastructure, placing economic and educational considerations in the fore-front of their policy initiatives.[28] The Department of Commerce has taken perhaps the most active role in providing support and direct funding for telecommunications infrastructure planning and development. Other federal departments and agencies providing support or direct funding for research and development on the NII include the Department of Defense, the Department of Education, the Department of Energy, the Department of Housing and Urban Development, the Department of Interior, the Department of Labor, and the National Aeronautics and Space Admin-istration. Under the Library Services and Construction Act (LSCA), the Department of Education's Office of Educational Research and Improve-ment (OERD) has provided $2 million in startup money to let the state of Maryland offer through its libraries free public access to the Internet.[29] Using a system called Sailor, Maryland citizens will have access to a full range of Internet services, including e-mail, file transfer, site-to-site con-nections known as telnet, and hundreds of special-interest electronic dis-courses called Usenet newsgroups. The free access is an important element in guaranteeing citizens universal access to the information superhighway. A commercial provider of full Internet services such as Digital Express Group, Inc., of Greenbelt, Maryland, for instance, charges $20 to set up the user, plus $250 in annual fees and $1 an hour to use the Internet for up to six hours a day. Of the major commercial services, America Online offers the most extensive range of Internet services, though still not a complete set of offerings as of April 1995. AOL charges $9.95 a month and $3.50 an hour after five hours of use.

STATE REGULATORS

The role of the states in shaping public policy on communication tech-nology has also been important, sometimes at least as important as that of federal agencies and institutions. A number of governors, such as Wis-consin's Tommy Thompson, for example, have announced ambitious programs to put their states into the forefront of the information super-highway. Public utility commissions (PUCs) have also served a vital role in shaping public policy on communication technology. In many cases, these PUCs have provided much needed direction in developing industry initiatives to create a new information infrastructure, and at other times they have put the brakes on programs proceeding at a pace the com-missioners felt was too fast. An interesting illustration comes from the Public Service Commission of New York. In May of 1994 the phone com-pany in Rochester, New York, agreed to link with a phone system Time

Warner Cable is creating from its cable TV operation in the city. Although staff of the New York Public Service Commission approved the agreement, the commissioners themselves must still rule. If they give their approval, the deal would make Time Warner Cable's phone service the first in the nation. The principle technical advantage of the arrangement is that cable TV lines have far more carrying capacity than the copper wires that typically deliver telephone services and will make it possible to provide high-speed data communications to households. In the deal, Rochester Telephone would no longer charge consumers for Touch-Tone service and would freeze basic service rates through 2001, saving Rochester consumers an estimated $21 million. In return, the phone company would no longer be required by state regulations to provide rebates to customers if the company earns more than a preset rate of return.[30]

INTERNATIONAL REGULATORY BODIES

The globalization of telecommunications and media has made international regulation and regulatory bodies of increasing relevance and importance in the world of new media technologies. Outside the United States, most countries' telecommunications systems are controlled by Post Telegraph and Telephone agencies (PTTs). There are also international bodies and agreements that regulate the development of transnational communications. There are, as well, important standard-setting bodies on an international level.

Two of the principal international regulatory bodies in the communications field are the International Telecommunications Union (ITU) and the World Intellectual Property Organization (WIPO). The ITU has responsibility for the international allocation of the radio spectrum and distribution of satellite slots, as well as overseeing basic telecommunications services between two or more countries. Its decisions are based primarily on the principles of first come, first served and universal service, although the latter is currently under debate. In its view, these information delivery technologies are best regulated because they constitute natural monopolies.

WIPO is responsible for protecting the intellectual property rights of authors whose works are being distributed internationally. Its fundamental position is that member states should grant the same protections to international copyright holders as they would to domestic authors. This position derives from the premise that creators of content have the right to control the distribution of that content.

Critical scholar Mark Alleyne, an assistant professor at Loyola University in Chicago, describes these agencies as the principle "regimes," or formal regulatory institutions, for controlling international communication. In contrast, nonregimes in international communication include primarily media organizations, including news, advertising, books and periodicals, films and television, and music producers. Unlike telecommunications, there is no international body that regulates the trade of these products. Likewise, there are no universally agreed upon norms or principles guiding international trade in this area.

It is worth noting that recent international trade agreements, including the European Union and the Maastricht Treaty, the GATT, and NAFTA do not provide comprehensive regulations regarding the areas of telecommunications and intellectual property rights, as well as other communication issues. This is largely because of the complexity and transitional nature of the technologies involved, which mandates that these areas be dealt with in subsequent trade agreement decisions when the technology is more settled. Moreover, the international players involved stretch far beyond the local participants (for example, Hollywood movie studios have sizable interests in Europe), thus making it difficult to reach a final agreement.

One distinguished telecommunications scholar has recently observed that the technological transformation of the world's telecommunications networks is pushing regulators away from the traditional monopoly model. Instead, governments are liberalizing their telecommunications policy and opening telecommunications industry to competition, explains Dr. Eli M. Noam, professor of finance and economics and director, Columbia Institute of Tele-Information (CITI), Graduate School of Business, Columbia University.[31]Although it may be painful to those designing this industrial restructuring, Noam adds, the integration of new telecommunications technologies has mandated the transformation and privatization of telecommunications. Importantly, the liberalization of telecommunications policy does not signal the end of regulation. Rather, it is the beginning of a new era in which telecommunications policy will emphasize a reformulation of the notion of universal service and access, and the continuing transformation of telecommunications networks into integrated systems of global communications.

Diplomacy, Technology, and International Communication Regulation

One media mogul learned the hard way the complexity and delicacy of international laws and managing new technology in early 1994. Rupert

Murdoch, who introduced in the early 1990s western-style television to Asia with StarTV, declared that he would use satellite technology to help bring an end to the rule of the many "despots" of the region. In short order, the result was not the end of the dictatorial rule of leaders of countries such as China, Singapore, or Indonesia, but the heightened regulation of satellite television in the region.

Western Europe has operated under a very different regulatory model, one that often places social needs ahead of the marketplace bottom line. As a result, new media technologies have evolved differently in most Western European countries. For example, France implemented its Minitel videotex service by using tax dollars to place a Minitel terminal in every French household. A market was instantly created, and services such as electronic telephone directories and online chat services flourished. Further, Minitel created some 350,000 jobs in just a decade.[32] In contrast, the tight regulation of the telecommunications industry in Western Europe (and most of the world outside the United States) has meant relatively slow growth in that sector of the economy. In the United States, the telecommunications industry, though regulated but to a lesser degree than in most of the world, has grown from about $75 billion in total revenues in 1974 to some $200 billion in 1994 and is estimated to surpass $300 billion by 2002.[33] Meanwhile, telecommunications revenues have grown much more slowly in Western Europe, rising from about $60 billion in 1974 to about $125 billion in 1994, and estimated at $155 billion in 2002. As members of the European Union ponder deregulation of the telecommunications industry, European investors and new media entrepreneurs are pondering the possibilities for new media industry growth.

CRYPTOGRAPHY AND THE CLIPPER PLAN CONTROVERSY

One of the most contentious issues in the world of new media technology is cryptography, now an important part of computer network security. Encryption is a form of communication and computing security that refers to the translation of data and communications into a secret code. To decode or read an encrypted file requires a key or password to decrypt the code.

As computer networks have become ubiquitous, and everything from banking to personal records are stored electronically, the need for computer security has grown exponentially. Although a variety of strategies have been developed for providing computer security, such as computer passwords, encryption is the equivalent of a digital deadbolt. Encryption is essentially an information age version of the ancient secretly coded message, a field known as cryptography. From Julius Caesar's Rome to Adolph Hitler's Germany, governments have used encryption systems to encode secret messages. During World War II, cryptography was taken to new heights, as the Germans used Enigma machines to encode their messages, and the Allies sought to break the code. Enigma started as a commercial product, but the Nazis pulled it off the market when they recognized its military value for encrypting messages. Allied intelligence eventually broke the code and helped win the war. Today, modern encryption techniques render computer messages indecipherable by using complex mathematical algorithms. Messages are unlocked using a passwordlike key. "It's the reversible transformation of a meaningful message to gibberish," says Michel E. Kabay, director of education for the National Computer Security Association.[34] In addition to the military and other branches of the government, the current domain of computer encryption users includes banking and big business, highly secure computer systems, software programming, and Internet power users.

The issue of cryptography did not arise in the U.S. public arena until Congress passed the Computer Security Act of 1987, as a reaction to electronic criminal activity and database violation.[35] The federal government regards cryptography—especially the encryption of computer-based communications—as a threat to national security, because it can be used by terrorists and other criminals to conceal their plans and activities from law enforcement agencies.

Although computer users in the United States have access to publicly available encryption technologies and can use them for domestic computer communications, the growing international dimension of computer networks complicates the situation. Users of the Internet are at risk of violating federal law if they use encryption technology, since the Internet transcends international boundaries, and it is illegal to export encryption technology. "Cryptographic products have been classified as munitions and controlled under the International Traffic in Arms Regulations," notes Stephen D. Crocker, area director for security with the Internet Engineering Task Force, which develops technical standards for the network, and vice president of Trusted Information Systems, a computer and network security company.[36]

From Purloined Letter to Codes for Kids

While cyberpolitics is in the grip of the debate over the scrambling and decoding of electronic communications, Microsoft has created a new software package to teach children the basics of cryptography. Creative Writer uses what is called a Caesar cipher, a form of cryptography originally used by Julius Caesar himself and later by lovers in Victorian England to send secret messages published in newspapers. The technique involves substituting a letter in the text by one a few notches down the alphabet. To illustrate, the software translates "codes for kids" into "htijx ktw pnix." Creative Writer is little more than a digital version of "cereal box decoder rings" notes the *New York Times*.[37] Nevertheless, under U.S. export laws forbidding the exportation of encryption software, Creative Writer technically cannot be shipped abroad.

Not the Yankee Clipper

While industry, academic, and other civilian computing groups generally favor an approach to encryption technology without a "back door" for government eavesdropping, the National Security Agency (NSA) is pushing for a single standard for electronically scrambling computer communications.[38] Called the Clipper plan, this single standard for computer encryption would make it easier for the government to crack electronic codes and eavesdrop whenever it suspects illegal activity to be underway. The system is based on an approach known as escrow key encryption. In this approach, the government holds in escrow a special master electronic key that would allow it to unlock any encrypted message, provided it first receives court permission. NSA, the federal agency responsible for electronic surveillance of international communications and which routinely listens to many of the world's telephone and computer conversations (919 calls were legally wiretapped in 1993), is usually not concerned with civilian communications within the U.S. borders and is seen by many as overstepping its bounds.[39] Some officials in the Clinton administration, for example, have stated that the NSA is premature, while privacy groups are concerned that it will give the government too much power to violate individual rights. "The proposal angers industry executives who believe that the agency is rushing to establish a de facto standard that will undercut efforts to adopt a competing commercial standard without the built-in back door," reports the *New York Times*.[40]

The data encryption plan was a source of heated debate among the five hundred persons attending the annual Computers, Freedom, and Privacy conference held in Chicago, Illinois, in March 1994. "Cryptography is an enormously powerful tool that needs to be controlled, just as we control bombs and rockets," said one conference attendee, David A. Lytle, of the President's Office of Science and Technology Policy.[41] "When cryptography is outlawed, only outlaws will have cryptography," a heckler responded. Writer Steven Levy reports that the most passionate foes of Clipper are the Cypherpunks, a group of computer hackers, cryptographers, and computer networks users who have recently joined forces to do battle against the pro-Clipper government forces. Levy reports that Cypherpunks share the assumption that cryptography is a liberating tool and, as such, should be protected. A leading commercial standard is being developed by RSA Data Security, a software company in Redwood City, California, which has received wide support by the country's leading computer makers, software developers, and telecommunications companies. Not everyone in government agrees that Clipper is the way to go to protect computer communications. Senator Pat Leahy (D-Vermont) is one. Leahy argues that the government should not be in the business of mandating particular technologies. Conversely, there are people outside of government who support the Clipper plan. Dorothy Denning, a cryptography expert who heads the computer science department at Georgetown University, is convinced that Clipper is needed to prevent crime on the Internet and elsewhere in cyberspace.

The Clipper plan would use a circuit card inserted into a personal computer and is based on a technology similar to the Clipper Chip, a telephone voice-scrambling device that allows law enforcement officials to eavesdrop. NSA officials call their device Tessera, officially known as MYK-78, a device not much bigger than a tooth.[42] Congress charged the National Institute of Standards and Technology with developing a national standard for computer communications encryption, but needing additional technical expertise in developing a secret code for public use, the institute asked the National Security Agency for help in 1989. Together, they created the Clipper plan. The Clipper plan was announced in April of 1993 by the Clinton administration. Although use of the Clipper Chip would be voluntary, computer and telecommunications executives and public policy groups have almost universally voiced their opposition to the plan. A group of thirty-eight of the nation's leading computer scientists, computer-security specialists and privacy experts sent a letter to President Clinton on Monday, January 24, 1994, urging him to stop the Clipper plan. The group is worried that federal agencies developed the plan in secret with no public review and that they are concerned primarily with electronic surveillance, not privacy. Signing the letter were most of the civilian pioneers of modern cryptography, including Ronald Rivest of the Massachusetts Institute of Technology, Martin Hellman of Stanford University, Ralph C. Merkle of the Xerox Corporation, and Whitfield Diffie of Sun Microsystems. These civilian cryptographers are troubled by NSA's refusal to disclose the mathematical formula, or algorithm, on which is based the Clipper or Tessera scrambling technology. Some are concerned that the government may use economic pressure to enforce compliance with the Clipper plan. For example, the federal government could require all companies intending to do business with the government to use the Clipper Chip in their computer systems.[43]

Conversely, government officials feel that civilians should not have access to secret government codes. "Should a secret algorithm developed by the intelligence community be used for unclassified civilian uses?" asks Stephen Walker, a computer security industry executive and a member of the government's Computer System Security and Privacy Advisory Board. "I think the answer is it should not."[44] NSA plans to purchase up to 70,000 of the Tessera chips for its use and for use by the Pentagon, but sees a vast array of civilian and government applications for secure computer communications, including the Internal Revenue Service, the Departments of Health and Human Services, Justice and State, and in the U.S. Congress. The Clipper Chip project "is a focal point for the distrust of government," admits Clinton Brooks, the NSA scientist who led the project. Proponents see the development of the Clipper Chip as a natural extension of telephone wire tapping to the next generation of communication in the online world and a necessary part of law enforcement. With the potential for money laundering activities, drug trade communications, and other illegal activities online, the case is compelling. The debate may ultimately hinge on the applicability of the First Amendment guarantees of freedom of speech to online communications. The First Amendment has not been applied broadly to the regulated world of telecommunications, although other constitutional tenets of privacy have been supported to a limited degree by the courts. If, however, the courts rule that the online world is more analogous to the printing press, and full First Amendment rights are granted, then the Clipper Chip will likely face a much more difficult test than in telephony. The issue is complicated by the uncertain status of e-mail as evidence in the courtroom. E-mail can easily be tampered with and leave no detectable trace of that tampering. Thus, electronic eavesdropping of online communications may prove to have little utility in the courtroom, even if gathered legally.

In the early 1990s, intense debate has arisen over whether the government's authority to wiretap telephone calls should extend to the realm of cyberspace and computer network communications. The debate has centered on the Clinton administration's proposal to implement the so-called Clipper Chip plan, which would provide through a technological device an eavesdropping mechanism for law enforcement agencies to listen in on criminal communications in the online world. Opponents of the plan argue that privacy will be threatened if the plan goes through and the chilling effect will be to destroy the free and open marketplace of ideas that has come to characterize the global web of computer communications known as the Internet. In early 1994, an AT&T Bell Labs scientist identified a major technical flaw in the Clipper Chip design, bringing into doubt even the technical value of the proposed technology. As a result, the Clinton administration abruptly reversed its policy position on July 20, 1994 and indicated its willingness to consider alternatives to the Clipper plan.[45]

Among those who argue that the Clipper Chip is needed is David Gelernter, associate professor of computer science at Yale and author of *The Muse in the Machine*. Gelernter explains that wiretapping, which has long been an integral part of law enforcement, has been made considerably more difficult because of new technology.

In the age of high technology, the wiretap is a dead duck. In the old days, all conversations associated with a given phone number were funneled through one physical pathway, and by spying on that pathway you could hear it all. Nowadays, cellular phones and call forwarding make it much harder to find the right spot and to attach a tap. New techniques coming into use will make it harder still: when many conversations are squished together and sent barreling over a high-capacity glass fiber, it's hard for wiretappers to extract the one conversation they are after from the resulting mush.[46]

Gelernter concludes that the Clinton administration's Digital Telephone and Communications Privacy Improvement Act will save wiretapping by instituting the use of the Clipper Chip plan and should be passed by Congress. "If Congress fails to pass the telephone bill," Gelernter cautions, "there is every reason to believe that crime, particularly terrorist crime, will get worse." The dilemma Congress faces is whether to enable law enforcement to fight crime in cyberspace or to preserve freedom and privacy on the electronic frontier. It's not an easy choice.

Public Key Cryptography
The alternative computer security system endorsed by many groups outside the government is called Public Key Cryptography, invented in 1976 by Stanford mathematician Whitfield Diffie, a computer scientist whose research began in the 1960s at the MIT Artificial Intelligence Laboratory.[47] By combining publicly available decoding algorithms (that is, keys) with private digital signatures, Public Key Cryptography creates a simple, secure, and, as of today, unbreakable system, one without an electronic "trapdoor" for government eavesdropping.[48] Writer Steven Levy notes that Diffie developed the notion of split-key cryptography in response to the inadequacies of the existing approaches to encryption developed by the NSA. Anticipating more than two decades ago the development of the personal computer, Diffie's cryptographic breakthrough puts control in the hands of every communicator. "The virtue of

cryptography should be that you don't have to trust anybody not directly involved with your communication," Diffie explains.[49]

"Encryption may be the only reliable method for securing privacy in the inherently public domain of cyberspace," says John Perry Barlow, a cofounder and board member of the Electronic Frontier Foundation (EFF) (and a former member of the Grateful Dead). "I certainly trust it more than privacy protection laws. Relying on government to protect your privacy is like asking a Peeping Tom to install your window blinds."[50] Beyond the Constitution, the key privacy protection laws pertaining to cyberspace are the Electronic Communications Act and the Foreign Intelligence Surveillance Act, which, although they mandate privacy protection, are full of legal loopholes that allow the government to eavesdrop in case of emergencies and threats to national security.

Since 1983, computer scientists at the MIT Athena project have been refining another computer network security system called the Kerberos authentication system. Kerberos works by avoiding "ever sending readable passwords across vulnerable networks."[51] To date, the developers of Project Athena have yet to see the Kerberos encryption protocols fail, despite the numerous hackers likely to be lurking on MIT's 10,000-computer network.

Breaking the Code

114,381,625,757,888,867,669,235,779,976,146,612,010,218,296,
721,242,362,562,561,842,935,706,935,245,733,897,830,597,123,
563,958,705,058,989,075,147,599,290,026,879,543,541

One of the most popular encryption technologies in use today on the nation's data networks was developed in 1977 and is known as RSA 129 after the initials of its creators, Dr. Ronald Rivest of the Massachusetts Institute of Technology, Dr. Adi Shamir of the Weizmann Institute of Science in Rehovoth, Israel, and Dr. Leonard Adelman of the University of Southern California, and the number of digits in the code. The code is based on a system of very large numbers that are divisible only by two similarly large prime numbers, or numbers that are divisible by only themselves and one. The system works like an electronic lock box with two mathematical keys. The first key is a large composite number, the product of two large prime numbers. Anyone may distribute this number publicly, and use that key to put a message in the lockbox. The box, however, cannot be opened again without the second key, the second factor in the composite number. Only the owner of the message knows both prime numbers, or factors, and thus controls security for the lockbox, or system.

Initially, the inventors proclaimed that the code, although not completely unbreakable, would take at least forty quadrillion years to factor, or decode.[52] But advances in computing power, networking, and the global community of scientists reachable by the Internet have made the assault on RSA 129 an intellectual challenge of the highest order, similar to the relentless pursuit by mathematicians of Fermat's eighteenth mathematical theorem, apparently solved only last year by a little-known Princeton mathematician. As a result, the code is almost broken, declare a growing number of scientists.

Digital Signatures

Also vital to the process of computer network security is the area of digital signature technology. Digital signatures allow each user to provide a unique "electronic signature" to any file or document, verifying to the recipient that the document has not been tampered with or altered. This is vital to the development of computer networked electronic commerce, ranging from ordering pay-per-view movies to electronic shopping, to democratic processes, such as online voting at electronic town meetings.

In May 1994, the federal government adopted another important standard for creating digital electronic signatures. Developed by the National Security Agency (NSA), the Digital Signature Standard, as it is called, works in tandem with the Clipper Chip. Some contend that the government's adoption of the signature standard, which it intends to mandate, is a veiled attempt to force compliance with the optional Clipper Chip plan. The adopted signature standard is also likely to be at odds with international electronic signature standards under development, which are largely compatible with the standard being developed by American private industry leader, RSA Security.[53]

Hackers, Cyberpunks, and Other Cybercrime

A growing number of crimes and illegal activity conducted in the venue of cyberspace reflect the relevance of government interest in controlling computer network communications. In San Francisco on April 5, 1994 the first arrest was made based on a crime committed on a consumer information service, when a man solicited for prostitution on America Online. Child abuse is another crime of growing concern in cyberspace. While many parents assume nothing more dangerous than Nintendo target shooting is going on as their child whiles away the hours on a computer, many children are being exposed to sexually explicit communications and content if not outright child abuse. Oftentimes children who are technically adept at exploring the online world may find their way into a "chat room" for adults. For example, one writer reports that her thirteen-year-old son wandered into a cybernetic singles bar on America

Online, where one conversationalist introduced herself as Angel and said she was a stripper.[54]

The Strange Case of Phiber Optik.   Perhaps the most perplexing criminal case in cyberspace is that involving a young computer hacker codenamed Phiber Optik. Phiber Optik is a twenty-one-year-old computer hacker recently convicted of computer intrusion and conspiracy for his role in electronically breaking into phone-company computers and conspiring to commit other computer crimes. Phiber, whose birth name is Mark, admitted to breaking into the computer network. He also insisted that he had never damaged or intended to damage any of the systems he broke into. As a result, Phiber had hoped for a relatively light sentence, one comparable to the probation received by Robert Morris, whose computer hacking nearly brought down the Internet. It wasn't to be. Justice Louis Stanton of the Southern District of New York handed Phiber a one-and-one-half year sentence in the federal penitentiary in Minorsville, Pennsylvania. "Hacking crimes," said Judge Stanton, "constitute a real threat to the expanding information highway."

While those in the telecommunications industry and government have cheered the sentence, many in the information highway underground think Phiber has been unfairly made a symbol to discourage other would-be hackers from threatening the economic interests of the information age. Phiber has emerged as "the digital age's first full-fledged outlaw hero," proclaims one writer.[55] "Phiber Optik is going to prison this week and if you ask me and a whole lot of other people, that's just a goddamn shame," writes Julian Dibbell in New York's *Village Voice*.[56] Will the Clipper Chip reduce the number of Phiber Optik renegades in cyberspace? Probably not, since such accomplished computer hackers will likely find a way around the technology anyway. Will it reduce the number of cases of online solicitation? Probably, although in one recent case, a man soliciting latchkey children masked the names of his victims by using publicly available encryption technology. Of course, the police were able to catch him by using traditional investigation techniques. Increasingly, computer hackers are using advanced techniques, such as "sniffer" programs that patrol the online byways electronically sniffing out user passwords, thus providing hackers easy access to otherwise secure computing environments. Government agencies have detected a growing number of electronic break-ins to hundreds of sensitive though not classified government and military documents stored on computer networks.[57] The compromised computer systems include those used for aircraft and ship design, ballistic weapons research, military payroll, and computer security research.

Some activity has taken the form of pranks and borderline crime. One example was a message posted anonymously on the Internet in late 1994 in the guise of an Associated Press (AP) news release stating that the Microsoft Corporation had agreed to acquire the Roman Catholic Church. Microsoft Corporation and the AP both denied any connection to the hoax, but showing a greater sense of humor, John A. McCoy, a spokesman for the Roman Catholic Church, said, "We thought our prayers had finally been answered."[58] Such messages can be posted anonymously simply by routing them through any of some two dozen remailers, Internet's version of electronic postal boxes, which strip off all traces of the author's identity, and forward them to other locations anywhere in the world.

RECONCEPTUALIZING PRIVACY

By restructuring the ways in which personal information is gathered, distributed, and controlled, new media technologies are mandating a complete reconceptualization of the very notion of privacy, contend the Aspen Institute's David Bollier and Charles M. Firestone.[59] Echoing this view is Professor Stefano Rodota of the University of Rome. He argues that privacy is no longer simply the classic formulation of Supreme Court Justice Louis D. Brandeis, which places the emphasis on maintaining the secrecy of private information, or "the right to be left alone—the most comprehensive of rights and the right most valued by civilized men."[60] Instead, new technologies require a new formulation of privacy based on "the right to maintain control over one's own data," Rodota adds. This view is fully articulated by Anne Welles Branscomb in *Who Owns Information?*[61]

Today's Privacy Threat: Government or Corporate Big Brother?

Invasions of privacy have often been thought of as the province of an overly intrusive and controlling government. In today's digital society, however, the biggest threat to personal privacy may come from the private sector, either from companies owning vast amounts of personal data about an individual, or from an employer who not only possesses such personal data, but may also conduct extensive, and legal, eavesdropping on employees. The U.S. Constitution does not specifically protect privacy. Courts have constructed legal concepts of privacy primarily as a safeguard against a prying government, not employers.[62] Federal protections are limited largely to civil rights laws barring discrimination and prohibiting employers from requiring employees to submit to lie detector tests. Although technologically enabled, much of the impetus for employer monitoring of employee communications comes from two sources: a desire to maximize work efficiency and minimize time spent on nonwork-related tasks, and the soaring costs of sexual harassment suits. A junior college in California, for example, has agreed to pay three students $15,000 each to settle charges of sexual harassment stemming from anatomically explicit comments posted on a men-only computer conference.[63] Moreover, with more office romances flowering over e-mail, employers have reason to be concerned. Still, the ability to eavesdrop on unsuspecting employees may be not only a violation of basic human rights, but may soon be a federal crime. Congress is considering legislation to ban employers from monitoring employees' electronic and voice mail and office telephone calls.

"Americans willingly have given up some privacy for convenience," observes former FCC chairman Al Sikes, now group head of the newly formed Hearst New Media and Technology group. "Eventually they will rise up against certain intrusions on their privacy," he adds, "And there will be a bill introduced to solve a specific problem."[64]

Public Opinion and Privacy

Privacy is of increasing concern to the public. A national poll conducted by Louis Harris and Associates in the spring of 1993 shows that concern about threats to individual privacy has climbed to an all-time high in the United States. The study was commissioned by *Privacy and American Business,* a publication of Equifax, Inc., the Atlanta-based credit-reporting company. African Americans and low-income persons are more concerned about threats to their privacy than the overall population, although this year's jump is largely a result of increased concerned in more affluent segments of the population. Four of five (83 percent) of those surveyed say they are concerned or very concerned about their own privacy. As Figure 8-1 shows, this is a significant rise in concern since the previous year, when 78 percent expressed concern about their privacy. The increasing apprehension about privacy is caused by two major factors, according to detailed Harris/Westin privacy surveys conducted in 1978 and 1990: "(1) distrust of institutions and government process and (2) public fears about misuses of computer technology by organizations."[65] Just a quarter of those surveyed are concerned about the privacy threats posed by computerized record keeping in President Clinton's proposed health-reform plan. Most of the public erroneously believes that

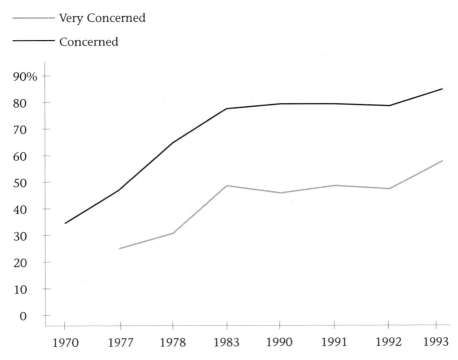

FIGURE 8-1   Public Concern About Privacy

Source: Louis Harris and Associates 1970–93.

there are strong medical confidentiality laws on the books. In reality, just seven states have any medical confidentiality laws at all.[66]

The 1993 Harris survey also shows that consumers say privacy protection is very important in the corporate sector. In fact, the majority of those surveyed feel it is very important to the public that businesses have strong privacy policies. More than half (53 percent) feel that it is very important for long distance telephone companies to have strong privacy policies, and another third (31 percent) say it is somewhat important. Few (14 percent) say it is not very important or not at all important for them to do so.

Other Indicators of Privacy Concern

Another indicator of the increasing concern about privacy is the increasing percentage of U.S. households with unlisted telephone numbers. The percentage of U.S. households with an unlisted phone number has increased from one in five (22 percent) in 1984 to nearly one in three (28 percent) in 1990.[67]

Privacy is also high on the agenda of Vice President Al Gore's initiative to promote a national information infrastructure. Pat Faley, the acting director of the Office of Consumer Affairs in the Department of Health and Human Services, heads a privacy working group within the Information Policy Committee on the NII Task Force. Faley has dealt with privacy issues since she served as head of consumer education at the Federal Trade Commission in the 1970s.

Traditionally, privacy has not been afforded high official status in public policy in the United States. One sign that this is beginning to change is the recent appointment of America's first so-called privacy czar. Carol M. Doeppers, a records administrator at the University of Wisconsin–Madison Hospital was named in late 1993 the first privacy advocate ever appointed by a governmental body in the United States. The position was created in Wisconsin by a privacy law passed in 1991. The world's first privacy ombudsman was created in the 1970s in the German state of Hesse. Today nearly all European nations and Canada have privacy commissioners at the federal level.[68]

Windows on Privacy

In one of Alfred Hitchcock's cinematic suspense masterpieces, actor Jimmy Stewart watches through his apartment's rear window the suspicious private activities of a neighbor. A strangely similar story has unfolded in the computer software world of Microsoft Word for Windows, a leading word processing package. Word for Windows has a design feature that allows a reader of a document to retrieve text that the writer deleted, or thought deleted. The recipient of a file sent via e-mail, disk, or shared on a network "may be able to read at least some of your original, raw remarks," reports Fred Langa, the editorial director of *Windows* magazine.[69] "For example, have you ever used Word to draft a contract, experimenting with various gambits? On its own, without your knowing it, Word may have saved some of your early, not-ready-for-prime-time drafts and deletions," Langa writes. Word for Windows automatically will save everything the writer has written if certain software settings are left in the default positions. Specifically, if the "Prompt for Summary Info" in the Tools menu is turned off, and the "Allow Fast Saves" feature is turned on, then Word for Windows will keep any earlier versions, despite saving over them. If you subsequently then view the file in a generic text program, such as the Notepad feature of Windows, some or all of the deleted material will appear. Although this may unnerve some unsuspecting users, it can serve as an electronic savior for anyone who has ever accidentally deleted or replaced a portion of a file, and thought the material irretrievably lost.

Privacy in the Electronic Workplace
Privacy has also traditionally had little legal status in the workplace. The Federal Electronic Communications Privacy Act of 1986 protects the privacy of electronic messages delivered via public networks such as the Internet and commercial services such as CompuServe and MCI Mail, to which individual consumers and companies subscribe. However, the act does not extend to a company's internal electronic mail. In an unexpected twist, however, the *Los Angeles Times* recalled in December 1993 a foreign correspondent assigned to its Moscow bureau for browsing through the electronic mail of his colleagues.[70] Such disciplinary action of a high-ranking employee has been rare in corporate America and signals a growing level of concern about privacy in the workplace.

Privacy in the International Arena
Privacy is on a slippery slope in the international arena, as is illustrated by the Internet, the global web of computer networks. "It is in the transborder nature of Internet traffic where the notion of privacy becomes slippery," notes Leslie Regan Shade of McGill University.[71] "The legal impact of such international flows has yet to be tested," she writes, "and the repercussions could be mind-boggling in a decentralized environment that is hard to regulate and manage, and that is further complicated by differing and often conflicting national laws."

A number of countries have formalized privacy protections for the individuals in the information age. In 1984, German courts upheld the fundamental right of informational self-determination. The European Union has established through two directives "a high degree of protection" for personal data, whether government or business-controlled.[72] But many of the world's countries have few or no laws protecting individual privacy, especially in the context of digital communications.

PROTECTING INTELLECTUAL PROPERTY RIGHTS

Ownership of information has long been an important issue central to notions of freedom of expression. For some three hundred years, copyright has been enshrined in the legal system of the Western world, since the passage of the 1709 Copyright Act, the first modern copyright law in England. Copyright directly and indirectly affects not just the creators of content, but those who make derivative works based on the content created by others, as well as lawyers, students of the law, and many others. The emergence of electronic, computerized information has only added to the complexity of the issue of the ownership of information. By eliminating the distinctions traditionally used to define different types of intellectual property, the digitization of information is turning the entire system of copyright on its head. Moreover, computerized networks and databases have raised a variety of troubling ethical and legal issues over who owns everything from an individual's name to his or her address. Many of these issues were first explored systematically by pioneering legal scholar Anne Wells Branscomb during her inaugural senior fellowship at the Freedom Forum Media Studies Center in 1985, where she wrote an occasional paper titled, "Who Owns Information?" leading to the publication of her book of the same title a decade later. Branscomb argues that the ownership of information hinges largely on the price and cost of information.

Intellectual Property Rights: Who Owns Electronic Information?

The acquisition and ownership of information has a price: a price to collect, a price to process, a price to distribute, and a price to store. Whether we consider information a resource, a commodity, or a basic right, there is a dollar value attached to it; and somebody or some institution has a proprietary interest in that monetary value. This is true whether we pay the price individually as consumers or collectively as citizens. Consider the following examples:

> *The federal census, first conducted by a handful of people in 1790, required the labor of 275,000 people in 1980 to conduct and $1.1 billion to process. The 1990 census cost an estimated $2.6 billion.*
>
> *The Library of Congress has a budget of $267 million a year to operate the largest collection of books in the world.*[73]

On the other side of the coin is the issue of individual rights, the right of an individual to control the use of her or his name, address, and other personal information. Branscomb asks, who owns your name, address, and telephone number? "Do these belong to you, to the telephone company, or to the many merchandisers who seek to sell you their wares?" The direct-mail advertising industry is a more than $20-billion-a-year business predicated on the ability to determine your name and address and to send you a catalog. Most mailing lists, such as consumer addresses and club memberships, are sold for a modest price per name and, in aggregate, add up to very large profits for the companies that sell them. There now exist on CD-ROM databases that contain the names, addresses, and telephone numbers for the entire population of the United States and Canada, with the only exceptions being the growing number of persons with unlisted telephone numbers. Moreover, these databases are widely available at affordable prices. A copy is available even in such remote places as the Field Library of Peekskill, New York, a sleepy Hudson River town of about 19,000, and famous as the original home of Crayola Crayons and the birthplace of Mel Gibson and Pee Wee Herman (and the author's home at the time of this writing). The database is extremely simple to use, as well. Simply type the name of the person you are looking for, and up pops the phone number and address. In the Field Library, all this is free to any one holding a library card (also available free to area residents). More sophisticated versions of the software can massage the data allowing direct marketing firms to target highly focused mailings. More frighteningly, burglars might use the data to target prospective victims, selecting well-to-do homes by zip code. The data might be merged with the U.S. Bureau of the Census Tiger mapping software to develop a nationwide grid including not just name and phone number, but typical household composition, average income, and other data. One might even tie in income tax data for a more complete demographic portrait. Ownership of information in the age of the information highway is everyone's concern. Consider the words of Dick Snyder, former head of Simon and Schuster, who described his company in these terms in 1992: "We are no longer just a publisher of books; we are exploiters of copyrights in all media."[74]

Some scholars contend that the emergence of digital technologies requires a complete reinvention of the prevailing system of intellectual property rights. Educator Don E. Tomlinson predicts that the existing overall copyright scheme currently favored by Congress is destined to complete failure. "Only a technology-specific approach to the monumental problems brought about by the use of digital technology in mass communication will prevent an utter breakdown in the system of intellectual property."[75] In agreement is Ethan Katsh, professor of legal studies at the University of Massachusetts. He argues that the digitalization of communications has blurred the lines between media to the extent that traditional legal distinctions between different forms of work no longer apply. He writes:

Any work that can be represented in other media can now be represented in digital form. In this form it can be used in a computer or other data processing unit, whether to be displayed or heard, or to perform some other function. Once in digital form, works protected by copyright are going to become less and less differentiated by type and more and more equivalent to one another because they will now all be in the same medium. This equivalence of works in digital form will make it increasingly easy to create a difficult-to-classify work by combining what have previously been thought of as separate categories of works. (What is an interactive annual report for a company? A literary work? A computer program? An audiovisual work?) Consequently, the elaborate distinctions copyright law has made among different kinds of work will lose much of the meaningfulness they had when media were more differentiated.[76]

Copyright and Fair Use in the Digital Age

Traditionally, copyright law has allowed authors and artists to build upon the intellectual property of others, while providing protection for the work of the original author or creator. Central to this provision in the digital age is the concept of "fair use." The Fair Use Doctrine has facilitated the use of privately owned material for publicly oriented activities, such as journalism and education. But determining whether unauthorized use of a copyrighted work is allowed by the Fair Use Doctrine has never been easy or simple. Four principles that have guided fair use decisions are

- the nature and purpose of the use (that is, not for profit or commercial use)
- the nature of the original copyrighted work (that is, unauthorized use of limited editions are less likely to be ruled fair)
- the portion of the work in relation to the whole
- the impact of the use on the potential market for the original work[77]

Complicating this framework is the global information superhighway, which greatly magnifies the potential for copying, eliminates geographic boundaries, and expands the marketing potential for both the original and derivative works. New York University professor Donna Demac, a leading lawyer and scholar in the field of intellectual property rights and the new technologies, argues that there are three important areas in which fair use takes on special significance in the digital age:

- interactive news
- electronic books
- musical sampling

These three areas are emerging rapidly as consumer applications, with wide implications for journalism and education. Although it is too early to make a definitive ruling on the Fair Use Doctrine as applied to these areas, Demac has identified some of the key questions.[78] In the area of interactive news, how does the fair use provision of the federal Copyright Act apply to the downloading of digital video by journalists and the public at large? To what extent should journalistic institutions be held liable in a digital era in which information is easily altered or pirated? How do we ensure people's right to privacy in an age of instantaneous global news distribution?

Regarding the electronic book, does fair use allow downloading entire books? Are libraries accountable for their patrons use or misuse of digital collections? Should the current copyright law waivers for libraries be revised or eliminated? For musical sampling, does current copyright law adequately balance the rights of music owners and the social benefits of new forms of music?[79] Should any unauthorized musical sampling be considered fair use?

Rewriting Copyright Law

As a consequence of the digitization of information, the Commerce Department has developed recommendations to rewrite existing copyright law in the United States. "Existing copyright law doesn't make it clear that it is a violation of the copyright owner's rights to distribute a protected work over the Internet," says Bruce A. Lehman, the Assistant Secretary of Commerce who is commissioner of patents and trademarks and chairman of the panel that developed the recommendations.[80] Lehman's recommendations would protect the intellectual property rights of creators of books, recordings, movies, and other forms of information in digital form, whether on compact disc or available online. The recommendations would also prohibit the use of technologies to pick the electronic locks copyright holders use to protect their works. A variety of industry groups have voiced concern about the increasing use of computers and computer networks to copy and distribute text, pictures, sound, and video in digital form. Record labels have objected to computer users who send unauthorized digital musical recordings over the Internet. In a major test case in district court, the Frank Music Corporation has charged CompuServe with enabling unauthorized recordings of the copyrighted song, "Unchained Melody." The class-action suit was filed in the United States District Court for the Southern District of New York on behalf of 140 music publishers. The outcome of the case may set the standard for copyright protection and digital recording distribution not only over the Internet but for all digital transmission systems, including cable

TV. Conversely, concern about copyright infringement and an inability to secure copyright permission has caused a number of multimedia projects to stall, especially in the educational arena. Multimedia business ventures have suffered the consequences of copyright, as well. Warner New Media's offering *Seven Days in August* cost $1 million to produce, most of which reflects the cost of securing permission to use copyrighted material from a variety of media sources. Still, many in the industry are opposed to lifting any copyright restrictions. Says Bernard R. Sorkin, senior counsel for Time Warner, "it is both unnecessary and undesirable to loosen copyright protections under any circumstances."[81]

Earlier generations of technology, including the photocopying machine and audiotape recorders, have presented challenges to existing copyright law, but none have posed the same threat as the digital age. Earlier technologies, although they may sometimes have made copying copyrighted material possible, did not have the copying advantages of digital technologies, which make instantaneous mass copying of exact duplicates on an international scale a matter as simple as pressing the Enter key.

Royalty Considerations: Land Grab on the Electronic Frontier

How to pay royalties to authors and copyright holders in the electronic publishing environment has been one of the most complex questions in the digital age. Should authors be paid every time someone else accesses something they have written? Should compensation be on the same basis as for printed publications?

One major publishing house has proposed an interesting solution. Random House has introduced a revised standard contract that will pay authors 5 percent of the amounts received from Random House's use of those rights, about half the royalty typically paid on trade paperback and hardcover books. Moreover, Random House would retain all electronic publishing rights from authors, including the rights for technologies not yet invented. The new contract has stirred much debate in the publishing industry. Alberto Vitale, Random House's chief executive officer, says the new contract will "protect the interests of both author and publisher." Robin Davis Miller, executive director of the Authors Guild, however, describes the plan as "a brazen attempted land grab on the electronic frontier."[82] The contract provides Random House with extensive control of electronic publications based upon the author's work, including the ability to adapt, abridge, add sounds and images, and combine an author's work with other's works in electronic edition, all without the author's approval.

Xanadu: Ted Nelson's Vision of Hypermedia

Ted Nelson, the creator of the hypertext concept, which in many ways gave birth to today's world of multimedia, has recently embarked on a massive publishing project called Xanadu, the name of the fabled home of the publishing baron depicted in the cinema classic, *Citizen Kane*. As envisioned by Nelson, Xanadu would be a digital global publishing environment, in which all documents, whether text-only or multimedia, would reside in their original form in only one location. All access to those documents would be electronically encoded in the account of the individual accessing them. Any quotation would be recorded electronically, and a charge would be made against the user's account, with royalties being deposited in the account of the author of the original document. Notably, the Xanadu system would maintain a permanent link between any document cited in a new file and that new file. Any subsequent user who might cite a quotation in the new file would have an electronic link with the original document automatically inserted in his or her file, with a royalty payment automatically made to the original author. If all this sounds complicated, it is. Xanadu may not be a practical solution to the royalty issue in the digital age, but it does reflect the complexity of the problem.

Patents

A third component of the intellectual property rights digital minefield is the area of patents. Traditionally, copyright and royalties were the only areas of intellectual property rights that applied to publishing. Copyright provided writers or publishers of original content with protection of the original expression of an idea. The idea itself was not protected. Royalty protection provided writers with a legal mechanism to collect payment for the publication of their copyrighted work. Patents, however, provide protection of inventions and procedures, areas traditionally outside the scope of copyrightable material. The computer age and digital publishing have changed all that. Recently, a patent was awarded for a computer program. Specifically, Patent No. 5,241,671 grants to Compton's New Media ownership of hypertext search techniques, which are the foundation for electronic search machines now used as the industry standard for multimedia publishing. As a result, any publisher whose multimedia product uses the patented hypertext search technique now must pay royalties to Compton's. This patent potentially means tens of millions of dollars, perhaps billions, in payments due to Compton's. Not surprisingly, many companies, including Microsoft, which uses the patented technique in its multimedia products, are challenging the patent award. The U.S. Patent Office is reviewing the patent award, and may reconsider its decision.

Electronic Piracy

Piracy of software has grown to Biblical proportions in the digital age, as electronic copying of commercial products has gotten easier and cheaper. According to one 1993 estimate, United States software providers would receive $65 billion in revenues if royalties could be collected on all intellectual property pirated throughout the world. GATT, the General Agreement on Tariffs and Trades approved in large part in December 1993 and signed into law a year later, contains a special provision for the collection of royalties on intellectual property. GATT requires all countries, including developing ones, to protect patents, copyrights, trade secrets, and trademarks. The greater problem, will be the enforcement of the law. In many of the world's developing regions, pirated software is so ubiquitous and ingrained that it would require a complete cultural revolution to change the system. In China, digital pirates have recently begun making illegal copies of musical compact discs (CDs) and selling them for the rock-bottom price of $2 a CD.[83]

Of course, software piracy is not unheard of in information societies, including the United States. A recent study commissioned by the Video Software Dealers Association (VSDA) found that the entertainment industry is losing some $242.5 million in revenues annually because of free viewings of pay-per-view movies via illegal cable converter boxes.[84] The VSDA study, which is based on telephone surveys of 1,000 heavy video viewer households, suggests that some 10 percent of all 20.2 million PPV households have illegal descramblers. In the case of one popular PPV movie, *Lethal Weapon III,* nearly half (0.5 million) of all PPV households that saw the movie (1.2 million) did so illegally. Although critics from the National Cable Television Association (NCTA) and others have criticized the study as biased and methodologically flawed, resulting in an extreme over-estimate of the amount of piracy, it is widely recognized that piracy of cable signals occurs at a significant level in the United States. Under the 1992 Cable Act, cable signal theft is a felony that carries a fine of up to $100,000. Wendell Bailey, engineer for Time Warner in charge of the design of the Orlando trial, says piracy of cable television signals is at one of its highest levels in the U.S. media capital, Manhattan. "People say the theft problem is 110 percent in Manhattan," he jokes, reflecting the view that in New York City, more people watch pirated cable than cable purchased legitimately.[85] Piracy of cable signals is easy in Manhattan's ubiquitous high-rise apartments where legitimate cable wiring enters the building and many apartment dwellers tap illegally into the line. About the only way to catch them is when a repairperson happens to make a service call to the building.

Preventing cable signal piracy requires cable programmers to scramble their signals, which is accomplished primarily through one of two ways. First is negative or positive trapping, an approach that involves the use of a mechanical device installed by the cable system operator. Negative trapping removes signals or channels the viewer does not subscribe to, and is used with high-penetration services, such as HBO. In this system, all the signals are delivered to the home, with only those not subscribed to being removed. Positive trapping is used for low-penetration services, such as the Disney Channel, and involves scrambling the signal at the head end where the cable system originates the signal, and then using a device at the subscribers set to descramble the selected channel or signal. Positive trapping is labor intensive and expensive, especially for pay-per-view events.

The second approach is interdiction. Interdiction is done electronically, and involves placing interference over the signal or channel not selected just before entering the viewer's home. This approach is little used, primarily because of its expense and the fact that it has been around for nearly a decade and many signal descrambling devices have been developed to defeat it.

On December 12, 1993, a federal grand jury indicted a San Jose, California, businesswoman in what is apparently the first case of piracy of software stored on CD-ROMs.[86] U.S. Customs Service agents seized nine hundred counterfeit CD-ROM disks imported from Hong Kong, along with eighteen thousand counterfeit user manuals. The pirated products included six multimedia titles produced by Software Toolworks, including a game designed by Lucasfilms Games. The government values the stolen software at more than $200,000.

Piracy Around the Globe

Intellectual property, consisting primarily of films, musical recordings, books, and computer software, has grown rapidly as an important American export. From 1991 to 1992, exports of American intellectual property grew by 9 percent, a rate exceeded by only the agriculture and aerospace industries. At the same time, piracy of intellectual property has also become increasingly significant. In 1993 alone, copyright-based industries in the United States lost at least $8 billion to piracy, report Gregory Stanko and Nisha Mody of the Economic Strategy Institute, an economic and trade policy organization.[87, 88] Among the world's worst offenders in the intellectual property piracy arena is China, which in 1993 heisted some $827 million in intellectual property from U.S. copyright holders.

The Office of the U.S. Trade Representative has identified fifteen laser and compact disk factories in China that produce counterfeit disks. Last year these factories produced fifty million pirated disks. Shenfei Laser Disk Optical Systems Company, Stanko and Mody report, is among the most brazen counterfeiters, having produced illegal copies of first-run blockbuster movies such as *Jurassic Park,* which as of this writing had not yet been released on video in the United States. Also pirated in China are U.S. computer software products. Among the pirates are some government-controlled institutions, including the Reflective Metals Institute at Shenzhen University. The institute recently produced sixty thousand holograms for a Taiwanese counterfeiter, who put the holograms on fake Microsoft products. Microsoft estimates such counterfeit products cost it as much as $150 million in 1993.

The mechanism to combat this piracy abroad is Special 301, a section of U.S. trade law dealing with American intellectual property. Under the law, the trade office must publish annually a list of companies involved in intellectual property piracy. The provisions of the law also enable the office to initiate investigations and impose sanctions against offending nations. The punch of the law may be weakened in the future as negotiations proceed on the so-called Uruguay Round of discussions on a world trade treaty. Some trade lawyers are lobbying that the sanctions called for under the treaty do not apply to intellectual property.

Libel in Cyberspace

Online communications are challenging many long-held notions of First Amendment law and theory. Who is responsible when a message is sent electronically? The sender or the provider of the conduit? How do principles of privacy apply in cyberspace? Does the Freedom of Information Act guarantee access to electronic public records? The answers to these puzzling questions are only beginning to emerge. "There is very little case law, and we can't tell for sure what the courts will say," says Shari Steele, director of legal services for the Electronic Frontier Foundation, an organization devoted to the defense of civil liberties in cyberspace.[89] Others are concerned about the legal implications of the digital alteration of images and sound. "Libel and false light cases will increase dramatically as manipulation becomes commonplace," warns professor Don E. Tomlinson.[90]

Cyberspace, Libel, and the Courts

Recent court cases begin to shed light on the legal status of libel in cyberspace. In a New Jersey federal court, a small medical-products company has filed a lawsuit against a user of a computer bulletin board service (BBS), charging him with libel. In the case, the Medphone Corporation charged Peter DeNigris with libel for allegedly posting messages on Prodigy's Money Talk BBS attacking the corporation for poor management and fraud.[91] The result of DeNigris's repeated accusations, the suit claims, caused the Medphone Corporation's stock to plunge 50 percent. In a $200 million electronic libel lawsuit filed in the New York State

Supreme Court in November, 1994, Stratton Oakmont, Inc., of Long Island, New York, has charged Prodigy Services Company with publishing a series of messages also on the Money Talk forum accusing the brokerage firm of numerous violations of Securities and Exchange Commission rules. Together, these cases may help determine whether a commercial BBS is more like a telephone company or a newspaper. As a legal monopoly, a telephone company serves as a common carrier of communications and as such is not legally responsible for the content. A newspaper can be held legally responsible for its content because it edits and organizes that content. Prodigy may be seen as a bit of both, since users post their own messages, but Prodigy does prohibit certain kinds of messages it finds offensive, and will remove them from its bulletin boards. Both Prodigy and CompuServe, another leading consumer online computer service, have argued in court that they should be treated as common carriers and not be held responsible for the content transmitted over their services. Yet, both services have also enforced their own content codes, censoring objectionable content. The prevailing climate in Washington, D.C., and across the fifty states today is inclined against granting full common carrier status to online information providers. The constitutional implications are equally significant, as potentially ever greater numbers seek legal protection behind the guarantees of the First Amendment, traditionally applied fully to print journalism, less vigorously to broadcast media, and even more weakly to commercial speech.

Libel and the Internet
In an unrelated case, a company marketing products on the Internet computer network recently filed a libel suit against a reporter who criticized the firm in an article distributed to other network users. It is the first time an Internet user has been sued for libel, says Bruce W. Sanford, a lawyer with the Washington, D.C., firm of Baker and Hostetler. Sanford is representing Brock Meeks, whose article about Suarez Corporation Industries of North Canton, Ohio, triggered the suit filed in March 1994. Suarez's suit seeks unspecified damages as well as an injunction prohibiting Meeks from writing about the company in the future.

Meeks, who is a reporter for *Communications Daily* in Washington, D.C., also writes stories on his own from his home in of Spotsylvania County, Pennsylvania, publishing them via the Internet. Earlier in 1994, Meeks published his story questioning an offer made by Suarez for free Internet access. Meeks's article said he responded to Suarez's solicitation, but received nothing more than an offer for a $159 self-help book and software package. Steven L. Baden, Suarez's general counsel, says Meeks should have also received an application to subscribe to the Electronic Postal Service, which Suarez is marketing. The owner of the company, B. Suarez, has been investigated previously in the state of Washington for illegal direct marketing activities.[92] How the courts ultimately rule on the suit is uncertain, but regardless of the outcome, the case is likely to have a chilling effect on reporting from cyberspace.

Electronic Access to Public Records

When Congress enacted the Freedom of Information Act (FOIA) in 1974, few observers even considered whether the act would apply to electronic, computer records. In recent years, the question of whether the act, which refers only to printed records, applies to electronic records has become of paramount concern. Today, not only are government printed records universally backed up electronically, but many are stored only in electronic form. "The new battleground is over purely electronic records that exist in no other form," writes Robert Ritter.[93] A federal judge's ruling in January 1993 stopped former president George Bush from destroying his administration's entire computer files, bringing an end to a five-year legal battle begun by the National Security Agency (NSA). The records at issue include the NSA's electronic mail files about Iran-Contra, computer tapes that may include details of the Persian Gulf war and President Clinton's passport controversy. White House officials wanted to release paper copies of the files, but Federal Judge Charles Richey said no, demanding the complete information. Invoking memories of Watergate, Richey asked, "What did officials know and when did they know it?" Without the judge's decision, a computer technician could have destroyed the files with a few simple keystrokes. "This decision cements the idea that electronic records are still subject to FOIA," concludes Rebecca Daugherty of the Reporters Committee for Freedom of the Press FOI Service Center.[94]

The Congress . . . Shall Make No Law: Freedom of Electronic Expression

Freedom of expression on the information highway is one of the great unsettled legal issues confronting communicators in the twenty-first century. Who will regulate the new media of the digital age; will the new media be guaranteed full First Amendment rights; and how will the principle of common carriage apply to the information highway are among the most critical questions.

The First Amendment to the Constitution of the United States declares, "Congress shall make no law . . . abridging freedom of speech, or of the press."[95] But the guarantees of free speech have been applied unevenly to media created since the passage of the First Amendment in 1790. Radio, and subsequently broadcast television, lost their full First

Amendment rights sixty years ago with the passage of the Communications Act of 1934, which both established the Federal Communications Commission (FCC) and required broadcasters to serve in the public interest. The FCC defends the constitutionality of its control over broadcasting largely on the basis of the notion of scarcity of the airwaves dating from the 1920s when broadcasters struggled for limited space on the broadcast spectrum. In the face of today's virtually unlimited channel capacity on the information highway, the notion of scarcity withers. Nevertheless, the FCC has shown little sign that it will weaken its hold over broadcasters and cable companies. Witness the reregulation of the cable television industry under the 1992 Cable Act, as well as the enforcement of "indecency" codes for cable operators, requiring them to group adult-oriented programming onto a single blocked channel, available only after written request from the subscriber.

Will the FCC apply these controls to the information highway? Section 10 of the 1992 Cable Act refers to programming, not to information services, and it is unclear whether these new controls prohibit obscene content in digital media.[96]

Will it matter who controls the information highway—the telephone companies, cable operators, broadcasters, or newspapers? "The kind of wire doesn't matter," says Linda Garcia of the Office of Technology Assessment (OTA) of the U.S. Congress. "What matters is whether we're talking about basic voice services or enhanced information services." Because the telephone companies have operated under the rules of common carriage, they have not been responsible for content. A very old legal notion, common carriage requires certain service providers, especially those granted monopoly status by the government, such as telephone companies, to provide service to anyone requesting it, without imposing unreasonable constraints, such as excessive pricing. "With many companies merging, some subject to common carrier rules and others subject to the rules that apply to print publishers, I don't think anybody can predict how this is going to sort itself out," says OTA's Garcia.[97]

Censorship in Cyberspace

Censorship reflects a society's lack of confidence in itself.
—POTTER STEWART[98]

Some argue that the principle of common carriage is central to any notion of freedom of expression on the information highway. "Without this assurance, people communicating unpopular ideas over the new digital infrastructure may have their path blocked by a 'censorious' decision of the network carrier," says Daniel Weitzner of the Electronic Frontier Foundation, a group devoted to promoting freedom of expression in the information age.[99]

While some look to the Clinton-Gore administration to build freedom of expression guarantees into their vision of the national information infrastructure, others go even further. Harvard Law School's Lawrence Tribe, a noted First Amendment theorist, has called for a Constitutional amendment to extend full First Amendment guarantees to all media, digital or otherwise.

Controlling Sex and Violence in New Media

Violence and sex have long permeated American culture, and they have always found a home in American media, from movies to books, from Hollywood to Times Square. Thus, it is no surprise that they are prevalent in the content of new media forms, from cable TV's "blue" channels to multimedia CD-ROMs to interactive online services.

Society and industry's response to sexual and violent content has tended to follow a consistent pattern. As a new medium develops and its popularity grows, along with its sexual and violent content, more attention and public scrutiny begin to focus on the controversial and potentially harmful effects of the undesirable content, especially on young consumers of that content and potentially unstable adults, especially males. As this controversy has grown, both in the press and the public, increasing scholarly attention has been devoted to the effects of the sexual and violent content, and subsequently, Congressional attention has slowly turned to the matter. Concurrently, industry leaders and concerned public citizens have mobilized to institute some form of control over the undesirable content. Industry leaders have joined to encourage self-censorship, while many in the public have called for governmental censorship, although some have questioned the constitutionality of such action, in light of the First Amendment. Finally, industry has acted to institute a form of labeling as a warning to consumers, especially parents, as to the violent and sexual content contained in particular media products, thus circumventing the need to take formal Congressional action.

This pattern has held for several media, including movies, comic books, and musical recordings. In the 1920s, many American movies were filled with violence and sex, although comparatively tame by today's standards. Scholarly attention came in the form of the Payne Fund Studies, which examined the effects of movies on children. Subsequently, the movie industry established a ratings council, which today warns parents about the sexual or violent content of movies in the form of G, PG-13, R, and NC ratings. Similarly, violence and sex were especially rampant in the comic books of the 1950s, which led to both Congressional hearings and scholarly study of "The Great Comic Book Scare," eventually leading to the establishment of the Comics Code Authority (CCA), sort of the equivalent to the Good Housekeeping Seal of Approval for comics books. As rock and other forms of music heated up in the 1960s and 1970s, an increasing segment of the public began calling for a halt to the production of violent and sexual popular music content. Some recordings have been confiscated in communities where the objectionable content has been deemed in violation of local obscenity laws, sellers and artists have been arrested. In response, the recording industry began putting labels on releases that are particularly strong in terms of violence and sex, such as some heavy metal and rap music.

The pattern is in its early stages for the new products of multimedia CD-ROMs and interactive online communications. As they grow in popularity and sex and violence become increasingly visible as a part of the new media environment, a growing chorus of critics have called for action. While many are members of the general public, some even come from industries whose products have come under similar criticism in the past. One such critic of new media content is Richard D. Heffner, chairman of the American film industry's rating system. Heffner believes the violence and sexuality of the emerging new media makes movie violence and sex pale in comparison. "The stunningly successful emergence of a revolutionary 'interactive entertainment' industry, with its video games and promise of 'virtual reality,' today brings violence and sexuality into homes with a lifelike intensity that had never been imagined."[100] Heffner has witnessed the growing cry against this content, and worries that too many of the critics "now naively turn to the movie rating system I head as a model of how to stem what may too likely become a plea for government censorship."[101] Heffner believes that a ratings approach is impractical for technologies that bring sex and violence directly into the home through an increasing abundance of channels and media. Heffner's alternative is borrowed from former first lady Nancy Reagan's battle cry against drugs, to "just say 'no.'" He hopes that new media producers and consumers will boycott sexual and violent content. This, too, seems hopelessly naive. New media producers reaping large and growing profits from sexually explicit and violent games and other content are not likely to stop selling their wares. Likewise, consumers, many of whom are young adults raised in a climate of electronic freedom of choice, are unlikely to give up what they are already used to.

Moreover, the video game and cable industries have already begun instituting ratings systems to reassure members of the public and Congress. Video games now come with the following ratings: early childhood, suitable for ages 3 and up; kids to adult, for ages 6 and up and may include some violence or crude language; teen, suitable for ages 13 and up, and may include violence, profanity and mild sexual themes; mature, suitable for ages 17 and up, with more intense violence, profanity, and sexual themes; and adults only, which may include graphic depictions of sex and violence.

It is likely that the producers of online and CD-ROM products are likely to follow the same course. The one exception may be freelance content producers who are able to distribute their materials over the Internet. This area of content production is a wildcard and is highly unpredictable. It may be the arena of new media content production most likely to produce truly creative products and to test the limits of acceptability and conventionality. It may also be the proving ground for censorship and the First Amendment in cyberspace. As legal scholar John Lofton wrote more than a decade ago, the guardians of the First Amendment have historically been the small, fringe publishers such as *The Progressive* in Madison, Wisconsin, not the mainstream behemoths, whose corporate interests rest on profits and public approval.

Censorship of new media content has been at least as much a part of the private, corporate sector as governmental action. In June of 1994, America Online shut down several feminist discussion forums over concern that young girls who would see the word "girl" in the forum's headline might enter into the discussion and find it inappropriate.[102] Supervisors on Prodigy have expanded their use of so-called George Carlin software, which locates messages containing objectionable words and warns those who sent them to delete them or face censorship.[103] The University of Florida revoked a student's access to the Internet after the student repeatedly posted electronic copies of a political polemic. In addition to the prohibitions of material by commercial online services such as Prodigy and CompuServe, the Interface Group recently banned X-rated CD-ROMs at its Comdex computer-industry trade shows. The ban, the company says, is in response to complaints from major exhibitors, including Microsoft Corporation.[104]

Circumventing Censorship. Conversely, online communications are also a vehicle for circumventing the censorship efforts of the world's governments. On the Internet, the Digital Freedom Net (DFN) is a forum for publishing material outlawed in authors' home countries. Formed in May of 1994, the New Jersey–based DFN has published excerpts from the works of Chinese dissident Wei Jingsheng, Indonesian novelist Pramoedya Ananta Toer, and Iranian Esmail Fassih.[105]

Digital Sex: Warning Label Required? Should digital sex come with a warning label? Some argue it should be banned completely. Many feminists, scholars, government officials, and others have challenged the burgeoning industry on the basis that its content may contribute to the objectification of women and even to violence against women. "What's wonderful about interactive media is also what's reprehensible about this kind of application: the idea of handing control over to the user," says Linda Jacobson, editor of *CyberArts.*[106] "Smut on paper or video is much more benign than interactive stroke books. These products show men that they can have control over women. You can force them to do your bidding and they do it willingly."

Moreover, electronic erotica may soon be challenged on legal grounds that it may violate laws against obscenity. Since the Comstock Act of 1873 outlawed the delivery of obscene materials through the mail, erotic materials have been treated as an exception to the First Amendment. The U.S. Supreme Court first considered the matter of obscenity in Roth v United States in 1957. In ruling against Roth, the court opined, "A thing is obscene if, considered as a whole, its predominant appeal is to prurient interest, i.e., a shameful or morbid interest in nudity, sex, or excretion."[107] In 1973, the court instituted a new test of obscenity in Miller v California. The court ruled that a work must exhibit "serious literary, artistic, political, or scientific value" (sometimes called the SLAPS test) to prove that it is not obscene. Miller also introduced the notion that erotic material should be judged in terms of "community standards." Justice Brennan provided a furious dissent, "any test that turns on what is offensive to the community's standards is too loose, too capricious, too destructive of freedom of expression to be squared with the First Amendment." The notion of community standards also raises complex issues when considering interstate and international distribution, which is increasingly common on the information highway. A "Decency" bill (S.314) was introduced in 1995 by Senator Jim Exon and is intended to eliminate erotic content on the Internet.

Controlling TV Violence: Technology to the Rescue.   Complementing the Clipper Chip is the less controversial V-chip, a part of Representative Ed Markey's (D-Massachusetts) legislation to control viewer access to TV violence. The so-called V-chip refers to a microchip inserted in every TV set to block programs containing more than a minimum level of violence. The technology would require all programming to have embedded an electronic code indicating the presence or level of violence, which the chip would decode and potentially block. Pay cable and premium networks would be exempt from the V-chip encoding requirements. Naturally, broadcast television industry groups are opposed to the technology. Leonard Hill of Los Angeles–based Hill/Field Entertainment, an independent television production company, worries that the technology could result in a "chilled" climate, one that would "sterilize the vital tribal fire" of the public airwaves.[108]

A New Regulatory Paradigm

New technology has provided the impetus for a new regulatory paradigm of the telecommunications and media sectors in both the United States and around the world. Although many suggest we are in an era of deregulation, others quickly respond that the new regulatory paradigm is simply one that puts more emphasis on competition and privatization, while building protections for privacy and universal access. In the United States, the Clinton administration has taken an active role in promoting the development of a new information infrastructure, emphasizing its potential benefits for both the commercial and public sector, especially to make America more competitive internationally and to build an improved environment for education and lifelong learning. The Congress is moving rapidly toward a new legislative framework that will treat telecommunications and cable TV providers in much the same fashion, in the hope of stimulating competition in all sectors. The FCC continues to play an important policy role, and will determine much of the future of a variety of new technologies, such as wireless and personal communication services, as well as existing industries such as cable TV through its interpretation of the 1992 Cable Act and other Congressional action. Finally, the Courts will serve as an important check against the actions of Congress and the administration, reinterpreting the constitutionality of new media law and the antitrust implications of a new era of corporate collaboration. In addition to the federal policy makers, however, states and local regulators will shape communication policy and the development of new media technologies by providing incentives to business to develop those new services in their local areas.

NOTES

1. Thomas Paine, The American Crisis, No. 1, 23 December 1776.

2. Everette E. Dennis, *Of Media and People*. Newbury Park, CA: Sage Publications, 1992.

3. Kim McAvoy, "Congressional Proposals at a Glance," *Broadcasting & Cable*, 3 January 1994:51.

4. Al Gore, "Forging a New Athenian Age of Democracy," *Intermedia*, April-May 1994:4–7.

5. John Carey, "From Internet to Infobahn," *Business Week*, Special 1994 Bonus Issue:32, 33.

6. Laura Dalton, *Executive News Summary*, 21 October, 1993:1.

7. Ibid.

8. Henry Geller, "Conversation on Ethics and Telecommunications," Donald McGannon Center, Fordham University, 1994.

9. Agis Salpukas, "Big Hopes Put on Electric Wires," *New York Times,* 6 July 1994:D1, D4.

10. Mark Thalhimer and Marcella Steingart, eds., *Media Industry News Roundup,* compiled from the Associated Press, the Freedom Forum Media Studies Center, 31 May 1994.

11. Ronald H. Brown, Mary L. Good and Arati Prabhakar, "Putting the Information Infrastructure to Work: A Report of the Information Infrastructure Task Force Committee on Applications and Technology," NIST Special Publication 857, Office of the Director, National Institute of Standards and Technology, U.S. Department of Commerce, Gaithersburg, MD 20899-0001, May 1994:4.

12. Kim McAvoy, "Markey's goal: Two Wires in Every House," *Broadcasting & Cable,* 15 November 1993:26.

13. "The National Information Infrastructure: A Key to America's Economic Growth and Global Competitiveness," a report from AT&T, August, 1993.

14. Charles M. Firestone, "A Preliminary Review of the Communications Act," January 1992, Aspen Institute; Charles M. Firestone, "Towards a Reformulation of the Communications Act," 1993, Aspen Institute.

15. Communications Act of 1934, U.S. Government.

16. Firestone, op. cit., 1993.

17. Ibid.:3.

18. Newton Minow, "Vast Wasteland Revisited," the Freedom Forum Media Studies Center, 1991.

19. Peter Passell, "F.C.C. 'Pioneer' Policy Under Attack," *New York Times,* 31 January 1994.

20. Ibid.

21. Ibid.:D1.

22. Ibid.:D7.

23. *Broadcasting & Cable,* 11 July 1994:32.

24. Chris Nolan, "Filling in the Blanks," *Cablevision,* 14 March 1994.

25. *Broadcasting & Cable,* 11 July 1994:32.

26. Thalhimer, *Media News Roundup,* 11 July 1994.

27. "The Sad-Truth Phone," *New York Times,* Sunday Magazine, 23 January 1994.

28. Brown et al., op.cit.

29. Tabitha M. Powledge, "Information Highway Without Tollbooths," *Washington Post,* 23 June 1994:1.

30. Mark Thalhimer, ed., *Media Industry News Roundup,* compiled from the Associated Press, the Freedom Forum Media Studies Center, 24 May 1994.

31. Eli M. Noam, "Beyond Liberalization: From the Network of Networks to the System of Systems," *Telecommunications Policy* 1994 18 (4):286–294.

32. Gail Edmondson, "Brave Old World," *Business Week,* Special 1994 Bonus Issue:42–43.

33. Ibid.:43.

34. Christopher J. Galvin, "The Digital Deadbolt," *CompuServe Magazine,* November 1993.

35. Richard Lipkin, "Making the Calls in a New Era of Communication," *Insight,* 12 July 1993.

36. David L. Wilson, "Threats to Internet Security," *Chronicle of Higher Education,* 30 March 1994:A26.

37. "HTIJX KTW PNIX,"*New York Times,* Sunday Magazine, 23 January 1994.

38. John Markoff, "U.S. Code Agency Is Jostling for Civilian Turf," *New York Times,* 23 January 1994:D1, D5.

39. Steven Levy, "We Have Seen the Content, And It Is Us," *The Media Studies Journal,* Winter, 1994.

40. Markoff, op. cit.:D5.

41. Peter H. Lewis, "Collisions in Cyberspace on Data Encryption Plan," *New York Times,* 26 March 1994:45.

42. Levy, op. cit.

43. John Carey, "Reality Check," *Business Week,* 4 April 1994:6.

44. Markoff, op. cit.:D5.

45. John Markoff, "Gore Shifts Stance on Chip Code," *New York Times,* 21 July 1994:D1.

46. David Gelernter, "Wiretaps for a Wireless Age," *New York Times,* 8 April 1994:E7.

47. Levy, op. cit.

48. Levy, op. cit.

49. Levy, op. cit.:51.

50. Levy, op. cit.:12.

51. Jeffrey Schiller, "Secure Distributed Computing," *Scientific American,* November 1994:72–76.

52. Gina Kolata, "The Assault on 12 . . . . ," *New York Times,* 22 March 1994:C1, C10.

53. John Markoff, "U.S. Adopts a Disputed Coding Standard," *New York Times,* 23 May 1994.

54. Felicity Barringer, "In Cyberspace, and Talking to Strangers," *New York Times,* 30 June 1994:D4.

55. Julian Dibbell, "Strange Loops: The Prisoner: Phiber Optik Goes Directly to Jail," *Village Voice,* 11 January 1994:44.

56. Ibid.

57. Peter H. Lewis, "Computer Snoopers Imperil Pentagon Files, Experts Say," *New York Times,* 21 July 1994:A1, B10.

58. Peter H. Lewis, "And the Spoof Begat a News Release, and Another," *New York Times,* 31 December 1994.

59. David Bollier and Charles M. Firestone, "The Promise and Peril of Emerging Information Technologies," report on the Second Annual Roundtable on Information Technology, Aspen Institute Communications and Society Program, 1993.

60. Ibid.

61. Anne Wells Branscomb, *Who Owns Information? From Privacy to Public Access.* New York: Basic Books, 1994.

62. Peter T. Kilborn, "The Boss Only Wants What's Best for You," *New York Times,* 8 May 1994.

63. Tamar Lewin, "Dispute Over Computer Messages: Free Speech of Sex Harassment," *New York Times,* 22 September 1994:A1.

64. Alfred Sikes, "Riding the Information Highway," speech, Center for Communication, 30 September 1993.

65. *Privacy & American Business: A Comprehensive Report and Information Service*, September/October 1993:3.

66. Anthony Smith, "New Communication Technology and Changing Political Boundaries," Technology Paper, the Freedom Forum Media Studies Center, October 1993.

67. John Carey, "Back to the Future: How New Communication Technologies Enter American Homes," Technology Studies Seminar, the Freedom Forum Media Studies Center, 26 October 1993.

68. *Privacy Journal*, November 1993.

69. Fred Langa, *Windows Magazine*, 1994.

70. Calvin Sims, "Reporter Disciplined for Reading His Coworkers' Electronic Mail," *New York Times*, 12 December 1993.

71. Leslie Regan Shade, "Computer Networking in Canada: From CA*net to CANARIE," *Canadian Journal of Communication, Vol. 19*, 1994:61, 53–69.

72. Ibid.:3.

73. Branscomb, op.cit.

74. Donna Demac, "Copyright and the New Electronic Media," midterm report, the Freedom Forum Media Studies Center, 29 December 1993.

75. Don E. Tomlinson, "Computer Manipulation and Creation of Images and Sounds: Assessing the Impact," monograph, the Annenberg Washington Program, Communication Policy Studies, Northwestern University, 1993.

76. Ethan Katsh, "Law in a Digital World: Computer Networks and Cyberspace," *Villanova Law Review*, vol. 38, no. 2, 1993:417.

77. Demac, op. cit.

78. Ibid.

79. Ibid.:6.

80. Teresa Riordan, "Writing Copyright Law for an Information Age," *New York Times*, 7 July 1994:D4.

81. Thomas J. DeLoughry, "Copyright Issues Said to Stall Many Multimedia Projects," *Chronicle of Higher Education*, 29 June 1994:A18.

82. Authors Guild, Inc., press release, 11 April 1994.

83. Adam Clayton Powell III, speech, Technology Studies Seminar, the Freedom Forum Media Studies Center, 5 April, 1994.

84. R. Thomas Umstead, "Stealing Cable," *Cablevision*, 6 December 1993.

85. Wendell Bailey, "Conversation on Ethics in Telecommunications," Donald McGannon Center, Fordham University, October 1993.

86. "Federal Jury Indicts Woman in a CD-ROM Piracy Case," *New York Times*, 12 December 1993.

87. Gregory Stanko and Nisha Mody, Special Report, Washington, D.C.: Economic Strategy Institute, 1993.

88. "Chinese Pirates Sail the Potomac," *New York Times*, 5 May 1994.

89. Robert Ritter, *New Media*, October 1993:24–25.

90. Don Tomlinson, *Digital Image Manipulation and Libel*, Northwestern, 1993.

91. Ritter, op. cit.

92. Mark Thalhimer, *Media Industry News Roundup,* compiled from the Associated Press, 3 May 1994.

93. Ritter, op. cit.

94. Ibid.

95. First Amendment to the U.S. Constitution, 1790.

96. The 1992 Cable TV Act, U.S. Government.

97. Suzanne Stefanac, "Sex & the New Media," *NewMedia,* April 1993:39.

98. Stefanac, op.cit.

99. Stefanac, op. cit.:46.

100. Richard D. Heffner, "The In-Your-Face Videos Bring the Censor Nearer," *International Herald Tribune,* Tuesday, 3 May 1994:7.

101. Ibid.

102. Peter H. Lewis, "Censors Become a Force on Cyberspace Frontier," *New York Times,* 29 June 1994:A1, D5.

103. Ibid.

104. "Porn File Not Found," *Newsweek,* 27 June 1994:59.

105. Barbara Kantrowitz, "Dissent on the Hard Drive," *Newsweek,* 27 June 1994.

106. Stefanac, op. cit.

107. Roth v. United States, 1957. 354 U.S. 476, 490, 775. Ct. 1304, 1312.

108. Jim Cooper, "From V-Chip to Hip Hop," *Broadcasting & Cable,* 28 March 1994: 22.

9

SOCIAL AND CULTURAL CONSEQUENCES

We believe that we live in the "age of information," that there has been an information "explosion," an information "revolution." While in a certain narrow sense this is the case, in many important ways just the opposite is true. We also live at a moment of deep ignorance, when vital knowledge that humans have always possessed about who we are and where we live seems beyond our reach. An Unenlightenment. An age of missing information.

—*BILL MCKIBBEN*[1]

It was the best of times. It was the worst of times.

—*CHARLES DICKENS*[2]

Understanding the consequences of new media technologies is at once both the most important and most difficult of tasks. It is the most important because the consequences of technological change are what makes technology matter. It is the most difficult because most of the technologies are still looming on the technological horizon, and have not yet taken their final shape or form. Even for a technology more than half a century old such as television, it is extremely difficult to determine its social consequences, despite thousands of studies by as many researchers all around the world. Even on specific topics such as television violence, few specifics are known with great certainty about audience effects.

Thus, this chapter sets out with an important caveat in its exploration of the social and cultural consequences of the new media frontier.

The consequences outlined here are largely speculative and are dependent on a variety of critical conditions and assumptions being met. Foremost, although current trends and past lessons will serve as guideposts for identifying potential consequences, the complexity and uncontrollable nature of the new media environment combine to make predicting the social and cultural impact of emerging technologies highly unreliable. This is especially true in the long term, although it is the long term that truly matters for society. Perhaps even more importantly, some of the most significant consequences are likely to be unexpected and unintended, and observable only with the benefit of historical perspective. Guiding the discussion in this chapter is a conceptual framework based on four major elements:

- Enduring topics and issues of major public and scholarly concern about the social consequences of new media technologies. These focus especially on the simultaneous forces of social fragmentation and cohesion, as well as the development of an electronic public space where virtual communities flourish. Also included here is an examination of the impact of new technologies on social institutions ranging from government and democracy to education and libraries, medicine and religion, with an emphasis on access to technology at the core of these effects. Finally, this discussion reviews the sociological implications of new technology and the nature and consequences of computer-mediated communication.
- Cultural consequences of emerging new media technology, such as the implications of new technology for the coverage of war, the video game as a cultural force and the intersection of new media technology and art.
- Theoretical perspectives on the social and cultural impact of new media technologies, including the uses and gratifications perspective, systems theory, critical perspectives, and a perhaps emerging paradigm based on the convergence of interactivity, online communications, and multimedia.
- International and intercultural perspectives on the social consequences of new media technologies, especially the implications for national development, intercultural communication and public diplomacy.

SOCIAL CONSEQUENCES IN NEW MEDIA TECHNOLOGY: ENDURING ISSUES

So with a hundred "modern improvements"; there is an illusion about them; there is not always a positive advance. The devil goes on exacting

compound interest to the last for his early share and numerous suc-
ceeding investments in them. Our inventions are wont to be pretty toys,
which distract our attention from serious things. They are but improved
means to an unimproved end.

—HENRY DAVID THOREAU[3]

New technology's social and cultural consequences have long been a subject of study and debate.[4-7] Advocates of technological change have often
argued that new technologies can lead to improvements in social institutions, citing examples from education to medicine. In religion, for
example, the development of Ecunet, the Ecumenical Network, has provided a global electronic gathering place for religious leaders from a variety of faiths and religions. It is estimated that some ten thousand
participants regularly log onto Ecunet. Similarly, the advent of telemedicine has enabled major medical centers such as Minnesota's Mayo Clinic
to connect with rural hospitals and clinics throughout the United States,
bringing advanced medical technology and expertise to patients and
physicians in remote locations. Some have argued that information technology is one of the greatest tools for fostering freedom and democracy,
citing examples from Moscow to Beijing.[8]

Critics of new technology contend that technological change frequently brings with it a variety of social and cultural evils, including the
loss of human employment, environmental damage, and increased control over information. Among the most outspoken critics of new technology was Jacques Ellul, the late French Protestant theologian and professor
of history and law. Ellul argued in his classic, *The Technological Society,*
written in the 1950s but published in the United States in 1964, that modern society valued technical efficiency as an end in itself, regardless of the
social, political, or environmental costs.[9, 10]

Those opposed to technological change sometimes have been called
Luddites, from the mid-1800s movement in England led by the fictional
character Ned Ludd, invented by a group opposed to the introduction of
new technology in the textile industry because it would replace human
labor. More recently, the negative human consequences of new technology have often been explored in venues of popular culture, never more
eloquently than in Rod Serling's television series, *The Twilight Zone.* Serling often explored the human consequences of new technology as a dramatic theme in the Emmy award-winning series. One episode showcased
the effects of computerized automation in the workplace, as more and
more workers found themselves out of work being replaced by a computer. Even the plant manager who first brought in the computer ultimately was replaced by a robot.

Canadian communication scholars Harold Innis and his most
famous pupil, Marshall McLuhan, studied the consequences of the

technology of communication on the society in which it exists. Innis and McLuhan argued that there is a direct correlation between the longevity of a society's communication medium and the speed of social change. Innis proposed that the long-lasting social structure of ancient Egypt was directly linked to the Egyptian's use of stone tablets as a medium of communication.[11] When the Egyptians began to write on papyrus, a much less permanent and much more portable communication medium, their society began to undergo much more rapid social change. McLuhan echoed Innis's observations, summing up this hypothesis of technological determinism in the now-famous phrase, "The medium is the message."[12] The printing press, telegraphy, and today's information highway have led to a global society dominated by instant communications and rapid social change.

Many agree that the development of these new information technologies is profoundly altering our social, political, and economic landscape. Among them is business guru and author John Naisbitt, who writes that the information society is more than an intellectual abstraction.[13] It is an economic reality with important implications for society. He suggests several important consequences of the information society:

- New communication and computer technology bring about a faster flow of information.
- New information technologies give rise to new activities, processes, and products.
- Social and political change proceeds at an ever more rapid pace, as real-time multimedia communications on a global scale become ever more common.

Many leaders of the world's so-called information societies agree with this assessment of the advanced digital information infrastructure that has emerged in the past decade. Among them are the members of the Club of Rome, a collection of leaders from business, industry, education, and government. "Microelectronics, through miniaturization, automation, computerization, and robotization," they write, "will fundamentally transform our lives and impinge on most of its facets: at work, at home, in politics, in science, at war, and at peace."[14]

Social Consequences of ITV: A Case Study

Hypothesizing about the social effects of interactive TV is tantalizing, fun, and dangerous—dangerous because the forecast, like those of all new technologies, is sure to be wrong. Lessons from the past are sometimes helpful, although they are by no means a reliable barometer. The earliest adopters of the VCR (videocassette recorder) were businesses. The next adopters tended to be technophiles (people who love technology and crave anything new) and users of pornography. Finally, the VCR came down in price and diffused to a general consumer market. Interactive TV is likely to follow a similar path, with early consumer users being those interested enough to pay the high price tag and to use a system that may not yet work perfectly—the technophiles and users of pornography (sexual gratification has especially high potential for truly interactive TV—it could allow people separated by oceans to come together for cybersex). If the technology catches on, then it will be adopted by a wider general audience. A key will be the development of quality software.

Interactive TV has the potential to be even more addictive than conventional TV. This could turn even more people into couch potatoes. Society could experience the electronic nightmare scenario envisioned by William Gibson and others in which everyone lives in a digital, interactive world populated by cyberpunks wreaking havoc. Conversely, truly interactive TV could open up a variety of new social uses linking people around the world into what Marshall McLuhan called the Global Village. That could make us all "village people."

Social Fragmentation, Digital Isolation, and the Multichannel Environment

Scholarly study of the social consequences of new media technology has frequently centered on the question of the potential fragmentation of society. Until the widespread development of cable television and the advent of a multichannel viewing environment, most television programming and viewership was dominated by three networks—ABC, CBS, and NBC. Through these three networks, American viewers tended to have regular common or shared viewing experiences, whether via the *CBS Evening News with Walter Cronkite,* from 1962 to 1981, *Bonanza,* NBC's Sunday night offering aired from 1959 to 1973, or ABC's *The Addams Family,* which ran from 1964 to 1966.[15] Certain major events could capture virtually the entire viewing audience, even the whole country, such as the assassination of President John F. Kennedy on November 22, 1963, which was captured on 8 mm film by amateur photographer Abraham Zapruder and aired on all three networks. Scholars have studied this event widely in the context of a shared viewing experience.

Today, the deployment of millions of miles of optical fiber, the convergence of computers, television, and telecommunications, and the emergence of a five-hundred-channel, interactive video environment are producing an entirely new media landscape in which shared viewing experiences may become little more than a fond memory. As a result, many are concerned that technological developments may erode one of the most important positive social functions television has served during its brief half-century existence: the nurturing of a common culture.

Conversely, others present compelling evidence that the new media landscape still presents opportunities for common mediated experiences, while at the same time offering a much richer, diverse range of programming alternatives for a variety of audiences often poorly served by network television in the past, such as women, minorities, and gays. Consider, for example, the Perot-Gore debate over NAFTA (North American Free Trade Agreement) broadcast via cable television on CNN's *Larry King Live* on Tuesday night, November 9, 1993. Promoted through a variety of media, this debate drew the largest rating ever, an 11.9, for any regularly scheduled program in the history of cable television.[16] This represents approximately 11,209,800 homes, with each rating point representing 942,000 homes. The rating was even higher, at 18.1, in homes that receive CNN. CNN is available in 62 million of the 94 million U.S. households that have television. The 11.9 rating does not include additional viewers who may have seen the debate on any broadcast stations that carried the debate live. CNN let broadcast stations carry the debate if they subscribe to the CNN news service. Moreover, more than two million viewers tried to phone in to the call-in program, said Steve Heyworth, CNN's director of public relations. The previous cable TV ratings high was also set by *Larry King Live* during the 1991 Persian Gulf war, which captured an 11.5 rating. These data demonstrate that it is still possible for a highly fragmented media system to provide a shared viewing experience.

Keep Going, O.J.

Or, consider a more recent and infamous example of the media providing a common shared viewing experience. In June 1994, former football and movie star O.J. Simpson was charged with the double murder of his ex-wife, Nicole Brown Simpson, and her male companion. After agreeing to surrender to the police, Simpson briefly became a fugitive, eluding police for several hours. The manhunt reached a national crescendo in the late afternoon of Friday, June 17, when Simpson and a friend, former football player Al Cowlings, led a police entourage across the highways of Los Angeles for more than an hour on a spectacular low-speed auto chase to Simpson's Brentwood estate. Anyone watching television that afternoon will likely never forget the scene, as live images of the vehicle carrying Simpson, Cowling's white Ford Bronco, led the squad of police cars to Brentwood. Shot from helicopter, the chase was carried not only on CNN and the major networks of CBS, NBC, ABC, and Fox, but on all of their LA affiliates, independent stations in LA, Spanish-language networks Telemundo and Univision, and even on ESPN, the Capital

Cities/ABC–owned sports channel. The spectacle drew a near record audience of some 95 million American viewers, rivaling the 118 million American viewers who tuned in during the early moments of the war in the Persian Gulf. Attention to the case continued after Simpson's arrest, as well, with one in four U.S. homes tuning in to the opening day of Simpson's court hearing. "That would be supplemented, of course, by a significant out-of-home audience, since it ran in the lunch hour for most of the country," says David Poltrack, CBS's top audience researcher.[17]

Although many shared viewing experiences may help build national consensus or cohesion or create a common frame of reference on matters of public importance, others may have a negative effect, at least according to many critics of television content, especially TV violence. One such critic is U.S. Attorney General Janet Reno, who testified before the U.S. Congress in 1993 that television violence viewing is a principal cause of real-life violence. Her argument is supported by a growing body of scholarly evidence that viewing TV and other mediated violence is related to real-life aggression. Unfortunately, Reno's criticism was largely directed at network television, which is arguably the most responsible in limiting violent content during hours when child viewers are likely to be present. Ironically, the two most notorious cases linking media and real-world violence in 1993 had nothing to do with network television. *Beavis and Butt-Head,* which was linked to a case of a five-year-old who set a fire in his home in which his two-year-old sister died, airs on cable TV's MTV. Similarly, several teenage boys were killed while imitating a scene depicted in *The Program,* a film produced by Buena Vista Films, a subsidiary of Walt Disney Productions, and in no way connected to network television.

Consonance in the New Media Environment

The issue of social fragmentation is complicated by the nature of the media system, at least in North America. Here, despite the growing number of television and other media channels, there is still a high level of consonance in media content. Recall the 1994 case of Olympic figure skaters Tonya Harding and Nancy Kerrigan. Kerrigan, who was clubbed on the knee after a skating practice a few weeks before the winter Olympics were to begin, and Harding, whose former husband admitted to helping to plan the assault, were covered widely in virtually every American medium, from network news to tabloid television to the pages of daily newspapers, the airwaves of talk radio, and even on electronic bulletin boards. Thus, whether individual consumers tuned to one channel or another, they could hardly help but come in contact with the Kerrigan-Harding saga. On the other hand, the particular slant or spin may have varied widely from one medium or program to another.

Similarly, although many point to the so-called five-hundred-channel TV environment, others are quick to point out that while the average channel environment rose from a half-dozen in the 1960s to several dozen in the 1980s, most people still watch only six or seven channels on a regular basis. Veteran television producer Adam Clayton Powell III, however, notes that there are many different sets of six or seven channels. Of course, even in a five-hundred-channel viewing environment, relatively few of those channels will be devoted to basic cable programming. Most will likely be premium services and pay-per-view alternatives. In this sense, the multichannel environment really will be more akin to putting today's video store online. In fact, the notion of a five-hundred-channel TV environment is misleading. It originated in a 1993 press conference with TCI's John Malone, where a reporter pressed him to say how many channels would be possible on the information superhighway. Somewhat exasperated by the reporter's persistence, Malone said that with 10:1 compression and an average of fifty channels now on the typical cable system, the information superhighway might bring five hundred channels to the average home. The number stuck.

Digital Isolation

Some are concerned about the effects of an apparently growing national obsession with new communication technology. "Soon, blessed with fax, voice- and e-mail, computer hookups and TVs with hundreds of channels, we won't have to leave our lonely rooms—not to write a check, work, visit, shop, exercise, or make love. We will have raced at incredible speeds to reach our final destination—nothing," writes Bill Henderson, director of the Lead Pencil Club, a subsidiary of the Pushcart Press publishing house.[18] Henderson is not the first to have voiced this concern about the isolating effects of new technology. As long ago as 1849 Henry David Thoreau wrote, "We are in a great haste to construct a magnetic telegraph from Maine to Texas, but Maine and Texas, it may be, have nothing important to communicate. . . . We are eager to tunnel under the Atlantic and bring the Old World some weeks nearer to the New, but perchance the first news that will leak through into the broad, flapping American ear will be that the Princess Adelaide has the whooping cough."[19] Today, it is just as likely that the hottest news traveling the transatlantic information superhighway will be latest sex scandal among the British aristocracy or on Capitol Hill.

Globalization and Cultural Homogenization

Others are rightly concerned that the globalization of media through satellite-delivered television and online communications present the distinct possibility of an increasingly homogeneous single global culture.

Rupert Murdoch, founder of the global News Corp and StarTV, summed this up eloquently at the 1994 Communicator of the Year Award luncheon hosted by the Center for Communication in New York. "Thanks to CNN," Murdoch said in jest of the global television news service created by the year's award recipient, "happy peasants in North Korea get to see happy peasants in Cuba, thanks to happy peasants in Atlanta."[20] CNN, which broadcasts from Atlanta, has a nonunion staff paid considerably less than their unionized counterparts at the New York–based networks.

An Electronic Public Space: The Virtual Community

Perhaps the most profound social consequence of the world of online communications is the development of virtual communities. The virtual community refers to a social collective, or community, that forms in the online, electronic world of computer communications known as cyberspace. Virtual communities are not defined by many of the boundaries that sociologists and others traditionally have used to define communities, especially geography and political boundaries. For example, traditional notions of geographically or politically defined communities include the city, the city-state, or the nation-state. Instead, in the world of cyberspace, virtual communities exist in an ethereal electronic space defined by digital networks, computers, and the people who use them. Of course there are physical boundaries in this electronic world, but they are not the same geographic and political boundaries we are most familiar with. The boundaries that apply are the telecommunications lines, ubiquity of computers, and electronic on-ramps that may or may not exist in any particular locality. The Internet, where the greatest number of virtual communities exist, is global in its reach, but tends to have very limited reach into certain heavily populated parts of the world, such as sub-Saharan Africa, Eastern Europe, and much of East Asia. Technological advances, such as wireless networks are rapidly changing this situation, however. And in Africa, the Pan African News Agency announced in June of 1994 the establishment of an Internet link.[21] Still, much of the developing world's population is excluded from the boundaries of any virtual community. Even in the most advanced information society, many of the poor and minority groups, inner city populations, rural residents, and the elderly and the young lie beyond the physical limits of virtual communities. Moreover, there are other limits such as cost that keep vast populations from joining any virtual communities.

Nevertheless, the estimated thirty million worldwide users of the Internet increasingly belong to a vast array of virtual communities. These communities represent profoundly different types of communities than one might find outside cyberspace. Not only are these communities frequently global, but they can form quickly around specific issues. At the

same time, virtual communities also share many qualities and characteristics of their real-world counterparts. They develop their own rules,
regulations, mores, and patterns of behavior. Consider the following
recent example of how one virtual community responded to the tragic
loss of a member.

Grieving Online
Cyberspace has even become a venue for grieving over the death of members of on-line communities. In one recent case, a regular participant in
an online forum was shot and killed, an innocent bystander during an
attempted robbery. The victim, David Alsberg, was a forty-two-year-old
computer programmer, who, ironically, only recently before had partici-
pated in a heated online debate about gun control. Alsberg argued force-
fully for stricter controls on firearms. After his death, members of his
online community expressed their regrets and sense of loss in an online
wake that lasted weeks.[22] "Much more than a crime statistic," one writer
later observed, "Mr. Alsberg has come to symbolize the new social
dynamic of computer networking."[23] The compassion reflected here is
not limited to the tragic case of Mr. Alsberg. Forums have emerged for
people with AIDS, for people who do not have AIDS but carry HIV, the
AIDS virus, and for cancer patients. Networks have formed for victims of
child abuse, even for those abusers in recovery. One accident victim,
Brendan P. Kehoe, who was severely injured in an auto accident on
December 31, 1993, has received a flood of electronic get-well cards from
friends on the Internet.[24] News of Kehoe's accident traveled rapidly
throughout the Internet, with many learning of his accident within hours
of its occurrence. Kehoe, who is well known on the Internet for having
penned "Zen and the Art of the Internet," has received messages in a variety of languages, including English, Spanish, French, and Russian, and
has received more than $1,000 in financial support.

A similar outpouring of grief was expressed on BRASNET, an Internet
forum including Brazilian and Portuguese-speaking subscribers worldwide, on learning of the death of Brazilian race car driver Ayrton Senna
de Silva, who was killed in a practice run in Italy.

Electronic mail, or e-mail, has emerged as the glue that often holds
these virtual communities together. The use of e-mail has grown profoundly since it first traversed the Arpanet in 1969. The Electronic Messaging Association (EMA) estimates as many as thirty to fifty million
people now use e-mail worldwide. In the business community alone, e-
mail users have swelled from one million in 1984 to sixteen million in
1993, reports EMA cofounder Walter Ulrich.[25] Still, little research has been
conducted on the nature and social consequences of e-mail and little is
known about how it affects human communication. Professor Bruce

Redford, a professor at the University of Chicago, proclaims that "the advent of electronic mail is fostering a revival of 'the familiar letter,'" popular in the eighteenth century.[26] Many management consultants see e-mail as an enabling technology for corporate reform, increasing organizational communication efficiency to such a great degree that the ranks of middle management can be significantly thinned. Despite these alleged virtues, e-mail has proven elusive. One writer observes,

> *E-mail is written, yet its language typically embodies a shift toward oral speech patterns. It is the most ephemeral of written mediums, lacking the material form of books or letters and capable of being erased in a keystroke, yet it can be archived and retrieved with unprecedented ease. It has occasioned an astonishing effusion of warm-hearted social interaction outside work settings, yet at work it is the medium of choice for employees who don't like each other and wish to minimize their interactions . . . And e-mail can just as easily promote workplace centralization as decentralization, for while workers may find e-mail gives them unaccustomed access to resources throughout their company, their superiors enjoy enhanced means of tracking their performance.[27]*

The Virtual Voter

As technology has helped transform notions of community based on geography to community based on interests, there are important implications for democracy and the democratic process. Most fundamental is perhaps the use of new technologies to facilitate an informed public citizenry, and the ability to increase and improve public participation in the political process. This has traditionally been a primary role of the press in a democracy. The advent of new media technologies can enhance this function by giving the public more, faster, and easier access to an increased array of information sources.

Concurrently, new technologies hold the promise of improving public participation in the political process and reducing political alienation. On a practical level, new technologies can make it easier to register voters using electronic means or even to allow voting or public opinion polling by online methods. Participation can also be enhanced through the development of electronic town meetings or town halls.

Conversely, there are political dangers in the electronic new media. One such danger is the creation of electronic mobs. Immediate or direct access to information and political sources, without the traditional journalistic filter, means the citizenry may be increasingly subject to biased information, or propaganda not labeled as such. Such rapid access to information may also lead to action without thoughtful deliberation, warns Charles M. Firestone of the Aspen Institute.[28] The public may be more easily stampeded and manipulated. Like talk radio, electronic, online forums may provide a venue for vocal minority or majority viewpoints to overwhelm more dispassionate and informed debate, warns William Joveway of E. M. Warburg, Pincus, and Company.[29]

The Virtual Public

The emergence of virtual communities also has important implications for traditional media and media support institutions, such as public relations or advertising. In the realm of public relations, the growth of virtual publics is transforming how organizations relate to their internal and external audiences. The concept of a virtual public derives from sociologist John Dewey's view of the public as a community that develops around a shared problem or concern.[30] Public relations scholars James Grunig and Todd Hunt, using Dewey's framework, have identified three levels or stages of publics: latent, aware, and active, with each level of mobilization representing a greater threat or concern to an organization.[31] Because of the limitations of traditional media of communication, the process of mobilizing a public from the latent to aware stage, or even from a nonpublic into a latent public, was relatively slow, typically taking weeks or months to develop. The virtual public completely redefines the mobilization time frame. In a matter of minutes, even seconds, a worldwide public, potentially numbering in the millions, can mobilize electronically around a problem perceived initially by even just a single computer user. In addition, more than six thousand latent, virtual publics already exist in the form of user groups, bulletin boards, and newsnets, which exist on a variety of topics and subjects ranging from the environment to health care. The largest Internet newsnet, Usenet, is estimated to have some ten million participants. The notion of the virtual public also has similar implications for the notion of publics defined by their organizational linkage, as conceptualized by scholars James Grunig and Todd Hunt.[32] These publics, based on functional, enabling, normative, and diffused organizational linkages may be mobilized much more rapidly in a distributed electronic cyberspace. For example, a diffused public, one that arises when an organization produces external consequences (for example, when a petroleum company has an oil spill), may be mobilized in a matter of hours, even minutes, on the Internet. Similarly, such publics can develop in cyberspace on an international scale much more readily than in the so-called real world, where communications might occur via "snail mail" (what those on "the net" call traditional postal service) or via expensive long-distance telephone calls or faxes.

Virtual publics possess potentially great power, as attests the recent online campaign a virtual public waged against the Arizona law firm that conducted an unsolicited advertising campaign on the Internet in violation of traditional values and beliefs of many network users. Similarly, reflecting the grass-roots nature of the Internet, a virtual public developed in the spring of 1994 around the landmark case of Brock Meeks, the first journalist sued for libel for a story published exclusively on the Internet. A freelance journalist who found himself in the uncomfortable situation of having no resources to mount a legal defense against the suit, Meeks sent electronic messages to friends and colleagues in cyberspace, who quickly mobilized into a virtual public dedicated to creating a legal defense fund to support the Meeks case. While such grassroots activism is no stranger to public relations or public relations research, it has not been studied in the realm of cyberspace and has important implications for public relations theory and practice.[33–35]

Virtual Consequences

Virtual reality and communications is the subject of increasing scholarly inquiry. The respected *Journal of Communication,* an official journal of the International Communication Association, recently devoted an entire issue to the subject.[36] In this issue, professor Frank Biocca suggests that virtual reality may be not only the next dominant medium, supplanting television, but the "ultimate medium." He asks, "should we not consider the implications now?"[37] Some scholars believe that virtual reality will become a battleground within the academy. "Virtual reality/cyberspace is the arena in which the extremists—technophobes and technophiles—will wage their information war," writes Canadian educator W. Lambert Gardiner. "Communication studies can provide a balanced middle ground between those two extremes."[38]

INSTITUTIONAL CONSEQUENCES OF NEW TECHNOLOGY

As the adoption and diffusion of new media technologies accelerates, virtually every social institution is inexorably altered. Whether the world of politics, education, or libraries, journalism, government, or religion, medicine, law, or the military, every major social institution is touched by the new media technologies. Their influences are varied and unpredictable, although certain common patterns emerge. These patterns include the sometimes complementary and sometimes contradictory forces of decentralization and multidirectional communication, as well as a drive for increased efficiency, productivity, and adaptability. For purposes of illustration, the consequences of new media technologies are examined for two major social institutions:

- the political system, including democratic processes, governmental services, and political participation

- education, including schools, libraries, and access to information technology

New Media Technology, Social Control, and Democracy

Those who deny freedom to others deserve it not for themselves, and, under a just god, cannot long retain it.

—*ABRAHAM LINCOLN*[39]

One of the world's keenest observers of the social consequences of new technology, Anthony Smith, president of Oxford's Magdalen College and author of *Goodbye Gutenberg*, offers another view of the social consequences of information technology. Smith sees the advance of information technology as redefining not just the media but society itself on a global level. Today's digital revolution, he argues, is as significant as Gutenberg's invention of movable type five centuries ago.[40] Just as Gutenberg's invention coincided with the rise of the modern nation state, the digital revolution is transforming the notion of nationhood. "With digitization there emerged a new unit of knowledge—no longer the word or unit of type but the bit and byte of computer data," Smith writes. "Digitization heralded new ways of knowing things and also of organizing both physical and intellectual processes. It insisted upon procedural rather than inspirational thinking. For some, the information revolution was a control revolution, a nirvana of management without mistakes."

To some, advances in information technology are destroying the ability of elites to control what people know, hear, or read. Information technology has irrevocably changed society, says technology visionary Walter Wriston.[41] Wriston, the former chief of Citicorp, one of the world's great banking institutions, says new technology has changed the way wealth is created and the concept of sovereignty. "The pathways open to the transmission of data and information are now so prolix as to make national borders totally porous and old regulatory distinctions meaningless." Information has become the new form of wealth. "The information standard has replaced the gold standard," Wriston adds. These effects, he notes, are positive for society, because they all lead toward greater democracy and freedom. And even if they are not entirely for the good, he concludes, "There are no U-turns on the road to the future."

In agreement are many others, including consumer activist Ralph Nader, who says, "Information is the currency of democracy."[42] Media mogul Rupert Murdoch, chairman of the Australian-based News Corp, also agrees. "Advances in the technology of telecommunications have proved an unambiguous threat to totalitarian regimes everywhere,"

Murdoch says. "Fax machines enable dissidents to bypass state-controlled print media; direct-dial telephone makes it difficult for a state to control interpersonal voice communications. And satellite broadcasting makes it possible for information-hungry residents of many closed societies to bypass state-controlled television channels."[43] *Revolution in a Box,* a 1989 video documentary by ABC's Ted Koppel, credits the presence of satellite dishes, as well as bootlegged videocassettes, in Poland and elsewhere in Eastern Europe with allowing citizens of these countries to bypass official government censorship to learn about international news.

Mitchell Kapor, founder of the Electronic Frontier Foundation and creator of Lotus Corporation, believes that the information highway could completely remake democracy. "This type of medium could enable a Jeffersonian revolution in our civic life" by allowing full, direct participation in public decision making, he says.

Adding to this view is Anthony Smith, who writes, "Television, today extended by video recorders, cable, satellite, and teletext, has become the principal instrument of our citizenship. . . . But it is the graveyard of subtlety, the executioner of taste, the mangler of passion."[44]

Echoing this sentiment is Lawrence Grossman, former president of NBC News, former president and CEO of PBS, and founder of Horizons TV, a new cable channel devoted to cultural and educational programming. Grossman says we are in the midst of the third great stage in the evolution of democracy since the Greeks invented it more than two thousand years ago and the United States created representative democracy more than two hundred years ago. Technology and the information highway, Grossman argues, have spawned an era of direct, electronic democracy.[45, 46] "There is a tremendous change going on in our political system, a change that has been little discussed and appreciated, perhaps because it seems to be so new," Grossman says. "The confluence—the coming together—of television, telephone, fax, computers, and satellites, now enables the American people instantaneously to express their views, for better or worse, to their leadership-representatives . . . with the advent of telecomputers, people will soon punch buttons at home, informing their representatives how they feel, at that instant, on any particular issue."

The Internet and Democracy

The Internet is the first medium that allows the democratic principles of free speech and self-governance to play themselves out unhindered, says David Sobel, a lawyer for the Electronic Privacy Information Center, a Washington, D.C., public interest lobbying group.[47] Conversely, many see even the Internet rapidly being subjected to the same commercial forces that have controlled traditional communication media.[48]

Everette E. Dennis notes that we now have the technological tools to make electronic democracy happen on a national scale. But, he cautions, "two overarching questions arise: (1) Will these innovations be readily accessible to all people, perhaps through such intermediate institutions as schools, churches, and community organizations, or to only some? And, (2) once we get the technology in place and get access to it, are we going to know how to use it?"[49]

One potential application of the information highway is to allow electronic voting by computer.

Technology and Political Campaigns

Gadgets do just about everything else for us these days, so we see no reason why they won't end up electing our presidents.

                                                                —ERIC SEVAREID[50]

Technological advances have helped close the gap between the voter and the candidate by providing a more direct link between the individual citizen and the candidate for office.[51] This was particularly evident during the 1992 presidential campaign.[52] Voters and candidates frequently used technologies such as electronic mail, videotaped messages and call-in talk shows to come in direct contact, essentially pulling an end-run on the traditional news media. At the same time, there are potentially onerous consequences of the application of new technology to political campaigning. As opinion polling is transformed by new technology and marketing utilizes computerized databases to zero in on the undecided voter, the individual is threatened by a loss of privacy, even control, in the political process. The manipulation of the media and public opinion becomes frighteningly real when candidates begin faxing to reporters and voters responses to their opponent's latest speech, even before they have delivered it.

"With all the electronic computers . . . and the flashing numbers and percentages, one can lose sight of the essential fact of any election. And that is the mind of the voter," said Eric Sevareid in a CBS News commentary, November 2, 1958.[53]

New communication technologies have also played an important role in the erosion of the political parties.[54]

De-Technology

Although it is not a book about technology, Roderick P. Hart's *Seducing America* offers one of the most eloquent examinations of the impact of the technology of television on the political process.[55] F. A. Liddell Professor of Communication and Government at the University of Texas at Austin, Hart argues that the technology of television is actually "a de-technology."[56] It is a medium that removes the space between members of the public on a global scale. "Through television, we can touch persons who live elsewhere; we can read their distant hearts." As a result, individuals are insulated from the feelings of massness in a mass society. Instead, viewers can act globally, while still thinking locally. They can even hear a more primitive voice.

> *And, look, this campaign is over. There's no hard feelings about that. The American people are smart. They know a tough-fought campaign on both sides when they see it.*
> —GEORGE BUSH[57]

Delivery of Government Services via the Information Superhighway

The largest of all social institutions, government is also undergoing a metamorphosis in part driven by new media technology. Government transactional records are almost universally stored in digital form, with public access increasingly in electronic, online form. Government services, once available only to those citizens willing to stand in line for many exhaustive hours, are increasingly available electronically online. Maryland, for example, recently became the first state to announce a program to make available free of charge to all its citizens access to the Internet. Wisconsin has similarly announced an ambitious plan to put all its citizens on the information highway. Although many of these technological applications have been developed at the state and federal level, the information highway can be used to address important issues on the urban agenda, as well. K. Kendall Guthrie argues that technology applications on the information highway have the potential to promote economic development and even help to reconnect the urban poor.[58] Internationally, a growing number of countries are expressing interest in putting governmental services online, much as France has done through the videotex service known as Minitel.

Advancing Education Through Technology

Education is one social institution that has the potential to benefit greatly from the development of new media technology. The government plays perhaps the lead role in ensuring that the benefits of technology reach America's educational institutions and classrooms. Vice President Gore and others including Commerce Secretary Ron Brown have been particularly outspoken in their advocacy of the educational benefits of a new national information infrastructure. While committing some federal funding to achieve this broad goal, they have called on the private sector to play an even greater role. In speaking to communications industry leaders on January 11, 1994, Vice President Al Gore said, "I challenge you . . . (communication industry leaders) to connect all of our classrooms, all of our libraries, and all of our hospitals and clinics by the year 2000."[59]

In a report issued in May of 1994, Commerce Secretary Brown outlined the possible educational and lifelong learning applications of the proposed NII. Consisting of the current and evolving telecommunications infrastructure, including telephone, broadcast, cable, and electronic networks, the NII may enable:

- multimedia interactive learning programs for students of all ages, whether delivered to classrooms or directly to the home
- simulated learning activities, such as laboratory experiments or archeological digs, featuring immersive, realistic simulations
- universal access interfaces to allow students, workers, and those with disabilities to fully participate in the learning experience

Government-funded research demonstrates the educational value of new media technology, as well. A Congressionally mandated study comparing multimedia and more conventional instruction found time savings of 30 percent, cost savings of 30 percent to 40 percent, improved student achievement, and a direct, positive link between interactivity and instructional effectiveness.[60] Other research has confirmed the instructional effectiveness of new technology in the classroom and beyond. A 1993 survey of studies on technology in schools demonstrated that "courses for which computer-based networks were used increased student-student and student-teacher interaction, increased student-teacher interaction with lower-performing students, and did not decrease the traditional forms of communications used."[61] Reviews of computer-based teaching in military applications found that students reach similar levels of achievement in 30 percent less time than those using more traditional teaching methods.[62]

Despite the effectiveness of new technology in the classroom, most classrooms are poorly equipped with those technologies, such as computers, especially multimedia technologies and online services. The installed based of computers in American elementary and secondary schools is generally unable to support multimedia computing, concludes the Information Infrastructure Task Force in its May 1994 report.

Eighty percent of the base includes 55 percent Apple IIs and 24 percent IBM PCs, XTs, ATs, or similar class machines, with limited graphic or multimedia capabilities; the part of the base made of 10 percent

Apple Macintoshes and 8 percent IBM compatible 386s or 486s is capable of supporting high level applications. The number of computers in the schools, 2.5 million, equivalent to one per classroom. In a 1993 survey of NEA members, only 4 percent of teachers reported having a modem in their classrooms, while 38 percent reported having access to a modem somewhere in the school building. Another survey found that among 550 educators who are actively using telecommunications, less than half have access to the Internet.[63]

Certain instructional technologies are available more widely in America's schools. For instance, 75 percent of America's schools have cable television, and half of all teachers use video material in the classroom.[64] More than twelve million Americans access daily at least some of the sixty thousand electronic bulletin boards available on the Internet, and the Department of Education estimates that much of this usage is for educational purposes. This usage is growing rapidly. In fact, the annual growth rate of Gopher traffic on the Internet, which reflects educational research information requests, is 1,000 percent.[65] In Texas, one-quarter of teachers regularly signs on to the Texas Education Network to share information, exchange e-mail, and find resources. Similar educational systems are in use in other states, as well. Distance learning and the "virtual classroom" are also increasingly in use in the United States. Another fascinating distance learning project is based at the University of Texas at Austin. Through the World Wide Web, the university has created a "Worldwide Lecture Hall," giving students the world over electronic access to a virtual university offering scores of courses online.

A word of caution is in order here. Advocates of television in classrooms have long heralded the potential of TV as a tool for enhancing learning. Research to date, however, has shown that by itself, TV will not work wonders on the educational process. Teacher involvement, full student interactivity, and richness of content are all prerequisites for effective use of technology in the classroom.

Governmental Objectives
The NII Task Force has outlined several educational objectives and goals for use of new media technologies for education and lifelong learning. Among these are:

- convenient and equitable access, by connecting to every classroom, public library, and other learning location, and providing affordable access in the workplace and home
- high-speed transmission capability, to permit multimedia applications and interactivity

- easy use to facilitate broad use among all educational markets and social segments
- technological simplification, with the ultimate goal to make connecting to the NII as simple as plugging in a telephone
- accessibility, to accommodate the diverse needs of American society
- security to protect privacy, safeguard intellectual property rights, and provide effective educational resources
- content in the form of rich and diverse material
- portability to insure system interoperability and to achieve the same level of "plug and play" found in high fidelity audio systems

Industry's Role

Although progress has been slow, a number of information highway builders as well as content providers are already stepping up to meet the Administration's challenge to provide new products and services for education. Pacific Bell Corporation and Jones Intercable have announced that they will connect schools to broadband networks, allowing a convenient on-ramp to the information superhighway. Pac Bell, as it is known in the West, provides telephone service to most of California, and will spend $100 million to install advanced telephone lines in schools, libraries, and community colleges in that state.[66] These digital lines will provide access to the Internet for users at some 7,400 public institutions by the end of 1996. Pac Bell has also pledged to keep access to the technology affordable for these public institutions. They have promised to wire two locations in each institution free of charge and will waive usage fees for one year after installation. They also promise to cooperate with the California Public Utilities Commission to establish a special low-cost education-access rate to keep educational institutions on the information superhighway.[67]

Two media giants, Liberty Media Corporation and Reuters NewMedia, have joined forces to create Ingenious, a daily multimedia news package for classroom and home use.[68] Reuters will provide the news content, while Liberty Media will deliver it to personal computers through Liberty's cable system, currently available in eighteen thousand schools and some twenty-eight million homes.

At the same time, the benefits of new media technologies may just as likely elude the educational arena, or be very selective in their impact, access, and availability. The above examples notwithstanding, there has been traditionally little financial incentive for companies to invest heavily in new technologies and education. This has been especially the case for many poor inner city and rural schools and school systems. Although many talk about the benefits of the information superhighway in the classroom, one recent study showed that only 5 percent of public school classrooms have a telephone line. Without this telecommunications lifeline, the information superhighway and its accompanying new media technologies hold little value or potential for most of America's schools. This situation presents both an irony and a dilemma for educational institutions. Commercial enterprises such as Chris Whittle's Channel 1 beams news programming directly into schools. Whittle provides all the needed equipment, including television monitor and satellite dish, free to the schools, many of which are in dire financial straits and cannot afford to buy such equipment.

Not surprisingly, Whittle's program is very controversial because the feeds include commercial messages. Moreover, to date, research has demonstrated little real educational value for Channel 1. Nevertheless, the dilemma for school administrators is that many lack the resources to get much needed equipment for their schools, but they find it difficult if not impossible for political reasons to accept Whittle's offer. Ironically, few question the role in the classroom of such "old" media as newspapers or news magazines, which also contain commercial messages. Nor do many voters who oppose Whittle's effort offer the public funds needed to put electronic on-ramps into all public schools. Further, while Channel 1 contains advertising messages, teachers are free to use the Whittle equipment for purposes other than receiving Channel 1. They can use it to receive programming such as CNN in the Classroom, a special news feed designed specifically for students and containing no advertising. Recent reports indicate that Whittle's enterprise may be in imminent danger of collapse because of an impending financial crisis (that is, the inability to repay a $100 million loan).[69]

Profnet: Linking Higher Education and the Press

Profnet is an interesting network service developed in 1992 that brings together the universe of higher education and journalism.[70] Until recently, journalists in need of an expert source turned most often to a well-stocked Rolodex and several hours on the telephone, not always successfully locating the needed specialist. Profnet is an online service created by Dan Forbush, associate vice president for university affairs at the State University of New York at Stony Brook. Reporters send queries by e-mail, fax, or toll-free number to Profnet headquarters, and in turn, the query is relayed by e-mail to public information (PI) officers at some six hundred colleges, universities, and research centers participating in the network. The PI officers then find resident experts on the needed subject, and quickly get in touch with the reporter placing the query. The Profnet system currently receives about twenty queries a day, all processed at no charge. Network costs to run the system totaled about $2,500 in 1993, not including the time of the various individuals involved. Profnet, and services like it, may help bridge the gap between the academy and the public.

The Electronic Library

Instead of fortresses of knowledge, there will be an ocean of information.
—JOHN BROWNING[71]

New technology has profound implications for one of society's most cherished educational institutions, the public library. Since the days of Andrew Carnegie, the public library has provided free and easy access to information of all types to the public, whether in the form of books, newspapers, or magazines. In today's new media environment, libraries still play a vital role in providing universal access to digital information.

At the same time, the arrival of digital technology has begun to profoundly transform the public library. Its impact has been both complex and subtle. "The computer plays a strategic role in the reorganization of all the institutions in which it arrives," writes Anthony Smith.[72]

"It is not a silent visitor, but an active agent of change, bringing with it the inexorable sense of its own modernity—inexorable, but with incalculable consequences. Like an epidemic, you cannot be sure where it will strike or what it will spare, only to return later." Smith argues that libraries will find themselves going through a variety of changes as a result of the introduction of digital technology. Among them:

- Libraries will turn into "a kind of print-house, since readers will want to create more and more of their hard-copy material within the library and then remove it."
- Computerization will permit unlimited revision of works including perishable or time-dependent information. Libraries may treat such a work "as a database and offer the reader, at appropriate cost, the chance to log onto it."
- Online communications and digital repositories will create virtual libraries that each user can create from any computer workstation connected to the global data network.

There are also a number of troubling questions that arise. "But what happens when a publisher decides that the task is no longer financially viable?" Smith asks. "Who then holds the database for purposes of public record? And at whose cost? Who holds the copyright? *Who* protects *whom* against acts of plagiarism from such a work?"

From Scriptoria to Virtual Books.   In the beginning, libraries were vast repositories of the world's knowledge, run and controlled by monks in scriptoria. Because knowledge often is power, access to libraries and their collections was fundamental to the control of society and the preservation of the status quo. As a result, libraries held tight rein over their hold-ings. Consider one example from England's Hereford Cathedral. "Books were chained to the shelves. Although books were sometimes lent to other monasteries, the consequences for failing to return them were severe, as the inscription from this twelfth century manuscript makes clear: 'This book belongs to the monastery of St. Mary of Robert's Bridge, whoever shall steal it, or mutilate it, let him be forever cursed. Amen.'"[73] Today's technology of the information highway is poised to change all that. From a local Internet terminal anyone can now search the catalogs of thou-sands of libraries around the world, including the vast collection of the Library of Congress and twelve to fifteen million items in the British Library.

Prospects for a Digital Library of Congress.   One of the greatest libraries ever created is the United States Library of Congress in Washington, D.C., just opposite the Capitol. With its collection of more than one hundred million items, it exceeds by more than a thousandfold even the great Alexandrian library of ancient Egypt.[74] As proponents push for a new national information infrastructure, one of the promises is to open elec-tronic pathways to the massive collection of the Library of Congress. The Internet already allows users to browse electronically the Library of Con-gress card catalog. But major hurdles remain. One of the most difficult and costly to overcome is the simple fact that the vast majority of items in the Library of Congress are in analog form, many in print and others on videotape or film. The collection includes more than twenty million books, more than four million maps and atlases, fourteen million prints and photographs, and more than six hundred thousand films and video-tapes. The cost and complexity of the Herculean task of converting all this material to machine readable form is almost incalculable, although a consortium of U.S. organizations has begun the process of raising pri-vate capital to fund the digital conversion of the Library of Congress's holdings.

The Vatican Library Goes Digital.   Founded in the mid-1400s by Pope Nicholas V, the Vatican Library holds some of the rarest books and antique manuscripts in the world, including a beautifully illustrated copy of Dante's *Divine Comedy,* Ptolemy's *Geography,* and the four oldest sur-viving manuscripts of Virgil's poems. The library houses more than 150,000 manuscripts and a million printed books, including 8,000 books published in the initial fifty years of Gutenberg's printing press. In early 1994, the Vatican and International Business Machines Corporation (IBM) announced a joint project to bring the five-hundred-year-old library into the computer age.[75] Using optical scanning technology, the pilot project will capture the pages of the collection in digital form, store the images in computer readable form, and open the door to worldwide scholarly access to the works through online communications. The project holds the promise of not only increasing access to the priceless collection, but will preserve and protect the fragile ancient holdings, which are jeopardized by repeated handling. Through image enhancement technology, it might also be possible to scrutinize certain works even more closely.

Many university libraries are also beginning the process of converting their holdings to digital form. A number of major universities have received multimillion dollar funding from the National Science Foundation as well as from private partners to undertake digital library projects, including Carnegie Mellon; the University of California at Berkeley; the University of Michigan; the University of California, Santa Barbara; Stanford University; and the University of Illinois.[76]

A Scholar's Electronic Paradise.   The electronic library has important implications for scholarly research and teaching. A number of major academic publishers have begun publishing scholarly journals on the Internet, on computer disk, or on CD-ROM, and others are considering such projects, including the MIT Press, the University of California Press, and the University of Chicago Press. Electronic journals may provide scholars with both more timely and complete access to research information and at a potentially lower cost, at least to the publishers.[77]

One of the greatest scholarly research resources in the United States is the Online Computer Library Center (OCLC), whose services are used by seventeen thousand libraries. Until recently, however, libraries have been unable to access the OCLC Online Union Catalog system for cataloging items and arranging interlibrary loans without paying fees to use OCLC's private telecommunications network.[78] In April of 1994 the OCLC began a one-year trial designed to let librarians access the OCLC through the Internet, which will allow access to the online catalog without network fees. Since fewer than a third of the libraries that use OCLC services have access to the Internet, however, the company will still maintain access through its private network.

Libraries in Crisis.   Patricia Glass Schuman, president of Neal-Schuman Publishers and former president of the American Library Association, however, is concerned that the economics of new technology may be contributing to the transformation of information from a public good into a commodity. Schuman cautions that we are rapidly moving into an era when we will pay an increasingly expensive fee for information that in the past the federal government provided free to public libraries.[79] In Vice

President Gore's "Reinventing Government" report, he recommends disbanding the Government Printing Office, which has for decades provided government publications free to the system of depository libraries.[80] The likely replacement will be publication of government data via electronic information services provided to libraries by private vendors who will charge a fee. "How many of you have ever paid for an online search yourself," Schuman asked the seminar participants, largely long-time journalists, media analysts, and communication scholars. "Perish the thought," was the response of one participant, followed by general laughter. Most had frequently used online database searches, but had exclusively relied on their employers to pay for the searches. Libraries face a "silent crisis," warned Schuman. There are 115,000 libraries in the United States, noted Schuman, including school, public, and private institutions. But the library is an "endangered public space," she added. Half the school libraries have closed in the last decade in California. One hundred public libraries are now being run by private companies, including some foreign companies. Many now cost more to run. "Is information a public good?" Schuman asked. "Does it contribute to education, culture, and the democratic process?" The answer is "yes," Schuman declared.[81]

Improving Educational Resources. A number of companies have announced they are developing digital libraries to serve the education market.[82] Three companies, Infonautics, Inc., Tandem Computers, Inc., and MRJ, Inc., have joined forces to create Homework Helper, an electronic library aimed at primary and secondary school students. The library will include information from a variety of sources, such as Compton's *Multimedia Encyclopedia, USA Today,* the *Los Angeles Times, Forbes,* Reuters, and *Time* magazine.[83] Journal Graphics and Cable News Network will provide transcripts of television news and information programming, and Simon and Schuster will provide a variety of content. Homework Helper will also include seven hundred works of literature and will be accessible through a variety of networks and commercial online services, including the Internet and Prodigy Services Company. Homework Helper will also feature an intuitive user interface. Students will be able to access the system by typing questions in plain English. For instance, typing "Where is Sri Lanka" will bring up a variety of types of information, including a map, an encyclopedia article about the country, and other related information.

Pulitzer Publishing Company has announced a new nationwide educational service that will link two thousand schools in thirty-three states and the District of Columbia. Called IDEAnet, for Interactive Distance Education Alliance, the interactive television service will carry a broad range of programming developed by several school systems and universities. Programming will include language classes, CNN Newsroom, and preparation courses for the Preliminary Scholastic Aptitude Test (PSAT). IDEAnet will also serve as a gateway to the Internet, Satlink On-Line, and Pulitzer's online newspaper, *Post-Link.* The IDEAnet system has reduced the costs of transmission by utilizing advances in compression to reduce satellite load. "By combining four established, successful TV education networks and utilizing digital compression technology, we can deliver multiple channels of programming using only one satellite transponder," says Briant L. Talbott, superintendent of District 101, one of the school systems participating in the IDEAnet.[84]

Access to the Information Highway

Fundamental to the technological transformation of every social institution, whether political, educational, or governmental, is universal access to technology. In *The People's Right to Know: Media, Democracy, and the Information Highway,* Frederick Williams and John V. Pavlik argue that guaranteeing access to all people is a fundamental prerequisite to the design of the information highway. "We have nearly achieved our goal of 'universal service' in voice telephony; why not a twenty-first-century upgrade to universal service in access to essential information and transactions?" they ask.[85] In late October 1993, a group of 71 nonprofit groups joined forces to urge policy makers to bring the public interest to the forefront of the design of the national information infrastructure. "It is not enough for the public to react to plans once they've been put in place. The public must be at the table when the plans are made," said the group's Kathryn C. Montgomery, president of the Center for Media Education. Called the Telecommunications Policy Roundtable, members of the group are concerned that a national information highway developed by market forces will bypass the poor and minority communities, and exclude information services of value to educators, librarians, people with disabilities and others. Most central to the Roundtable's mission is the issue of universal access. Roundtable members urge policy makers to consider these seven principles in the design of the information highway:

- free access to information needed to fully participate in a democratic society
- freedom of expression for network users—protection of copyright to content creators and library patrons' use of materials
- an "electronic commons" for public discussion and debate
- a marketplace of ideas accessible to all and not controlled by telecommunications carriers

- an opportunity to improve the quality of work and equity in the workplace
- privacy protection of users
- an opportunity for full public involvement in policies regarding the data network[86]

If these policy imperatives are met, Roundtable members suggest, then the information highway will foster robust communication, which has been the foundation of democracy in the United States for more than two hundred years. "We cannot begin to afford to allow people not to speak on this information highway," said Roundtable participant T. Andrew Lewis, executive director of the Alliance for Community Media. "Nothing could be more clear than the need for communication in our communities today."

The implications of universal access are profound for the democratic process, which rests on the principle of a government responsive to and in touch with the people. To be responsive, the government must communicate with the people. "One cannot talk about communications from citizen to government—or any other kind of communications—in this information age without discussing the role of technology," says Harvard University political scientist Sidney Verba in the 1993 James Madison Award Lecture. But many are already excluded from the emerging information highway, and as a result are disenfranchised from the process of political communication and, thus, from full participation in our democracy. "Those of us plugged into networks—that sometimes burden us with information coming in and the sense that we ought to be sending things out in reply—forget how many people are outside of such networks," Verba explains. "People like us receive many computer-generated communications about public matters and requests for action or contributions. Our data show, however, that a large proportion of Americans never receive a piece of mail soliciting support for a political cause. Networks are very selective," he concludes.[87]

Not everyone agrees that equal access to new media technology and the information superhighway should be the first priority for public policy. Dr. Eli Noam, founding director of the Columbia Institute for Tele-Information and a well-known expert on communications policy and economics, suggests that while universal access is important, encouraging competition among service providers is a better way to ensure low prices and the development of new services.[88] Many in industry are in agreement, including Eric Rabe, director of media relations for Bell Atlantic and a member of the executive committee that had been charged with planning the ill-fated Bell Atlantic–TCI merger. Rabe, whose company has always been a heavily regulated monopoly, would welcome increased competition over additional regulation. "Equity is a red herring," says Nancy Hicks Maynard, president of Maynard Associates, a new media technology consulting firm and a veteran newspaper publishing executive.[89] Noting that new technologies are almost always relatively expensive when they are introduced but invariably come down quickly in price and become widely available, Maynard suggests that the equity imperative should not be so great that it inhibits the development of new information services and technologies.

CULTURAL CONSEQUENCES OF NEW MEDIA TECHNOLOGY

From the evolution of storytelling to electronic art, new media technologies are steadily exerting their influence on cultures both in the United States and throughout the world. Moreover, the use of new media technology is itself leading to the growth of computer-mediated culture, much of which is based on traditional culture, but other aspects of which are unique.

Hyperfiction

One of the most dramatic effects of new media technology derives from the creation of hypertext, or nonlinear, nonsequential writing. As the concept of nonlinear writing, or writing that is nondirectional without any preset beginning, middle, and end, has taken hold, an entirely new form of literature, that of hyperfiction, has emerged. Hyperfiction is a form of writing in which the author creates characters, environments, and motivation, but not a single predetermined plot. Rather, each reader is a participant in a simulated reality that he or she helps define through his or her decisions, actions, and communication. In many ways, the creator of the original hyperfiction is like a filmmaker who finds him or herself in the role of despot, almost playing god in creating a world. How that world evolves, however, is left to the interaction of the qualities of the world created and the participants who enter into it. Like snowflakes, no two experiences in hyperfiction are alike. Each is unique. Nevertheless, there are common experiences and meanings to be shared across "readers" or participants in hyperfiction. What disappears in hyperfiction is the notion of a single narrative line, not narrative itself. Stories are still read, it's just that the author is truly both reader and the original creator. As hyperfiction evolves and becomes an increasingly significant cultural force, its reach and impact will extend beyond the specialized realm of computer enthusiasts, and into the mainstream of society, through educational venues, advertising, and the commercial sector. Hyperfiction may even evolve into an important part of how cultural values and mores are transferred from generation to generation. Much as many oral cultures have not relied greatly on technology in storytelling and cultural transference, and written cultures have relied on the written word, society's next generation may come to increasingly rely on computer-based hyperfiction as an important tool for sharing and transferring cultural symbols and meaning.

Related to contemporary society's shift toward a hyperfiction communication environment is the development of a culture of random access and remote technological control. The ubiquity of computers has led their users to become increasingly comfortable with the concept of random access to information. In older media, such as radio, television, movies, books, and newspapers, the presentation of content has always been determined by a central content provider. It has been presented for consumption at a particular time and in a preset order and must be consumed as it is packaged. Although a newspaper reader is not required to begin with the first story on the first page, it is not possible to conduct a keyword search to immediately jump to just the story or item of interest. New, digital media have changed all this. Users of new media can go directly to any desired content. It is rapidly creating a cultural generation that not only expects but increasingly demands information and entertainment on demand.

Although typically associated with the TV set, remote control technology is a much broader concept that applies increasingly to all mediated experience. The next generation expects to remotely control its answering machines, its voice mail, its electronic mail, its bank accounts. Coupled with the growth of remote control technology, tomorrow's media consumer will demand remote access to and remote control of any media content whenever, wherever, and however they want. Anything less will leave them frustrated and seeking alternative sources of news, information, and entertainment.

Connecting Concepts in Hyperspace

Hypertext and hypermedia also change the way we access information. Not only can we gather information more rapidly and efficiently through nonlinear media, but they allow us to make unexpected connections between concepts, almost in a spiderweb fashion. No longer must we search information organized the way someone else has decided. We are not limited by the alphabetic system of classification of books envisioned centuries ago by Herbert Maunsell. Instead, we can make connections by our own concepts and ideas, sometimes in unexpected ways. Anthony Smith, for example, described how he was recently using an encyclopedia on CD-ROM and came across the word *Orangutan*.[90] He noticed the word had a Hottentot origin. Curious about the extent of the African language's impact on Western culture, he queried the CD-ROM about how many English-language words have a Hottentot origin. The answer: 27.

Some might claim that in creating hypertext information systems or virtual libraries, something intangible is lost. There is no longer a sense of being there, of placing one's hands on an original manuscript. This may be true, as in the case of a somewhat sterile corporate library where all information is stored electronically, but the advantage is that it makes all information available at once.[91]

Multimedia Art Forms

Multimedia technology and online communications also present important implications for contemporary culture. Increasingly, artists are finding a new palette in multimedia technology. Since the late Lejaren Hiller pioneered the use of the computer as a medium for musical composition with the creation of the *Illiac Suite* in 1956, digital technology has produced profound effects on music and other art forms.[92] Today, artists following in the footsteps of John Cage and others are using digital technology not only to present their musical compositions, but as a creative environment. Italian composer Nicola Sani has employed a variety of electronic, multimedia technologies to synthesize new compositions and to combine music with full-motion video images. The result is a digitally generated interactive multimedia artform reminiscent of Walt Disney's classic *Fantasia* composition. Sani's musical video art has been distributed electronically via CD-ROM, communication satellite, and online. Sani's efforts reflect the convergence of visual and aural arts in a multimedia creative environment. Digital technology has also provided an opportunity for entrepreneurial artists to both create a new medium for artistic expression as well as a venue to display their work and hold public discourse on art and artistic expression. One such effort has been pioneered by multimedia producers Emily Hartzell and Nina Sobell, creators of Parkbench, an online arts environment designed for the discussion, creation, and display of electronic art. Run out of a new media lab at New York University in Greenwich Village, ParkBench is available free to all comers at @large.cs.nyu.edu.

The Virtual Art Gallery

The advent of online communications is also emerging as an important vehicle to provide worldwide public access to art. Institutions ranging from the White House to the Smithsonian have developed online art tours available free of charge to the public. An increasing number of museums around the world are putting their collections in digital form onto the Internet, as well as CD-ROM. Examples include the World Wide

Web servers at the Museum of Paleontology at the University of California at Berkeley or Krannert Art Museum at the University of Illinois, which allow visitors from dozens of countries to view text and images of exhibits via the Internet, or the "virtual reality" exhibit at Carnegie Mellon University's Studio for Creative Inquiry at which visitors wear a virtual reality helmet to tour the Egyptian Temple of Horus.[93]

Of concern to some is the increasing corporate interest in capturing the rights to publish electronically a variety of works of art and art collections. Reminiscent of the late publishing baron William Randolph Hearst in his quest to own vast collections of the world's art is computing software king Bill Gates, chairman and founder of Microsoft. Gates has been quietly and systematically buying the rights to store and publish electronically a huge collection of art masterpieces ranging from classic paintings by Vincent Van Gogh to contemporary artists as well. Gates has even spent some $30.8 million to acquire the *Codex,* Leonardo da Vinci's rare manuscript. Some are worried that public access to digital art collections will be severely limited or subject to cost restrictions, if electronic art is controlled by corporate interests. Offering some poetic justice, *Millenium Auction* offers via CD-ROM a twenty-first-century marketplace where would-be collectors can bid on art works such as Manet's *Déjeuner sur l'Herbe* and Picasso's *Guernica.*

Popular Artists
A variety of popular artists are also turning to multimedia platforms, especially CD-ROM and CD-I, to produce and release their commercial products. One interesting area is the emergence of interactive rock 'n' roll. Veteran rock singer and producer Todd Rundgren, once known for his 1970s hit "Then I Saw the Light" and more recently for his experimental applications of computer technology in rock music, is one of the most innovative pioneers in the developing area of interactive rock. In "No World Order," Rundgren has created "the first do-it-yourself album," proclaims *Time* magazine.[94] Listeners can use their CD-I (compact disc-interactive) players to customize any of the songs to their tastes, change the tempo, the mix ("natural," "spacious," or "Karoake"), even the mood ("bright," "happy," or "thoughtful"). They can create virtually new music by digitally sampling any of the 933 musical snippets in the database. "This is your chance to talk back to the music," explains Rundgren.

Technology and Fractal Geometry
The intersection of art and technology has often been unexpected, as in the fascinating case of the development of fractal geometry. Discovered by French mathematician Dr. Benoit B. Mandelbrot some forty years ago, fractal geometry has helped provide a "measure of order in physical,

mathematical, and social phenomena that are characterized by abundant data but extreme variability."[95] Fractal geometry has had surprising aesthetic value and utility in a variety of media and communication applications. The striking visual patterns created in fractal geometry have been widely acclaimed for their beauty and for the synergy they reflect between worlds of mathematics and art. Fractal patterns, which because of their complexity often require powerful computers to execute their calculations and draw the resulting images, frequently suggest organic and naturally occurring objects and images, such as trees, snowflakes, and shorelines. Mandelbrot has argued that nature itself reflects the principles of fractal geometry. A number of filmmakers have employed fractal geometry applications to create coastlines and other terrain on fictional planets in science-fiction movies.

Video Games as Cultural Force

A growing number of scholars, policy makers, and members of the public voice concern about the cultural implications of an emergent media form known as video games. Australian scholar McKenzie Wark argues that the Nintendo generation is experiencing the world through a new cultural lens, that of the video game.[96] He suggests that video games are to today's youth what television and cinema were to earlier generations. "Pac-Man, Donkey Kong, and the new release of Mortal Kombat ('16 megs of mayhem!') have to be seen as the start of something new, not merely something to be reduced and subsumed under past cultural, regulatory, and theoretical experiences of the media."[97] The implications of this emergent media form are profound not just in the United States but internationally, especially in Japan and East Asia where much of the hardware and software for video games is being created and consumed. "The challenge mounted by the emerging cultural technology of games to the dominant ones of cinema and television is felt also in Hong Kong— one of the world's great cinema capitals," writes Wark.[98] "Fight games like Street Fighter II cannibalize another great non-Western pop genre, the Hong Kong martial arts film, in much the same way the latter ate up traditional Chinese performance and martial art forms." Notably, much of the content or software being produced for video games comes not just from the United States, which in general dominates the world's media software market, but from Japan.

Moving-Image Technology and Perceiving Reality

Advances in moving-image technology, some have argued, have profound implications for more than just what we see. They can alter our perceptions of reality and how we interact with it. "With each new technology, there come new techniques for duplicating the world," suggests Oxford's Anthony Smith.[99] Two parallel lines of image technology are now coalescing, Smith argues. From the paintings of Leonardo da Vinci of the fifteenth century to the high-definition TV of today, one line has striven for increasing realism in the moving image. A parallel line began with French filmmaker Méliés and has reached its pinnacle in virtual reality, in which "The surreal dissolves into the real," Smith observes. However, in virtual reality, the lines between fantasy and reality become indistinguishable, and a new theoretical view of the moving image emerges. It is one based on the fusion of Da Vinci's realism and Méliés's fantasy. Smith cautions that the inevitable impact of this fusion may be the erosion of the credibility of the image, especially in television news, where viewers already have frequent reason to doubt the veracity of what they see.

SOCIOLOGICAL PERSPECTIVES ON NEW MEDIA TECHNOLOGY

Understanding the social and cultural importance of new media technologies also requires a close examination of the sociological transformation those technologies are triggering. To those living in the final years of the second millennium, it has become increasingly apparent that new media technologies offer important implications for how we live, work, and play. The following discussion turns a sociological prism on the growth and impact of new media technologies. Focusing first on the transformation of the workplace, the discussion includes a look at the role of gender, race, age, and social class in the use and impact of new technology, as well as the nature and consequences of computer-mediated communication.

Telecommuting: Transforming the Workplace

Five years ago we moved to Telluride, Colorado, a tiny mountain village in the southwest corner of the state. Our house and our town (population 1,200) are at 9,000 feet in a box canyon where the mountains all around us soar to 13,000 and 14,000 feet. It looks a little like the Swiss Alps.

Although we are six hours from Denver, with our computers, telephones, fax machine, and Federal Express we are as in touch with the rest of the world as if we were in downtown Tokyo or London.
—JOHN NAISBITT AND PATRICIA
ABURDENE[100]

Just as the automobile and the national highway system helped transform the sociological landscape of America by fostering a more mobile society, so too will the information highway and new media technologies have important sociological effects.[101] One of these effects is the growth of telecommuting, the ability to conduct one's work from a remote location. Advances in telephony, networked computing, and the fax machine have enabled some ten million people nationwide to set up shop at home.[102]

What do Buffalo, Wyoming, Sun Valley, California, Pullman, Washington, and Steamboat Springs, Colorado, have in common with a growing number of other out-of-the-way places? One answer is new media technology: they are all fast emerging as the test sites for tomorrow's telecommunities. In Telluride, Colorado, an old mining town turned into a ski resort, the Telluride Institute has set up a new communications program called InfoZone. By providing access to voice, data, and video through advanced cable television and telephone technology, the two-year program will establish a communitywide information system connecting residents with schools, the library, a health clinic, and other community centers. In addition to the computer technology already in most residents' homes (50 percent have a home PC versus 24 percent nationwide), Apple computer has donated equipment for public places, such as the library. US West is laying optical fiber to service new subdivisions and the town is rapidly becoming fully wired. Richard Lowenberg, program director of the Telluride Institute, hopes that InfoZone will help answer some of the critical questions about the nature of the new telecommunity. "How does this affect the quality of life over the next twenty years? Are people going to be more alienated and have less face-to-face communication? Does it create a real economic engine for small communities or just keep costing more?" he asks.

In other communities, telecommunications systems are being upgraded to provide enhanced telecommuting capabilities. Two hundred fifty miles east of Seattle, officials of four counties near Pullman, Washington, are negotiating with GTE Corporation to provide telecommunications improvements in order to create attractive telecommuting opportunities for laid-off high-tech workers. The ranching community of Buffalo, Wyoming, has received dozens of inquiries from people who want to telecommute from the town where Owen Wister wrote *The Virginian*. Meanwhile, a nonprofit group in Durango, Colorado, is working to build a backup communications system for area telecommuters. The nonprofit is negotiating with AT&T to buy thirty abandoned microwave towers to serve as a backup system for the community.[103]

A growing number of studies are beginning to document the social and environmental benefits of telecommuting and its positive influence on overall quality of life, both for individuals and their communities, as well as for enhancing work performance and worker productivity, sometimes by as much as 100 percent.[104]

Gender and Technology Use

Gender often has been a defining factor in the emergence and use of new media technologies. Males tend to have higher usage of new media technologies, and they have designed much of the communication software and hardware. Although there have been notable exceptions, such as Bell Atlantic's Vivian Horner, who is the creator of much new video programming for children, including Nickelodeon, much of the history of new media technology has been a story of men, from Alexander Graham Bell to William Gates. A telling recent example is Battletech, one the first and most successful networked virtual reality simulations; it appeals almost exclusively to males.[105] Created by Dungeons and Dragons aficionados Jordan Weisman and Russ Babcoc, the first commercial Battletech center opened in Chicago in 1990 and almost immediately reaped a profit. Walt Disney's grandson Tim and his partners bought the rights to Battletech in 1992 and transformed it into Virtual World Entertainment, a string of urban arcades featuring Battletech and other proposed offerings. "We knew Battletech was limited," Disney admits.[106] "It plays to a 92 percent male audience. If a couple walks up to a Battletech Center, they begin arguing; then the man goes inside and the woman walks away."[107]

Transcending Gender

The information superhighway holds the promise of opening up the doors to women. One illustration comes from the world of cyberspace. Within the Internet, New York's Stacy Horn has created her own East Coast Hang Out (ECHO), founded in 1989. As one writer describes it, ECHO "is a metropolitan oasis, an electronic gathering place for writers, artists, and culture mavens, closer to a literary salon than the usual online techno-jock boys' club."[108] Although most information services tend to be male-dominated, ECHO appeals nearly equally to women. Of ECHO's four thousand subscribers, nearly half (40 percent) are women, says Horn. In contrast, only 10 percent of CompuServe's subscribers are women.[109] ECHO's users pay a monthly fee of $13.75 to $52.43 and have access to online discussions of topics ranging from American mythologies to writing. They also have access to several women-only conferences, including WAC, run by the Women's Action Coalition, coordinating worldwide prochoice, child support, and anti–date rape political actions and WIT, the Women in Telecommunications conference, which Horn likens to "a pajama party." In true media convergence form, every Thursday at 11 P.M. Manhattan Cable viewers tuning in to a program called Electronic Neighborhood can read Echo keyboard conversations displayed on their TV screens, and listen to separate three-way telephone conversations.[110]

Reflecting the democratic potential of the information superhighway, Horn launched Echo with nothing more than the severance pay she received from Mobil Oil when the company moved to Virginia and she resigned. "It's just text, so we run Echo with two 486-based computers that we're planning to upgrade to Pentiums. I employ two part-time people. We have thirty-five phone lines and we're planning on adding ten. We also have a high-speed connection to the Internet," Horn says.[111]

Other women who through their leadership and vision are making a difference in both the private and public worlds of new media technology include:

- Ellen Hancock, senior vice president, IBM
- Mary Burnside, chief operating officer, Novell
- Michele DiLorenzo, executive vice president, Viacom New Media
- Sueann Ambron, vice president, Paramount Technology
- Jacqueline Woods, chief executive officer, Ameritech, Ohio
- Audrey Well, vice president, America Online
- Terry Hershey, president, Time Warner Interactive
- Carlene Ellis, senior vice president, Intel
- Patricia Seybold, president, Patricia Seybold Group
- Patty Stonesifer, vice president, Microsoft
- Susan Ness, FCC commissioner, communications attorney, and vice president/group head at American Securities Bank
- Rachelle Chong, FCC commissioner and a communications attorney, from San Francisco
- Mary Lowe Good, undersecretary for technology, U.S. Commerce Department
- Arati Prabhakar, director, National Institute of Standards and Technology, Commerce Department[112]

Research also has helped to identify several important questions on women and new technology.[113] Australian communications scholar Bernadette Flynn says we should consider these questions in the context of women and new technology:

- Who has access to the technology and in whose interests is it designed?

- What positions might be adopted in relation to female/machine exchanges rather than human(male)/machine relations?
- What positions might feminists adopt in relation to their technology in constructing new meanings and cultural positions?
- What strategies can be employed by the female artist for oppositional and transgressive positions that privilege a feminist agenda?

MIT professor Sherry Turkle adds an extra dimension of insight into how technology and gender interact in her landmark book, *The Second Self*.[114] Turkle's research suggests that boys and girls tend to bring different cognitive styles to their computer interactions. Girls tend to engage in a form of soft mastery in which the computer is understood as sensuous and tactile. In contrast, boys tend to engage in a form of hard mastery characterized by a competitive approach to working with computers and an attempt to impose their will over use of the machine.

People of Color and New Media Technology

"Future archaeologists, studying the documentary record of the present," writes new media expert Adam Clayton Powell III, "would have reason to conclude that people of color were bypassed by the information highway."[115] Not only have people of color been bypassed by the information, but, as with women, they have had only a limited role in the development of new media in general. The reasons for this limited involvement are many, including historical forces and the fact that high-tech fields tend to be dominated traditionally by white males, and even the government has been less than fully inclusive of people of color in the process of building policy on the National Information Infrastructure. However, the situation is beginning to change, as attitudes shift, new media enter the mainstream, and educational institutions known for their technology leadership enroll record numbers of women and minority-group students. Some minority-group leaders in the new media field are listed below.

- Stan Thomas, president and CEO of Time Warner's new interactive Sega Channel
- Susan Bokern, associate director of Gannett New Business
- Robert Johnson, founder of Black Entertainment Television
- Eduardo Gomez, president and general manager of KABQ Radio in Albuquerque
- Jorge Schement, a Rutgers University professor, who is preparing a report on universal service for the Federal Communications Commission

Generational Issues in New Media Technology

Once the battle cry of hippies, yippies, and many 1960s radicals, "Don't trust anyone over thirty" could easily be adapted to "Just ask someone under thirty" in today's new media environment. New media technology is the province of the young, especially the worlds of cyberspace and multimedia technology. Teenagers are among the heaviest users of online communication services. They are also the first to explore most new video games, CD-ROM products, and virtual reality creations. If not for the little matter of cost, their usage of these technologies would be even higher. Of course, the youthful nature of new media technologies is nothing new. A classic example from the modern era of media technology is the creative force that founded Apple Computer, a team including a youthful Steve Jobs, Steve Wosniak, and others, all in their early twenties at the time. Today's parallel is the creators of Mosaic, the popular window onto the Internet, created by a team of computer programmers all also in their twenties.

Implications for the Individual: Empowerment Through Technology

Although new media technologies pose many threats to the cherished values of privacy, intellectual property, and access to information, they also hold promise of a better future. One of the most likely benefits of the emerging communication technologies is personal empowerment. As the personal computer has become increasingly common and powerful, millions of individuals around the world have been empowered to act, communicate, or participate in the broader society and political process. "Because it enhances the abilities of a single person so dramatically," writes Steven Levy, author of *Artificial Life*, "the computer is a great equalizer. Individuals or small groups can duplicate efforts that previously could only be performed by large institutions or governments. A single college student in a dormitory room or a lone political dissenter in a basement apartment can produce a document that glistens with professional authority—the electronic rebirth of the 'lonely pamphleteer' that helped incite American democracy in the first place."[116]

Computer-Mediated Communication

Computer-mediated communication (CMC) not only has emerged as a much more efficient and rapid form of one-on-one communications than traditional hard-copy letters, "It's a populist form of broadcasting as well."[117] Those using CMC have moved beyond the traditional paradigm of broadcasting used by the mass media of television, radio, and newspapers, which emphasize a one-to-many approach. "Instead, they *participate,*" notes Levy. CMC incorporates the one-to-one interactivity of the telephone to create a new form of many-to-many online communications carried out in real time and across political and cultural divides. Electronic mail and computer bulletin boards make it just as easy to send a message to one person as to thousands connected to the network anywhere in the world. Recent research confirms that messaging, or sending electronic messages between or among individuals, is the most popular use of computer networks of all types.[118] An illustration of the use of a computer bulletin board called the WELL has interesting implications for traditional providers of news and other media content. One of the oldest computer bulletin boards, the WELL is run from the modest headquarters of the Whole Earth collective in Sausalito, California, and serves as an electronic commons. Howard Rheingold, author of *The Virtual Community: Homesteading on the Electronic Frontier,* recalls how he tapped into the WELL after finding a tick on his two-year-old daughter's scalp.[119] While his wife phoned the pediatrician, Rheingold logged onto the WELL via his computer modem. Before his wife could reach the doctor, a physician reading messages posted on the WELL encountered Rheingold's query and provided a response indicating how to safely remove the tick. Science and technology writer Steven Levy relates a similar experience from a session on the WELL. Someone posted a message discussing the reporting of ABC News correspondent Cokie Roberts, prompting another "WELL being" to respond by expressing admiration for Ms. Roberts' work and pondering how she ever got the name, "Cokie." Rather than visit the local library in search of biographical data about Ms. Roberts or pay for an expensive search on NEXIS, the WELL provided the answer. One of the so-called "lurkers" on the WELL happened to know a relative of Ms. Roberts. A quick phone call to his friend produced an answer, which was then relayed over the WELL: "an early propensity for Coca-Cola led to Cokie Roberts' nickname."[120]

The implications for the traditional providers of media content are profound and far-reaching. As was evidenced in the 1992 presidential campaign, new media such as computer bulletin boards are providing increasingly direct access to a variety of information sources, sometimes supplanting or even replacing the traditional news media.[121] As new media grow in popularity and reach an ever-greater portion of society, old media will need to adapt. One important strategy of adaptation may be by participating in the online communications world sometimes referred to as cyberspace. This means going online as an equal participant with thousands of others. An advertiser, for example, might utilize this new medium by participating in online forums related to her business and providing information about the company's relevant products or services. News organizations might similarly enter the online world by sponsoring public computer bulletin boards oriented to news and public affairs. In July 1993 *New York Newsday* did just that, setting up an online bulletin board with interested readers to provide a forum for discussing a series the paper was running on the information highway. *Time* magazine and *U.S. News and World Report* among others have set up similar online forums as part of their online editions.

Replacing Interpersonal with Mediated Communication
Historians have documented the role of new technology and the emergence of mediated communication in the nineteenth century in supplanting interpersonal communication as the principle means of the diffusion of news. Historian Richard Brown, for example, has shown how news about the Battles of Lexington and Concord and George Washington's death spread largely along well-traveled networks of interpersonal communication.[122] News about the assassination of President Abraham Lincoln, in contrast, spread rapidly along impersonal media of communication, especially the telegraph, newspapers, and tolling bells atop church towers. This was particularly the case in the North, while in the South, word spread more sporadically and slowly often along interpersonal networks.

Romancing the Electronic Stone.   As it transforms the most fundamental aspects of human society, the information superhighway is also changing the nature of romance. Or rather, the way romance is carried out, at least in the workplace. One happy couple carried out a year-long courtship via e-mail before their wedding in 1993.[123] Burke Stinson and Nancy J. Smith, executives at AT&T in New Jersey, traded some four hundred pages of confessions and passions through interoffice e-mail, sometimes sending two or three love letters and notes a day. "It's such a thrill to bare one's soul right on the screen, see it, save it, reread it, then swallow hard, and push the send button," says Ms. Smith.[124] Writer Avodah Offit uses e-mail as a vehicle of sexual healing in her first novel, *Virtual Love*, in which a San Francisco therapist communicates with a colleague in New York by computer and modem. The messages become increasingly erotic, as the therapist describes his fantasies about a troubled patient, a prostitute he describes as "thirty-two years old, single, Native American, part Swede, and extraordinarily attractive."[125]

Even traditions such as writing letters to Santa Claus have found an electronic replacement on the new media landscape. Novalink, based in Westborough, Massachusetts, happily forwards all electronic letters sent to santa@novalink.com straight to the North Pole.[126]

THEORETICAL PERSPECTIVES
ON THE SOCIAL CONSEQUENCES

Emerging alongside these digital wonders are a number of important theoretical perspectives and models aimed at critically evaluating the impact of these technologies as well as enhancing scholarly and public understanding of their role in society. These perspectives include the uses and gratifications model, systems theory, a knowledge hierarchy model and critical perspectives.

Uses and Gratifications Research

Uses and gratifications research suggests that people watch, read, and listen to the media to meet certain social and psychological needs.[127] Typical uses of the media include reading a newspaper in order to stay connected to society or watching television to avoid loneliness. From a uses and gratifications perspective, one might expect new media technologies to help people satisfy a range of social and psychological needs. For example, much of the development and use of new media technologies for erotic communications may be derived from sexual drives or needs of audience members. One might similarly explain the use of electronic mail and online communications in terms of the need to maintain social ties over great distances and political boundaries. This is especially apparent in electronic communications among so-called virtual communities that exist over vast geographic regions all linked in cyberspace.

Media uses and gratifications also vary by medium. Les Brown, a leading television journalist, critic, and author, has observed that his forty years of experience lead him to conclude that television, despite its efforts to the contrary, is an emotional medium, one that produces visceral responses in viewers.[128] When people saw the horrors of prisoner of war camps in Bosnia in 1993 it elicited such a strong response that it affected American foreign policy. A recent eight-country public opinion survey by Times Mirror similarly found that Americans ranked among the poorest in knowledge of public affairs issues but among the highest in viewership of television news. Thus, Brown concludes that television is the least intellectual of all media and the most emotional. Radio, he suggests, is somewhat more intellectual, and because of its low cost and portability, it is the future of news in the age of the information superhighway. Newspapers and news magazines are even more intellectual. But the most intellectual is the computer, where active information seeking is the norm. In contrast, television usage tends to be much more passive. These views are confirmed through a variety of scholarly studies, as well, although little uses and gratifications research has focused on interactive TV.[129] As a result, the role of television in the digital age may be to produce the entertainment superhighway, while computers may become the on-ramp to the information superhighway. Confounding all this is the telephone. Telecommunications scholar Frederick Williams, a professor at the University of Texas, believes that the screen phone may be one of the best information highway on-ramps, because of its low cost, ease of use, and potential for universality.[130] Of course, the screen phone is limited by the amount of information that can be displayed both visually or aurally. Most likely, there will emerge multiple on-ramps each serving different information needs for different audiences, perhaps even varying by the situation each consumer finds him- or herself in through the day or a lifetime.

Les Brown is also concerned about the culture of the television industry, both cable and broadcast, and the likelihood that it can ever produce a product that delivers more than the core killer applications of the information superhighway, including movies on demand, home shopping, and video games, and the even less socially redeeming gambling and pornography.[131] As cable companies vied for cable franchises in the 1970s and 1980s, many companies promised spectacular systems featuring interactive services and extensive public access. But when the companies obtained the franchises, few actually delivered on their promises. The overselling of cable in the 1980s has many parallels in today's highly charged environment, as some of these same companies promise highly developed systems of interactive television but are already experiencing delays in delivering services. Even if they do deliver on some of the so-called killer applications, such as movies on demand, home shopping, and video games, and some of the more socially questionable services such as gambling and pornography, Brown is concerned that there will be little priority placed on developing a central place for journalism, education, and other services that may have high social value but little commercial attractiveness. This commercial development may limit the uses and gratifications new media will provide.

On an even more fundamental level, communication scholar John Phelan suggests that computers may be altering the very minds of those who use them. He argues that ever-increasing computing speed enhances the computer user's feeling of computational control and integration with the computer itself.[132] Increasingly fast computers become as transparent as the biological senses of sight, smell, touch, and taste. As a result, people use computers without even thinking about how they work or recognizing their consequences. Computing speed, then, is far more than merely a computing improvement—it helps transform the computer into an extension of the human mind.

A Systems Theory Perspective

Fundamental to a systems theory perspective on new media technology is the notion of complexity. Complexity, which refers to the level of differentiation or heterogeneity in a system, is a fundamental quality of all systems. It acts as a critical mechanism in determining how any system responds to input, stimuli, or change in its environment. One of the pioneers in the study of complexity in systems theory is Dr. Murray Gell-Mann, a Nobel-prize winning author and the founder of the Sante Fe Institute, an independent research organization dedicated to understanding the behavior of complex systems. Gell-Mann suggests there are two types of complex systems.[133] The first type has no ability to learn or evolve biologically. Illustrative of such complex systems are galaxy or solar systems. The second type is capable of adaptive behavior. Such complex adaptive systems are especially relevant to an understanding of new media technologies. This is apparent with the advent of artificial intelligence and artificial life, the interplay between complex systems of business, government and other institutions, and media technology and the fundamental role of feedback, as communication, in complex adaptive systems. Each complex system is interdependent upon evolving media technologies in a process of coevolution.

Knowledge Hierarchy

One of the fundamental consequences of new media technologies is that they have increasingly created a knowledge hierarchy, theorize David Bollier and Charles M. Firestone (see Figure 9-1).[134] In their view, knowledge in its most elemental form is data. A step up on the knowledge hierarchy is information, where data are organized and defined in some intangible fashion. True knowledge emerges when information is interpreted and synthesized, reflecting certain values. Found at the knowledge hierarchy summit is wisdom, knowledge that carries spiritually profound, transhistorical insight. To this knowledge pyramid the author

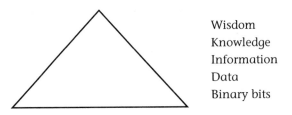

Wisdom
Knowledge
Information
Data
Binary bits

FIGURE 9-1   The Pyramid of Knowldege

adds a digital precursor to data—the bits and bytes, 1s and 0s, to which all data are reduced for storage in a computer for electronic storage or transmission in a digital network.

Critical Perspectives

> *This instrument can teach, it can illuminate; yes, and it can even inspire. But it can only do so to the extent that humans are determined to use it to those ends. Otherwise it is merely wires and lights in a box.*
> —*EDWARD R. MURROW*[135]

Murrow spoke these words about television, but today he might just as well have said them about computers or the emerging information super-highway and its many technical devices for accessing and receiving multimedia communications. Although some argue that technology—any technology—is inherently value laden, it is ultimately how we humans use that technology that determines its social effects. Critical philosopher Jacques Ellul argued in favor of a stronger view, in which technology is almost autonomous in its development and in the spread of its influence.[136] Ellul even suggests that technology is like a religion whose god is efficiency, whose high priests are economists and whose loyal servants are engineers. This view has been popularized in modern fiction, as well, by such writers as Ira Levin in *The Stepford Wives* or Rod Serling in *The Twilight Zone*. Horror novelist Dean Koontz examined the darker side of the information highway in his runaway bestseller *Midnight*. In the novel, he created a master villain whose vision of a utopian society was a world peopled by genetically engineered human-computer mutants, drained of all emotion except fear and driven by an unquenchable thirst for efficiency.[137] Twenty-five years earlier science-fiction author Anne McCaffrey articulated a similar view, writing of giant spaceships peopled by physically helpless humans hard-wired into a central computer.[138]

James Beniger, author of *The Control Revolution,* has sought a middle ground, arguing neither for technological determinism nor technological rationalism.[139] In his view, technological innovation is called on to solve problems brought about by previous technological creations.

Others have challenged and refined some of these notions, suggesting that often driving technological change is the class phenomenon of economic and political power. Joseph Schumpeter and Nikolai Kondratieff are economic geographers who subscribe to the notion of long wave theory, in which economic, political, and technological change are seen as coming in long-term cycles highly interrelated. The so-called Fifth Kondratieff represents the coming economic upswing driven by widespread innovation based on computer and information technology—the information superhighway. In this view, some will experience "gales of destructive force" based on factors in the competitive marketplace, while others will experience profound gains.[140] Moreover, certain technologies will be seen as more appropriate or essential in the new world economic order. In today's context, multimedia, interactive, digital technologies are part of the coming wave of such winning technologies.

Cybernetic Capitalism

Even farther along the critical continuum lie neo-Marxist scholars such as Frank Webster, Kevin Robins, and Oscar Gandy, who see the current generation of technological change as less a revolution and more an extension of capitalist influences in a postindustrial society, a sort of "cybernetic capitalism."[141] In *The Panoptic Sort,* Gandy describes an "all-seeing . . . model" derived from technology.[142] Dan Schiller, a University of California at San Diego communication professor, suggests that new technology has contributed directly to the "commoditization" of information. To Schiller, information is "the making of meaning in capitalist society," and a commodity is "a resource produced for the market by wage labor."[143] Therefore, the making of meaning is synonymous with the making of money in a capitalist society. Schiller argues that the processes of commoditization have "repeatedly congealed around new means of information production: the whole succession of technologies of information objectification, beginning with printing and continuing through lithography, photography, film, audio recording, video, and currently, digital signal processing."[144] Schiller further argues that it is to these purposes that the new media technologies must be put. "The suggestion that, to the contrary, such technologies can be put to other uses, seems to me doubly spurious. . . . In historical terms—the only terms that truly matter—such technologies have provided indispensable sites of capitalist accumulation."[145]

The Road to Utopia or Simply a Digital Toll Road?

Much of what we understand about the information highway is filled with the same kind of illusion, deception, and slight of hand found along L. Frank Baum's fictional yellow brick road, contends media studies scholar Oscar Gandy, a professor of communication at Annenberg School for Communication at the University of Pennsylvania.[146] The information age, much less the information highway, is a utopian tale, Gandy writes, promising an end to adversity, discrimination, and want. What they will deliver, unfortunately, is just the opposite, he says. Not at all a truly yellow brick road, the information highway will be a toll road with a pay-as-you-go philosophy designed not to further the public good or provide universal access. Rather, the companies building the information highway are doing so for one purpose: to create their own cities of gold, an El Dorado of the digital age, where el Camino Real leads not to Silicon

Valley, but to Cebolla, the lost city of gold once sought by Spanish conquistador, Hernan Cortes. The situation brings to mind a joke sometimes told by the Emmy-award winning ABC-TV network executive Julius Barnathan. Barnathan whimsically recalls the three great lies: "Sure, baby, I'll still love you in the morning," "The check is in the mail," and, "Hi! I'm from the phone company. I'm here to help you."[147]

Echoing this skeptical view are some communication scholars who question the intentions of many of the principal players on the information highway, not just those of the phone companies. Jerry Salvaggio, a Rutgers University professor, has studied the promotion of the technology of the information age. He concludes that companies promoting those technologies do so primarily in their own interest. It is in their interest to "hasten the arrival of the information society by fostering a technological ideology," one emphasizing the benefits and not the costs of the technologies.[148]

Recent advertising campaigns by such leading telecommunications firms as AT&T and MCI demonstrate the role of corporate communications in this process. MCI has drawn much attention from industry ad watchers by creating a surrealistic campaign about the coming information highway in which international child star Anna Paquin, the eleven-year-old New Zealander who won an Oscar for her supporting performance in 1993's *The Piano,* describes the virtues of the coming digital data network. "The information highway will have no speed limits . . . It will have no gas stations . . . This is not about data, digits, technology. It's not even about highways," Paquin declares in the ethereal ads, "It's about you and me and uncle Jack and everybody." The impact of the ad is subtle, yet powerful, contends one psychologist. Carol Moog, president of Creative Focus, Bala-Cynwyd, Pennsylvania, and a psychologist who has served as an advertising consultant since 1982, says the ad is a "powerful metaphor" that "resonates with a psychological place in all people."[149] Moog explains, "In most of the MCI spots, this little girl [Anna Paquin] is at the beginning of a completely new virgin world, but she is a genius."

Social Inequality and Society's Have-Nots

New media technologies are likely to produce more, not less, inequality in the distribution of wealth in society argue neo-Marxist scholars. These effects are especially likely to be felt among women and minorities, who will be disproportionately displaced by computer technologies in the workplace. Studies already indicate that a variety of media technologies have often bypassed the poor, especially women and minority group members, inner-city dwellers, and rural residents.[150] One resident of City Hill, Kansas, pointedly concludes that the phone company had relegated his town of 1,800 not to the information highway but to "the information cowpath."[151] Data from the Bureau of Labor Statistics also reveal a steady increase in long-term unemployment as a proportion of overall unemployment. Gandy suggests this trend "reflects a growing deficit . . . in the information age."[152]

Technological Bypass: Redlining on the Information Superhighway

The so-called information superhighway is already bypassing poor areas of society, especially society's minority neighborhoods, reports a study released in May 1994. Funded by a collection of civil rights and citizens groups, the study revealed that many of the interactive TV trials and other early efforts to build a new information infrastructure target relatively affluent regions. Sponsors of the study have charged that telephone companies building the information superhighway are systematically avoiding less lucrative markets, in the same way that some in the banking industry have avoided making loans to residents of such markets, especially to Black or other minority residents, an illegal discriminatory practice called "redlining." It is called redlining because unscrupulous bankers would draw a notorious red line on a map indicating which geographic regions they would not serve, areas often defined not by income but by race. Sponsors of the 1994 study charge the phone companies with exclusionary "electronic redlining" in construction of the information superhighway. The study examined a dozen detailed plans filed by four regional bell companies, including Ameritech, Bell Atlantic, Pacific Telesis, and US West. The areas targeted by the companies include Washington, D.C., and its suburbs, Toms River, New Jersey, Chicago, Illinois, Denver, Colorado, and its suburbs, San Diego and Orange County, California, and Portland, Oregon. The plans "systematically underrepresent" poor and minority neighborhoods, says Jeffrey Chester, executive director of the Center for Media Education, a Washington, D.C. policy group and a sponsor of the study. "These video dial-tone networks could become the primary communications system for millions of Americans," Chester added. "They must be made available in an equitable and nondiscriminatory manner."[153] He urged regulators at the FCC to consider revising their rules on video dial-tone trials to address more directly the issue of minority group access. Spokespersons for the RBOCs admit their plans are not fully representative of the U.S. population at large, but argue that they are sensitive to the needs of all groups in society. "To say that we're going to stay out of areas permanently is dishonest and ridiculous," says Jerry Brown, a spokesman for US West, Inc. "But we had to start building our network someplace. And it is being built in areas where there are customers we believe will use and buy the service. This is a business."[154]

Constructing a Technology Gap

Historically, new technological infrastructures, such as the railroad system or the national highway system, have tended to serve society's elite first, and only later have the benefits trickled down to the masses. This has been due largely to the high cost usually associated with the use of these new technologies. It is also likely that the information superhighway, a new national information infrastructure, will likely benefit society's elite first, the information rich. Thus, one might expect the gap between the information rich and poor to widen. Research by Tichenor, Donohue, and Olien among others demonstrates that information often diffuses differentially among the information rich and poor, contributing to an ever widening knowledge gap. Only under limited circumstances does the pattern not hold, such as situations of high involvement for the information poor and lower socioeconomic status (SES) groups or when there is high conflict. We might expect the information highway to trickle down especially slowly to society's underclass for an additional reason. To effectively use the information highway or even to recognize its value may require knowledge and skills that many in lower SES groups simply don't have. As Jannette Dates, Howard University's Dean of the School of Communication, has observed, the government will need to take special steps to ensure that those excluded from society's information upper class see the value in the information superhighway and that they be empowered to effectively use that highway through educational efforts to enhance their skills in the electronic information environment. This is especially important if the information superhighway is the key to the economic fortunes of the global economy in the twenty-first-century. Of course, some members of the information poor will find their own on-ramps to the information highway.

International Perspectives

Globalization has become almost cliché in contemporary discussions of new media technologies. Nevertheless, media technologies truly are global in their reach and impact. The following section looks at the role of new media technology in the very important international arenas of national development and public diplomacy. Though much of the application of technology for development and public diplomacy is planned, many uses are surreptitious and unexpected, often the product of local ingenuity and efforts to bypass government restrictions, economic limitations, and traditional technological, political, and geographic boundaries.

New Media Technology and National Development

Scholars, policy makers, and economic analysts widely view communication technology and telecommunications as central to the needs of developing countries. *The Missing Link,* the Maitland Commission report prepared for the International Telecommunication Union in 1984, made it very clear that telecommunications is an engine for economic and social development.[155] "It is now generally accepted by most countries around the world that very little economic and social growth can take place without an adequate telecommunications infrastructure," concludes David Wright, manager for regional programs at Inmarsat, the international cooperative that provides global mobile satellite communications.[156] Today, many would broaden this notion to suggest that the information superhighway is fundamentally important in serving the communication needs of developing societies, not just to improve communication in cities, but also in remote and rural areas as a mechanism to slow the sometimes overwhelming migration to urban areas, where poverty, slums, and overcrowding await. The information superhighway can serve the communication needs of a variety of groups in developing countries, including farmers, those in natural resource industries, government officials at remote outposts, construction workers building railways, roads, and pipelines, medical practitioners providing health care services, journalists reporting from remote locations, civil protection forces, disaster relief agencies, and many more who rely on fast, efficient communication to perform their work.

The seemingly intractable telecommunications problem facing most developing nations, Wright argues, involves an economic "Catch-22." They need advanced communications technology to facilitate economic growth, but the required technologies—microwave towers, optical fiber, or even copper wire—are beyond most developing countries' reach. The dilemma, Wright contends, is not insoluble, however. One alternative is to develop mobile satellite communications networks in developing nations. The cost of creating mobile satellite services (MSS) in these countries is substantially less than land-based telecommunications infrastructures. This strategy of "leapfrogging" intermediate technologies has become increasingly popular in many of the world's developing regions, including Africa, Eastern Europe, and Latin America.

Scholars and policy makers generally agree that new media technologies are essential tools for growth in the developing world. Heather Hudson, director of the Telecommunications Management and Policy Program, McLaren School of Business, University of San Francisco, suggests that new telecommunication technologies provide increasingly instantaneous communication and, thus, facilitate development through three primary mechanisms:

- increased efficiency, defined in terms of the ratio of output to cost
- enhanced effectiveness, defined as the extent to which development goals are achieved

- greater equity, defined in terms of the distribution of development benefits throughout the society[157]

A variety of telecommunications technologies contribute to this process, Hudson notes, including:

- small satellite earth stations to improve rural telephony
- new radio technologies, which offer an affordable means to reach rural residents
- facsimile, for low cost transmission of text and graphics
- CD-ROM, for distributing large databases or multimedia information
- audio and video conferencing to link remote locations for a variety of applications such as project administration or distance learning
- electronic mail, for low cost instantaneous communications both domestically and internationally
- computer conferencing to provide interactive online forums for many users simultaneously
- desktop publishing, to produce low-cost newsletters
- access to databases, which is especially useful for research purposes in agriculture, providing low-cost, instant access to remote databases such as the Food and Agricultural Organization (FAO) database in Rome
- electronic transactions, such as the transfer of funds between banks, airplane reservations, including tourist bookings, or trading commodities electronically, especially agricultural goods
- voice messaging, possibly providing a voice mailbox for rural residents who lack individual telephones but have access to a public phone

In the Asia-Pacific region, new technology clearly plays a crucial role in economic development. Among those who have recently argued for the importance of new media technologies for development in the Asia-Pacific region are Hugh Leonard, secretary-general of the Asia-Pacific Broadcasting Union, Kuala Lumpur, Malaysia; Meheroo Jassawalla, an economist at the East-West Center, Honolulu, Hawaii; and, Georgette Wang, professor in the Graduate School of Journalism, National Chengchi University, Taiwan. Leonard writes that although there is no "typical" country in the region, the winds of change are blowing, primarily due to the combination of new technology and deregulation.[158] The number of television households in Asia has increased by 70 percent since 1988, and new technologies, especially satellite television available via Asiasat, have transformed the viewing landscape. Combined with the relaxation of rules governing broadcasting in many Asian countries, broadcasting has taken on a vitally new significance in the economic development in the region.

Telecommunications also plays a critical role in the development in the Asian region, writes Meheroo Jussawalla.[159] "The prospects for growth of the telecommunication market in the Asian region are so promising . . . in terms of overall regional economic development," Jussawalla notes.[160] He explains that the technologies adding value to the gross domestic product (GDP) of the region have been optical fiber, facsimile, cellular telephony, and satellite earth receiving equipment. Nevertheless, the technological development of the region varies greatly country by country. Indonesia, for example, has the lowest density of telephones per hundred population at 0.8 (in 1991). Singapore, by contrast, is at the forefront of new media technologies, and is known as the "intelligent city."

Georgette Wang agrees that satellite television has revolutionized communications in the Asia-Pacific. She notes that the "reach" of modern communications satellites is "staggering."[161] Asiasat 1's footprint covers most of Asia and much of the Pacific. "However, satellite television is not the only new medium that has taken hold in Asia," she adds.[162] Cable TV and the VCR have also made significant inroads in the region.

Government responses to satellite television in the Asian region fall into four categories, reports Joseph Man Chan:

- virtual suppression, such as in Singapore and Malaysia, where citizen access to satellite television is prohibited
- regulated openness, as in Hong Kong and the Philippines, where access is permitted, but government regulates the redistribution of programs
- illegal openness, such as in Taiwan and India, where government regulations merely discourage redistribution of programs via satellite
- suppressive openness as seen in China, where the communist government prohibits private ownership of satellite receiver dishes and permits no access to "foreign television signals"[163]

At the same time, it is important to maintain a critical eye on the application of new media technologies in developing nations. Anwar Ibrahim, Minister for Finance, Malaysia, observes that for decades information technology has been viewed as largely value-free.[164] Technology has been judged largely from a utilitarian perspective, with economic benefits far outweighing any cultural costs. Ibrahim argues that "Asia needs to achieve material prosperity, with a reflowering of culture at the same time. This will contribute to the heritage of mankind in the same way we have seen the West, since its ascendancy in the sixteenth century, produce some of the most remarkable cultural achievements in human history."[165] As the pace of technological change quickens, however, the value of diversity must be maintained, he cautions. "In the final analysis, the communication order we seek must not only expand our mental horizons, increase our range of choices, facilitate our decisions, it must also enrich our cultural experience and enlarge our freedom."[166]

Expecting the Unexpected: The South African Experience

Not all uses of new media technology in developing regions fall into the category of planned applications. Many are both unexpected and ingenious. Consider the case of South Africa, as that country emerges from decades of apartheid. Under the apartheid state, the government of South Africa's official position was that no significant economic activity existed in the black townships, from Soweto to Lesotho. But recent trips to those townships immediately dispelled that notion, reports Adam Clayton Powell III, who made six trips to South Africa between 1991 and the official end of apartheid in 1994. "Many parts of the townships I have visited look like Palo Alto (part of high-tech and wealthy Silicon Valley in California)," Powell says. Although official government sources denied the presence of any economic prosperity in these townships, people in corporate sales, however, knew the true level of activity. "Sony sells a lot of VCRs in the townships where there is officially no electricity," Powell notes.[167] There is a thriving battery business there, though. The government has even published on CD-ROM a "complete" set of economic data for South Africa, excluding any data about the townships. Moreover, the South African census officially reports the population of the country to be some thirty-eight million, but the data from the townships are based on nothing more than a crude population estimate derived from aerial photographs of the regions. Putting these data into electronic form and distributing them via the information highway will not only fail to improve their accuracy, but could compound the problem by making them widely available.

Public Diplomacy and New Technology

New media technology has not escaped the ever-watchful eye of diplomats and world leaders eager to reach an increasingly electronic audience. With the dawn of international television systems, especially CNN, the global news network, the international scene has witnessed the advent of "media pervasiveness" as well as electronic public diplomacy.[168] The pervasiveness of the media was demonstrated for the world to see during the Tiananmen Square demonstrations when CNN pioneered real-time news coverage for a global audience. The impact of media pervasiveness is clear in the process of international diplomacy.

"For policy makers, the nonstop coverage of CNN (also coming in the future from the BBC and others) presents opportunities to constantly monitor news events and disseminate timely diplomatic information," writes James F. Hoge, Jr., the editor of the distinguished journal *Foreign Affairs*.[169] Although there may be earlier examples, none were more dramatic than the public diplomacy carried out on CNN by Iraq's Saddam Hussein and the U.S.'s George Bush during the Persian Gulf War. No witness to the historic Middle East conflict will ever forget the image of Hussein patting on the head a British child being held hostage in Bagdad. However inept, Hussein's efforts to sway the international court of public opinion were enabled by the global presence and reach of satellite-based television technology. By virtue of its universal presence, CNN became the medium of choice for carrying out this telediplomacy.

Beyond CNN, other new media technologies are influencing the process of international diplomacy, as well. By creating an environment of instantaneous global communication, technologies such as the Internet, fax communications, and satellite television have increased the pace and public visibility of diplomacy. "Today's correspondents employ laptop computers, wireless telephones that transmit directly to satellites and mobile satellite dishes to broadcast vivid pictures and commentary from the scenes of tragedy and disorder without the transmission delays, political obstructions, or military censorship of old," explains James F. Hoge, the former publisher of the *New York Daily News*.[170] No longer can diplomats and heads of state take several days to ponder foreign policy matters as President John F. Kennedy did during the Berlin Wall crisis of August 1961. ". . . politicians are more concerned than elated by global, real-time broadcasting," adds Hoge. "They worry about a 'loss of control' and decry the absence of quiet time to deliberate choices, reach private agreements, and mold the public's understanding. They point with nostalgia to how those opportunities helped President John F. Kennedy respond safely to the discovery of Soviet missiles in Cuba."[171] Instead, the global communications grid now necessitates policy decisions, actions, and communications on an almost equal instantaneous basis. If a world leader delays in responding to a widely known crisis situation, perhaps made visible through television, as images of prisoner of war camps did in Bosnia in 1992, he or she will likely look indecisive, weak, or worse in the international media and court of public opinion. Moreover, lack of rapid policy making or public diplomacy in this hyper-information environment can have significant economic implications. By delaying to respond to an important international development, financial traders, for example, who have access to vast real-time information services around the world, may make momentous decisions profoundly affecting the world's currency. Conversely, policy makers run an equal risk of setting off a financial stampede by acting too impulsively.

Social Consequences and Public Policy

All too frequently public policy decisions about new media technologies flow largely from the commercial interests surrounding those technologies, with social and cultural consequences carrying little weight in the policy debate. This occurs for several reasons, including the fact that like all areas of public policy, commercial interests have the greatest resources to support lobbying in Washington. In addition, however, scholarly study of the social and cultural consequences of emerging technologies is scarce and difficult to undertake both because of limited funding and because the technologies of concern may not even exist.

A FRAMEWORK FOR UNDERSTANDING THE SOCIAL CONSEQUENCES OF NEW MEDIA TECHNOLOGY

This chapter has outlined a conceptual framework for understanding the likely social and cultural consequences of new and emerging media technologies. The framework rests on four major themes:

- enduring topics and issues of major public and scholarly concern about the social consequences of new media technologies, including potential social fragmentation, privacy concerns, and the growth of virtual communities, as well as implications for social institutions and computer-mediated communication
- cultural consequences of emerging new media technology
- theoretical perspectives on the social and cultural impact of new media technologies
- international and intercultural perspectives on the social consequences of new media technologies

Students, practitioners, and users of new media technology can use this framework to evaluate not only the commercial implications of the evolving communication environment, but the social and cultural implications as well. Decisions and debate based on such a framework will thus benefit from an enriched understanding of how new technologies may transform not just the media industries themselves, but those who consume and are touched by them.

NOTES

1. Bill McKibben, *The Age of Missing Information*. New York: Random House, 1992.

2. Charles Dickens, *A Tale of Two Cities*. London: J.B. Lippincott, 1930.

3. Henry David Thoreau, *Walden*. New York: T.Y. Crowell, 1849.

4. Jacques Ellul, *The Technological Society*. New York: Alfred A. Knopf, 1964.

5. I. de Sola Pool, *Technologies of Freedom*. Cambridge: Belknap Press of Harvard University, 1983.

6. I. de Sola Pool, *Technologies Without Boundaries: On Telecommunications in a Global Age*. E. M. Noam, ed., Cambridge: Harvard University Press, 1990.

7. Daniel Bell, *Post Industrial Society*. New York: Basic Books, 1973.

8. de Sola Pool, op. cit., 1983, 1990; Walter Wriston, "Public Opinion: 'Mistress of the World.'" Inaugural address in the Freedom Forum Media Studies Center Technology Lecture Series, 25 October 1993.

9. Ellul, op. cit.

10. Peter Steinfels, "Jacques Ellul, French Critic of Technology, Is Dead at 82," *New York Times,* 21 May 1994.

11. Harold Innis, *Empire and Communications*. Oxford: Clarendon Press, 1950.

12. Marshall McLuhan, *Understanding Media: Extensions of Man*. New York: McGraw-Hill, 1964.

13. John Naisbitt, *Megatrends*. New York: Warner Books, 1982.

14. Club of Rome, *Microelectronics and Society: For Better or Worse*. New York: Pergamoff, 1982.

15. Les Brown, *Les Brown's Encyclopedia of Televison,* ed. 3. Detroit, MI: Gale Research Inc., 1992.

16. "TV Debate Set a Cable Record," *New York Times,* 11 November 1993.

17. Mark Thalhimer, ed., *Media Industry News Roundup,* compiled from the Associated Press, the Freedom Forum Media Studies Center, 6 July 1994.

18. Bill Henderson, op ed page, *New York Times,* 16 March 1994.

19. Thoreau, op. cit.

20. Rupert Murdoch, keynote address, Center for Communication Communicator of the Year Award Luncheon, 11 April 1994.

21. Howard W. French, "Linked to Internet, Could Africa's Voice Be Heard?" *New York Times,* 1 October 1994.

22. Peter H. Lewis, "Strangers, Not Their Computers, Build a Network in Time of Grief," *New York Times,* 8 March 1994.

23. Ibid.:A8.

24. Ibid.

25. Jacques Leslie, "Mail Bonding: E-Mail is Creating a New Oral Culture," *Wired,* March 1994:42.

26. Ibid.

27. Ibid.

28. Charles M. Firestone, "Towards a Reformulation of the Communications Act," the Aspen Institute, 1993.

29. Ibid.:15.

30. John Dewey, *The Public and Its Problems*. Chicago: Swallow, 1927.

31. James E. Grunig and Todd Hunt, *Managing Public Relations*. New York: Holt, Rinehart, and Winston, 1984.

32. Ibid.

33. Ibid.

34. Larissa A. Grunig, "Activism and Organizational Response: Contemporary Cases of Collective Behavior," paper presented to the Association for Education in Journalism and Mass Communication, Norman, OK.

35. P. Murphy and J. Dee, "Du Pont and Greenpeace: The Dynamics of Conflict Between Corporations and Activist Groups," *Public Relations Research Annual,* 4(1), 1992:3–20.

36. Mark Levy, ed., "Virtual Reality: A Communication Perspective," *Journal of Communication,* 42(4), Autumn 1992.

37. Frank Biocca, "Communication Within Virtual Reality: Creating a Space for Research," *Journal of Communication,* 42(4), Autumn 1992:5–22.

38. W. Lambert Gardiner, "Virtual Reality/Cyberspace: Challenges to Communication Studies," *Canadian Journal of Communication,* vol. 18, 1993:387–396.

39. Abraham Lincoln, letter to H.L. Pierce, 6 April 1859.

40. Anthony Smith, "New Communication Technology and Changing Political Boundaries," Technology Paper, the Freedom Forum Media Studies Center, October, 1993.

41. Walter Wriston, inaugural address, the Freedom Forum Media Studies Center Technology Lecture Series, 25 October 1993, New York.

42. Leonard Davis, "The Customer Is Always Right," *Omni,* November 1993:24.

43. Jonathan Karp, "Prime Time Police: China Tries to Pull the Plug on Satellite TV," *Far Eastern Economic Review,* 21 October 1993:72–73.

44. Anthony Smith, "Is TV's Web of Images Strangling Our Hearts?" *New York Newsday,* 3 January 1994:33.

45. Lawrence Grossman, speech at "Newsroom Technology: The Next Generation," the Freedom Forum Media Studies Center, 15 September 1993.

46. Lawrence Grossman, "Toward a New Era of Direct Participatory Democracy" in Don W. Stacks, ed., *Seminar on Direct Electronic Democracy,* School of Communication, University of Miami, 1993:3–9.

47. Peter H. Lewis, "Anarchy, a Threat on the Electronic Frontier," *New York Times,* 11 May 1994:D1, D7.

48. John M. Phelan, "The Inner Face of Interface," unpublished essay, June 1994.

49. Everette E. Dennis, *Of Media and People.* Newbury Park, CA: Sage Publications, 1992.

50. Eric Sevareid, CBS Radio News commentary, 26 August 1952.

51. Gary W. Selnow, *High-Tech Campaigns: Computer Technology in Political Communication.* Westport, CT: Praeger, 1993.

52. The Research Group, *The Media and Campaign '92.* The Freedom Forum Media Studies Center 1992.

53. Sevareid, op. cit.

54. Selnow, op. cit.:169.

55. Roderick P. Hart, *Seducing America: How Television Charms the Modern Voter.* New York: Oxford University Press, 1994, p. 63.

56. Ibid.

57. Ibid.

58. K. Kendall Guthrie, "How Information Highways Can Address the Urban Agenda: Promoting Economic Development and Reconnecting the Urban Poor," paper presented at the 43rd Annual Conference of the International Communications Association, Washington, DC, 27–31 May 1993.

59. Ronald H. Brown, Mary L. Good and Arati Prabhakar, "Putting the Information Infrastructure to Work: A Report of the Information Infrastructure Task Force Committeee on Applications and Technology," NIST Special Publication 857, Office of the Director, National Institute of Standards and Technology, U.S. Department of Commerce, Gaithersburg, MD 20899-0001, May 1994:4.

60. Ibid.

61. Software Publishers Association, "Report on the Effectiveness of Technology in Schools, 1990–1992," conducted by Interactive Educational Systems Design, 1993:2.

62. J. Orlansky and J. String, "Cost-Effectiveness of Computer Based Instruction in Military Training," IDA Paper P-1375, Institute for Defense Analyses, Alexandria, VA, 1979.

63. Brown, et al., op. cit.

64. Ibid.

65. Ibid.

66. "On Line," *Chronicle of Higher Education,* 2 March 1994.

67. Ibid.

68. Mark Thalhimer and Marcella Steingart, eds., *Media Industry News Roundup,* compiled from the Associated Press, the Freedom Forum Media Studies Center, 31 May 1994.

69. *Advertising Age,* 18 July 1994.

70. Jonathan Rabinovitz, "Computer Network Helps Journalists Find Academic Experts," *New York Times,* 21 May 1994.

71. John Browning, "Libraries Without Walls for Books Without Pages," *Wired,* Premier Issue 1993.

72. Smith, op. cit.

73. Browning, op. cit.:63.

74. Marilyn Gell Mason, "More Than a Library for Congress: Making LC the Nation's Library," *Library Journal,* 1 November 1993:40–43.

75. "I.B.M. Project For Vatican," *New York Times,* from Reuters 12 April 1994.

76. Robert Pool, "Turning an Info-Glut into a Library," *Science,* vol. 266, no. 7, October 1994:20–22.

77. Leigh Hafrey, "At Cyberspace University Press, Paperless Publishing Looks Good," *New York Times Book Review,* 30 October 1994.

78. *Chronicle of Higher Education,* 4 November 1994.

79. Patricia Glass Schuman, "Information Justice," Fellows Seminar, the Freedom Forum Media Studies Center, 1993.

80. Albert Gore, "Reinventing Government," The Office of the Vice President of the U.S., 1993.

81. Schuman, op. cit.

82. Gary H. Arlen, "Education Networks to Go Online Later This Year; Content Providers to Offer 'Electronic Printing Press,'" *Information & Interactive Services Report,* 25 February 1994:17.

83. Ibid.

84. Ibid.

85. Frederick Williams and John V. Pavlik, *The People's Right to Know: Media, Democracy and the Information Highway.* Hillsdale, NJ: Lawrence Erlbaum Associates, 1994, p. xi.

86. Thomas J. DeLoughry, "Guaranteeing Access on the Data Highway," *Chronicle of Higher Education,* 3 November 1993.

87. Sidney Verba, "The 1993 James Madison Award Lecture: The Voice of the People," delivered at the American Political Science Association Annual Meeting, Washington, DC, 3 September 1993, edited version published in Robert J. P. Hauck, ed, *PS: Political Science & Politics,* vol. XXXVI, no. 4, December 1993:684.

88. Eli Noam, speech, Technology Studies Seminar, the Freedom Forum Media Studies Center, 5 April 1994.

89. Nancy Hicks Maynard, speech, Technology Studies Seminar, the Freedom Forum Media Studies Center, 5 April 1994.

90. Smith, op. cit.

91. John W. Verity, "The Information Revolution: How Digital Technology Is Changing the Way We Work and Live," *Business Week,* Special 1994 Bonus Issue: 14.

92. Allan Kozinn, "Lejaren Hiller 69, First Composer To Write Music with a Computer," *New York Times,* 1 February 1994.

93. Thomas J. DeLoughry, "Museums Go High-Tech," *Chronicle of Higher Education,* 14 September 1994:A47.

94. Richard Corliss, *Time,* 4 October 1994:58, 59.

95. Benoit B. Mandelbrot, "The Beauty of Fractals and Their Usefulness—Relations Between Geometry, Art, and Technology," the Inaugural Magill Lecture in Science, Technology, and the Arts, Columbia University, 7 April 1994.

96. McKenzie Wark, "The Video Game as an Emergent Media Form," *Media Information Australia,* February 1994, No. 71.

97. Ibid.:22.

98. Ibid.:28.

99. Anthony Smith, "From Méliés to Virtual Reality," speech, Technology Studies Seminar, the Freedom Forum Media Studies Center, 23 February 1994.

100. John Naisbitt and Patricia Aburdene, *Megatrends 2000.* New York: Morrow, 1990.

101. Eli M. Noam, keynote address, the Everette Parker Luncheon, 1993.

102. Sandra D. Atchison, "The Care and Feeding of 'Lone Eagles,'" *Business Week,* 15 November 1993:58.

103. Ibid.; Jared Sandberg, "Up in Flames," *Wall Street Journal Reports,* 15 November 1993:R12.

104. Mary Van Sell and Sheila M. Jacobs, "Telecommuting and Quality of Life: A Review of the Literature and a Model for Research," *Telematics and Informatics,* vol. 11, no. 2:81–95.

105. Michael Krantz, "Dollar a Minute," *Wired,* May 1994:107.

106. Ibid.:107.

107. Ibid.

108. Steve Ditlea, "Female E-Mail: Computer Networks Put Women On-Line," *New York Daily News,* 3 November 1993.
109. Gary H. Arlen, "Who Uses CompuServe?" *Information & Interactive Services Report,* 11 February 1994:4.
110. John Markoff, "An Electronic Salon," *New York Times,* 27 March 1994:F10.
111. Ibid.
112. Bronwyn Fryer, "Sex & the Superhighway," *Working Woman,* April 1994:51-61.
113. Bernadette Flynn, "Woman/Machine Relationships," *Media Information Australia,* May 1994, no. 72:11–19.
114. Sherry Turkle, *The Second Self: Computer and the Human Spirit.* Simon and Schuster, New York, 1984.
115. Adam Clayton Powell III, "On-Ramps to the Information Superhighway," *Media Studies Journal,* Summer 1994:viii, 113–121.
116. Steven Levy, *Artificial Life: The Quest for a New Creation.* London: Penguin Books, 1993.
117. Ibid.
118. William Dutton, "Lessons from Public and Nonprofit Services," in Frederick Williams and John V. Pavlik, eds., *The People's Right to Know: Media, Democracy and the Information Highway,* Hillsdale, NJ: Lawrence Erlbaum Associates, 1994.
119. Howard Rheingold, *The Virtual Community: Homesteading on the Electronic Frontier.* New York: Simon & Schuster, 1993, pp. 19, 26.
120. Steven Levy, "We Have Seen the Content, and It Is Us," *The Media Studies Journal,* Winter 1994.
121. John Pavlik and Andras Szanto, "Mutiple Method Research in Media Studies: The Case of the 1992 Presidential Campaign," the Freedom Forum Media Studies Center, 1994.
122. Richard D. Brown, *Knowledge Is Power: The Diffusion of Information in Early America, 1700–1865.* New York: Oxford University Press, 1989.
123. Kirk Johnson, "Office Romance: Love On Line at Speed of Light," *New York Times,* 26 March 1994.
124. Ibid.:21.
125. Christopher Lehmann-Haupt, "Plumbing the Recesses of Psyche and Cyberspace," *New York Times,* 14 April 1994:C21.
126. Elizabeth Weise, "Santa's Elves Check E-Mail for Your Merry Messages," Associated Press wire service, 13 December 1994.
127. Jay Blumler and Elihu Katz, *Uses and Gratifications Research in Mass Communication.* Newbury Park, CA: Sage Publications, 1974.
128. Les Brown, speech, Technology Studies Seminar, the Freedom Forum Media Studies Center, 6 April 1994.
129. Blumler and Katz, op. cit.
130. Williams and Pavlik, op. cit.
131. Les Brown, op. cit.
132. Phelan, op. cit.

133. Murray Gell-Mann, *The Quark and the Jaguar: Adventures in the Simple and the Complex.* New York: W. H. Freeman, 1994.

134. David Bollier and Charles M. Firestone, "The Promise and Peril of Emerging Information Technologies," a report on the Second Annual Roundtable on Information Technology, Aspen Institute Communications and Society Program, 1993.

135. Edward R. Murrow, on "See It Now," CBS News, 1958.

136. Ellul, op. cit.

137. Dean Koontz, *Midnight.* New York: Berkley Books, 1989.

138. Anne McCaffrey, *The Ship Who Sang.* New York: Walker, 1969.

139. James R. Beniger, *The Control Revolution: Technological and Economic Origins of the Information Society.* Cambridge, MA: Harvard University Press, 1986.

140. Oscar H. Gandy, Jr., "The Information Highway as Yellow Brick Road," speech, Santa Clara University, 27 January 1994.

141. Ibid.

142. Oscar H. Gandy, Jr., *The Panoptic Sort.* Boulder, CO: Westview, 1993, p. 10.

143. Dan Schiller, "From Culture to Information and Back Again: Commoditization as a Route to Knowledge," *Critical Studies in Mass Communication,* 11 (March 1994):92–115.

144. Ibid.:99.

145. Ibid.

146. Gandy, op. cit., 1994.

147. Julius Barnathan, speech, Technology Studies Seminar, the Freedom Forum Media Studies Center, 12 December 1992.

148. Jerry L. Salvaggio, *Telecommunications.* New York: Longman, 1983.

149. Laura Loro, "Do MCI's Ads Offer a Genius Child?" *Advertising Age,* 14 March 1994:29.

150. Gandy, op. cit., 1994:12, 13.

151. Shinji Morukama, "The Information Superhighway," *Forum Magazine,* May 1994:4.

152. Gandy, op. cit., 1994:13.

153. Mark Thalhimer, ed., *Media Industry News Roundup,* compiled from the Associated Press, the Freedom Forum Media Studies Center, 31 May 1994.

154. Steve Lohr, "Data Highway Ignoring Poor, Study Charges," *New York Times,* 24 May 1994:D3.

155. David Wright, "Mobile Satellite Communications in Developing Countries," *Telecommunications Policy,* January/February 1994.

156. Ibid.:5.

157. Heather E. Hudson, "Maximizing Benefits from New Telecommunications Technologies: A Development-Based Approach to Communications Planning," *Media Asia,* vol. 20, no. 3, 1993:133–139.

158. Hugh Leonard, "Asian Broadcasting: The Changing Scene," *Media Asia,* vol. 20, no. 3, 1993:123–126.

159. Meheroo Jussawalla, "Information Technology and Economic Development in the Asia-Pacific," *Media Asia,* vol. 20, no. 3, 1993:127–132.

160. Ibid.:130.

161. Georgette Wang, "Satellite Television and the Future of Broadcast Television in the Asia-Pacific," *Media Asia,* vol. 20, no. 3, 1993:139–148.

162. Ibid.:141–2.

163. Joseph Man Chan, "Satellite Television and the Infosphere: National Responses and Accessibility to STAR TV in Asia," paper presented to the Ninth World Communication Forum, the Japan Society of Information and Communication Research, Tokyo, Japan, 19–20 November 1992.

164. Anwar Ibrahim, "Communication, Technology and Development: Alternatives for Asia," *Media Asia,* vol. 20, no. 3, 1993:157–158.

165. Ibid.:157.

166. Ibid.:158.

167. Adam Clayton Powell III, Technology Studies Seminar, the Freedom Forum Media Studies Center, 6 April 1994.

168. James, F. Hoge, "Media Pervasiveness," *Foreign Affairs,* July/August 1994, vol. 73 no. 4:136.

169. Ibid.

170. Ibid.

171. Ibid.:137.

10

THE FUTURE: THE AGE OF RANDOM ACCESS

If I were to give you an army of ten thousand people, could you build a pyramid? A computer gives the average person, a high school freshman, the power to do things in a week that all the mathematicians who ever lived until thirty years ago couldn't do.

—ED ROBERTS[1]
Designer of the first personal
computer

ON THE HOLODECK

Emerging technologies are rapidly transforming the media landscape. Advances in computer-based online communications, interactive television and personal communication services are creating an entirely new communication environment in which the roles of media consumer and content creator often blur and interactivity becomes a reality. Multimedia technology, virtual reality, and flat panel displays are redefining the media experience, transforming the narrative structure of media images, sound, and text into nonlinear, hypertext communication. Media consumers will have unprecedented choice and control over the media experience, selecting not just what they watch, read, or hear, but when and where they do so. The commercial media system itself is undergoing a "mediamorphosis," as well, moving away from passive, scattershot content delivery toward highly targeted messaging. A double-edged sword, this new media engine may present both a marketer's paradise and a consumer's privacy nightmare.

Much media content will still consist largely of packaged products of news, information, entertainment, and advertising manufactured by highly centralized media organizations, but tomorrow's media will increasingly target in real time the demands, tastes, and preferences of ever more specialized niche audiences spread over diverse geographic regions. The new media system will not rigidly divide along the traditional lines of delivery such as print, broadcast, and cable, but will become true multimedia technologies, involving new forms of mediated communication, ultimately embracing the tactile technology of emerging virtual reality systems. Shared media experiences, although increasingly rare on a mass scale, will take on an entirely new meaning, one in which audiences anywhere around the globe will be enveloped in a total sensory media experience created at least in part by those audiences. Increasingly, each member of the new media audience will have direct access to this information superhighway through lightweight, portable, wireless multimedia devices, totally enveloping multisensory data suits, or communal media technologies featuring multidimensional images and stereophonic sound not unlike the holodeck on the starship *Enterprise* featured in *Star Trek: The Next Generation*.

Of course, not every media experience will be of this Buck Rogers' type. Consumers will spend much of their media time reading newspapers printed on traditional newsprint. They will still read leather-bound and paperback books. They will still listen to the radio, watch TV, and get advertising circulars in the mail. And the Publisher's Clearinghouse will probably still proclaim half of America "Winners" in its multimillion dollar lottery. Moreover, legal and regulatory frameworks will continue to evolve mechanisms to monitor and control the new media system. Freedom of expression issues will take on even greater significance in the new media environment. Although Thomas Jefferson's words still ring true, "Freedom of the press belongs to those who own one," the Internet and other media technologies are empowering members of virtual communities around the globe. They are providing a new electronic age printing press that costs little to operate and reaches audiences of millions in almost instantaneous fashion. John Siegenthaler, a Pulitzer-prize winner newspaper editor and chairman of the Freedom Forum First Amendment Center, says the information superhighway already is being dominated by eighteen-wheelers, including the baby Bells, cable TV companies, and other corporate players who are used to working in a regulated environment.[2] These companies are likely to compromise on First Amendment issues, he cautions. News organizations, journalism educators, and other guardians of the First Amendment will need to be vigilant in the new media environment if we, as a society, are to preserve free speech values. This is especially important, Siegenthaler adds, if it is true that a free press is one of the cornerstones of democracy.

The social and cultural consequences of these new media technologies are profound. They are creating unprecedented opportunities for political participation, through electronic town halls, direct-access to political leaders, and, potentially, online voting. At the same time, issues of equitable access and cost considerations are challenging the very political viability of creating a new information infrastructure. Social fragmentation is only one of the many potential negative consequences of the new technologies that are increasingly leading media consumers into online worlds and away from their geographically defined communities.

User Control and User Choice: New and Improved Media

For the media consumer, perhaps the most important difference between old and new media is greater user choice and control. Unlike any time before, media audiences will have ever greater choice and control over media content and the media experience in general. Video on demand, including pay-per-view movies, news on demand, educational programming, and documentaries will all be available over the information superhighway. The shift in the media paradigm is from strict source or media control over content delivery to increasing user control.

Simultaneously, media audiences will enjoy increasing interactivity on the information highway. They will have opportunities to interact with media content, selecting different options from preset video library menus to battling enemy starships in video games. Audience members will also be able to participate in the process of content creation, sending messages, home video, or data files to anyone else on the system. Over time, the superhighway will offer increasing opportunities for moving beyond two-way communication and into an n-way media environment in which hundreds, thousands, even millions will participate in a rich communication smorgasbord. Virtual worlds will be created by media audiences around the world in which the dimensions of that world are limited only by the imaginations of those within it. The seeds of this n-way communication world can already be seen in online bulletin boards, tele- and videoconferences, multiuser dungeons (MUDs) and the Internet. On the World Wide Web, virtual reality and three-dimensional graphics are likely to transform the online landscape as the new Virtual Reality Modeling Language (VRML) takes hold in 1995.

Does all this mean the end of the couch potato? Not at all. Not only will traditional passive media consumption continue, but it will thrive in an increasingly complex and stressful world demanding occasional if not frequent mindless escape. But the interactive world will become a ready choice. Of course, too much interactivity could produce the era of the mashed potato.

Driving this user-controlled, interactive, multimedia world are the technological forces of digitization, compression, and the broadband switched telecommunications network. Through advances in computer technology, we are rapidly moving toward a united state of media in which all communications, from voice to data to full-motion video, are available in digital form, computer readable 1s and 0s. Compression technology has made it possible to compact that digital data, especially full-motion video, into smaller and smaller packets. The convergence of telecommunications and cable, along with the deployment of advanced optical fiber, has provided a high-capacity electronic superhighway to transmit and provide access to all that compressed digital data.

A final technological factor contributing to the transformation of the media landscape is wireless communications. As the forces of digitization and compression have inexorably advanced, research has helped create an increasingly broadband switched network that is not dependent on wires. Instead, we are moving toward a telecommunications highway universally available over the high-frequency wavelengths of the radio spectrum. By connecting to satellite and wired networks, this wireless network will provide a complementary and perhaps competitive alternative multimedia information superhighway. Although engineers have not yet achieved the necessary compression algorithms to distribute full multimedia communications via the wireless spectrum, it is ultimately very likely. As a consequence of this wireless broadband network, a phenomenon called nomadic computing will emerge. Nomadic computing means using a portable computer to access the information superhighway from any location, anywhere, anytime. Someday, we may see emerge global media nomads.

PARALLEL OR DIVERGENT UNIVERSES?

What price will a digital universe exact? No one really knows. Projected costs to build the new communication infrastructure range from hundreds of billions to several trillion dollars, for just the United States. Cost estimates are also in the hundreds of billions to create new information infrastructures in Japan and many other countries. Those developing new media products and services say that the actual price the consumer will pay will be modest. If it isn't then none of the products will succeed. Telecommunications expert John Carey suggests that the estimates for the new information infrastructure may not really be as expensive as some in the industry claim. In the area of interactive television, "it turns out that much of the cost associated with building the new infrastructure, particularly for telephone companies, involves investments that the companies would make regardless of any interactive television services," Carey explains.

> *In other words, the incremental costs of building a network for interactive television are a modest addition to normal replacement and upgrading costs for their networks. So, when a telephone company says that it will spend $17 billion to build a telecommunication superhighway for ITV and other advanced services, it usually means that they plan to spend $2 billion more than they would otherwise spend for normal replacement and upgrading of their network. Further, the plans typically allow them to scale back the additional costs if market demand for new services is lower than expected. For cable operators, incremental costs are greater. However, they too can scale back investment if demand is lower than expected. Further, the investment will yield other benefits such as lower operating and maintenance costs.*[3]

But there are other costs, perhaps more significant than dollars. Among these are issues of access to the technology. Two principles that have guided public communication policy for most of the century are universal and equitable access. Unless these two principles apply equally well in the new media environment, the social costs will be high. Among the likely losers will be women, minority groups, inner city and rural dwellers, children, the elderly, the homeless, and persons with disabilities. Other social costs may include social fragmentation, digital isolation, and a falloff in political participation.

The Consequences of Technology Convergence

One of the most basic trends in the new media environment is the convergence of multimedia and online, or networked, communications. As these systems converge, a truly unique and powerful new medium of public communication will emerge. Its commercial and cultural implications are as profound as they are remarkable. It is likely to transform virtually every social institution, from education to government, medicine to law. This new medium will influence the process of human communication, the process by which social change occurs and the processes and mechanisms controlling both the U.S. and the world economy. The three most significant unanswered questions are:

- Will these changes be for the better or worse?
- What will be the cost and for whom?
- What will be the timetable for change?

Countervailing Forces

Countervailing technological forces may also be at work, however, in the new media universe. One of the almost sacred primordial forces driving technological change during the past quarter century has been the dramatically falling price of computing power. Recent evidence suggests this trend may soon be slowing down, if not drawing to a close completely. As computer chip manufacturers have created ever-smaller chips capable of ever-greater calculation, the price of computing has fallen remarkably. Manufacturers today, however, may be reaching the theoretical limit to computer chip miniaturization. "The problem is that life gets harder for chip makers as dimensions shrink below a micron in size," reports Gary Stix.[4] "At about 0.05 micron, the dimensions of the individual devices will be so small that quantum effects will disrupt their behavior. Then a new technology based on probabilistic laws will be needed." Producing reliable chips has also become increasingly complex and costly, as reflected in the initially flawed, super-fast Pentium chip. State-of-the-art chips now house some sixteen million memory bits and require two hundred processing steps. By 2001 reliable production techniques may require manufacturing devices as small as 15 to 50 nanometers, "less than the width of a coiled DNA molecule."[5] Moreover, as the cost of chip manufacturing has fallen, the cost of chip design and manufacturing technology has risen. Gordon Moore, the former chairman of Intel, the world's largest chip manufacturer, noted that his company's first chip manufacturing plant in the late 1960s cost $3 million.[6] "Today that is the cost of one piece of equipment in one of our plants," Moore observes. The next generation of chip manufacturing plants will exceed $1 billion in price, and by 2000 may cost ten times that. The effect on the semiconductor business is that returns on investment are threatened, and the drive to manufacture even smaller chips may stall.

If this trend toward chip miniaturization does draw to a close, projections for the future will change dramatically. It will not be safe to assume that super-powerful computing devices will become ubiquitous in at least the early twenty-first century. Information appliances will not become the consumer standard many hope for. The potential for video delivery and processing will fall dramatically, and the price will stabilize.

Commercial investment in the new media, as a result, will slacken and economic growth will slow.

How likely is this dire scenario? Unless there is a breakthrough in chip design, it is fairly likely. Optical technology, however, though still in the laboratory research stages, is one of the most intriguing avenues for the future of computing. Optical, or photonic, computing, based not on the flow of electrons in a silicon-based computer chip, but on pulses of light in a new silicon environment, may unleash vast new opportunities to decrease the cost of computing power and dramatically increase computing power and speed—the theoretical limit is the speed of light, 186,000 miles per second. Moreover, if optical technology can be combined with some preliminary but theoretically sound research on organic neural networks, the next generation may reach new thresholds in computing power and intelligence. As an alternative to such designs, some companies are experimenting with three-dimensional microchips. Unlike traditional two-dimensional designs in which the chip is approximately 5 microns in height and the conducting wires and transistors lie across the insulating silicon base, Mitsubishi, IBM, Siemens, and Toshiba are developing chips 20–30 microns in height with wires, conductors, and transistors all layered atop an insulating base of silicon.[7] Such chips could eventually lead to the development of supercomputers the size of a sugar cube.

If computer speed, processing power, and memory do continue to increase, the possibilities are seemingly boundless. Some predictions include:

- 2002—Personal "Crays" capable of emulating any desktop, from Macintosh to PC with the power of today's supercomputer
- 2005—Smart TVs that remember past viewing patterns and suggest new shows that match tastes and preferences
- 2008—Telephones that instantaneously translate messages from callers speaking in any of a dozen or more languages
- 2011—Artificial intelligence applications so smart and humanlike that they can replace entire corporate departments such as accounting or finance[8]

DIGITAL PUBLISHING

The evolution of multimedia products in an online environment will push traditional and new media providers to explore new publishing frontiers. New media publishers will not only have opportunities to reach global audiences with multimedia products in real time, but will also be able to completely rethink their relationship with advertisers and audiences. Further, they will have the unique opportunity to completely rethink their internal processes of content creation. No longer will they be constrained by traditional modes of product development. Conversely, the world of digital publishing will present considerable uncertainty for companies already unsure of themselves and their business future. All bets are off in the business of new media. Competitors will arise from every corner of the market and the world. Even the audience will be inclined and able to get in on the action in a computer-driven media world.

Publishers or "Content Providers"?

One of the growing debates in the new media world involves what values dominate the content production process. Will content producers continue in the tradition of the great publishers of the newspaper or magazine publishing world, placing concerns about freedom of expression, privacy, and democratic processes high on the communication agenda? Will the values of the broadcast industry prevail? Where will concern about the public interest fit in this new scenario? Will everyone be reduced to the role of "content provider"? At a conference held in early 1994 in Atlanta, heads of several hundred media publishing interests gathered to discuss the prospects for publishing on the information superhighway. When one participant encountered the president of one of the two oldest National Football League franchises, he asked him why he was attending the conference. His response was a simple, "Because we are a content provider."[9]

Verifying Information

Journalism also faces another imminent threat on the global information grid. On a digital information superhighway characterized by a laissez faire marketplace where information is openly exchanged and computer network security is difficult if not impossible to guarantee, how does a media organization—or any other organization—verify the accuracy of data? How does it protect its intellectual property? The world's largest news service recently ran headlong into this problem. On Monday, April 4, 1994, a remarkable news story appeared exclusively on the global Reuters news service. In the wake of the assassination of Colosio, the leading presidential candidate in Mexico's 1994 elections, the story alleged that President Salinas was about to rewrite the Mexican constitution to allow him to run for another term in office. The story, however, was false. Someone had cracked the Reuters network and placed the fictitious report on the news wire.

An "FBI" Solution

One possible solution has recently been introduced by a British company offering an electronic signature ID. Nottingham-based MOR Ltd. has developed a digital technique it calls FBI that combines a header, electronic "fingerprints," and an alphanumeric ID sequence imprinted throughout an image or data file.[10] The digital ID is completely transparent and hidden from view and is nearly impermeable to tampering. When used, it would provide a nearly permanent encoding system that publishers and other new media content providers could use to verify the source of a message and to determine whether a video or audio segment was pirated from an original feed.

The Confluence of Information and Entertainment

Despite the allure of digital technology, it is important not to get caught up in the hype surrounding the information superhighway and new media technologies. Media entrepreneurs have been drawn by the siren call of new technology in the past, only to lose millions of dollars on failed technology applications. Many are already urging caution in investing huge sums in as yet unrealized technologies. Mark Stahlman, president of New York–based New Media Associates, is one entrepreneur sounding the alarm. He recently wrote in *Wired* magazine:

> All the headlines about the digital, interactive, 500-channel, multi-megamedia blow-your-socks-off future are pure hype. Yes, all the wild Wall Street, through-the-roof, Crazy Eddie, cornucopia, shout-it-out-loud promo jobs are pure greed. It's all a joke.
>
> It's now official. I'm announcing the beginning of convergence backlash. There will be no convergence. There will be no 500-channel future. There will be no US$3 trillion mother of all industries. There will be no virtual sex. There will be no infobahn. None of it—at least not the way you've been reading about it.
>
> Sure the technologies are real. Digital compression and digital phone lines are real. Those 100-MIPS micros are real. Multimedia and high-speed networks are real. In fact, the technology is so real that it's almost obvious. Unfortunately, the businesses to exploit these technologies are anything but obvious.[11]

Tomorrow's News

Although newspaper readership has been declining steadily for nearly four decades, does this mean people are less interested in reading the news? Does the decreasing audience for network television news mean people want to watch less televised news? Research suggests the answer to both these questions is no. One recent study shows that three out of four adults in the United States are still "very interested" in getting the latest news about current events. There is also much anecdotal evidence to suggest that people still have an insatiable appetite for news. Today there are more newsletters (ten thousand in print and even more in electronic form), magazines (ten thousand), ethnic newspapers (five hundred), and other successful printed news products than ever before. Moreover, the national newspaper *USA Today*, the Cable News Network (CNN), C-SPAN, the ever-vigilant eye on Congress and Washington, and CourtTV were all launched after 1980. Although few of these news and information products capture major audience shares, they have all carved out important niches.

If you are still not convinced, consider this scenario for one possible news product of the not-too-distant future. Imagine pulling out of your book bag a one-pound electronic tablet about the size of a notepad. As you unfold the flexible tablet, you say, "Let's see this morning's paper." As the tablet's voice recognition software interprets your command and identifies your voice pattern, the screen is quickly transformed into a full-color electronic version of your local newspaper, if you still wish to call it a "newspaper." It's really a hybrid news product. The design still looks like a newspaper, with a front page, headlines, text, pictures, and graphics. But, it's really much more. A touch with the attached light pen, and a news photo comes to life, with full-motion video and audio. Another touch brings up a detailed historical analysis of today's top news story. Reading a related editorial, you react strongly. Again using the light pen, you activate the tablet's microphone, which allows you to record a voice-mail message to the editorial page editor, letting him or her know how you feel. PCS technology integrated into the tablet automatically sends your voice mail to the editor, who later hears your response and sends you an equally strongly worded voice-mail response. A classified ad catches your eye, and you use the light pen to extract more information about the product for sale. After seeing a three-dimensional picture of the product, you decide against making the purchase. As you look up, you see that you've reached the 116th stop on the number 1 line, and you put your tablet back in your bag and exit the subway, heading off to your graduate seminar in journalism at Columbia University in New York.

Network TV Online
NBC TV went online in May 1994 on America Online (AOL) and GEnie, two leading commercial online services. Every Friday on AOL, a star from

an NBC program talks via computer with up to five hundred subscribers for an hour in the online NBC "auditorium," with others "listening in." Additional NBC online features include downloadable color photos, ten-second video clips, ticket information about show tapings, and more.[12]

The rise of electronic, online information services does not signal the end of traditional print forms of communication, such as newspapers and magazines. "On-line services will coexist with print for the foreseeable future and maybe forever," says Stephen B. Shepard, editor in chief of *Business Week*.[13] Print is still highly portable and relatively inexpensive, and previous predictions of a paperless office have failed to materialize. In fact, the opposite has occurred. By the end of the 1980s, after a decade of computerization in the workplace, "we had four times the amount of paper being created in offices," says Rich Karlgaard, editor in chief of *Forbes ASAP*, a technology supplement to *Forbes* magazine.[14]

Dial N11 for News

Entry into the new media marketplace is remarkably simple and inexpensive, although this may rapidly change as competition heats up. Illustrative is the recent lottery for three-digit phone numbers Southern Bell held in May of 1994. Several Florida businesses won three-digit telephone numbers awarded in the first-ever such lottery. Southern Bell, a unit of BellSouth Corporation, awarded the numbers 211, 311, 511, 711, and 811 in Miami, Fort Lauderdale, and Orlando to a number of companies, including the *Miami Herald,* the *Sun-Sentinel of Fort Lauderdale,* the *Orlando Sentinel,* the Yellow Pages division of BellSouth, and several other businesses. The lottery was open to anyone willing to pay a $25,000 startup fee and a minimum $10,000 per month. Regulators, other phone companies, and others interested in entering the expanding telecommunications market are watching to see how the so-called N11 services develop in Florida. Companies have filed petitions for N11 numbers in most states, but no utility regulators outside Florida have endorsed the commercial service, and BellSouth is the only regional Bell operating company to push for such sales. Bell Atlantic has planned a field trial using an N11 number to let residents of New Jersey have free telephone access to news and other information. Beginning in October of 1994, callers in the 201 and 908 area codes can dial 211 to hear a menu from which they can select a newspaper or other information source for a variety of information, including news, sports scores, or classified ads. Information providers will likely include the *Star-Ledger* of Newark, the *Record* of Hackensack, the *Philadelphia Inquirer*, the *Asbury Park Press* of Neptune, the *Burlington County Times* of Willingboro, *Neighbor News* of Denville and the Recorder Publishing Company, as well as Market Link-Infodial and the Trenton office of the federal General Services Administration.[15]

The Texas Public Utility Commission decided on April 27, 1994 that newspapers and other businesses cannot use three-digit telephone numbers for commercial purposes. The commission agreed with an administrative law judge who ruled that permitting businesses to use the scarce numbers would give them an unfair commercial advantage. The FCC has yet to weigh in on the issue. Most well-known among these services is the widely available 911 emergency line. Phone companies typically use 411 or 611 for directory assistance and service calls.

Winners of the Florida lottery can charge consumers per call or offer services to callers for free, as well as add advertising to those services. Newspapers might offer, for example, sports scores, sponsored by a pizza parlor or local sportswear shop. The *Atlanta Journal* and *Constitution* newspapers in Georgia and the *Palm Beach Post* of West Palm Beach, Florida, also have experimented with three-digit numbers to offer information services.[16]

A BUSINESS MANAGER'S GUIDE
TO DIGITAL PUBLISHING

Although no one knows the exact parameters of the emerging new media environment, the basic topography of that world has begun to take shape. New media products, regardless of their content, audience, or means of delivery, will be in digital form. Products will migrate rapidly toward the multimedia format. Content will evolve more slowly from extensions of the old media into more experimental and novel categories. Today's online services "are the Model Ts, the horseless carriages of the information future," says Bob Ingle, executive editor of the *San Jose Mercury News*.[17] Content providers will respond to the intellectual property challenges of the digital age in a number of ways, including branding, electronic signature identification, and international partnerships. Audiences are likely to be defined not as much by geography or political boundary, as much as other lifestyle, psychographic, and generational factors. Perhaps more importantly, audience members will become important providers and shapers of content. Although most will remain in the passive, couch potato mode, many, especially in the younger audience segment, will enter into an interactive, participatory mode, much as now prevails on the Internet. Content delivery will evolve increasingly toward a networked environment. Initially, many products will be on CD-ROM and other optical media, although magnetic formats will persist. Still, the efficiency of online delivery and the growing reach of online technologies, especially with the advent of wireless technologies, in concert with improved compression, encryption, and legal protections for intellectual property rights, will help online technologies prevail and become the dominant mode of delivery.

To sum up, publishers should consider the following ten new media guidelines:

- **Digital multimedia,** including a combination of full-motion video, audio, hypertext, and data, all fully manipulable on either optical, CD-ROM or online format.
- **Video on demand,** with full VCR features, such as pause, rewind, fast forward, and scan.
- **Online versions** of media products do not seem to cannibalize print or broadcast version. Experience, in fact, suggests that use of online products on the World Wide Web on the Internet generally enhances interest in traditional format products, especially when the online and traditional versions are not strict duplicates of each other.
- **True interactivity,** featuring "upstream" capability.
- **Flexible cost structure,** to allow consumers extensive choice in designing their own information system.
- **Intellectual property rights protections and limitations,** to insure the integrity, credibility, and maximum lifespan of their content creations—many multimedia projects have already stalled over the complexities and cost of copyright considerations.
- **Security,** including encryption, to protect communications in a public network environment.
- **International partnerships,** which will enable domestic companies to effectively enter and succeed in foreign markets where local expertise is essential.
- **Original, quality content,** without which consumers will have no significant reason to turn to new media offerings—this will cost more to produce, but ultimately will be worth the extra investment.
- **Freedom of expression protections,** without which, the new media environment will be destined to wither and die.

Although these general guidelines may suggest an optimistic view of the future, those entering the world of digital publishing would be wise to exercise caution. As of this writing few of the technologies examined in this book are settled. Most are in an active process of evolution. Technical standards vary not only from region to region, but from country to country, and show little chance of settling down anytime soon. Legal and regulatory structures are rapidly evolving and the competitive environment is in a great state of flux. Much of the audience has almost no idea what to make of the new technologies. Many audience members find them fascinating, but are unsure whether they will be worth the cost or have any real advantages over existing sources of media entertainment, news, and information. Content creators are also uncertain of how to proceed. So far, there are few truly original offerings in the new media environment. Most are simply adaptations and extensions of existing products and have about as much appeal as movie sequels, if that much. The new rules of content production are also up in the air. No one knows exactly what a multimedia "script" is worth, how long it will take to produce, and whether it will ultimately turn a profit. One thing is certain: many entrepreneurs bold enough to leap into the new media world will lose much of their investment. Some will probably make a great deal of money. As one experienced corporate sponsor once said: "Half of my advertising is extremely effective. I just don't know which half." It may be that half of the new media products put into the market will succeed; unfortunately, no one knows which half.

The Intrepid Entrepreneur

The intrepid new media entrepreneur will integrate a considerable amount of research into his or her marketing efforts. Using both formative (that is, diagnostic) and summative (that is, end results) evaluation will greatly increase the efficiency of any new media marketing efforts and provide the competitive edge and adaptability needed to survive and even thrive in a highly volatile market.

A variety of media entrepreneurs have offered their prognosis for the future. Among the most visionary of the new media entrepreneurs is Reese Schonfeld, president and CEO of the National Food Network. Schonfeld, the cofounder of CNN, has been promoting the virtues of the information highway since the mid-1980s, long before most had even heard of the idea. Schonfeld admits he does not know what final shape the information superhighway will take, but he knows what it should be: It should be digital, packet switched, and designed with an open architecture to allow everyone to produce content for it.[18]

In agreement is John Malone, president and CEO of TCI and "the most powerful man in television," says premier media critic Ken Auletta.[19] "A full-access universal network is really what we're talking about—broadband, fully interactive, bidirectional, and universally available," says Malone.[20] "I see it happening in the next three to five years."

James C. Kennedy, chairman and chief executive officer of Cox Enterprises, Inc., of Atlanta, is convinced that newspapers have a place on the information superhighway, but to secure that place they will need to demonstrate creativity and commitment to change.[21] "If we don't have the courage and creativity to take these risks, we won't have to worry about the public trust we enjoy today," Kennedy told members of the Newspaper Association of America on June 27, 1994.

Amidst the swirling hype and hope of the digital revolution, Neal B. Freeman, a Peabody Award–winning television producer and chairman of the Blackwell Corporation, stands among those convinced of the promise of the information highway. "The digital era of communications is here, and its essence is this: vastly more people will have vastly improved access to vastly more information."[22] Freeman's conclusion is based on an analysis of the political economy of the digital era, in which he believes we are at "one of those rare moments in techno-economic history when it becomes clear that some players will win big and many other players will win at least a little. The zero-sum, scarce-spectrum game is over, and real growth is at hand." What does he base his analysis on? Five factors:

- the increased power of special interests, with dozens of groups having formed, for example, their own networks, ranging from the Caribbean Satellite Network to the Crime Channel to the Gaming Network
- the retreat of telecommunications regulation, as the Clinton-Gore administration continues the momentum built during the Reagan-Bush years marked by the 1984 Modified Consent Decree divesting the baby Bells from behemoth AT&T
- the loss of America's cultural hegemony, as the global information network slowly erodes U.S. dominance in the creation of popular culture
- the rise of the multinational corporation, making once-exotic "supranationals" such as Rupert Murdoch the norm, as it is the exceptional company that does not systematically move its rising young executives around the global markets
- the emergence of the digital press, as online, multimedia newspapers and magazines take hold, redefining the concept of news and markets no longer limited by geographic or political boundaries

At the same time consumers will have access to an increasing flow of raw data feeds from electronic media of all types. The need for information filters will rise dramatically. Traditional news media organizations will have an opportunity to expand their interpretation function.

The new media will also offer promising new tools to business leaders and others tuned into the information superhighway. These new tools may offer a variety of competitive edges to the corporate risk taker. One example comes from a new service offered by CNN and Intel. The television news network and chip manufacturer have teamed up to test transmission of TV news to personal computers. Cable News Network and Santa Clara, California–based Intel launched their test service in May 1994. Using Intel's multicast video technology, video signals are compressed and delivered to PCs via local area networks, or LANs. The technology does not require special computer monitors or decompression hardware and involves programming from CNN and Headline News.[23]

Careers in the New Media: The Educational Mandate

Anyone planning a career in new media should be prepared for change, adaptation, and convergence. Few new media technologies are settled into their final form. As the technology continues to evolve, content production processes will continue to change. Moreover, as the new media of the digital age grow in importance, individuals with a rich understanding of technology convergence will have an advantage. New media products will become increasingly multimedia in format, with text, data, audio, and motion video blending in a single communications environment. Students preparing for new media careers should take courses both in the liberal arts and in all aspects of human communication. Medium-specific courses or degrees will have decreasing value in the emerging new media environment. Instead, the next generation of students will need to combine basic skills in thinking and writing with new media coursework emphasizing all aspects of human communication, from interpersonal and group communication to mediated and networked communications.

The Business Forecast

> *"You acted unwisely," I cried, "as you see*
> *by the outcome." He calmly eyed me;*
> *"When choosing the course of my action,"*
> *said he, "I had not the outcome to guide me."*
>
> —AMBROSE BIERCE[24]

Against a backdrop of considerable optimism and enthusiasm for the coming new media age, there is still profound commercial and cultural risk in investing millions, even billions, of dollars in staking out territory on the new media business frontier. Although there is no way to completely remove the risk from entering the new media marketplace, there are ways to minimize that risk. One set of tools comes from the field of financial analysts, commercial high rollers accustomed to risk taking. One of the premier financial analysts specializing in the media is J. Kendrick Noble, a veteran media analyst, who recently completed a senior fellowship at the Freedom Forum Media Studies Center. Noble's fellowship research included developing a methodology for conducting a business forecast for the media industry. Based on an examination of data for a variety of media and communication fields, including newspapers, magazines, cable TV, and telephony, for much of the twentieth century, Noble suggests that reliable forecasts for new media technologies are possible, at least under limited circumstances. Perhaps most importantly, the forecasts must be based on accurate historical time-series data. Moreover, any forecast should be extended for no more than one-third the time frame of the original data. That is, if historical data are available for thirty years, then any forecast or prediction, should be limited to the next ten years. For example, if data are available for 1965–1995, then a reliable forecast can be made through 2005. Beyond that period, the forecast is subject to many unexpected factors and likely to vary widely from the observed or actual pattern. Noble further notes that mathematical curves known as "S" curves are among the most commonly used tools for such forecasting. Such so-called growth curves are based on mathematical models for describing growth rates among biological organisms, such as humans or microorganisms. Logistic (or Pearl) and Gompertz curves are among the most widely used growth curves, and Noble argues they are effective for conducting new media forecasts.[25, 26] Others have used such biological models in describing media growth patterns, as well, including studies of media specialization and niche publishing. In Noble's research, a logistic curve provided an accurate description of the household penetration of the telephone from 1877 to 1931, but as a result of the Great Depression, underestimated the ultimate penetration level of the telephone in the 1980s (that is, the model predicted telephone penetration would top out at about 40 percent, when it actually reached close to 95 percent in the 1980s). Use of a Gompertz curve provided a somewhat less accurate description of the adoption level of the telephone during the first half of the twentieth century, but accurately forecast the penetration level of the 1980s. Assuming the Gompertz curve provides a more reliable long-term forecast for media household penetration, Noble's analysis suggests that cable TV will achieve in 2040 the same household penetration achieved by telephony in 1994 (that is, roughly 95 percent).

Given the utility of these financial forecasting methods, new media entrepreneurs should consider employing logistic and Gompertz curves to project the possible market for new media technologies. The results might help steer them away from huge financial blunders and into more productive returns. Still, a word of caution comes from an unlikely theological source. The Rev. Donald Shriver, former president of the Union Theological Seminar in New York, warns that a forecast for the future of the media, an institution central not only to the functioning of our economy but to our cultural and political process, may have greater value if it is contrasted against an alternative prediction, or based on clearly outlined conditions in an if/then fashion.[27] Typically, Noble observes, financial analysts must forecast a single projection, because it is what the clients demand. If their forecasts are right, they will succeed and make a lot of money. If they are wrong, they will need to find a new line of work. Intrepid new media investors should consider both the best and worst case forecasts before investing heavily in new media technologies.

A CONSUMER'S GUIDE TO DIGITAL COMMUNICATION

As the world of digital communication continues to evolve, media consumers will need to develop a new form of electronic media literacy. Central to this literacy is understanding the dimensions, grammar, and commercial nature of multimedia and cyberspace communications. As these two forms of digital communications converge, or collide, in the emerging information superhighway the new literacy will also continue to evolve. The rules and guidelines offered here are merely a starting point and will require continual updating as the technology and its uses evolve.

"Seeing is believing" is an adage many have subscribed to for centuries. But in today's digital media age it can no longer be relied on. Digital image processors have made synthetic video commonplace. As a result, new media consumers need to be both aware of the new rules of the game, as well as how new media content producers will respond. Outlined below are ten rules, or commandments, to guide consumers navigating the world of digital communications. The first three rules apply generally to digital media, and the rest apply to cyberspace and beyond.

Rule number 1: Question everything that is seen, heard, read, or watched in the new media environment. Digital processors and those who own one make detecting synthetic content impossible, and there is no government agency like the Federal Drug Administration (FDA) charged with evaluating media content, partly as a result of the First Amendment, partly a result of the complexity and scope of the existing communication system, and largely because of technology itself.

Rule number 2: Conclude that almost everything in the new media environment is created to make money for someone. The few media products that truly do not have a commercial basis are as rare as a VCR that never blinks "12:00."

Rule number 3: Assume that every new technology is a potential threat to your privacy. Every interactive system from your cable TV to the telephone has the ability to record every interaction you engage it in. The question you must ask yourself is: Is the convenience it provides worth the loss of privacy? The questions to ask the service provider are: What information about me and my use of your service are you recording, how will you use it, and will you make the information available to anyone else, to whom, and for what price?

Exploring the Limits of Cyberspace: The Possible and the Impossible

Cyberspace is the domain of networked communications that today encircle the globe, and tomorrow may stretch well beyond planet Earth. Although its beginnings were meager and the applications generally limited to electronic mail and file transfers, today the boundaries of cyberspace are rapidly expanding. Electronic bombs are sometimes as frequent as electronic mail, commercial transactions are almost as common on some systems as document transfers, and electronic publishing is challenging commercial printing as the state of the art in reaching both niche and mass markets. Moreover, the frontier nature of cyberspace also abounds with villains, outlaws, and heroes. Together, these patterns lead to **rule number 4:** Assume there are no boundaries in cyberspace, other than your own or someone else's imagination.

The following rules are especially important for parents, but apply to anyone concerned about the digital world. **Rule number 5:** Apply all the rules of conventional media literacy to digital communications. In other words, be aware of what your children are tuned into, whether going online, exploring multimedia, or simply playing video games. Guide them in their selections, but also let them explore and enjoy freedom in making their own decisions. Debrief them periodically on their new media encounters.

Rule number 6: Expect the unexpected. Because the limits of cyberspace are unknown and expanding, there will always be surprises. This is much of what attracts young people to explore the online world. It is participatory, evolving, and allows connections to people all around the world. There are many benefits possible, including cultural enrichment, education, and cognitive development. But there are also dangers, some of which are outlined below.

Rule number 7: Never assume that if your child is using his or her computer that he or she is necessarily engaged in something educational.

Although it is tempting to think that using the computer is better than watching television, it's not necessarily the case. Pedophilia in the online world is rampant. Sexual content is among the most commonly transmitted digital material on the Internet. Children should always be monitored when using their computers, especially if their system has an online connection, including a modem and a phone line. It's wise to talk to your child after he or she uses the computer to find out what your child has been doing. Or, better yet, join your children in their computer explorations and game playing. When buying computer games, always read reviews and make sure that the content is suitable for your child. Many games are fun, educational, and harmless. But many are equally filled with violence, sexual exploitation, and even racism. Many of both the best and worst games can be obtained through cyberspace. Monitor your child's computer use to make sure the material he or she may be downloading is appropriate for your child and meets your standards. Also, make sure that your child is not obtaining pirated material, such as digital recordings of copyrighted music or video. This is not only potentially dangerous but is illegal. If you do find pirated material, talk to your child about how he or she received it, and delete the files.

Corollaries to rule number 7:

- Beware of anyone bearing uninvited gifts, anything free, or anything that sounds too good to be true—because it probably is. The Internet is filled with hucksters, charlatans, con artists, and worse. The discussion below examines the dimensions of the lawless nature of the electronic frontier.
- Never give out your name, address, or phone number, and instruct your children to do likewise and to never give out the name of their school.
- Don't respond to angry or obscene online messages; report them to the manager of the online service you or your child uses.
- Know the online service(s) your child uses, and see if blocking is available.

Rule number 8: Encourage the spirit of the First Amendment in cyberspace. Freedom of expression is perhaps the strongest positive force to countervail against many of the potentially negative forces at work in cyberspace. By promoting more communication, not less, participants in the global online community will enjoy a more robust communication environment, one in which truth will likely prevail over falsehood. Such platitudes may seem naive in today's somewhat cynical age, but they reflect the importance of reaffirming the Constitutional guarantees on the electronic frontier.

Rule number 9: Think twice before buying the first, or even second generation of any new media technology. Chances are great that the early generations may have bugs or technical problems. Subsequent versions are likely to be considerably less expensive and to work better, often having more features and being less complicated. Also, new technologies will tend to evolve toward a more unified set of standards, allowing greater compatibility among software from different companies or suppliers. This is not a hard and fast rule, but it tends to be the case.

Rule number 10: Experiment with and enjoy the technology. Test and explore the limits of cyberspace. If you have children, encourage them to do the same, and don't be afraid to *ask them* for help and advice. Chances are your children may know more about using many of the new media technologies than you do. Seeking their advice will not only be educational, but it will show them respect, help build their self-esteem, and encourage them to share future electronic discoveries with you. Research at the Pathways for Women in the Sciences program at Wellesley College suggests three ingredients are especially important in creating a user-friendly environment that will encourage girls to explore new media technology: hands-on experience, teamwork, and relevance.[28] Following these rules may not ensure a safe, enjoyable, and learning new media environment, but they will increase the chances of electronic success.

Scenario for Tomorrow: Knowbots, Virtual Reality, and Cyberpunks

Because it is neither owned and controlled by anyone, nor regulated by government, the Internet has served as a hotbed for unrestrained communication and an information free-for-all. Although philosopher John Locke may have been pleased to see his notion of a marketplace of ideas come to digital fruition, he may have been equally concerned about some of the emerging patterns of abuse.

Anarchy and Lawlessness on the Electronic Frontier

Technology reporter Peter H. Lewis writes that "Turks and Armenians have brought their decades-old hatred to the digital stage, accusing one another of using electronic mail forgeries and software that seeks and destroys an enemy's messages to the broader community."[29] Elsewhere on the "net," computer programmers are preparing "electronic mail bombs" to damage other users' computers, pedophiles are going online to recruit young boys for sex, and pornographic images are transmitted in large volume. Many long-time users are worried that the free and open atmosphere that has existed on the Internet and fostered an intellectual climate rich in diversity will be replaced by one chilled by obscenity and pandering to the lowest common denominator, where prejudice and promiscuity become the norm.

Strategies to protect the Internet community have been few, and some have given up hope. "Certainly there will never be any consensus to establish a regulatory body for Usenet (largest news groups on the Internet)," writes Mr. Botz in an e-mail.[30] "And no, the existing defenses are clearly not adequate. So what will happen? The Net as we know it will die."

Others see a technological solution. "What people will probably do is invent 'site kill files,'" writes David Hayes, a Usenet participant who works at the National Aeronautics and Space Administration's Jet Propulsion Laboratory in Pasadena, California.[31] "Site kill files" allow a user to block selected computer messages or specific parts of the network. At the same time, site kill files could be used to censor politically unpopular views, not just obscene messages or unsolicited advertisements.

Virtual Reality

Jaron Lanier, the creator of the first virtual reality device, says that passive entertainment will always have a place in the media world, but he believes there is also a much more engaging place for virtual reality. Virtual reality is in use in a variety of industries and applications, including training, design, education, medicine, art, and entertainment. In Germany, virtual reality technology is helping in the redesign of the city of Berlin, with VR technology controlling construction robots. In Japan, department store shoppers use VR applications to design their own kitchen, try it out, and have it delivered. In the United States, Medical Media Systems of New Hampshire is using virtual reality to enhance surgical tools. Here, VR technologies integrate magnetic resonance imaging (MRI) with live sensory data to give a surgeon a three-dimensional view of the body. Conjuring up images of the science fiction film classic *Fantastic Voyage* starring Raquel Welch, surgeons also use an instrument called endoscopic surgery, in which a tiny optical fiber is inserted into the body to control microinstruments. By remotely controlling this device, the surgeon virtually experiences the interior of the body. "It is like a zone for a fighter pilot," says Lanier.[32]

Although the passive couch potato may not quickly become a thing of the past, historians of the next millennium may someday need to write a virtual media history. Shaping that future is research scientist Brenda Laurel, whose work at Interval Research, a new Palo Alto, California, think tank, is creating virtual reality products generally not held in high regard in the commercial sector because they do not involve killing.[33]

Laurel's virtual reality creations include a "virtual environment for two" at the Banff Center for the Arts in Canada that lets visitors don computerized helmets and hand sensors to take a simulated trek to a mountain cave and step into the bodies of a snake, fish, spider, or crow.

Sonification

As we move into an era dominated by information, we are threatened by an increasingly complex and bewildering array of data. While T. S. Eliot once asked, "Where is the wisdom lost in knowledge? Where is the knowledge lost in information," Anthony Smith asks, "Where is the information lost in data?" "Sonification" may provide at least a partial answer. "Sonification" refers to the notion of making scientific data audible. Introduced into the technical literature in 1952, the notion has surfaced from time to time since then. Recently, a sonification research program emerged at the National Center for Supercomputing Applications (NCSA) at the University of Illinois. "If you work in the field of computer music, representing data with sound is a pretty obvious idea," says Illinois composer Robin Bargar.[34] The group at NCSA has developed sonification software that uses an IBM-compatible PC and a MIDI synthesizer to turn just about any data into sound. Gregory Kramer, a musician similarly intrigued by the notion of sonification, has developed a system in which sound represents several variables at once. Clarity, the company he founded in Garrison, New York, is designing a sonification system for operating rooms that will broadcast the patient's vital signs, including blood pressure and oxygen levels. The trick to sonification systems is developing a trained ear for sound, but it's a problem that training can overcome. Says Kramer, "You know when your car is running well just by listening to it. A certain noise, like a rattle, might also tell you what's wrong. Sounds in a well-designed sonification system could be interpreted in much the same way.[35] In the next decade, specialized applications of sonification technology might allow physicians to analyze complex patient data simply by listening to their audio representation. Perhaps sports fans one day may digest complex sports statistics simply by listening to an audio representation of the data on their personal digital appliance.

Artificial Life

Notions of artificial life, or living beings created by human hands, have been in our imagination for more than a century. Victorian novelist Mary Shelley envisioned an artificial life-form in her classic novel of Gothic horror, *Frankenstein*. More recently, Hungarian mathematician John Von Neuman described the automaton, a robotic machine capable of self-replication and other lifelike qualities. Logician Alan Turing outlined the foundation for machine-based life in his creation called the Turing Machine.

As a scientific discipline, the field of artificial life is in its infancy, however, with the first formal conference held in 1987.[36] Nevertheless, a number of computer scientists have conducted pioneering research to create computer-based life forms, artificial life, or a-life, which exhibit many of the qualities commonly associated with "real" life. These qualities include the ability to see, to eat, to reproduce and engage in sexual activity, to make decisions, to adapt to a changing environment, to demonstrate processes of natural selection. Since these artificial beings are capable of dying, then conversely, they are also capable of living. Tomorrow's media world may be populated more heavily by electronic a-life forms than by their human counterparts. Many of these a-life forms will be acting as personal assistants, or knowbots, to go in search of the information their human masters desire, to make or break appointments, or even conduct transactions at the bank or the supermarket based on rules that we have established for them. At the same time, many of these electronic creatures may be less socially acceptable. One of the most notorious forms of artificial life is the computer virus. Although invented as an academic exercise, the computer virus has evolved to become a powerfully destructive force. Beyond the computer virus, future forms of a-life may exceed even a science-fiction writer's most devilish imagination.

Most Wanted in Cyberspace

When Willie Sutton once was asked why he robbed banks, he replied: because that's where the money is. If cyberspace's most wanted cyberpunk were asked why he turned computer hacker, would he respond in like fashion: because that's where the information is? We may soon find out. Computer hacker Kevin Mitnick recently captured national headlines when he was arrested for allegedly stealing software and data from more than a half dozen cellular telephone manufacturers.[37] He was hunted in a much-celebrated FBI case for violation of a federal probation requirement that he not enter computers illegally. Technology reporter John Markoff reports that as a teenager, Mitnick used a computer and modem to:

- secretly read electronic mail of computer security officials at MCI Communications

- access telephone company central offices in Manhattan and the phone switching centers in California, allowing him to listen in on phone calls and engage in high-tech hijinks such as reprogramming home phones so that callers would hear a recording asking for a deposit of 25 cents
- break into a North American Air Defense Command computer, fore-shadowing the 1983 movie *War Games*

Digital Security

Protecting against computer hackers, criminals or cyberpunks, or virulent forms of a-life is rapidly becoming big business in the online world. Reflecting its deep concern, the Clinton administration released on July 8, 1994 a plan to help businesses protect their material on the information highway. Patent commissioner Bruce Lehman has recommended changes in the Copyright Act, designed to give owners of digital information greater ability to collect royalty payments from those who use their electronic work.

Security in cyberspace will become a dominant issue in the years ahead. Consumers and businesses will need to be vigilant in protecting their communications, electronic products, and commercial transactions in cyberspace. The cost of publishing online will rise as a result of security concerns and measures, at the same time increasing the cost of downloading electronic products and conducting electronic transactions and communications for the consumer. Similarly, the demand for electronic security will spawn new industries and trigger growth in existing companies involved in computer security. One possible new field will be insurance for electronic products, as a guard against electronic theft, vandalism, or destruction of electronic property.

THE GLOBAL INFORMATION INFRASTRUCTURE: GII

One of the emerging benefits of the new information age is the development of a global information infrastructure (GII). The GII refers to the emerging network of advanced telecommunications, computing, and information technologies around the world. Although the GII will not reach all communities, countries, and computers simultaneously, it will—in fact, it already does—reach many millions of persons around the world. GII will make it possible for persons in even remote regions to stay in constant electronic touch. It will enable low-cost, high-speed commercial transactions from any location in the world, as long as they are connected to the GII. It will provide electronic access to diverse resources located throughout the world.

Important questions about the GII include:

- Who will have access?
- What will be the cost of access and use?
- Who will pay for the construction of the GII?
- How will the GII be controlled or regulated?
- What guarantees for freedom of expression will exist in the GII?

A Global Virtual Digital Library

From a cultural perspective, one of the most important opportunities the GII affords is the creation of a global virtual digital library. Such a library is already developing, as electronic resources such as those at the OCLC, the U.S. Library of Congress, and at countless libraries and public institutions connected to the global network of networks known as the Internet. This library is virtual in the sense that its collection, as it were, is housed in no single physical location. Rather, it exists in digital format in many decentralized locations, in computers in libraries, schools, offices, and elsewhere. Each digital location acts as a communication portal, or file server, providing electronic access, browsing, or downloading of material to any location in the world connected to the GII. Important questions about this global virtual digital library are many, and parallel those outlined above regarding the GII.

A New Athenian Age of Democracy

Perhaps even more important than the development of virtual libraries are the implications of digital communications for the political system. For more than a century, political pundits have pondered the role of electronic media in the democratic process.[38] Today, Vice President Gore proclaims that networked communications may signal the beginning of a new Athenian age of democracy. Lawrence Grossman, former president of NBC News and PBS, echoes this view, suggesting that new media technologies are rapidly transforming the democratic system from one of representation to direct democracy. Armed with their computers, modems, and interactive television sets, citizens increasingly have direct access to the political process. Not only can they communicate directly with political candidates and elected officials, but they can vote on referenda and other legislative issues. Such a political transformation may be both a good and a dangerous thing. Although direct access technologies may enhance political participation, they may also lead to political decisions based on little more than the emotions aroused by dramatic television images.[39] More alarmingly, the selective development and diffusion of new technologies, the lack of access to the poor, and the difficulty in using many new technologies may also lead to political tyranny of the majority, with minority voices being lost in a digital cacophony.

Electronic Town Meetings

For two centuries, town meetings have been a vital part of democracy in America, making the electoral process a participatory rather than a spectator sport. French philosopher Alexis de Tocqueville observed how town meetings gave Americans a hands-on education in democracy. Brandeis University professor Jeffrey Abramson notes that the town meeting was originally designed to meet three purposes:

- to educate citizens about common concerns
- to empower citizens to self-government
- to engage citizens in an open and universally accessible process[40]

Of course, since their inception, town meetings have failed to fully meet these goals, restricting participation based on race, gender, church membership, and property. Still, the town meeting has been pursued as a democratic ideal. In its most recent incarnation, it emerged during the 1992 presidential campaign in a new, technologically driven form as the electronic town hall. Texas businessman Ross Perot trumpeted the electronic town hall as the platform for a new era of democracy. Others hailed the electronic town hall as a twenty-first-century technique to reintroduce face-to-face communication in a media society. But electronic town meetings are not necessarily a panacea. Not everyone may have access to the technology needed to participate fully. There is a tendency for "push button" democracy to take hold, where rather than meet and discuss, participants may do little more than push a button on a telephone handset or a remote control to indicate approval or disagreement.

Abramson argues that three conditions are necessary for effective deliberation at a town meeting:

- Citizens should be able to explore political messages of substance at length and in depth, without limiting exchanges to ever-shrinking soundbites.
- Citizens must be able to reflect on those messages, and not respond instantaneously.
- Citizens should be able to interact and exchange views and ideas, to test each other's reactions, and weigh their opinions against those of others.

Although face-to-face meetings can clearly satisfy these conditions, how well electronic town halls fare is a matter of how they are designed and executed.[41, 42] Technology may make it possible to bring together many participants at remote and scattered locations, but it can also encourage instantaneous response and a lack of substantial communication.

Abramson outlines six critical issues in designing electronic town meetings to satisfy the above criteria for effective political deliberation.

- **Venue.** New media technologies enable us to hold electronic town meetings on a national, regional, or local level. The choice of venue depends on both the issue or political campaign, as well as citizen access to the relevant technology.
- **Issue.** Every electronic town meeting should be devoted to a single, clearly stated issue, such as national health care or the federal deficit.
- **Agenda-setting/editorial control.** Setting the issues for the town meeting is a complex matter and research by Abramson suggests two models. The primary model is for the organization hosting the meeting, such as a television station, to choose the issues and plan the event, including selecting moderators, experts, and so on. Alternatively, it is sometimes effective for a nonprofit group to set the agenda.
- **Audience/participants.** Rarely will a town meeting, electronic or face to face, satisfy the demands of scientific sampling and representativeness of the broader population. Instead, audience members are typically self-selected and represent only politically active groups. Thus, Abramson recommends building an audience in two stages. First, there will naturally be the primary, self-selected audience, often limited to those who can come to a TV studio. Second, a broader audience should be invited to participate through the use of interactive technology such as the telephone through 800 or 900 numbers or through online communications. In one test, a preselected random sample of the population of San Francisco used confidential phone numbers to call in their responses during a 1987 town meeting.
- **Choice of interactive technology.** Interactive technology provides three main options for providing audience involvement and participation. First is Touch-Tone telephone dialing, particularly 800 and 900 networks provided by carriers such as AT&T and MCI. These networks can process more than ten thousand calls in ninety seconds. For national town meetings, it is essential to provide sufficient 800 network capacity. The CBS "America Online" special during the 1992 campaign frustrated many callers by providing too little capacity— only 314,786 calls got through out of some 24.6 million attempts.

The second option is two-way cable systems, which were inaugurated in the Warner Amex Qube experiment in the 1970s in Columbus, Ohio, and are today increasingly common. Interactive systems in San Antonio, Texas, Minneapolis, Minnesota, Portland, Oregon, Upper Manhattan, New York, Reading, Pennsylvania, Orlando, Florida, and Fairfax, Virginia, all allow the viewer to send messages upstream using a remote control, as well as receive TV programming. Lack of access to nonsubscribers is a limitation of this approach.

Finally, online services provide a third technological option for electronic town meetings. Online computer forums are in fact already common on the Internet and on commercial services. They allow in-depth discussion of issues, as well as direct communication and exchange of ideas. Moreover, through the Internet it is possible to provide a forum for holding for the first time an electronic town meeting in an international global venue. As we move toward McLuhan's global village, this may become an increasingly important issue. Moreover, online forums are inexpensive, since telecommunication charges are only local. The biggest drawback to online network approaches is the limited availability of computers and online services among the general citizenry. Even in an information society such as the United States, only some 20 percent of U.S. households have a computer, and even fewer have a network connection. This situation, however, may rapidly change with the proliferation of powerful, inexpensive video game players and the convergence of telecommunications, cable, and computers. Other emerging technologies such as DBS and PCNs may also provide a technological infrastructure for electronic town meetings by the end of the decade. Importantly, pioneering online voter information services were implemented via the Internet during the 1994 elections in California, including the Voter Online Information and Communications Exchange (VOICE) sponsored by two major national organizations, the League of Women Voters, and Project Smart Vote.[43] Preliminary evidence suggests VOICE received heavy usage by California's online electorate.

- **Voting from home or other audience locations.** This is in many ways the natural conclusion of the electronic town hall. One of the most significant problems in electronic voting, however, is the ability of individuals to vote multiple times. Similarly, it is important to provide multiple individuals at a *single location* the ability to each cast individual votes. A potential solution to these problems is to provide a personal identification number (PIN) to each participant to electronically monitor voting, assuring that each town hall participant could vote only once, and that each person at a location could cast a vote. Moreover, this approach would lay the foundation for full voting activity electronically, assuring that each ballot cast was entered by a registered voter. The security of each PIN would become imperative in such a system. Advanced systems could use optical scanners to verify voter identification through finger prints or retinal scan, although at present the cost of the necessary technology would be prohibitive. One of the important limitations of voting at electronic town meetings is generalizability beyond the meetings' participants. Participation in town hall meetings, whether traditional or electronic, is not representative of the population at large, and any results from a vote cannot be fairly generalized to the broader population.

Cities also play a central role in this digital future. One excellent example is The City of the Future project in San Diego, California, that is creating a vision of communication technology central to the economic and cultural life of the San Diego and Baja regions.

Freedom of Expression and Censorship in Cyberspace

Among the thorniest but most important issues confronting the electronic frontier is freedom of expression and censorship. How these issues are resolved will ultimately determine the value and contribution of networked communications in the political system and beyond. Although some First Amendment absolutists would shrug and say, "no law means no law," others perhaps more realistic will realize that there will always be limitations placed on speech, regardless of the venue or medium. Although no individual or group directly controls the Internet, a variety of corporate groups, individuals, and governmental agencies have already placed constraints on freedom of expression, whether in the form of direct censorship, chilling activities and threats, or electronic eavesdropping. Commercial online services such as Prodigy and America Online have censored some bulletin boards, removing comments deemed offensive or objectionable. Some individuals have dispatched electronic bombs to incapacitate the computers of individuals whose communications they found undesirable. Law enforcement agencies have assigned officers to patrol electronic cyberspace beats, posing as latchkey children in an attempt to lure potential online pedophiles. Many would agree that catching online criminals is a good thing. Others might draw the line at corporate censorship. The bottom line is that online freedom of expression is in a state of uncertainty. Since no one controls the online world, no one or no institution is in a position to offer any legal guarantees or protections for free electronic speech.

THE NEXT GENERATION:
CHILDREN AND TECHNOLOGY

Understanding the uses and consequences of new media technology ultimately hinges on understanding the next generation. Today's children and youth are the heaviest users of new media technology. They enjoy the highest comfort level with the technology. For them, many seemingly foreign and obtuse technologies are second nature and completely transparent. They often have an intuitive grasp of new media technologies. Whether programming a common house device like a VCR or accessing the Internet, many youth travel in and out of the cyberworld as easily as most adults get in an out of a car. To many older adults, the idea of talking to your computer, much less a banking machine, may seem like fanciful science fiction if not downright dangerous. But to the next generation, calling in to an automated banking machine and simply telling the computerized system what transactions you wish may be as simple as using an ATM is to most Americans today. One major bank in New York, Chemical Bank, is already conducting a test with voice-response telebanking. You dial in and simply say "representative" for the operator, or any of a number of other terms to select those banking options. The system works simply, easily, and reliably. What's around the corner is anybody's guess. But one thing is certain: the next generation will glide as easily through this seemingly high-tech world as today's average household gourmet operates a microwave oven. The next generation's new media habits will also continue the transformation of new media technology. Their behavioral preferences and patterns and content choices will influence the design and future look and feel of tomorrow's media. The nature of interactivity will reflect the next generation's lifestyle and attitudes.

Jaron Lanier, the recognized "father" of virtual reality offers this view of the importance of the next generation:

> *The digital superhighway is much more than a highway system. It's actually the construction of an entirely new virtual continent in which the highway runs. In the future, we will live part of our lives in cyberspace, in the world of virtual reality. We could bequeath few gifts to future generations more important than getting this right. It's critically important to balance public and private interests, much as it's very important to do so in land use, where even private land owners have certain obligations to the public.*[44]

No one can predict with any certainty the future of the media world. Many elements will be new and unexpected, while perhaps most will continue to reflect the best and worst of today's media system. Commercial interests will no doubt continue to dominate, but there will be room for cultural forces. As we already see in the Internet, the role of an electronic public space will be profound. The future of the media world may not be ours entirely to shape, but it is ours to discover. Lord Tennyson once offered these encouraging words:

Come, my friends, 'Tis not too late to seek a newer world.
—ALFRED, LORD TENNYSON[45]

NOTES

1. Steven Levy, "We Have Seen the Content, and It Is Us," *Media Studies Journal,* Winter 1994.

2. John Siegenthaler, Leadership Institute, the Freedom Forum Media Studies Center, 23 June 1994.

3. John Carey, "Media Research and the Information Highway: Setting a Research Agenda," speech, the Freedom Forum Media Studies Center, 14 February 1994.

4. Gary Stix, "The Wall: Chip Makers' Quest for Small May Be Hitting It," *Scientific American,* July 1994:96, 98.

5. Ibid.:96.

6. Ibid.

7. John Markoff, "Chip-Making Towers of Power," *New York Times,* 8 November 1994:C1.

8. *Business Week,* special report, "Some Gigachip Milestones to Look For," 4 July 1994:88.

9. Everette E. Dennis, Technology Studies Seminar, the Freedom Forum Media Studies Center, 6 April 1994.

10. Mark Fitzgerald, "Invisible Digital Copyright ID," *Editor & Publisher,* 25 June 1994.

11. Mark Stahlman, "Backlash: The Infobahn Is a Big, Fat Joke," *Wired,* March 1994:73.

12. Executive News Summary, *USA Today,* 6 May 1994:10.

13. Glenn Rifkin, "Seeing Print's Future in a Digital Universe," *New York Times,* 9 May 1994:D8.

14. Ibid.

15. Mark Thalhimer, ed., *Media Industry News Roundup,* compiled from the Associated Press, the Freedom Forum Media Studies Center, 6 July 1994.

16. Ibid.

17. Philip Moeller, "The Age of Convergence," *American Journalism Review,* January/February 1994:22.

18. Reese Schonfeld, speech, IRTS seminar, 11 February 1994.

19. Ken Auletta, "John Malone: Flying Solo," *New Yorker,* 7 February 1994.

20. Daniel Tynan, "PC Meets TV," *PC World,* February 1994:139.

21. Thalhimer, op. cit.

22. Neal B. Freeman, "Populism + Telecommunications = Global Democracy," *National Review,* 15 November 1993:50.

23. Mark Thalhimer, ed., *Media Industry News Roundup,* compiled from the Associated Press, the Freedom Forum Media Studies Center, 3 May 1994.

24. Ambrose Bierce, *The Collected Works of Ambrose Bierce.* New York: The Neale Publishing Co., 1909.

25. Joseph P. Martino, *Technological Forecasting for Decision-Making* ed 3. New York: McGraw-Hill, 1993.

26. J. Kendrick Noble, Jr., "U.S. Daily Newspapers: Past, Present and Prospects, 1958–2008," research report, presented at Fellows Seminar, 26 May 1994.

27. Rev. Donald Shriver, speaker, Fellows Seminar, the Freedom Forum Media Studies Center, 26 May 1994.

28. Katie Hafner, "Getting Girls On-Line," *Working Woman,* April 1994:61.

29. Peter H. Lewis, "Sneering At a Virtual Lynch Mob," *New York Times,* 11 May 1994:D7.

30. Ibid.

31. Ibid.

32. Jaron Lanier, "Virtual Reality," chapter in John V. Pavlik and Everette E. Dennis, eds., *Demystifying Media Technology,* Mountain View, CA: Mayfield Publishing, 1993.

33. Francine Hermelin, "Feminizing Virtual Reality," *Working Woman,* April 1994:54.

34. Steve Nadis, "Artificial Intelligence: The Sound of Data: Data May Fill Your Ears Rather Than Your Eyes," *Omni,* January 1994:26.

35. Ibid.

36. Steven Levy, *Artificial Life: The Quest for a New Creation.* London: Penguin Books, 1993.

37. John Markoff, "Cyberspace's Most Wanted: Hacker Eludes F.B.I. Pursuit," *New York Times,* 4 July 1994.

38. James Carey, *Communication as Culture.* London: Unwin Hyman, 1989.

39. Michael Schudson, "The Limits of Teledemocracy," *The American Prospect,* 11 (3), 1992:41–45.

40. Jeffrey B. Abramson and Charles M. Firestone, *Electronic Town Meetings: Democratic Design for Electronic Town Meetings,* the Aspen Institute, 1992.

41. F. Christopher Arterton, *Teledemocracy.* Beverly Hills, CA: Sage, 1987.

42. Theodore Becker, "Teledemocracy: Gathering Momentum in State and Local Governance," *Spectrum: The Journal of State Government,* 66 (2) 1993:14–19.

43. Peter H. Lewis, "Electronic Tie for Citizens and Seekers of Office," *New York Times,* 6 November 1994:15.

44. Daniel Tynan, "PC Meets TV." *PC World,* Feburary 1994:139.

45. Alfred Tennyson, *Ulysses.* London: Moxon, 1869.

APPENDIX A[1]

TABLE A-1 Top Media Companies Worldwide

Company	Media turnover (in millions)
Viacom	$9,300
Time Warner	$7,309.5
Sony (Columbia), Japan	$5,702.8
Matshushita Electrical Industrial	$4,651
Capital Cities/ABC	$4,329.8
NHK, Japan	$4,029
ARD, Germany	$3,580.2
Philips (Polygram NV), Netherlands (Holland)	$3,380.1
Fininvest, Italy	$3,330.9
Fujisankei e, Japan	$3,259.2
TCI	$3,206
Bertelsmann, Germany	$3,187.9
General Electric (NBC)	$3,120.2
CBS	$3,035
News Corporation, Australia	$2,750.7
RAI, Italy	$2,727.1
Walt Disney Company	$2,594.1
BBC, UK	$2,576.5
Thorn EMI, UK	$2,455.4
Nintendo, Japan	$1,702.9
Tokyo Broadcasting System Japan	$1,586.4

TABLE A-2   Top Cable System Operators Worldwide

Company	Revenue (in millions)
TCI	$3,206
Time Warner	$1,935
Continental	$1,039
Deutsche Bundespost Telekommunications	$1,030
Comcast	$ 647
Cox Enterprises	$ 610
Sci Holdings	$ 607
Cablevision	$ 603
Rogers Cable	$ 449
Times Mirror	$ 322

TABLE A-3   Leading U.S. Telecommunications Companies

Equipment and services	Market value (in millions)
AT&T	$75,700
MCI Communications	$12,284
McCaw Cellular Communications	$ 6,688
Sprint	$ 6,494
LIN Broadcasting	$ 4,216
Contel Cellular	$ 1,599
Telephone & Data Systems	$ 1,536
Century Telephone Enterprises	$ 1,493
Fleet Call	$ 1,365
U.S. Cellular	$ 1,204

TABLE A-4 Telephone Companies

Company	Market value (in millions)
GTE	$33,588
Bellsouth	$27,529
Bell Atlantic	$23,685
SouthWestern Bell	$22,399
Ameritech	$20,026
Nynex	$18,796
Pacific Telesis Group	$18,786
US West	$17,356
Alltel	$ 4,478
Centel	$ 3,440

TABLE A-5 Leading U.S. Computer Companies

Major systems	Sales (in millions)
IBM	$67,045
Hewlett-Packard	$15,918
Digital Equipment	$13,952
Unisys	$ 8,628
Apple Computer	$ 7,087
Sun Microsystems	$ 3,690
Harris Corporation	$ 3,046
Amdahl	$ 2,170
Tandem Computers	$ 2,037
Wang Laboratories	$ 1,896

TABLE A-6   Leading U.S. Computer Software Companies

Software	Sales (in millions)
Microsoft	$2,996
Computer Associates	$1,688
Oracle Systems	$1,241
Computervision	$1,132
Lotus Development	$ 903
Novell	$ 860
Policy Management Systems	$ 478
Borland International	$ 474
ASK Computer Systems	$ 441
Mentor Graphics	$ 374

TABLE A-7   Leading U.S. Newspaper Companies

Gannett Company
 USA Today, 87 other dailies
Knight-Ridder, Inc.
 Philadelphia Inquirer, Miami Herald, 27 others
Newhouse Newspapers
 Staten Island Advance, Portland Oregonian, 24 others
Tribune Company
 Chicago Tribune, New York Daily News, 7 others
Times Mirror
 Los Angeles Times, New York Newsday, Baltimore Sun, 5 others
Dow Jones & Company
 Wall Street Journal, 22 Ottaway newspapers
International Thomson
 120 dailies, mainly Canada
New York Times Company
 New York Times, 26 others
Scripps-Howard Newspapers
 Denver Rocky Mountain News, 22 others
Hearst Corporation
 San Francisco Examiner, 13 others
Cox Enterprises
 Atlanta Journal and Constitution, 19 others
News Corporation Ltd.
 Boston Herald, New York Post, 2 others

TABLE A-8 Leading Television Programming Companies

Company	Sales (in millions)
Viacom	$3,800
Turner Broadcasting	$1,641.4
QVC Networks	$1,070.6
Home Shopping Network	$1,053.9
Walt Disney Company	$ 761
King World Productions	$ 503.1
Gaylord Entertainment	$ 392.2
Spelling Entertainment	$ 258.5
Liberty Media	$ 156.5
Westwood Inc.	$ 137.7
International Family Entertainment	$ 131.7
BET Holdings	$ 61.7
RHI Entertainment	$ 56.5
All American Communication	$ 45.3

NOTES

1. Television Business International, March 1993; *TBI Yearbook 93; Broadcasting & Cable,* "Top 100 in Electronic Communications," June 21, 193; Renaud, Jean-Luc (1993). "Who Are Europe's Biggest Media Companies?" *TBI Yearbook 93; Screen Digest* (August 1993). "The World's Top AV Companies: The IDATE 100," Lee, M. and N. Solomon (1980), *Unreliable Sources,* New York: Carol Pub. Endicott, R. Craig, "100 Leading Media Companies: Relaxed rules, solid values trigger flurry of media acquisitions," *Advertising Age,* v. 64: no. 20, 16 August 1993. *Fortune,* "The 500 by Industry," 19 April 1993. *Business Week,* "The 1993 Business Week 1000: U.S. Companies Ranked by Industry," Comte, Elizabeth, "Entertainment & information: Movie companies, television networks and publishers felt a mild recovery from the recession," *Forbes,* 4 January 1993:142–3. Pitta, Julie, "Computers & communications: For years, nimble PC clonemakers have nibbled away at IBM and other industry leaders. In 1992 the giants fought back," *Forbes,* 4 January 1993:114, 115, 118. *Cable TV Financial Databook,* "The Largest Cable TV Deals in History," June 1993. *Cable TV Financial Databook,* "Cable TV Banking Ranking," June 1993. *Media Industry Newsletter,* "MIN's Exclusive Review of Group Publishers' First-Half-1993 Ad Pages: The Gains Are Shrinking, but the Majority of Publishers Remain Up," 2 August 1993, vol. 46, no. 31. *Media Industry Newsletter,* "Monthly Stock Watch," 9 August 1993, vol. 46, no. 32. *Cable and Satellite Europe (C&SEu),* "Top 50 Cable and Satellite Companies," 1993.

GLOSSARY OF NEW MEDIA
TECHNOLOGY TERMS

Road Signs on the Information Superhighway

Agents, or interface agents, are computer programs that employ artificial intelligence to help users operate various computer applications. They act much as a personal assistant. Agents can learn by observation, make decisions, and filter incoming information, such as select news items based on personal preferences or search a database looking for selected pieces of information or conduct transactions, such as electronic banking or making an airline reservation.

Artificial intelligence (AI) refers to computer-based technologies that replicate behaviors associated with human thinking, such as making decisions, evaluating options, or developing new ideas. AI applications have been developed in the areas of computer vision, robotics, language processing, and expert systems (for example, agents).

Asymmetrical digital subscriber line (ADSL) is an emerging telecommunications transmission technology that uses advanced packet switching (as opposed to the traditional circuit switching technology) to make the distribution of full-motion video possible using twisted-pair telephone lines.

Asynchronous transfer mode (ATM) is a new packet switching technology that will allow all types of networks, both local and wide area, to seamlessly interconnect and to transmit all forms of information, including voice, data, and full-motion video, via packet switching (that is, in bunches) rather than circuit switching (that is, over a dedicated line).

Bandwidth refers to the capacity of an electronic medium, such as an optical fiber, to carry information or data. The greater bandwidth of optical fiber allows it to carry full motion video, which contains large amounts of information compared to text or audio.

C and Ku-band satellites refer to medium-power, common carrier satellites that operate in the 12–14 gigahertz region. They are widely used to deliver television programming.

CAR, or CAIR, refers to computer-assisted (investigative) reporting pioneered in 1967.

CCD refers to a charge-coupled device used in electronic cameras to capture images without the use of emulsion, or chemical-based, film stock. CCD chips operate under low light conditions and have no delay for processing time.

Common carrier traditionally refers to the legal requirement that a regulated medium such as a telephone company provide open access at a fair price to all content providers seeking to use the telephone infrastructure. It is unclear whether new services such as consumer online services will be treated as a common carrier. Common carriers are not responsible for the content they carry from third parties, nor can they legally censor that content.

Compact disc–read only memory (CD-ROM) and Compact disk–interactive (CD-I) refers to an optical storage medium similar in format to music CDs. Designed with text storage in mind, a single CD-ROM can store more than 250,000 pages of text. CD-ROMs can also be used to store multimedia information, including audio and full-motion video, and are now being used by a variety of media companies to publish multimedia products ranging from electronic encyclopedias to news magazines. CD-I offers an interactive format for other kinds of products, such as games.

Compression refers to a technical process through which large amounts of data are condensed, or compressed, in digital format for transmission or storage. Many multimedia products would not be feasible today if not for advances in compression technology that reduce the digital information needed to replicate an image on a video monitor. This process has important implications for the creation of a video dial tone and for the storage of video signals, especially full-motion video, on CD-ROM or laserdisc devices.

Cyberspace is a termed developed by science fiction writer William Gibson to refer to a place similar to what many now call virtual reality. In *Neuromancer,* (1984) Gibson described cyberspace:

> *A consensual hallucination experienced daily by billions of legitimate operators, in every nation. . . . A graphic representation of data abstracted from the banks of every computer in the human system. Unthinkable complexity. Lines of light ranged in the nonspace of the mind, clusters and constellations of data. Like city lights, receding. . . .*

Digitization refers to the process of storing any information or communication in computer-readable format of 1s and 0s, or digits. It is the driving force behind the multimedia convergence of text, data, audio, and video.

Direct broadcast satellite (DBS) is a distribution medium that can transmit full-motion video direct to home compact satellite dishes no more than 18 inches across and costing about $700, replacing the large, expensive backyard dish. Initially launched in 1975, DBS systems have only recently begun to succeed commercially in the United States.

Electronic bulletin boards (BBS) are electronic message posting places widely available in the online world. There are thousands of electronic bulletin boards on the Internet dealing with as many subjects.

Electronic/digital photography refers to a new generation of cameras and photographic technologies that capture and store images in digital format. It makes possible the complete processing of any images—still or full motion—in a computerized, nonlinear environment. With wide commercial applications in advertising, public relations and journalism, it also raises a variety of thorny ethical questions about the veracity and credibility of the image. Digital cameras do not store images at as high a level of resolution as emulsion-based film cameras; state-of-the-art digital cameras can store images with some 10 million pixels (the smallest picture element in a computer image), as opposed to 35 million in film.

Electronic mail or e-mail is a form of computer-to-computer messaging that has existed since the first computer networks in the 1960s, allowing users to send and receive electronic mail at very little cost all around the world. It is among the heaviest uses of most computer networks, including the Internet.

Encryption is a communication security procedure referring to the encoding of messages in secret form and requiring subsequent decoding for interpretation. An ancient technique once used by Julius Caesar, emperor of Rome, encryption is a controversial topic in computer communications, as U.S. governmental agencies push for an encryption standard that would allow the authorities to eavesdrop and private groups push for a totally secure alternative.

Federal Communications Commission (FCC) is the principal federal communications regulatory agency in the United States. Created under the 1934 Communications Act, the FCC enforces and interprets laws pertaining to telecommunications, new media technology, and the existing electronic media, such as the 1992 Cable TV Act.

Flat panel displays refer to a new class of computer displays using liquid crystal (LCD), plasma, and other technologies (for example, diamond-coated displays) to present images on a flat screen. Many predict that the development of a high-resolution, color flat panel at low cost (about five to ten years in the future) will transform the computer into an effective and portable communications device, making possible new information services such as a multimedia electronic newspaper.

Full service network (FSN) is the term Time Warner and other corporations are using to describe the information superhighways currently under construction in places such as Orlando, Florida. The FSN consists of optical fiber networks, driven by Silicon Graphics computers, and will offer a full range of new information services such as interactive TV and PCNs.

High-definition television (HDTV) refers to the next generation of television technology, featuring a wide-screen aspect ratio similar to that of the cinema, high-resolution images, advanced color rendition, and stereophonic sound all processed digitally.

High-8 millimeter video/camcorders are lightweight, low-cost, highly portable imaging technologies that are transforming how full-motion images are captured, processed, and stored. They are in use at a variety of media organizations, such as New York One, Time Warner's twenty-four-hour cable news channel in Manhattan.

Hypertext means nonlinear text. Coined by technology visionary Ted Nelson, hypertext is the foundation for the next generation of multimedia computing.

Icon is a graphic representation of a computer function that appears on a display, such as a microcomputer monitor.

Information society refers to a society in which knowledge and information increasingly become the dominant source of wealth, power, and employment.

Information superhighway means many things to many people, but in general it refers to the various emerging electronic data networks of advanced telecommunications technologies that make possible a variety of new information services ranging from video on demand to home shopping to computer-to-computer communications around the globe. Vice President Al Gore envisions an information superhighway based on the Internet model of networked computing, while telephone companies see it as a broadband switched telecommunications network capable of delivering everything from video on demand to personal communications.

Information technology refers to the acquisition, processing, storage, and dissemination of vocal, pictorial, textural, and numerical information by a microelectronics-based combination of computing and telecommunications.

Integrated services digital network (ISDN) is a telecommunications technology that brings together in a single medium of distribution all types of information, including data, voice, text, and video.

Intellectual property rights refers to the rights to ownership, marketing, and licensing of computer software and other information products. Includes questions of copyrights and patents.

Interactive media embrace telecommunications, computer, broadcast, and cable systems that allow direct exchanges among people or machines via one or more communications channels such as voice, writing, or vision.

Interactive television refers to a coming revolution in television viewing technology in which viewers will have access to a variety of two-way services and will be able to select and control what they view and when. The first interactive television actually can be traced to a 1950s television show called *Winky Dink and You,* and subsequently appeared in the 1970s in Warner Communications' Qube experiment in Columbus, Ohio, which gave birth to many of today's cable networks and programs, including MTV and Nickelodeon.

Internet refers to the global web of some ten thousand computer networks all linked electronically via computer university gateways and commercial services such as CompuServe, Prodigy, and America Online. The Internet provides free or low-cost access to some fifteen million users worldwide to global electronic mail (e-mail), file transfers, and databases ranging from the U.S. Library of Congress card catalogue to the four-thousand-page federal budget. Internet grew out of the Arpanet, created by the Defense Department as the first national computer network in 1969.

Modem refers to MOdulate-DEModulate, the device that allows computers to communicate over a wide-area network.

MPEG refers to the Motion Picture Experts Group, which sets standards for digital television images.

MSS refers to mobile satellite services, such as Inmarsat.

Multimedia refers to the integration of text, images, audio, and data in a digital environment.

NTSC refers to the National Television System Committee, one of three international systems of television standards, commonly used in the U.S., Japan, and a number of other countries. Named after the federal committee that originally established the United States monochrome TV standard in 1936, the committee was reconstituted in 1950 to recommend a compatible color system.

Online communications is the generic term for communications over a computer network.

Optical fiber is a silicon, or glass, medium for transmission of digital information. Optical fiber, or fiber optics, has transformed modern telecommunications primarily because it has more than one thousand times the carrying capacity of conventional, twisted-pair telephone lines.

Packet switching is a technique of switching digital signals with computers wherein the signal stream is broken into packets and reassembled in the correct sequence at the destination.

PCN refers to personal communication networks and services (PCS) that will be developed under the FCC forthcoming high-frequency spectrum auction. PCNs will allow for widespread wireless communications beyond cellular communications.

Personal digital appliances (PDAs) refer to a new class of computer-based communications devices such as the flat panel, personal communication device or pocket computers, such as the Apple Newton.

Pixel refers to the smallest picture element in a computerized imaging system.

RAM refers to random-access memory in a computer.

RBOC refers to Regional Bell Operating Company, one of seven firms that emerged from the 1984 AT&T divestiture as prime distribution channels for office phone and computer systems. RBOCs are: NYNEX, Bell Atlantic, Bell South, PacTel, Ameritech, SouthWestern Bell, US West.

Remote sensing technologies refers to a class of high-resolution electronic cameras in orbit around the earth. They involve two primary sensor systems: one is a television camera that takes pictures of the earth using visible light. The other is a multispectral scanner that uses both visible and infrared light. Advances in the technology and the end of the Cold War have made remote sensing an increasingly important technology for a variety of civilian applications, such as gathering visual information about the earth for weather forecasting, news gathering, and environmental monitoring.

Screen phone is the next generation of telephone handsets that will feature a liquid crystal display capable of providing textual information or data, making possible a variety of new information services on a mass scale and at a low cost.

Speech synthesis and recognition refer to technologies for computer voice processing, including understanding and responding to the spoken word as well as computerized speech. Applications are available for a variety of fields including medicine and journalism, but are especially important for making media technologies available for persons with disabilities.

S-VHS (Super-Home Video System) describes lightweight, low-cost, highly portable imaging technologies that are transforming how full-motion images are captured, processed and stored. They are in use at a variety of media and news organizations, such as industrial production houses, local television stations, and Fox Television Network News.

Transactional services refer to a variety of computerized, interactive information services including electronic or home shopping, making airline reservations, banking, and bill paying.

Video dial tone or video on demand (VOD) refers to a new form of interactive television in which the viewer has direct electronic access to digital libraries of full-motion video, including movies or news on demand. The video dial tone is the television analog to the telephone dialtone.

Virtual reality (VR) is for some the ultimate communication medium: a total sensory experience in which the user (or users) can interact with or create their own multidimensional universe by using a data glove, data suit, and data visor. When immersed in virtual reality, users see, feel, interact with, and manipulate a computer-generated world not necessarily related in any way to the so-called real world we all live in. VR applications have been developed for entertainment and arcade games, medicine, and employee training.

Virus—the computer virus is the digital equivalent of an organic virus that can infect a living being, such as a human. Computer viruses, however, are created by humans and are designed to disrupt computer applications. Computer viruses, a form of artificial life, are spread by inserting infected disks in other computers or by transferring infected files electronically over a computer network; the viruses then attach themselves to software applications, sometimes causing immediate damage and other times operating on a delayed basis.

Wireless transmission, including personal communication networks or services (PCN or PCS), is a new technology that uses a portion of the radio spectrum formerly thought impractical for communication uses, but now desirable because of advances in telecommunications, digitization, and compression. The Federal Communications Commission (FCC) is auctioning off the wireless spectrum estimated at a value in excess of $10 billion.

BIBLIOGRAPHY

"The ABC's of DBS." *Broadcasting & Cable,* 6 December 1993:38.

Abramson, Jeffrey B. and Charles M. Firestone. *Electronic Town Meetings: Democratic Design for Electronic Town Meetings.* The Aspen Institute, 1992.

"A day in the 'virtual' life of a Chiat/Day executive." *Advertising Age,* 14 March 1994.

Advertisement. *Omni,* January 1994:75.

Advertising Age. 18 July 1994:16.

Alpert, Mickey. "DBS." In John Pavlik and Everette E. Dennis, eds., *Demystifying Media Technology: Disk Edition.* Mountain View, CA: Mayfield Publishing, 1993.

American Demographics. February 1994:36.

Amstrong, David. "Ziff Happens." *Wired,* June 1994.

Andrews, Edmund L. "A Satellite System Is Planned to Link Most of the Globe." *New York Times,* 21 March 1994:A1, D2.

Andrews, Edmund L. "Betting on Small-Dish TV." *New York Times,* 15 December 1993:D1, D7.

Andrews, Edmund L. "Sudden Synergy Among Communications Rivals." *New York Times,* 21 October 1993:D1, D10.

Andrews, Edmund L. "Time Warner's 'Time Machine.'" *New York Times,* 12 December 1994:C1, C7.

Apple, R. W., Jr. "Policing a Global Village." *New York Times,* 13 October 1993:A1.

Arlen, Gary H. "America OnLine Continues Meteoric Growth, Signs Consumer Magazine Publisher." *Information & Interactive Services Report,* 19 November 1993.

Arlen, Gary H. "Education Networks to go Online Later This Year; Content Providers to Offer 'Electronic Printing Press.'" *Information & Interactive Services Report,* 25 February 1994:17.

Arlen, Gary H. *Information & Interactive Services Report.* 17 December 1993:5.

Arlen, Gary H. "LucasArts Charts Digital Path Between Film, Interactivity." *Information & Interactive Services Report,* 11 March 1994:11.

Arlen, Gary H. "RBOCs Finally Deploy ISDN." *Information & Interactive Services Report,* 25 February 1994:11.

Arlen, Gary H. "Washington Post Picks Ziff Interactive to Publish Its Online Newspaper." *Information & Interactive Services Report,* 25 March 1994.

Arlen, Gary H. "Who Uses CompuServe?" *Information & Interactive Services Report,* 11 February 1994:4.

Arterton, F. Christopher. *Teledemocracy.* Beverly Hills, CA: Sage, 1987.

Arthur, Brian. "Positive Feedback in Economic Modeling." *Scientific American,* May 1991.

Asimov, Isaac. *I, Robot.* New York: Gnome Press, 1950.

AT&T. "The National Information Infrastructure: A Key to America's Economic Growth and Global Competitiveness." A report from AT&T, August 1993.

Atchison, Sandra D. "The Care and Feeding of 'Lone Eagles.'" *Business Week,* 15 November 1993:58.

Auletta, Ken. *Three Blind Mice: How the Networks Lost Their Way.* Random House, 1991.

Auletta, Ken. "John Malone: Flying Solo." *New Yorker,* 7 February 1994.

Authors Guild, Inc. Press release, 11 April 1994.

Baer, Walter. Technology Studies Seminar, the Freedom Forum Media Studies Center, 1991.

Bailey, Wendell. "Conversation on Ethics in Telecommunications." Donald McGannon Center, Fordham University, October 1993.

Baker, Edwin. "Tollbooths on the Information Superhighway." *New York Times,* 26 October 1993.

Barnathan, Julius. Speech, Technology Studies Seminar, the Freedom Forum Media Studies Center, 12 December 1992.

Barringer, Felicity. "In Cyberspace, and Talking to Strangers." *New York Times,* 30 June 1994:D4.

Becker, Theodore. "Teledemocracy: Gathering Momentum in State and Local Governance." *Spectrum: The Journal of State Government,* 66, 1993,(2):14–19.

"Bell Atlantic Chairman Sketches Map of Information Superhighway." *Information & Interactive Services Report,* 5 November 1993:9.

Bell, Daniel. *The Coming of Post-Industrial Society.* New York: Basic Books, 1973.

Belsie, Laurent. "Info Superhighway: Metaphor in Concrete." *Christian Science Monitor,* 23 February 1994:A1.

Beniger, James R. *The Control Revolution: Technological and Economic Origins of the Information Society.* Cambridge: Harvard University Press, 1986.

Benjamin, Burton. *Niemen Report.* Summer 1986.

"The Best Products of 1993." *Time,* 3 January 1994:76.

Bierce, Ambrose. *The Collected Works of Ambrose Bierce.* New York: The Neale Publishing Co., 1909.

Biocca, Frank. "Communication Within Virtual Reality: Creating a Space for Research." *Journal of Communication,* 42(4), Autumn 1992:5-22, 9.

Bloomberg, Michael. "The Next Generation." Technology Studies Seminar for Newsroom Managers, the Freedom Forum Media Studies Center, 15 September 1993.

Blumler, Jay and Elihu Katz. *Uses and Gratifications Research in Mass Communication.* Newbury Park, CA: Sage Publications, 1974.

Bohrman, David and Larry Wood. "Hypermedia at ABC News: Magna: An Electronic Anchor Information System." In John V. Pavlik and Everette E. Dennis, eds., *Demystifying Media Technology,* Mountain View CA: Mayfield Publishing, 1993.

Bollier, David and Charles M. Firestone. "The Promise and Peril of Emerging Information Technologies." A Report on the Second Annual Roundtable on Information Technology, the Aspen Institute Communications and Society Program, 1993.

Braman, Sandra. "Contradictions in Brilliant Eyes." *Gazette* 47:177–194, 1991.

Brand, Stewart. *The Media Lab: Inventing the Future at MIT.* New York: Viking, 1987.

Branscomb, Anne Wells. *Who Owns Information? From Privacy to Public Access.* New York: Basic Books, 1994.

Brender, Mark E. "High Resolution in Remote Sensing by the News Media." *Technology in Society* 22:89–98, 1989.

Broad, William J. "Spy Data Now Open for Studies of Climate." *New York Times,* 23 June 1992:C1, C10.

Broadcasting & Cable, 11 July 1994:32.

Brown, Les. *Les Brown's Encyclopedia of Televison,* 3d ed. Detroit, MI: Gale Research Inc., 1992.

Brown, Les. Speech, Technology Studies Seminar, the Freedom Forum Media Studies Center, 6 April 1994.

Brown, Rich. "BellSouth Makes Another Move into Cable." *Broadcasting & Cable,* 13 December 1993.

Brown, Richard D. *Knowledge Is Power: The Diffusion of Information in Early America, 1700–1865.* New York: Oxford University Press, 1989.

Brown, Ronald H., Mary L. Good, and Arati Prabhakar. "Putting the Information Infrastructure to Work: A Report of the Information Infrastructure Task Force Committee on Applications and Technology." NIST Special Publication 857, Office of the Director, National Institute of Standards and Technology, U.S. Department of Commerce, Gaithersburg, MD 20899-0001, May 1994:4.

Browne, Malcolm W. *New York Times,* 28 September 1993:C1.

Browning, John. "Libraries Without Walls for Books Without Pages." *Wired,* Premier Issue 1993.

Buchman, Jeffrey. Speech. Technology Studies Seminar, the Freedom Forum Media Studies Center, 23 October 1993.

Bulkeley, William M. "Semi-Prose, Perhaps, But Sportswriting by Software Is a Hit." *Wall Street Journal,* 29 March 1994:1.

Burrus, Daniel with Roger Gittines. *Technotrends: How to Use Technology to Go Beyond Your Competition.* New York: Harper Business, 1993.

Bushkin, Kathy. Interviewed by the author. 13 April 1994.

Business Week, special report. "Some Gigachip Milestones to Look For." 4 July 1994:88.

Business Week, "The 1993 Business Week 1000: U.S. Companies Ranked by Industry." Special Annual Issue.

"Cable TV Banking Ranking." *Cable TV Financial Databook.* June 1993.

"Cap Cities/ABC TV Selects EON for Interactive Television Services." *Information & Interactive Services Report,* 8 October 1993: 4.

Carey, James. *Communication as Culture.* London: Unwin Hyman, 1989.

Carey, John. "From Internet to Infobahn." *Business Week,* Special 1994 Bonus Issue: 32, 33.

Carey, John. "Back to the Future: How New Communication Technologies Enter American Homes." Technology Studies Seminar, the Freedom Forum Media Studies Center, 26 October 1993.

Carey, John. "Field Testing the Information Superhighway." Speech, the Freedom Forum Media Studies Center, 5 April 1994.

Carey, John. "Media Research and the Information Highway: Setting a Research Agenda." Speech, the Freedom Forum Media Studies Center, February 14, 1994.

Carey, John. "Reality Check." *Business Week,* 4 April 1994:6.

Carey, John. "Thinking Flat in Washington." *Business Week,* 9 May 1994:36.

Carmody, Deirdre. "For Magazines, a Multimedia Wonderland." *New York Times,* 11 October 1993.

Chan, Joseph Man. "Satellite Television and the Infosphere: National Responses and Accessibility to STAR TV in Asia." Paper presented to the Ninth World Communication Forum, the Japan Society of Information and Communication Research, Tokyo, Japan, 19–20 November 1992.

"Chinese Pirates Sail the Potomac." *New York Times,* 5 May 1994.

Chronicle of Higher Education. 16 February 1994.

Clarke, Arthur C. "Extraterrestrial Relays." *Wireless World,* June 1945.

Clarke, Arthur C. *The Lost Worlds of 2001.* Boston: Gregg Press, 1979.

Clinton, W. J. and A. Gore. *Technology for America's Economic Growth, a New Direction to Build Economic Strength.* Washington, DC: Office of the President of the United States, February 1993.

Clinton, W. J. and A. Gore. *National Information Infrastructure.* Washington, DC: Office of the President of the United States, September 1993.

Club of Rome. *Microelectronics and Society: For Better or Worse.* New York: Pergaman Press, 1982.

Clyman, John. "PowerPC: Your Next CPU?" *PC Magazine,* 22 February 1994.

Commerce Department, U.S. Dept. of Labor, Bureau of Labor Statistics, Washington, DC 94-202116, 1994.

The Federal Communications Act of 1934. U.S. Government, Washington, DC 19 June, 1934.

Compaine, Benjamin. *Understanding New Media: Trends and Issues in Electronic Distribution of Information.* Cambridge: Ballinger, 1984.

Comte, Elizabeth. "Entertainment & Information: Movie Companies, Television Networks and Publishers Felt a Mild Recovery from the Recession." *Forbes,* 4 January 1993:142-3.

"The Consumer Multimedia Marketplace 2: Software." *Screen Digest,* May 1994.

Cooper, Jim. "From V-chip to Hip Hop." *Broadcasting & Cable,* March 28, 1994:22.

Coover, Robert. *New York Times,* Book Review, 29 August 1993.

Copyright Law of the United States of America, contained in Title 17 of the United States Code, Revised to March 1, 1991.

Corliss, Richard. *Time,* 4 October 1994:58, 59.

Crichton, Michael. Speech, the National Press Club, Washington, D.C. on 6 April 1993; *Mediasaurus* (1993) *Wired.*

Cuadra Associates. Directory of Online Databases. Boston, MA, 1994.

Daley, Richard J. Speech, Chicago, IL., 15 October 1993.

Dalton, Laura. *Executive News Summary,* 21 October 1993:1.

Davis, Leonard. "The Customer Is Always Right." *Omni,* November 1993:24.

de Sola Pool, I. *Technologies of Freedom.* Cambridge: Belknap Press of Harvard University, 1983.

de Sola Pool, I. *Technologies Without Boundaries: On Telecommunications in a Global Age.* E. M. Noam, ed., Cambridge: Harvard University Press, 1990.

Deitz, Paula. "All It Takes Is a Computer and Photos." *New York Times,* 31 March 1994.

DeLoughry, Thomas J. "Copyright Issues Said to Stall Many Multimedia Projects." *Chronicle of Higher Education,* 29 June 1994:A18.

DeLoughry, Thomas J. "Guaranteeing Access on the Data Highway." *Chronicle of Higher Education,* 3 November 1993.

DeLoughry, Thomas J. "Museums Go High-Tech." *Chronicle of Higher Education,* 14 September 1994:A47.

Demac, Donna. "Copyright and the New Electronic Media." Midterm report, the Freedom Forum Media Studies Center, 29 December 1993.

Dennis, Everette E. *Of Media and People.* Newbury Park, CA: Sage Publications, 1992.

Dennis, Everette E. Technology Studies Seminar, the Freedom Forum Media Studies Center, 6 April 1994.

Deutschman, J. Feature story on Larry Ellison. *Broadcasting & Cable,* 17 January 1994:3.

Dewey, John. *The Public and Its Problems.* Chicago: Swallow, 1927.

Dibbell, Julian. "Strange Loops: The Prisoner: Phiber Optik Goes Directly to Jail." *Village Voice,* 11 January 1994:44.

Dickens, Charles. *A Tale of Two Cities.* London: J.B. Lippincott, 1930.

Ditlea, Steve. "Female E-Mail: Computer Networks Put Women On-Line." *New York Daily News,* 3 November 1993.

Donegan, Jack. San Diego Supercomputer Center, Cities of the Future conference, 13 December 1994.

Dordick, Herbert S. and Dale E. Lehman. "Information Highways: 'Trickle Down' Infrastructure?" In Frederick Williams and John V. Pavlik, eds., *The People's Right to Know: Media, Democracy and the Information Highway.* Hillsdale, NJ: Lawrence Erlbaum Associates, 1993.

Dordick, Herbert S. and Georgette Wang. *The Information Society: A Retrospective View.* Newbury Park, CA: Sage Publications, 1994.

Dovaton, Scott. "While Other Agencies Talk, Bozell Acts." *Advertising Age,* 4 April 1995:20.

Dovaton, Scott. "Ad Council Finds a Niche in New Media." *Advertising Age,* 11 April 1995:18.

Dunkin, Amy. *Business Week,* 4 October, 1993:124–25.

Dutton, William. "Lessons from Public and Nonprofit Services." In Frederick Williams and John V. Pavlik, eds., *The People's Right to Know: Media, Democracy and the Information Highway,* Hillsdale, NJ: Lawrence Erlbaum Associates, 1994.

Edmondson, Gail. "Brave Old World." *Business Week,* Special 1994 Bonus Issue:42–43.

Eisenstadt, G. "That's Where the Money Is." *Forbes* 151 (2), 18 January 1993:56–57.

Ellul, Jacques. *The Technological Society.* New York: Alfred A. Knopf, 1964.

Elmer-DeWitt, Phillip. Space Technology Studies Seminar, the Freedom Forum Media Studies Center, 5 April 1994.

Elmer-DeWitt, Phillip. "Traveling the Information Superhighway." Speaking at a press briefing, the Freedom Forum Media Studies Center, 1 February 1994.

Endicott, R. Craig. "100 Leading Media Companies: Relaxed Rules, Solid Values Trigger Flurry of Media Acquisitions." *Advertising Age*, 16 August 1993.

Espanshade, Edward B., Jr., ed. *Goode's Rand McNally World Atlas*, 18th ed. Skokie,IL: Rand McNally, 1990.

Ewen, Stuart. *All Consuming Images*. New York: Basic Books, 1992.

Executive News Summary. *USA Today*, 6 May 1994:10.

Fabrikant, Geraldine. "$23 Billion Media Acquisition Reporter to Be Near Completion." *New York Times*, 13 October 1993:A1.

Featherstone, Mike, ed. *Global Culture*. Newbury Park, CA: Sage Publications, 1990.

"Federal Jury Indicts Woman in a CD-ROM Piracy Case." *New York Times*, 12 December 1993.

Felker, Clay. Fellows seminar, the Freedom Forum Media Studies Center, 13 October 1993.

Fenton, Tom. Freedom Forum report on a speech by Charles Brumback at the 47th World Newspaper Congress and FIEJ Annual General Meeting, 29 May–1 June 1994, Vienna, Austria.

Fidler, Roger. "Information Graphics." In John Pavlik and Everette E. Dennis, eds., *Demystifying Media Technology: Disk Edition*. Mountain View, CA: Mayfield Publishing, 1993.

Fidler, Roger. "Mediamorphosis." In Frederick Williams and John V. Pavlik, eds., *The People's Right To Know: Media, Democracy and the Information Highway*. Hillsdale, NJ: Lawrence Erlbaum Associates, 1994.

Financial World, 12 October 1994:56.

Firestone, Charles M. "A Preliminary Review of the Communications Act." The Aspen Institute, January 1992. Firestone, Charles M., "Towards a Reformulation of the Communications Act," the Aspen Institute, 1993.

First Amendment to the U.S. Constitution, 1790.

Fitzgerald, Mark. "Invisible Digital Copyright ID." *Editor & Publisher*, 25 June 1994.

"The 500 by Industry." *Fortune*, 19 April 1993.

Flaherty, Joseph. "High-Definition Television: Technical and Political Issues." In John V. Pavlik and Everette E. Dennis, eds., *Demystifying Media Technology*. Mountain View, CA: Mayfield Publishing, 1993.

Fleming, Michael. "Freeze Frame: Who Undressed Jessica Rabbit?" *Variety*, 14–20 March 1994.

Flynn, Bernadette. "Woman/Machine Relationships." *Media Information Australia*, May 1994, 11–19.

Flynn, Laurie. "A Multimedia Networking Challenge." *New York Times*, 14 December 1994.

Flynn, Laurie. "For Children, a Gift of Software." *New York Times*, 16 December 1994:C1.

Flynn, Laurie. "Thrills and Chills of Marketing a CD-ROM Adventure." *New York Times*, 27 November, 1994:F3.

"Forget the Big Mergers." *Newsweek*, 24 January 1994:44.

Frank, Reuven. *Out of Thin Air: The Brief Wonderful Life of Network News*. New York: Simon & Schuster, 1991, p. 7.

Freeman, Neal B. "Populism + Telecommunications = Global Democracy." *National Review*, 15 November 1993:50.

French, Howard W. "Linked to Internet, Could Africa's Voice Be Heard?" *New York Times*, 1 October 1994.

Fryer, Bronwyn. "Sex & the Superhighway." *Working Woman*, April 1994:51–61.

Gabriel, Trip. "A Visionary on the Border of Movies and Microchips." New York *Times*, 27 October 1993.

Galvin, Christopher J. "The Digital Deadbolt." *CompuServe Magazine,* November 1993.

Gandy, Oscar H., Jr. *The Panoptic Sort.* Boulder, CO: Westview, 1993, p. 10.

Gandy, Oscar H., Jr. "The Information Highway as Yellow Brick Road." Speech, Santa Clara University, 27 January 1994.

Gannett Executive News Summary, 5 October 1993.

Gannett Executive News Summary, 7 October 1993.

Gardiner, W. Lambert. "Virtual Reality/Cyberspace: Challenges to Communication Studies." *Canadian Journal of Communication,* vol. 18, 1993:387–396, 392.

Gelernter, David. "Wiretaps for a Wireless Age." *New York Times,* 8 April 1994:E7.

Gell-Mann. *The Quark and the Jaguar: Adventures in the Simple and the Complex.* New York: W. H. Freeman, 1994.

Geller, Henry. "Conversation on Ethics and Telecommunications." Donald McGannon Center, Fordham University, 1994.

Germain, Ellen. *Time,* 13 September 1993:61.

Gibbons, John H., ed. *U.S. Congress Office of Technology Assessment, Commercial Newsgathering from Space: A Technical Memorandum.* Washington, D.C.: Government Printing Office, 1987, pp. 39–44.

Gibbs, Wayt W. "When Cells Divide: Making Space for the Next Wave of Wireless Communications." *Scientific American,* December 1993:44–45.

Gibson, William. *Neuromancer.* New York: Ace Books, 1984.

Gilder, George. "Law of the Microcosm." *Forbes ASAP,* 1994.

Gilder, George. "Telecosm: Digital Darkhorse—Newspapers." *Forbes ASAP,* 25 October 1993:138–149.

Gipson, M. *Information & Interactive Services Report,* 8 October 1994.

Glasco, Tom. Information Director. Interview, EOSA,/NASA, Washington, DC, 1992.

Goodman, Walter. "Code Breaking and the Good It Does." *New York Times,* 18 January 1994.

Gore, Al. "Forging a New Athenian Age of Democracy." *Intermedia,* April–May 1994, 4–7.

Gore, Al. "Reinventing Government." The Office of the Vice President of the U.S., 1993.

Gore, Al. "Information for the Global Village." *Scientific American,* November 1991.

Great Geographical Atlas. Skokie, IL: Rand McNally, 1991, pp. 8–9.

Great World Atlas. Maspeth, NY: American Map Corporation, 1992, pp. 12–39.

Greenfield, Jeff. "American Agenda." *ABC World News Tonight with Peter Jennings,* 25 September 1993.

Greenfield, P. M. *Mind and Media: the Effects of Television, Video Games and Computers.* Cambridge: Harvard University Press, 1984, p. 108.

Grossman, Lawrence. "Toward a New Era of Direct Participatory Democracy." In Don W. Stacks, ed., *Seminar on Direct Electronic Democracy,* School of Communication, University of Miami, pp. 3–9.

Grossman, Lawrence. "Newsroom Technology: The Next Generation." Speech, the Freedom Forum Media Studies Center, 15 September 1993.

Grundner, Thomas. "Free-Nets: Networking Meets Middle America." *Link Letter,* September/October 1991.

Grunig, James E. and Todd Hunt. *Managing Public Relations.* New York: Holt, Rinehart and Winston, 1984.

Grunig, Larissa A. "Activism and Organizational Response: Contemporary Cases of Collective Behavior." Paper presented to the Association for Education in Journalism and Mass Communication, Norman, OK, August 1986.

Guthrie, K. Kendall. "How Information Highways Can Address the Urban Agenda: Promoting Economic Development and Reconnecting the Urban Poor." Paper presented at the 43rd Annual Conference of the International Communications Association, Washington, DC, 27–31 May 1993.

Hafner, Katie. "Getting Girls On-Line." *Working Woman,* April 1994:61.
Hafrey, Leigh. "At Cyberspace University Press, Paperless Publishing Looks Good." *New York Times Book Review,* 30 October 1994.
Hansell, Saul. "Banks Go Interactive to Beat the Rush of Services." *New York Times,* 19 October 1994:C1, C6.
Hardie, Mary. Executive News Summary, *Wall Street Journal,* 18 November 1993:A16.
Harris, Kathryn. "The Stupendous Seven—The New Masters of the Universe." *Media Studies Journal,* Winter 1994:81–93.
Hart, Roderick P. *Seducing America: How Television Charms the Modern Voter.* New York: Oxford University Press, 1994:63.
"Hear This." *International Herald Tribune,* 8 July 1994:8.
Heffner, Richard D. "The In-Your-Face Videos Bring the Censor Nearer." *International Herald Tribune,* Tuesday, 3 May 1994:7.
Henderson, Bill. Op ed page, *New York Times,* 16 March 1994.
Hermelin, Francine. "Feminizing Virtual Reality." *Working Woman,* April 1994:54.
Higgins, John M. *Multichannel News,* September 1993:1.
Hillis, John. Technology Studies Seminar, the Freedom Forum Media Studies Center, 15 May 1994.
Hilts, Paul. "RoundBook Rounds Up Russian Art Treasures." *Publishers Weekly,* 19 July 1993:24.
"Historical Premonitions of the Information Superhighway." *Wired,* August 1994:64.
Hoge, James F. "Media Pervasiveness." *Foreign Affairs,* July/August 1994, 136.
Holzmann, Gerard J. and Bjorn Pehrson. "The First Data Networks." *Scientific American,* January 1994.
"HTIJX KTW PNIX," *New York Times,* Sunday Magazine, 23 January 1994.
Hudson, Heather E. "Maximizing Benefits from New Telecommunications Technologies: A Development-Based Approach to Communications Planning." *Media Asia,* vol. 20, no. 3, 1993:133–139.
Hughes, Janice. "The Changing Multimedia Landscape." *Media Studies Journal,* the Freedom Forum Media Studies Center, Winter 1994.
Hunter, Jesse. "Authoring Literacy: From Index to Hypermedia." *Canadian Journal of Communication,* vol. 19, 1994:41–52.
"I.B.M. Project for Vatican." *New York Times,* from Reuters, 12 April 1994.
Ibrahim, Anwar. "Communication, Technology and Development: Alternatives for Asia." *Media Asia,* vol. 20, no. 3, 1993:157–158.
Information & Interactive Services Report, 27 September 1993.
"Information Highway Still a Mystery." *USA Today,* 8 May 1994:5B.
Innis, Harold. *Empire and Communications.* Oxford: Clarendon Press, 1950.
Jennewein, Chris. "Audiotext Gives a Growing Number of Dailies the Chance to Experiment with New Technologies." *ASNE Bulletin,* January/February 1994.
Jessell, Harry A. "For Time Warner, Software is Hard Part." *Broadcasting & Cable,* 28 March 1994:42.
Jessell, Harry A. "VOD, Gaming to Help Pave Superhighway." *Broadcasting & Cable,* 6 December 1993.
Johnson, Kirk. "Acorns Sprout Among the Oaks of the Telecommunications Field." *New York Times,* 5 July 1994:A1, B2.
Johnson, Kirk. "Office Romance: Love On Line at Speed of Light." *New York Times,* 26 March 1994.
Johnstone, B. "True Believers." *Far Eastern Economic Review,* 155 (51), 24 December 1993:70–71.
Jussawalla, Meheroo. "Information Technology and Economic Development in the Asia-Pacific." *Media Asia,* vol. 20, no. 3, 1993:127–132.

Kahrenburg, K. K. "Power of the Media in the Global System." *Journal of International Affairs.* 1993:i.

Kalb, Bernard. Speech, the Freedom Forum Trustees, February 1993.

Kantrowitz, Barbara. "Dissent on the Hard Drive." *Newsweek,* 27 June 1994.

Karp, Jonathan. "Prime Time Police: China tries to Pull the Plug on Satellite TV." *Far Eastern Economic Review,* 21 October 1993:72–73.

Katsh, Ethan. "Law in a Digital World: Computer Networks and Cyberspace." *Villanova Law Review,* vol. 38, no. 2, 1993:417.

Keizer, Gregg. "Debbie Does Silicon Valley: In Search of Sophisticated Electronic Entertainment." *Omni,* February 1994:24.

Kempton, Paul. "Who in the World Wants VOD?" *Cable and Satellite Europe,* 19 April 1994:26–34.

Kennedy, Daniel. "Lost in Space." *Boston Phoenix,* 7 May 1993:40.

Kilborn, Peter T. "The Boss Only Wants What's Best for You." *New York Times,* 8 May 1994.

Kim, James. "British Pioneer Launches Interactive Network." *USA Today,* 15 November 1994:7B.

Kiplinger Washington Letter, October 1994:2.

Kiplinger Washington Letter, 24 September 1993.

Klopfenstein, Bruce C. "The Diffusion of the VCR in the United States." In Mark Levy, ed., *The VCR Age: Home Video and Mass Communication.* Newbury Park, CA: Sage Publications, 1989.

Kolata, Gina. "The Assault on 12. . . ." *New York Times,* 22 March 1994:C1, C10.

Koontz, Dean. *Midnight.* New York: Berkley Books, 1989.

Kozinn, Allan. "Lejaren Hiller 69, First Composer to Write Music with a Computer," *New York Times,* 1 February 1994.

Kragen, Pam. "Copley Press Jumping on Info Superhighway." *Times Advocate,* November 1994.

Krantz, Michael. "Dollar a Minute." *Wired,* May 1994:107.

Kuckro, Rod W. "Studies Show Growing Demand for Interactive TV Services." *Information & Interactive Services Report,* 3 December 1993.

Landsat Spacecraft Data Sheet. EOSAT, January 1991.

Lang, Curtis. "The Pied Piper of Convergence." *Advertising Age,* 6 December 1993:16.

Langa, Fred. *Windows Magazine,* 1 March 1994.

"The Largest Cable TV Deals in History." *Cable TV Financial Databook.* June 1993.

Late Show with David Letterman, 7 February 1994.

Leary, Warren E. "French Team Develops Flexible, Electronic Transistor Made of Plastic." *New York Times,* 16 September 1994.

Lee, M. and N. Solomon. *Unreliable Sources.* New York: Carol Pub., 1980.

Lehmann-Haupt, Christopher. "Plumbing the Recesses of Psyche and Cyberspace." *New York Times,* 14 April 1994:C21.

Leonard, Hugh. "Asian Broadcasting: The Changing Scene." *Media Asia,* vol. 20, no. 3, 1993:123–126.

Lerner, Sid. "Lexicon for the Auto-Maga-Video Age." *New York Times,* 5 December 1993.

Leslie, Jacques. "Mail Bonding: E-mail is Creating a New Oral Culture." *Wired,* March 1994:42.

Levy, Mark, ed. *The VCR Age: Home Video and Mass Communication.* Newbury Park, CA: Sage Publications, 1989.

Levy, Mark, ed. "Virtual Reality: A Communication Perspective." *Journal of Communication,* 42(4) Autumn 1992.

Levy, Steven. *Artificial Life: The Quest For A New Creation.* London: Penguin Books, 1993.

Levy, Steven. *Insanely Great: The Life and Times of Macintosh, the Computer that Changed Everything.* New York: Viking, 1994.

Levy, Steven. "We Have Seen the Content, And It Is Us." *Media Studies Journal,* Winter 1994.
Lewin, Tamar. "Dispute Over Computer Messages: Free Speech of Sex Harassment." *New York Times,* 22 September 1994:A1.
Lewis, Peter H. "Anarchy, a Threat on the Electronic Frontier." *New York Times,* 11 May 1994:D1, D7.
Lewis, Peter H. "And the Spoof Begat a News Release, and Another." *New York Times,* 31 December 1994.
Lewis, Peter H. "Censors Become a Force on Cyberspace Frontier." *New York Times,* June 29, 1994: A1, D5.
Lewis, Peter H. "Collisions in Cyberspace on Data Encryption Plan." *New York Times,* 26 March 1994:45.
Lewis, Peter H. "Companies Rush to Set Up Shop in Cyberspace." *New York Times,* 2 November 1994:C1, C6.
Lewis, Peter H. "Computer Snoopers Imperil Pentagon Files, Experts Say." *New York Times,* 21 July 1994:A1, B10.
Lewis, Peter H. "Electronic Tie for Citizens and Seekers of Office." *New York Times,* 6 November 1994:15.
Lewis, Peter H. "Internet Users Get Access To S.E.C. Filings Fee-Free." *New York Times,* 17 January 1994.
Lewis, Peter H. "Preaching the Techno-Gospel, Al Gore Version." *New York Times,* 17 January 1994:D1.
Lewis, Peter H. "Radio Internet To Broadcast Around Clock." *New York Times,* 19 September 1994:A10.
Lewis, Peter H. "Sneering at a Virtual Lynch Mob." *New York Times,* 11 May 1994:D7.
Lewis, Peter H. "Strangers, Not Their Computers, Build a Network in Time of Grief." *New York Times,* March 8, 1994: D4.
Lewis, Peter H. *New York Times,* 13 December 1994.
Lewis, Peter H. "U.S. Begins Privatizing of Internet Operations." *New York Times,* 24 October 1994:A10.
Liebman, Hanna. "About Time for On-Line." *MEDIAWEEK,* 27 September 1993:32, 36–37.
Lincoln, Abraham. Letter to H.L. Pierce, 16 April 1859.
Ling, Ruth. "Try Before You Buy." *Satellite Communications,* November 1993:25.
Lipkin, Richard. "Making the Calls in a New Era of Communication." *Insight,* 12 July 1993.
Lohr, Steve. "Data Highway Ignoring Poor, Study Charges." *New York Times,* 24 May 1994:D3.
Lohr, Steve. "Pearson Enters Multimedia Software Arena." *New York Times,* 1 April 1994.
Lohr, Steve. "The Silver Disk May Soon Eclipse the Silver Screen." *New York Times,* 1 March 1994.
Lohr, Steve. "Americans See Future and Say, 'So What?'" *New York Times,* 7 October 1993.
Long, Elizabeth Valle. "To Our Readers." *Time,* 1 January 1994.
Long, Kim. "The Year Ahead." *American Demographics,* December 1993.
Loro, Laura. "Do MCI's Ads Offer a Genius Child?" *Advertising Age,* 14 March 1994:29.
MacDonald, Richard. "Patterns of Media Entrepreneurship." Fellows presentation, the Freedom Forum Media Studies Center, 15 December 1993.
MacDonald, Richard. Technology Studies Seminar, the Freedom Forum Media Studies Center, 6 April 1994.
Maggin, Bruce. "Riding the Information Highway." Speech at the Center for Communications, 30 September 1993.
Maher, Mike. "Electronic Gatekeeper for News." *Editor & Publisher,* 25 June 1994:70, 72.
Makulowich, John S. "Internet: Explore the 'Network of Networks." *Quill,* September 1993:28.
Malone, John. Speaking at the 1993 Cable TV Show.

Maltin, Leonard. *Entertainment Tonight,* 29 March 1994.

Mandel, Michael J. "The Information Economy: The Digital Juggernaut." *Business Week,* Special 1994 Bonus Issue:22, 23.

Mandelbrot, Benoit B. "The Beauty of Fractals and their Usefulness—Relations Between Geometry, Art, and Technology." The inaugural Magill Lecture in Science, Technology and the Arts, Columbia University, 7 April 1994.

Manly, Lorne. "The 6 Days of Creation." *Folio,* 15 June 1993:49, 92.

Marey, Kevin. "High Price May Create Initial Static. *USA Today,* 4 May 1994:10B.

Markoff, John. "Rear Adm. Grace Hopper Dies; Innovator in Computers Was 85." *New York Times,* 3 January 1992:A17.

Markoff, John. "'I Wonder What's on the PC Tonight.'" *New York Times,* 8 May 1994:F1, F8.

Markoff, John. "A Free and Simple Computer Link." *New York Times,* 8 December 1993:D1, D7.

Markoff, John. "A Magazine Seeks to Push the On-Line Envelope." *New York Times,* 31 October 1994:C6.

Markoff, John. "An Electronic Salon." *New York Times,* 27 March 1994:F10.

Markoff John. "A Phone-Cable Vehicle for the Data Superhighway." *New York Times,* 14 October 1993:A1.

Markoff, John. "Chip Makers' Competing Creed." *New York Times,* 11 March 1994:D1, D2.

Markoff, John. "Chip-Making Towers of Power." *New York Times,* 8 November 1994:C1.

Markoff, John. "Cyberspace's Most Wanted: Hacker Eludes F.B.I. Pursuit." *New York Times,* 4 July 1994.

Markoff, John. "Gore Shifts Stance on Chip Code." *New York Times,* 21 July 1994:D1.

Markoff, John. "Intel's Crash Course on Consumers." *New York Times,* 21 December 1994:C1.

Markoff, John. "Microsoft Organizes Its Interactive TV Team." *New York Times,* 2 November 1994.

Markoff, John. "New I.B.M. Laser Method Stacks Data on Disks." *New York Times,* 12 May 1994.

Markoff, John. "New Venture in Cyberspace by Silicon Graphics Founder." *New York Times,* 7 May 1994:B1.

Markoff, John. *New York Times,* 1994:47.

Markoff, John. "Toys Now, Computers Tomorrow." *New York Times,* 20 April 1994:D1, D6.

Markoff, John. "Traffic Jams Already on the Information Highway." *New York Times,* 3 November 1993.

Markoff, John. "U.S. Adopts a Disputed Coding Standard." *New York Times,* 23 May 1994.

Markoff, John. "U.S. Code Agency Is Jostling for Civilian Turf." *New York Times,* 24 January 1994:D1, D5.

Martino, Joseph P. *Technological Forecasting for Decision-Making,* ed 3. New York:McGraw-Hill, 1993.

Marx, Andy. "Interactive Development: The New Hell." *Variety,* March 1994:1.

Masefield, John. *Salt Water Ballads and Poems.* New York: MacMillan, 1923.

Mason, Marilyn Gell. "More Than a Library for Congress: Making LC the Nation's Library." *Library Journal,* 1 November 1993:40–43.

Matthews, Len. Special Report, *Next Century Media,* 1994:6.

Maxwell, Charles T. "U.S. Blunders on Computer Screen Subsidy." Letter to the editor, *New York Times,* 11 May 1994.

Maynard, Nancy Hicks. Speech, Technology Studies Seminar, the Freedom Forum Media Studies Center, 5 April 1994.

McArroll, Thomas. "Betting on the Sky." *Time,* 22 November 1993:57.

McAvoy, Kim. "Congressional Proposals at a Glance." *Broadcasting & Cable,* 3 January 1994:51.

McAvoy, Kim. "Markey's Goal: Two Wires in Every House." *Broadcasting & Cable,* 15 November 1993:26.

McCombs, M. E. and C. H. Eyal. "Spending on Mass Media." *Journal of Communication* 30(1), 1980:153–158.

McCombs, M. E. and J. Nolan. "The Relative Constancy Approach to Consumer Spending for Media." *Journal of Media Economics* 5(2), 1992:43–52.

McKibben, Bill. *The Age of Missing Information.* New York: Random House, 1992.

McLuhan, Marshall. *Understanding Media: Extensions of Man.* New York: McGraw-Hill, 1964.

McWilliams, Gary. "Computers are Finally Learning to Listen." *Business Week,* 1 November 1993.

Mediaweek, 27 September 1993.

Meyrowitz, Joshua. *No Sense of Place: The Impact of Electronic Media on Social Behavior.* New York: Oxford University Press, 1985.

Miller, David. "The Many Faces of the Internet." *Internet World,* October 1994:34–38.

Minow, Newton. "Vast Wasteland Revisited." The Freedom Forum Media Studies Center, 1991.

"MIN's Exclusive Review of Group Publishers' First-Half-1993 Ad Pages: The Gains Are Shrinking, but the Majority of Publishers Remain Up." *Media Industry Newsletter,* 2 August 1993.

Mitchell, Susan. "Technophiles and Technophobes." *Demographics Magazine,* October 1993.

Moeller, Philip. "The Age of Convergence." *American Journalism Review,* January/February 1994:22.

"Monthly Stock Watch." *Media Industry Newsletter,* 9 August 1993.

Morain, Stanley A. *Remote Sensing: Instrumentation for Nondestructive Exploration of Cultural Resources,* No. 2 in *Remote Sensing: A Handbook for Archaeologists and Cultural Resource Managers.* Washington, DC: Cultural Resources Management Division, National Park Service, U.S. Department of the Interior, 1978.

Morukama, Shinji. "The Information Superhighway." *Forum Magazine,* May 1994:4.

"Motif Unveils New Flat-Panel Technology, Largest Manufacturing Plant in U.S." *Video Technology News,* 11 October 1993:8.

"Movie Magic." Discovery Channel, 16 June 1994.

Mowlana, Hamid, George Gerbner and Herbert I. Schiller. *Triumph of the Image: The Media's War in the Persian Gulf: A Global Perspective.* Boulder, CO: Westview Press, 1992.

"Multimedia Announces Strategic Initiatives to Strengthen Competitive Position and Give Access to Superhighway." SNPA Bulletin, 1 March 1994.

Multispectral Imagery report, EOSAT, January 1991.

Murdoch, Rupert. Keynote address, Center for Communication, Communicator of the Year Award Luncheon, 11 April 1994.

Murphy, P. and J. Dee. "Du Pont and Greenpeace: the Dynamics of Conflict Between Corporations and Activist Groups." *Public Relations Research Annual,* 4(1), 1992:3–20.

Murrow, Edward R. "See It Now." *CBS News,* 1958.

"The Mysterious Case of the Missing Troops." *St. Petersburg Times,* 30 November 1990.

Nadis, Steve. "Artificial Intelligence: The Sound of Data: Data May Fill Your Ears Rather Than Your Eyes." *Omni,* January 1994:26.

Naisbitt, John. *Global Paradox.* New York: Morrow, 1994.

Naisbitt, John. *Megatrends.* New York: Warner Books, 1982.

Naisbitt, John and Patricia Aburdene. *Megatrends 2000.* New York: Morrow, 1990.

Nelson, Clark, Director for Corporate Communication. SPOT Image, interview by author, Reston, VA, 1992.

"A New Fee Structure to Share On-Line Data." *New York Times,* 6 April 1994:D1, D6.

New York Times, 12 May 1994:D2.

News Inc., 4 October 1993:1.

Nichols, Peter M. "Home Video: What Exactly Is 'Multimedia'?" *New York Times,* 1 April 1994:D17.

Nichols, Peter M. "Mini-Series Blazes Trail in High-Definition TV." *New York Times,* 19 April 1994:D10.

Noam, Eli M. Keynote address, the Everette Parker Luncheon, 1993.

Noam, Eli M. "Beyond Liberalization: From the Network of Networks to the System of Systems." Telecommunications Policy 1994 18 (4):286–294.

Noam, Eli. Speech, Technology Studies Seminar, the Freedom Forum Media Studies Center, 5 April 1994.

Noble, J. Kendrick, Jr. "U.S. Daily Newspapers: Past, Present and Prospects, 1958–2008." Research report, presented at Freedom Forum Center Fellows Seminar, 26 May 1994.

Nolan, Chris. "Does HDTV Compute?" *Cablevision,* 6 December 1993:94.

Nolan, Chris. "Filling in the Blanks." *Cablevision,* 14 March 1994.

Noll, Michael. "Is All That Fiber Necessary?" *New York Times,* 19 October 1993.

"On Line." *Chronicle of Higher Education,* 2 March 1994.

Orlansky, J. and J. String. "Cost-Effectiveness of Computer Based Instruction in Military Training." IDA Paper P-1375, Institute for Defense Analyses, Alexandria, VA.

Ostry, Sylvia. "The Domestic Domain: The New International Policy Area." *Transnational Corporations 1,* February 1992:7.

Page, Bruce. Meeting, 12 February 1994.

Paikert, Charles. "CD-ROM Next Best Hope." *Variety,* 28 February–6 March 1994.

Paine, Thomas. *The American Crisis.* No. 1, 23 December 1776.

Palmer, Allen W. "On the Limits of a Free Press: Remote Imaging and Commercial News Gathering." *Gazette* 49:159–176, 1992.

Paris, Hilton. NASA Teacher Resource Center, City College of New York, 17 June 1992.

Passell, Peter. "F.C.C. 'Pioneer' Policy Under Attack." *New York Times,* 31 January 1994.

Pavlik, John. *Media Technology Chronology.* Software published by Wayne Danielson Software, 1992.

Pavlik, John. "Newsroom Convergence." In John V. Pavlik and Everette E. Dennis, eds., *Demystifying Media Technology,* Mountain View, CA: Mayfield Publishing, 1993.

Pavlik, John and Andras Szanto. "Coverage of the Information Superhighway." In *Separating Fact from Fiction on the Information Superhighway,* the Research Group, the Freedom Forum Media Studies Center, May 1994.

Pavlik, John and Andras Szanto. "Mutiple Method Research in Media Studies: The Case of the 1992 Presidential Campaign." The Freedom Forum Media Studies Center, 1994.

Pavlik, John and Everette E. Dennis. "Traveling the Information Superhighway." The Freedom Forum Media Studies Center, 1994.

Pavlik, John V. and Mark A. Thalhimer. "A Brief History of Computer-Assisted Investigative Reporting." The Freedom Forum Media Studies Center, 1992.

Peers, Martin. *New York Post,* 5 November 1993:23.

Phelan, John M. "The Inner Face of Interface." Unpublished essay, June 1994;

Piirto, Jennifer. *American Demographics.* November 1993:6.

Pitta, Julie. "Computers & Communications: For Years, Nimble PC Clonemakers Have Nibbled Away at IBM and Other Industry Leaders. In 1992 the Giants Fought Back." *Forbes,* 4 January 1993:114, 115, 118.

"Poached By Sonic the Hedgehog." *Economist,* 20 February 1993:326.

Pollack, Andrew. "From Korea, a Challenge to Japan." *New York Times,* 12 May 1994:D1, D5.

Pollack, Andrew. "Matsushita, in Lab Test, Reduces Disk to a Dot." *New York Times,* 19 September 1994:C2.

Pollack, Andrew. "Organizers Captivate Japanese Girls." *New York Times,* 22 December 1994:C1.

Pool, Robert. "Turning an Info-Glut into a Library." *Science,* October 1994:20–22.

"Porn File Not Found." *Newsweek,* 27 June 1994:59.

Port, Otis. "Wonder Chips: How They'll Make Computing Power Ultrafast and Ultracheap." *Business Week,* 4 July 1994:86–92.

Postman, Neil. *Amusing Ourselves to Death.* New York: Penguin Books, 1986, p. 86.

Postman, Neil. *Technopoly: The Surrender of Culture to Technology.* New York: Random House, 1992.

Powell, Adam Clayton III. "Getting the Picture." In John V. Pavlik and Everette E. Dennis, eds., *Demystifying Media Technology.* Mountain View, CA: Mayfield Publishing, 1993.

Powell, Adam Clayton III. Meeting, 6 May 1994.

Powell, Adam Clayton III. "On-Ramps to the Information Superhighway." *Media Studies Journal,* Summer 1994: viii, 113–121.

Powell, Adam Clayton III. Speech, Technology Studies Seminar, the Freedom Forum Media Studies Center, 27 October 1994.

Powell, Adam Clayton III. Technology Studies Seminar, the Freedom Forum Media Studies Center, 6 April 1994.

Powledge, Tabitha M. "Information Highway Without Tollbooths." *Washington Post,* 23 June 1994:1.

Privacy & American Business: A Comprehensive Report and Information Service, September/October 1993:3.

Privacy Journal, November 1993.

Quinlan, Joe. Interview with the author, 1992.

Quittner, Josh. "Johnny Manhattan Meets the FurryMuckers." *Wired,* March 1994:92.

"Rabbit Is Naked." *New York Times Magazine,* 27 March 1994:22.

Rabinovitz, Jonathan. "Computer Network Helps Journalists Find Academic Experts." *New York Times,* 21 May 1994.

Ramirez, Anthony. "An Infrastructure Without Structure." *New York Times,* 7 January 1993:D1.

Ramirez, Anthony. "Computers Reach Out and Touch." *New York Times,* 18 January 1994:A20.

Ramstad, Evan. "Interactive TV Gets Another Moment in the Sun." Associated Press, 11 December 1994.

Ramstad, Evan. "Whoa, Slow Down! Metaphor Abuse Causing Whiplash on Information Highway." Associated Press, 3 February 1994.

Raskin, Robin. "Inside." *PC Magazine,* 22 February 1994:4.

Research Group, *The Media and Campaign '92.* The Freedom Forum Media Studies Center, 1992.

Rheingold, Howard. *The Virtual Community: Homesteading on the Electronic Frontier.* New York: Simon and Schuster, 1993:19, 26.

Rifkin, Glenn. "Seeing Print's Future in a Digital Universe." *New York Times,* 9 May 1994:D8.

Riordan, Teresa. "Writing Copyright Law for an Information Age." *New York Times,* 7 July 1994:D4.

Ritter, Robert. *New Media,* October 1993:24.

Rohter, Larry. "Florida Entrepreneur Plans to Challenge Disney World." *New York Times,* 4 April 1994.

Rose, Cynthia. "Neville Brody: How to Be a Graphics Guru." *International Herald Tribune,* 8 July 1994:24.

Roth v. United States. 354 U.S. 476, 490, 77 S.Ct. 1304, 1312, 1957.

Rothenberg, Jeff. "Ensuring the Longevity of Digital Documents." *Scientific American,* January 1995:42–47.

S C Research International. "Professional Video Marketplace." Cited in *Video Technology News,* 14 March 1994.

"The Sad-Truth Phone." *New York Times,* Sunday Magazine, 23 January 1994.

Salpukas, Agis. "Big Hopes Put on Electric Wires." *New York Times,* 6 July 1994:D1, D4.

Salvaggio, Jerry. *Telecommunications.* New York: Longman, 1983.

Sandberg, Jared. "Up in Flames." *Wall Street Journal Reports,* 15 November 1993:R12.

Schiller, Dan. "From Culture to Information and Back Again: Commoditization as a Route to Knowledge." *Critical Studies in Mass Communication* 11 March 1994:92–115.

Schiller, Herbert I. "Transnational Media: Creating Consumers Worldwide." *Journal of International Affairs,* Summer 1993.

Schiller, Jeffrey. "Secure Distributed Computing." *Scientific American,* November, 1994:72–76.

Schmit, Julie. "High Tech Has Phones Humming." *USA Today,* 23 April 1994.

Schonfeld, Reese. Speech, IRTS seminar, 11 February 1994.

Schramm, Wilbur. *The Story of Human Communication: Cave Painting to Microchip.* New York: Harper & Row, 1988.

Schudson, Michael. "The Limits of Teledemocracy." *The American Prospect,* 11 (3), 1992:41–45.

Schuman, Patricia Glass. "Information Justice." Fellows seminar, the Freedom Forum Media Studies Center, 1993.

Schwartz, Evan I. "The Cleavers Enter Cyberspace." *Business Week,* 11 October 1993:142.

Schwartz, John and Tracy Thompson. "The On-Line Link to a Natural Disaster." *Washington Post,* 19 January 1994.

Schwartz, Mischa. "Telecommunications Networks and Multimedia." Fellows seminar, the Freedom Forum Media Studies Center, 2 February 1994.

Selinger, Iris Cohen. "Cerritos Test Shows There's More to Learn About Interactive Television." *Advertising Age,* 25 October 1993:25.

Selnow, Gary W. *High-Tech Campaigns: Computer Technology in Political Communication.* Westport, CT: Praeger, 1993.

Seminar, the Freedom Forum Media Studies Center, 23 February 1994.

Sevareid, Eric. CBS Radio News commentary, 26 August 1952.

Seybold Report on Desktop Publishing, 1993.

Seybold Report on Desktop Publishing, 7 March 1994.

Seymour, Jim. "Pentium PCs: Pentium: The Second Wave." *PC Magazine,* 25 January 1994:110

Shade, Leslie Regan. "Computer Networking in Canada: From CA*net to CANARIE." *Canadian Journal of Communication,* vol. 19, 1994:61, 53–69.

Shakespeare, William. *Othello,* act 3, sc. 4, line 69 (1621). George L. Kitredge, ed., Ginn, 1941.

Shaw, Donald L. "The Rise and Fall of American Mass Media." *Journal of Communication,* 1993.

Shaw, Russell. "Pac Bell Offering Video, Audio over Phone Lines." *Electronic Media,* 22 November 1993:10.

Sheehan, Henry. "Philip Noyce Plays 'Patriot Games' with the CIA." *Satellite TV Pre-Vue,* 28 June–4 July 1992:5, 25,.

Shefrin, David. "History of the Fax Newspaper." In John Pavlik and Everette E. Dennis, eds., *Demystifying Media Technology: Disk Edition.* Mountain View, CA: Mayfield Publishing, 1993.

Shriver, Rev. Donald, speaker, Fellows seminar, the Freedom Forum Media Studies Center, 26 May 1994.

"SI Diamond Plans Flat-Panel Display Project Using Diamond-Based Technology." *HDTV Report,* 13 October 1993.

Siegenthaler, John. Leadership Institute, the Freedom Forum Media Studies Center, 23 June 1994.

Sikes, Alfred. "Riding the Information Highway." Speech, Center for Communication, 30 September 1993.

Simon, Herbert A. Interview, *Omni*, November 1994:71, 72.

Sims, Calvin. "Reporter Disciplined for Reading His Coworkers' Electronic Mail." *New York Times*, 12 December 1993.

Smith, Anthony. *Age of Behemoths*. New York: The 20th Century Fund, 1992.

Smith, Anthony. "From Books to Bytes: The Computer and the Library." In John V. Pavlik and Everette E. Dennis, eds., *Demystifying Media Technology*, Mountain View, CA: Mayfield Publishing, 1993.

Smith, Anthony. "From Méliés to Virtual Reality." Speech, Technology Studies, the Freedom Forum Media Studies Center, 19 December 1994.

Smith, Anthony. *Goodbye Gutenberg*. New York: Oxford University Press, 1980.

Smith, Anthony. "Is TV's Web of Images Strangling Our Hearts." *New York Newsday*, 3 January 1994.

Smith, Anthony. "New Communication Technology and Changing Political Boundaries." Technology Paper, the Freedom Forum Media Studies Center, October 1993.

Smith, Ralph Lee. *The Wired Nation: Cable TV: The Coming Information Highway*. New York: Harper & Row, 1972.

Software Publishers Association. "Report on the Effectiveness of Technology in Schools, 1990–1992." Conducted by Interactive Educational Systems Design, 1993:2.

Sommer, Francine, panelist. "Media Mania." Columbia Business School Alumni Day, 13 November 1993.

"Sony and Philips Design CD's for Movies." *New York Times*, 17 December 1994.

"Soviet Art via CD-ROM." *Publish*, January 1994:13.

Stahlman, Mark. "Backlash: The Infobahn Is a Big, Fat Joke." *Wired*, March 1994:73.

Stanford Resources, San Jose, CA, 1994.

Stefanac, Suzanne. "Sex & the New Media." *NewMedia*, April 1993:39.

Steinfels, Peter. "Jacques Ellul, French Critic of Technology, Is Dead at 82." *New York Times*, 21 May 1994.

Stephenson, Neal. "Smiley's People." *New Republic*, 13 September 1993:26.

Stix, Gary. "The Wall: Chip Makers' Quest for Small May Be Hitting It." *Scientific American*, July 1994, p. 96, 98.

"Study Suggests Wireless Could Transform Communications Industry." *The Sampler*, Response Analysis Corp., Princeton, NJ, pp. 1, 4.

"Superhypeway Backlash." *Marketing Pulse*, 31 January 1994.

T Leaves, "Bulletins from the Information Highway: John Evans on New Media, Roadkill and More," March 1994. Published by the Newspaper Association of America.

"Talks Set on Digital VCR." *New York Times*, 12 April 1994.

"Technophobia Emerging as the Malady of the '90s for Half of Americans." Knight-Ridder Newspapers, 12 June 1994.

Television Business International Yearbook, March 1993; *Broadcasting & Cable*, "Top 100 in Electronic Communications," 21 June 1993.

Tennyson, Alfred. *Ulysses*. London, Moxon, 1869.

"Test Set for Digital Movies." *New York Times*, 21 March 1994:D2.

TFPL Publishing, Washington, DC, 1994.

Thalhimer, Mark. "The Virtual Newsroom." *Media and Campaign '92: The Homestretch*, the Freedom Forum Media Studies Center:70, 1992.

Thalhimer, Mark. *Media Industry News Roundup*, compiled from the Associated Press, 3 May 1994.

Thalhimer, Mark and Joanna Campbell. *Media Industry News Roundup,* compiled from the Associated Press, 19 April 1994.

Thalhimer, Mark and Marcella Steingart, eds. *Media Industry News Roundup,* compiled from the Associated Press, the Freedom Forum Media Studies Center, 31 May 1994.

Thalhimer, Mark. "Origins of the Information Superhighway Metaphor." In *Separating Fact from Fiction on the Information Superhighway,* the Research Group, the Freedom Forum Media Studies Center, May 1994.

Thalhimer, Mark, ed. *Media Industry News Roundup,* compiled from the Associated Press, the Freedom Forum Media Studies Center, 6 July 1994.

Thalhimer, Mark, ed. *Media Industry News Roundup,* compiled from the Associated Press, the Freedom Forum Media Studies Center, 24 May 1994.

Thalhimer, Mark, ed. *Media Industry News Roundup,* compiled from the Associated Press, the Freedom Forum Media Studies Center, 31 May 1994.

Thalhimer, Mark. "Online News Services." *The Race for Content, The Media Studies Journal.* Winter 1994.

Thalhimer, *Media News Roundup,* 11 July 1994.

Thoreau, Henry David. *Walden.* New York: T.Y.Crowell, 1899.

Tierney, John. "Pornography and Technology." *New York Times,* 16 January 1994.

Todd, Russell G. Communication and Society Seminar, the Freedom Forum Media Studies Center, 1992.

Tomlinson, Don E. "Computer Manipulation and Creation of Images and Sounds: Assessing the Impact." Monograph, the Annenberg Washington Program, Communications Policy Studies, Northwestern University, 1993.

"Top 50 Cable and Satellite Companies." *Cable and Satellite Europe (C&SEu),* 1993.

"Top 50 Cable and Satellite Companies." *Cable and Satellite Europe (C&SEu),* 1994.

"Treasure Hunters." Discovery Channel, 1 February 1994.

Turkle, Sherry. *The Second Self: Computer and the Human Spirit.* New York: Simon and Schuster, 1984.

Turner, Ted. Speaking at the 1993 Cable TV Show.

"TV Debate Set a Cable Record." *New York Times,* 11 November 1993.

Tynan, Daniel. "PC meets TV." *PC World,* February 1994:139.

Umstead, R. Thomas. "Stealing Cable." *Cablevision,* 6 December, 1993.

"U.S. Industrial Outlook '92: Business Forecasts for 350 Industries." U.S. Department of Commerce, January 1992.

U.S. International Trade Commission, 1993. "Global Competitiveness of U.S. Advanced-Technology Industries: Computers." Washington, DC: USITC, Pub. no. 2705, December 1992.

Van Der Leun, Gerard. "'This is a Naked Lady.'" *Wired,* Premiere Issue 1993:74.

Van Sell, Mary and Sheila M. Jacobs. "Telecommuting and Quality of Life: A Review of the Literature and a Model for Research." *Telematics and Informatics,* vol. 11, no. 2:81–95.

Verba, Sidney. "The 1993 James Madison Award Lecture: The Voice of the People," delivered at the American Political Science Association Annual Meeting, Washington, DC, 3 September 1993, edited version published in Robert J. P. Hauck, ed., *PS: Political Science & Politics,* vol. XXXVI, no. 4, December 1993:684.

Verity, John W. "The Information Revolution: How Digital Technology is Changing the Way We Work and Live." *Business Week,* Special 1994 Bonus Issue:14.

Via Satellite, 4 April 1994.

Video Technology News. "Active-Matrix LCD Will Stay a Flat Panel Technology with Large Markets." 3 January 1994.

Wall Street Journal, 17 March 1994:B5.

Wall Street Journal, 6 May 1994:B10.

Walley, Wayne. "Grossing Out at New Levels: Stern PPV Event Posts Strong Buy Rates." *Electronic Media,* 10 January 1994.

Wang, Georgette. "Satellite Television and the Future of Broadcast Television in the Asia-Pacific." *Media Asia,* vol. 20, no. 3, 1993:139–148.

Wark, McKenzie. "The Video Game as an Emergent Media Form." *Media Information Australia,* February 1994.

Washington Post, 17 March 1994:B14.

Weber, Bruce. "Why Marilyn and Bogie Still Need a Lawyer." *New York Times,* 11 March 1994.

Weiner, Norbert. *Cybernetics: The Human Use of Human Beings.*

Weiner, Tim. "C.I.A. Considers Allowing Sale of Spy Technology." *New York Times,* 13 November 1993:A8.

Weise, Elizabeth. "Santa's Elves Check E-Mail for Your Merry Messages." Associated Press wire service, 13 December 1994.

White, Jan V. *Graphic Design for the Electronic Age.* New York: Watson-Gruptill Publications, 1988.

"Who Are Europe's Biggest Media Companies?" *TBI Yearbook 93.*

Wicklein, John. *Electronic Nightmare.* New York: Viking Press, 1981.

Wiggins, Richard W. "Examining Mosaic." *Internet World,* October 1994:48–51.

Williams, Bill. "FaxPaper." In John Pavlik and Everette E. Dennis, eds., *Demystifying Media Technology: Disk Edition.* Mountain View, CA: Mayfield Publishing, 1993.

Williams, Frederick. *The New Telecommunications.* Free Press: New York, 1991.

Williams, Frederick and John V. Pavlik. *The People's Right to Know: Media, Democracy and the Information Highway.* Hillsdale, NJ: Lawrence Erlbaum Associates, 1994.

Williams, Frederick. The Freedom Forum Media Studies Center Leadership Institute, 22 June 1994.

Wilson, David L. "Compatible at Last? Alliance of Apple and IBM Leads to New Machines, but Differences Remain." *Chronicle of Higher Education,* 16 March 1994:A19.

Wilson, David L. "Threats to Internet Security." *Chronicle of Higher Education,* 30 March 1994:A22.

Wilson, Kinsey. "Your Life as an Open Book." *New York Newsday,* 21 July 1993:46.

Winkler, Matthew, speaker. "Real-Time Information Services." Technology Studies Seminar, the Freedom Forum Media Studies Center, 15 September 1993.

Winkler, Matthew. Technology Studies Seminar, the Freedom Forum Media Studies Center, 6 April 1994.

"Wired." *Wall Street Journal Reports,* 15 November 1993.

Wiseman, Paul and Dottie Enrico. "Techno Terror Slows Info Highway Traffic." *USA Today,* 14 November 1994.

"With Phones Out, Computer Networks Provide Key Link." Gannett Suburban Newspapers, 18 January 1994.

"The World's Top AV Companies: The IDATE 100." *Screen Digest,* August 1993:181

Wright, David. "Mobile Satellite Communications in Developing Countries." *Telecommunications Policy,* January/February 1994.

Wriston, Walter. *Twilight of Sovereignty: How the Information Revolution is Transforming Our World.* New York: Scribners, 1992.

Wriston, Walter. "Public Opinion: 'Mistress of the World.'" Inaugural address in the Freedom Forum Media Studies Center Technology Lecture Series, 25 October 1993.

INDEX

Note: Bold page numbers indicate figures and tables.